*For the students in my
graduate and undergraduate seminars
in German history,
Columbia University, New York, 1980,
and
University of East Anglia, Norwich, 1976–86*

RETHINKING GERMAN HISTORY

Nineteenth-Century Germany and the Origins of the Third Reich

RICHARD J. EVANS

Professor of European History
University of East Anglia

HarperCollins*Academic*
An imprint of HarperCollins*Publishers*

Published by
HarperCollins_Academic_
77–85 Fulham Palace Road
Hammersmith
London W6 8JB
UK

First published in 1987
First published in Paperback in 1990
Second impression 1991

British Library Cataloguing in Publication Data

Evans, Richard J.
Rethinking German history : Nineteenth-Century Germany
and the Origins of the Third Reich.
1. Germany – Social life and customs – Historiography
I. Title
943'.07'072   DD204
ISBN 0–04–943051–3
ISBN 0-00-302090-8

Library of Congress Cataloging in Publication Data

Evans, Richard J.
Rethinking German history.
Essays, most of which were published in various journals
between 1978 and 1985.
Includes index.
1. Germany – History – 1789–1900. 2. Germany – History – 20th
century. I. Title.
DD204.E88 1987 943'.07 87–975
ISBN 0–04–943051–3 (alk. paper)
ISBN 0-00-302090-8

Typeset in 10/12 Garamond by Computape
and printed in Great Britain
by Biddles Ltd, Guildford

Contents

Acknowledgments   *page* iv

Introduction   1

PART ONE   *Historiographies*

1 Wilhelm II's Germany and the Historians   23
2 From Hitler to Bismarck: Third Reich and   55
   Kaiserreich in Recent Historiography
3 The Myth of Germany's Missing Revolution   93

PART TWO   *Mentalities*

4 Religion and Society in Modern Germany   125
5 In Pursuit of the *Untertanengeist*: Crime,   156
   Law and Social Order in German History

PART THREE   *Movements*

6 The Sociological Interpretation of German   191
   Labour History
7 Liberalism and Society: the Feminist   221
   Movement and Social Change
8 'Red Wednesday' in Hamburg: Social   248
   Democrats, Police and *Lumpenproletariat*
   in the Suffrage Disturbances of 17 January
   1906

Index   291

Acknowledgments

Of the contents of this collection, the Introduction has been specially written, and Chapter 5 is previously unpublished. Of the rest, the original places of publication were as follows:

Chapter 1: Richard J. Evans (ed.), *Society and Politics in Wilhelmine Germany* (London: Croom Helm, 1978), pp. 11–39; and *West European Politics*, vol. 4, no. 2 (1981), pp. 134–48 (London: Frank Cass and Co.).

Chapter 2: *Historical Journal*, vol. 26, no. 2 (1983), pp. 485–97, and vol. 26, no. 4 (1983), pp. 999–1020 (Cambridge University Press); *History*, vol. 68 (1983), pp. 364–5.

Chapter 3: *New Left Review*, vol. 149 (Jan./Feb. 1985), pp. 67–94.

Chapter 4: *European Studies Review*, vol. 12, no. 3 (1982), pp. 249–88 (SAGE Publications Ltd).

Chapter 6: Richard J. Evans (ed.), *The German Working Class 1888–1933: The Politics of Everyday Life* (London: Croom Helm, 1982), pp. 15–53.

Chapter 7: Richard J. Evans (ed.), *Society and Politics in Wilhelmine Germany* (London, Croom Helm, 1978), pp. 186–214.

Chapter 8: *Social History*, vol. 4, no. 1 (1979), pp. 1–31 (Methuen and Co. Ltd).

Introduction

I

Most general books on German history consist of straightforward narratives of political events, with a strong emphasis on German unification, the origins of the First World War, the rise and fall of Nazism and the emergence of the 'two Germanies' after 1945. Within the narrative framework they tend to concentrate on presenting the factors that led to the catastrophe of Hitler's Third Reich.[1] If they make any concessions to social history at all, it is either by adducing 'social factors' to explain political events, or by adding on a few statistics at the end of the book, as a kind of afterthought.[2] Another, very different tradition of writing in broad, general terms about German history takes its cue from literature, and depicts German society and German values through the use of novels, drama, poetry, autobiography and other kinds of literary evidence. Here the stress is on the drift of the 'German mind' towards authoritarianism, militarism and eventually National Socialism.[3] Inevitably, this kind of literary social history concentrates heavily on the small élite of well-educated people who produced the great bulk of the literary evidence on which it relies. Just as much as the history of high politics, it leaves the majority of German people in the past out of the picture.[4] In this book, I want to argue that social history, the history of German society as a whole, and not just its thin upper crust, cannot be relegated to a few statistical tables in an appendix, or confined to the illustration of a handful of literary texts. Social history belongs in the centre of German history, and it is when we put it there that the rethinking process really begins.

The essays collected in this book seek to illustrate and exemplify this basic argument in a number of ways. The first part charts the work that has gone on since the end of the Second World War in an attempt to understand the course that German history took from the eighteenth century to the twentieth. It tries to explain how historians' views of the central issues have changed, and to suggest some of the limitations to which the work of the 1960s and 1970s in particular was subject. Part 2 of the book turns to attitudes and values, and questions how far they have really persisted over the century and a half since Germany's industrial revolution began. The examples of the 'spirit of submission' and of religious belief suggest the difficulties of explaining political developments solely or even mainly by reference to the persistence of what French historians like to call *mentalités*, or structures of thought and belief in the widest, often barely articulated sense. Finally, the third part of the book presents three studies which concentrate on challenges to authority in Imperial Germany – the Social Democratic Party, the feminist movement, and popular disturbances. Here the intention is to question the stereotype of the 'orderly German', and to suggest that the *Kaiserreich* was not a rigid, immobile, hierarchical society yearning for authority, but a society in an active state of ferment and flux. It was out of such social upheaval, seen in a general sense, and not out of social stagnation, that Nazism was eventually born.

Because they form a collective argument in favour of social history, the essays published (or republished) in this book inevitably have a strongly historiographical slant. They can be seen as assessments of the contributions made by a number of different approaches to our understanding of the German past, ranging from biographical and organizational history (Chapter 2) through Gramscian neo-Marxism (Chapter 3), and sociology (Chapter 6), to quantification (Chapter 5) and the 'social history of politics' (Chapter 1). The book also offers general critical accounts of major areas of German history including labour history (Chapter 6), women's history (Chapter 7), the history of religion (Chapter 4), the history of crime and 'social protest' (Chapter 5) and of course the major problems of political developments and structures in the German past (Chapters 1, 2 and 3). It therefore provides an introduction to recent German and Anglo-American work in these fields, and conveys to an English-reading audience, accustomed to thinking of European social history mainly in terms of Britain and France, something of the rich variety of socio-historical work now being done on Germany.

II

Although all the essays were written in the last ten years (the earliest being Chapter 8, which originated in a conference paper first presented in January 1977), the research on which they are based, or from which they ultimately derive, goes back a lot further. It began at the end of the 1960s, as a whole generation of British history graduates began to pursue PhD. research projects in modern German history. Unlike the much less numerous older generation of historians of Germany then teaching at British universities, some of whom were German exiles, others of whom had been drawn to the subject through their work in military intelligence and other areas in the Second World War,[5] most of us had no prior connection with Germany at all. We all grew up in the 1950s, in an atmosphere that was universally referred to as 'postwar'. Germany and the war were frequent topics of conversation among our elders, while on the wireless, in the newsreels and later on television, the topic was almost impossible to avoid. All around us, too, was the physical evidence of the war – overgrown bomb sites in the cities, crumbling air-raid shelters in the gardens, rotting gas-masks in the lumber-rooms. To anyone with a degree of intellectual curiosity it became important to find out why the Germans had fought the war, and why Hitler had come to power.

No one who was an undergraduate in the late 1960s could have failed to have been affected by the intellectual ferment that was going on in the universities, not even those who were not active in student politics themselves. Among the many broader political questions which played such a major role in the student movement of those days, were a good number that reinforced an interest in German history. The Vietnam War, which raised the whole question of the roots of imperialism and foreign aggression and popularized concepts like the 'military–industrial complex', was perhaps the most obvious of these issues, directing attention inexorably to the two world wars of our century, in which Germany had played so decisive a role. What seemed like the looming danger of the Third World War focused the mind powerfully on the origins of the First and Second World Wars. In domestic politics, the rise of the National Front in this country, and the phenomenon of the neo-Nazi National Democratic Party in West Germany, both raised the spectre of a revival of fascism in our own time and made the question of the origins of Nazism appear one of considerable political urgency. The late 1960s were also a period of significant new developments in historical research in the area of fascism and its prehistory. Two breakthroughs were especially exciting. In the first place, there was a veritable explosion of theoretically innovative historical research on the phenomenon of fascism in general, for example in the work of Ernst Nolte (1965), Barrington Moore (1966), Walter Laqueur and George Mosse (1966), and Stuart Woolf (1968).[6] Secondly, this was also the moment at which the work of Fritz Fischer was first received and discussed in England with the publication of an English translation of his book *Germany's Aims in the First World War* in 1967. Fischer's first appearance in Oxford, in 1969, was a major event; his lecture was attended by all the leading lights of the Oxford historical scene, and people were cramming the aisles to hear what he had to say. It was clear that German historiography was in a state of ferment, and, more exciting still, it was also apparent from the violent controversy that Fischer's work (which is discussed in more detail in Chapter 1) aroused that interpretations of recent German history still had real political relevance and meaning.

Finally, the sudden outburst of British work on German history that began around 1970 can be seen as part of a far wider reorientation of British intellectual life consequent upon the end of Empire during the previous decade and the turn towards Europe cemented in the British accession to the European Community in 1973. On the Left, this was a

3

time when events on the European continent, above all the student movements of the late 1960s in France and Germany, had a power and fascination of which it seemed impossible to reproduce more than a faint echo in Britain. The leading radical journal, *New Left Review*, had only recently begun its work of familiarizing the British Left with continental Marxism. And in Oxford at least, and probably beyond its boundaries too, the work of Richard Cobb, who had only recently started publishing in English, exerted a seductive influence.[7] Cobb took the view that to understand a foreign country you had to live in it, speak its language fluently, indeed eventually *become* a foreigner, so to speak, acquiring a 'second identity' – in his case, French – as well as your original British one.[8] Older British historians, by contrast, tended to see Germany very much from the outside, in an 'us and them' sort of way. Although by this time anything but Marxist, Cobb's work on the popular movement in the French Revolution, and his concentration on the everyday life of the poor and on the experience of dearth, violence, deviance and revolt, combined with his distaste for the powerful in the past to exert a strong appeal for postgraduates beginning work on Europe. Cobb, and, in his more detached way, Theodore Zeldin, whose revolutionary work *France 1848–1945* did not begin to appear until 1973,[9] but whose doctoral students were already thick on the ground in the late 1960s, helped foster an awareness that the most exciting ideas and innovations going on in the field of history were French. The work of the *Annales* school was already being widely discussed in the 1960s, and since, partly for institutional reasons, partly as a sort of defence mechanism against the dominant school of English history, European history postgraduates tended to stick together, a growing familiarity with French work, with historians like Goubert, Ladurie, Braudel, Le Goff and Duby, was the inevitable result. The French historians taught that nothing was impossible, no subject could be ruled out of court: not only demographic and family history, but also the history of love and fear, of time and space, was all grist to their mill, and their work opened up whole new possibilities of understanding the past.[10]

The 1960s were also a time of tremendous excitement in British historical scholarship, particularly since it was in that decade that British Marxist historians like Christopher Hill, Eric Hobsbawm, E. P. Thompson and others were producing some of their most celebrated works.[11] They showed that Marxist history need not be dull, difficult or dogmatic, and that it was about far more than simply ascribing economic motives and causes to historical events. Here too there was an interest in exploring values and attitudes, whether of seventeenth-century Puritans, eighteenth-century Methodists, or nineteenth-century bandits, and treating them seriously in their own terms, while at the same time never losing sight of their ultimate social determination. There was a sense of rediscovery, as the focus broadened to include whole social groups, classes, even major-

4

ities, like the peasantry, previously neglected by historians. There was a strong conviction that the common people in the past had a dignity and sense of their own worth that did not allow them to take oppression and exploitation without protest or resistance, even if it was expressed in ways that previous historians had seldom understood as rational or meaningful (and it was part of the excitement of this new work that it showed that such actions could be so understood). The culmination of this trend was the foundation of the History Workshop movement in Oxford, in the late 1960s, which took it even further, so that among its offerings (in the beginning, indeed, central to them) were shop-floor workers, miners, agricultural labourers and others writing their own history themselves. No one who attended those workshops could fail to be impressed by the excitement and enthusiasm for history which they generated.[12]

All these influences helped shape my decision, after some initial hesitation, to choose as a research topic what many both then and subsequently have found an unusual, even an eccentric subject, namely the feminist movement in Germany from 1894 to 1933. It seemed, however, to offer a whole range of possibilities to the serious student. It was completely neglected – the women's liberation movement had not even begun in Germany at the time, and was only just getting under way in Britain and the USA – and so was ideal for an exercise in reconstructing history from the sources. It was an oppositional, progressive, popular movement for the emancipation of a large section of the population (well over half, in fact). It seemed to open up questions of attitudes and values in a very promising way. And from the point of view of German history it provided an example of a liberal movement of social reform which was large enough to be important but compact enough to follow over a long period of time and so be used as a test case to find out when and how liberal values in Germany declined or were transformed in a way that allowed the liberal bourgeoisie, both men and women, to vote for Hitler and welcome the Nazi seizure of power.

The research, which eventually appeared as a book in 1976,[13] forms the point of departure for Chapter 7 in the present volume. It aroused a good deal of interest among feminists, though the chequered history of its subsequent reception by feminist historians suggests that this was probably not unqualified even at the beginning.[14] And it was well received in England and the USA. But it had no impact on the West German historical profession, attracted only one review in a serious historical journal, and has never been mentioned in any work on the history of German liberalism as far as I know.[15] To German historians, liberalism meant, and still means, the liberal political parties; the notion of liberal values in a wider sense – of a whole general package of attitudes and assumptions which one might describe as the liberal mentality – seemed to be largely absent. Except, that is, in the work of those who sought to argue for a

Shows how cliff.
Historians accepted his works.

5

continuity of *il*liberal values in German history. Yet the rise of a numerically strong, active and vocal feminist movement in the 1890s, with a variety of radical policies, ranging from female suffrage and entry into the universities and professions to equal rights in property and divorce law and the abolition of police controls over prostitution, brought such a continuity into question. Although at least one German historian tried to dismiss all this as an irrelevance ('what difference did a handful of emancipated women make?'), it soon became clear in comparing notes with other British contemporaries working on the same period that the rise of the feminist movement was only part of a far broader political mobilization of German society, including workers, peasants, nationalists, anti-Semites, agrarians and many others, that was going on in the 1890s.

The implications of this view of the 1890s as a decade in which the profound social and economic stresses attendant upon Germany's transformation into an urban–industrial society undermined the hold of local notables on politics, and brought new, politically dynamic and sometimes volatile masses on to the scene, were far-reaching. Wilhelmine Germany appeared not as a static social and political system locked into a pre-programmed authoritarian rigidity, but as a rapidly changing, turbulent society in which new developments of all kinds were possible.[16] This view suggested that the *Kaiserreich* deserved closer attention in its own right, not merely as an antechamber of the Third Reich. New developments seemed as important as old structures in leading ultimately to Nazism, as even my own work, which argued a sharp swing to a new form of nationalist and illiberal politics on the part of the feminist movement just before the First World War, suggested. And the war itself, the subsequent revolution of 1918–19, and the economic disasters of the Weimar Republic, regained their importance as factors in the ultimate triumph of Hitler. Fascism began to look like the product of Germany's complex and uneven transition to modernity – as the convoluted history of that most modern of social movements, feminism, once more seemed to indicate – and not as an outcome of persistent political backwardness.

Although these ideas were at that time by no means fully worked out, there seemed enough of a common approach to the history of the *Kaiserreich* among British historians of my generation to bring them together in a book of essays which I edited in 1978, called *Society and Politics in Wilhelmine Germany*.[17] Not all of the ten contributors were in agreement on the central issues at stake, but enough of them were to ensure that the book had an impact far beyond the expectations of its authors. It received widespread attention in Germany and provoked a lively debate, providing the starting-point for a considerable quantity of later research, above all in the USA.[18] As Chapter 1 of the present book, which originated as the introduction to that collection, shows, the contributors were united in the critical stance which they adopted towards the interpretation of German history dominant in the Federal Republic (and widely held in Britain and America too) in the 1970s. The unifying concept of the book was the idea of 'history from below'. Subsequently this phrase has been much misunderstood. In 1978, however, it seemed clear enough. As defined in Raphael Samuel's introduction to the first volume of essays to emerge from the History Workshop movement,[19] 'history from below' meant above all a change of perspective, in which the historian examined what was happening not from the point of view of the government in Berlin, but from the point of view of the great mass of ordinary people in the rest of the country, not through the eyes of those who wrote the official documents on which we all so much depend, but through the eyes of those at the receiving end of the policies they were formulating. While this did mean widening one's vision to encompass all of society, it did not, as critics have sometimes mistakenly supposed, mean turning one's attention away from politics, or from government at the top. It simply meant interpreting them in a wider context and with different questions in mind. That is why the phrase is 'history *from* below' and not 'history *of* below'. For some strange reason, this point of view has frequently been described by its critics as 'populist', as if it had something to do with the agrarian and petty-bourgeois politics of demagogy to which that concept is most usually applied. It is better described as 'democratic'. In so far as it puts forward the not unreasonable argument that people, within limits, make their own history, and do not simply have it foisted on them from above, it represents a corrective to the élitist view which so many political historians adopt, without neglecting the constraints which existed on the freedom of action of the subordinate classes in the past.

Soon after the publication of *Society and Politics in Wilhelmine Germany*, two of the volume's contributors, David Blackbourn and Geoff Eley, brought out their own monographs, on the Catholic Centre and the nationalist movement respectively, in which it was clear that they had already taken the implications of the revaluation of the 1890s and the nature of the Wilhelmine empire for the interpretation of the whole course of German history even further.[20] Meanwhile, increasing quantities of literature on the subject were pouring off the presses, and it was clear that 'history from below' was after all only one of a number of approaches, still practised by a relatively small minority, as the discussion of some of this literature in Chapter 2 makes clear. The culmination of the debate was the publication in 1980 of Blackbourn and Eley's *Mythen deutscher Geschichtsschreibung*, issued in a much expanded and improved English version as *The Peculiarities of German History* five years later, and the subject of Chapter 3. The book, which caused a major row,[21] suggested among other things how fruitful the influence of French and particularly Italian neo-Marxism on British historians could be, although it also,

7

especially in David Blackbourn's contribution, bore traces of the Frank-furt school as well. It incidentally indicated another advantage of a British perspective on German history. Historians from Perry Anderson to Martin Wiener have been trying to locate the origins of Britain's long-term decline in the Victorian era, or even earlier in the failure of a full-scale bourgeois revolution.[22] Their work, and that of many others, has laid bare the undemocratic and illiberal side of Victorian and Edwardian Britain to an extent that makes it seem absurd to those of us brought up in the decades of British decline that modern British history should be held up by historians of Germany as an example from which it was Germany's entire misfortune to have deviated.

III

While this controversy was just beginning, an important chance had opened up to bring still further aspects of a British perspective to bear on the interpretation of the German past. One of the greatest surprises to a British historian coming to Germany from the ferment generated by the growth of social history in Britain and France was the discovery that the developments that made the British Marxist historians and the *Annales* school so exciting had no parallel at all on the other side of the Rhine. There was no sign of any serious interest in West Germany in the first half of the 1970s in social history as it was understood elsewhere. The new 'critical' approach of 'historical social science' advocated by Hans-Ulrich Wehler and others in the reinterpretation of the German past that took place in the years following on the Fischer controversy seemed in many ways like the old traditional German history, only presented in a different way. As Georg Iggers, one of the most perceptive observers of the German historiographical scene, has remarked, German historians includ-ing the post-Fischer 'critical school' still operated within the national paradigm of Bismarck's *kleindeutsch* concept of Germany; they still focused almost exclusively on political history, used mainly government records, and concentrated on the state, its actions and policies, and the history of those who brought direct political pressure to bear on it. 'Only after the middle of the 1970s', he notes, 'did there emerge a significant literature which explored the working and living conditions of ordinary men and women from a critical perspective'.[23]

The moment seemed right, therefore, to bring some influence to bear on this emergence of social history in Germany by setting up a series of working seminars in which the small, though steadily growing number of German specialists in key areas of social history could share their work, debate methodologies and hammer out controversial issues with British historians, both those specializing in the same areas and those with a more general interest in German social history. Fortunately the Social Science Research Council (now the Economic and Social Research Council) was able to offer financial support, and, when its budget fell victim to government cuts, first the Nuffield Foundation and then the University of East Anglia, Norwich, stepped in generously to fill the gap. Over the eight years from 1978 to 1986, a total of ten seminars, with twenty to thirty people taking part in each, including half a dozen or so at each meeting from the Federal Republic, was held at Norwich, on subjects ranging from the history of the family, the peasantry, the working class and the bourgeoisie to the history of crime, religion, popular culture, unemployment, health and medicine, and élites and ruling classes.

As part of the format of each meeting, the topic was usually introduced by a critical survey of research, and several of these surveys have served as introductions to the series of publications that has emerged from the papers presented to the seminars. Three of the chapters in the present book – Chapters 4, 5 and 6 – originated in this way.[24] These publications cover topics including *The German Family* (1981), *The German Working Class* (1982), *The German Peasantry* (1986) and *The German Unemployed* (1987), with *The German Underworld*, *The German Bourgeoisie* and possibly one or two others to come.[25] Taken together, they aim to provide an introduction to major areas of German social history and to tackle these areas 'from below', offering a new and critical perspective on aspects of German society neglected or given a narrowly political or legalistic interpretation by previous generations. For example, the recently published volume on the peasantry brought together a number of local studies to show that German peasants were not simply the passive objects of government policy or party-political manipulation, but made their own history and developed their own dynamic of social and political change. The village emerges not as an immobile, cohesive, timeless and united community, but as a social entity riven by internal conflicts and tensions which interacted with outside forces to produce a variety of historical developments to which the villagers themselves made a positive contribution, whether in the decay and collapse of serfdom at the turn of the eighteenth and nineteenth centuries, or the new volatility of peasant politics at the turn of the nineteenth and twentieth.[26]

This kind of approach made it clear that despite their rediscovery of neglected social movements in the German past, my book on feminism and its companion volume on the Social Democratic women's movement, published in German in 1979,[27] still concentrated too much on organizational history. Research on the feminist movement's activities in the north German port of Hamburg, which for various reasons can be regarded as the major centre of German feminism around the turn of the century, revealed the city's role as a bastion of bourgeois liberalism, mercantile rule, and laissez-faire, 'English' values in the nineteenth and early twentieth centuries, and the coincidence of a female suffrage campaign with a retrogressive revision of the local electoral system in 1906 provided the opportunity to begin exploring the connections between the city's political development and the social and economic structures that lay behind it. The result was an article, reprinted as the final chapter in this book, which focused on the suffrage riots that occurred in Hamburg in 1906. The article formed a preliminary exploration of many of the themes which recur in the much larger study of the city which has now been published under the title *Death in Hamburg*.[28]

Thinking about a major series of popular disturbances in a notorious 'criminal quarter' of Germany's second city before the First World War naturally led on to a broader consideration of the themes of authority and obedience in the German past, and the first conference of the International Association for the History of Crime and Criminal Justice, held in Washington in 1980, provided the opportunity to bring these thoughts together in a general critical survey, now published in a revised form as Chapter 5. This was not the only reason for becoming interested in this area, however. Even earlier, the frequent clashes of the 'radical' wing of the feminist movement with the police over the state control of prostitution had prompted an attempt to assess how far the police were really able to exert a close control over social behaviour in this way, and how far they were in fact at the mercy of wider processes and pressures rooted in dynamics of social change over which they had no power. Similarly, work on the Social Democratic women's movement had revealed the inadequacy of conventional approaches to German labour history, which seemed to stress the identity of the Social Democratic 'subculture' with working-class values and to argue, therefore, that the German proletariat was fundamentally reformist, orderly, respectable and even *embourgeoisé* long before the First World War. This seemed at odds both with the experience of Hamburg in 1906 and with the contradictions and conflicts which the rise of a socialist women's movement brought into the Social Democratic 'subculture'. The essay that now forms Chapter 6 of this book tried to draw out some of the wider implications of this work, and to argue that it was time to examine working-class values and working-class behaviour in a broader sense, and to realize that they were in many ways by no means identical with the culture of the Social Democratic labour movement.[29]

IV

By the beginning of the 1980s, the British contribution to reassessing the German past was attracting widespread attention, not all of it favourable, among historians in Germany and the USA as well as in Britain itself. Within the Federal Republic, it soon became taken up into a debate that had origins of its own in the change of intellectual atmosphere that accompanied the decay of the Social Democratic–liberal coalition, the accession of Chancellor Kohl to power in 1982, and above all the rise of the Green Party and allied social movements such as the new peace movement, the women's liberation movement and the ecological movement. The affluence and prosperity generated by the 'economic miracle' of the 1950s slowly turned sour, with rising unemployment making itself felt. The costs of economic success, above all massive environmental pollution, became increasingly clear. The failure of affluence to solve deep-rooted structures of inequality, discrimination and oppression in German society grew steadily more apparent. And the end of *détente* and the emergence of a new cold war put Germany in the front line of future hostilities once again. Among younger German historians, all this led to a questioning of the belief, which had become a dogma among the 'middle generation' of historians who rose to prominence in the 1960s and 1970s, that industrial prosperity inevitably brought social progress, democracy and freedom (even if, in Germany's case, it was argued that this conjuncture was fatally delayed until after 1945).[30]

Joining this new interest in social history and this new awareness of the victims of the 'modernization' process was a lively growth of popular interest in modern history particularly the history of everyday life in Germany over the past hundred years. The social and political background to this new development lay in the emergence all over Germany of innumerable local 'initiatives', covering a vast range of social problems, which sprang up as people despaired of the ponderous machinery of local government and political parties and began to organize themselves for single-issue campaigns on a local basis. So large is this 'alternative' constituency that it can sustain not only a whole number of small journals and magazines, as in Britain, but even an alternative, nationally distributed daily newspaper called *Die Tageszeitung*. It is not surprising, therefore, that this new constituency has also given rise to a new, widespread interest in an alternative history, 'history from below', in fact, a history whose practice also depends on local initiatives emerging from the alternative Left.

The emergence of a radical popular history movement has expressed itself in many ways: in the mounting of exhibitions on local historical topics, in the formation of small museums and study centres and in the eager collection of unused material on the recent past.[31] An interest in labour history and the history of the working class has been complemented by a concern with everyday life under Nazism and the daily experiences of ordinary working-class people under the Third Reich. In 1981 some of the interested parties got together to discuss the foundation of a new journal that would cater for the growing interest in a politically radical, locally based social history. The discussions resulted, however, not in an academic journal, which was felt to be too remote from the practice of the local initiatives, but in the foundation of an organization that aimed to bring together the initiatives and interested academic historians in a practical, democratic way: in fact, a History Workshop. This move was helped by a tremendous upsurge of local historical initiatives during the fiftieth anniversary year of the Nazi seizure of power, as the massive publicity given to the subject in the media stimulated a lively new interest in the popular experience of the Nazi regime among activists in the alternative community. The German History Workshop (*Geschichtswerkstatt*), founded in Bochum in 1983, soon claimed over 400 members. In 1984 it celebrated its first anniversary with a widely advertised History Festival (*Geschichtsfest*), held in West Berlin, and a second one took place in 1985.[32]

In many ways, the History Workshop movement in West Germany is very different from its British counterpart, despite the obvious and explicitly acknowledged debt it owes to the British model. To judge from its first annual History Festival, held in 1984, its main concern is with methods, rather than with problems. Most excitement was generated by sessions on interview techniques in oral history, the use of photographs, films and videotapes, and the presentation of historical subjects through the medium of drama, museum exhibitions or 'alternative' historical guides and tours of significant places. There seemed to be very little interest in the written word, and a strong distaste for written sources, which were widely regarded as only giving official views of the past. Perhaps people were put off by the incomprehensible academic jargon used by most left-wing historians in the Federal Republic. Perhaps this was the TV generation coming into its own: the past is only 'real' if seen and heard. Use of such sources also bore witness to a lack of interest in the past beyond 1900. The overwhelming concentration was on the Third Reich and reconstruction after 1945. The celebration of radical traditions going back to medieval times that plays such an important part in the British History Workshops had no counterpart in the Berlin meeting. Moreover, the breadth of vision apparent in the British movement, with its interest in colonial and Third World history, was largely absent in the German History Workshop: the real interest was almost exclusively in locally based German History, despite a few pious hopes expressed to the contrary. Those who came from local initiatives of this kind were mainly young, often university-educated, in many cases unemployed school-teachers and the like. There was hardly a grey head to be seen, and the massive support the British History Workshop receives from trade unions, which gives it close contact with older workers, is not paralleled in Germany, where the industrial unions have their own historical traditions and are deeply suspicious of the anti-industrial elements among the Greens. Finally there were few practising university historians to be seen, a reflection of the lack of any long-established tradition of Marxist historiography in West Germany, and those few younger academic historians who did attend had to encounter a good deal of suspicion from the participants, particularly when they tried to defend the use of theory or advise caution in the interpretation of oral evidence. It remains to be seen, too, whether the German History Workshop, which so far has not been able to find the kind of institutional roots which its British counterpart enjoys, can convert the enthusiasm generated by the 1983 and 1985 anniversaries into a more permanent engagement with the past.

Even if the German History Workshop fails to last, however, the approach to history which it represents is surely here to stay. The presentation of history in ways other than, or at least additional to, the written word is of central importance in an age when not only the possibilities of doing this, but also the difficulties of conveying new kinds of historical evidence in verbal form, are greater than ever before. Moreover, the nearer we get to the present, as we move through the invention of the telephone, the wireless, the motion picture, the tape-recorder, the video cassette and so on, the more inadequate written evidence becomes. A concentration on modern and contemporary history is a feature not just of the German History Workshop, but also of university-based history, which is now rushing into the post-1945 period as the files become available under the thirty-year rule. And the interest of the History Workshop in what is known in Germany as *Alltagsgeschichte* (the history of everyday life), but has been familiar for much longer elsewhere as social history, *histoire sociale*, is shared by increasing numbers of academic historians as well.[33]

Two other varieties of social history (or *Alltagsgeschichte*) apart from the Workshop movement can be discerned in West Germany today. In the first place there is a sociological variety, politically neutral in orientation, and concerned mainly with quantitative studies of living conditions, groups of workers, family structures and the like. While this is producing a great deal of valuable work, it tends to ignore the political aspects of the subjects it tackles, and, like much quantitative history, it pretends to represent a 'balanced', or in other words 'objective' approach to the past that is belied by its strong inclination to suggest that everyday life has been getting steadily better for everyone since the rise of capitalism and the onset of industrialization. Thus it plays down social inequality and social conflict in the past, and directs the historian's attention towards abstract models of social change.[34] Secondly there is a more left-wing variety, which is strongly influenced by Anglo-American social anthropology, British Marxist history, and French theories and methods of demographic, family and community history. Here attention is focused not on the urban–industrial world, but on the world of the village, often going back to the Middle Ages, and not on broad generalization and the testing or establishment of sociological 'laws' but rather on micro-history, on teasing out historical meaning from the closely detailed study of small communities, groups of people or even individuals. Like the History Workshop, these historians deal with local or at most regional subjects, and so break with the national history paradigm dominant until now. They also share with the History Workshop a concern with the subjective experiences, perceptions and beliefs of those they study, a distrust of theories rigidly imposed on the evidence from outside, an interest in neglected groups in the past, and a concern to take seriously and if possible to explain actions and beliefs previously thought by historians to be trivial or irrational, and in neither case, therefore, worth studying.[35] It is not surprising, therefore, that they have provided the bulk of the professional historians involved in the Workshop movement, though their interest in history before 1900 and in the rural world means that they may in fact have less in common with the movement than might appear at first sight.

In the lively debate that has emerged in West Germany about the merits (or otherwise) of social history,[36] these three rather different approaches have sometimes been confused.[37] At other times, critics have failed to recognize that the phenomenon of *Alltagsgeschichte* is not exclusively German but part of a substantial international movement, in which West Germany has in many ways actually lagged behind other countries. This has led at times to an extraordinary parochialism of view, in which critics have accused micro-historians of doing something different just to make a name for themselves, as if this could be true of the established historians who have led the way in the field, such as Emmanuel Le Roy Ladurie, Natalie Zemon Davis, or Arthur Imhof, or have taken their stand on theoretical positions put forward by Droysen, Weber, or Dilthey, as if theorists outside the German tradition did not exist, or were irrelevant or inadmissible.[38] What is curious from the point of view of an outsider from another country is not only the vehemence of the debate on social history in West Germany but also its intolerance, as all sides advance their own approach as the only possible way of studying history, and condemn all others as outdated, pointless, or at best interesting without being really significant.[39]

Nevertheless, there are some very important issues at stake. Whether these include the continued monopoly of academically trained professional historians over the accumulation, teaching and presentation of historical knowledge, and whether this is the fundamental reason for the hostile reaction of some of them to the History Workshop movement, must remain an open question in view of the movement's limited scope and uncertain future. There can be no doubt, however, that both micro-history and regional social history on the one hand and the similar thrust of the History Workshop on the other are mounting a serious challenge to two central traditions of German historiography which – in contrast to Britain, France and the USA – have remained dominant right up to the

1980s: the primacy of political history and the assumption that Germa history has to be studied in the framewoık of the nation-state (or, moı precisely, the *kleindeutsch* boundaries of the Bismarckian Empire). Foı the generations that have grown up since the end of the Second World War, the concept of the nation-state has come to mean very little: the question of the costs and gains of industrialization and technological change is of far more importance; and correspondingly, the centrality of political history, seen in terms of the exercise of power at the national level, gives way to a focus on different problems which involve a concept of power as something both more intimate and more diffuse.[40] It is as an illustration of the way that power can be conceived of in social history terms that I have put together the three studies that make up the third part of this book; and as a reflection of the change in perspective that has taken place with the emergence of a German social history that I have structured the book so that it begins with the discussion of the development of the nation-state and ends with the analysis of the events of a single day in one particular German town.

What has fundamentally taken place over the last two decades can be seen as a *normalization* of German historiography. No one could deny the deforming and isolating effects of the experience of 1918, the Third Reich and the defeat of 1945 on the German historical profession, or the tremendous achievements of the 1960s and 1970s in bringing this isolation to an end. What we are witnessing in the 1980s are the full consequences of this achievement, as the study of German history has broadened its scope and its methods so that it is being carried on in much the same way as the study of history in other countries. Of course it still has its own peculiarities, and some of them, perhaps most of all the importance it accords to conceptual clarity and theoretical awareness, are exerting an influence on historians in other countries in their own right. But when one looks at the range of subjects on which German historians have recently published, it is hard to detect any really fundamental difference between the historiography of Germany and that of other countries any more. The reasons for this development lie above all in the history of contemporary Germany itself; but if it could be said that outsiders working in the field, such as the British historians of my own generation, had made even a small contribution to this process, it would be reward enough for our labours.

The arguments put forward in this book thus reflect in the first place the influence on my thinking exerted by the community of British historians working on Germany, above all as it has been thrashed out in the ten Research Seminars in Modern German Social History held over the years at the University of East Anglia. The discussions at those meetings (and on many other occasions) have influenced me in ways too numerous to mention. I owe a particular debt in this context, as will be readily apparent from some of the essays in this book, to David Blackbourn and Geoff

15

Eley, but also to Richard Bessel, Jane Caplan, David Crew, Dick Geary, Ian Kershaw, Robert Lee and James Wickham. Further back, I also owe a debt of gratitude to my friends and colleagues at St Antony's College, Oxford, from 1969 to 1972, especially those who introduced me to the *Annales* school and the History Workshop, and to Robin Law, with whom I taught a joint course on Marxist historiography in 1974 that had a crucial influence on my later thinking about methodology. My own institution, the University of East Anglia, has not only provided constant encouragement and support but also, in the late 1970s and early 1980s, with colleagues such as Ian Farr, Willi Guttsman, Paul Kennedy, Werner Mosse and Alice Teichova, formed an almost ideal environment for thinking and talking about German history. In Germany itself I have benefited from discussing history and historiography over the years with too many historians to mention here, and have been kept in touch with the scene by a constant stream of offprints and photocopies from sources even greater in number: I hope they will accept my thanks here, which are no less heartfelt for being necessarily anonymous. I learned a great deal from a sympathetic critique of my work by Robert Moeller, and from the criticisms and comments made by the audiences in various countries on whom many of these chapters were first tried out. Anthony Nicholls has been unstinting in his advice and support ever since he set me on the road to German history back in 1969. On a more practical level, Jane Harris-Matthews at Allen & Unwin has been a patient and understanding editor, while Elvi Dobie and Carol Haines at the University of East Anglia have been untiring in their help with the final stages of preparation and typing, and Lynn Abrams and Martin Pond have kindly assisted with the proof-reading. Finally, I owe in some ways most of all to my students, at Columbia University, New York, where I was fortunate enough to be able to teach a graduate class on German history in 1980, and above all at the University of East Anglia, where I have been teaching courses in German history and supervising postgraduate work in the field for the last ten years. My students' interest and enthusiasm has been vital in sustaining my own, and their critical reception of my ideas has done perhaps more than anything to help me define them and find an adequate form for their expression: I hope they will not think it presumptuous of me if I dedicate this book to them in appreciation.

NOTES

1 Good examples of this kind of work include W. Carr, *A History of Germany 1815–1945* (2nd edn., London, 1979); G. A. Craig, *Germany 1866–1945* (Oxford, 1978). Popular, but far less satisfactory, is G. Mann, *The History of Germany since 1789* (London, 1968).
2 See e.g. V. R. Berghahn, *Modern Germany: Society, Economy and Politics in the Twentieth Century* (Cambridge, 1982).
3 An outstandingly successful example of the *genre* is G. A. Craig, *The Germans* (New York, 1982), deservedly a best seller in both America and Germany.

4 For detailed substantiation of this point, see my review of E. Sagarra, *A Social History of Germany 1648–1914* (London, 1977), in *Journal of European Studies*, vol. 10 (1980), pp. 150–1.

5 Among the former category F. L. Carsten was particularly important; among the latter, H. R. Trevor-Roper, Alan Bullock and A. J. P. Taylor. The influence of a younger generation of German exiles, such as Volker Berghahn and H. Pogge-von Strandmann, was also beginning to make itself felt in the 1960s.

6 E. Nolte, *Three Faces of Fascism* (London, 1965); B. Moore, Jr., *Social Origins of Dictatorship and Democracy* (London, 1966); W. Laqueur and G. L. Mosse (eds.), 'International Fascism 1920–1945', *Journal of Contemporary History*, vol. 1 (1968); S. J. Woolf (ed.), *European Fascism* (London, 1968); Woolf (ed.), *The Nature of Fascism* (London, 1968). Also E. Weber, *Varieties of Fascism* (New York, 1964); F. L. Carsten, *The Rise of Fascism* (London, 1967); H. Rogger and E. Weber (eds.), *The European Right* (London, 1965).

7 R. Cobb, *The Police and the People* (Oxford, 1970); *Reactions to the French Revolution* (Oxford, 1972); *Paris and its Provinces* (Oxford, 1975).

8 R. Cobb, *A Second Identity* (Oxford, 1969).

9 T. Zeldin, *France 1848–1945*, Vol. 1, *Ambition, Love and Politics* (Oxford, 1973), Vol. 2, *Intellect, Taste and Anxiety* (Oxford, 1978).

10 Introductory surveys to the work of the French historians are now very numerous. Among them one of the most useful is the special issue of the *Journal of Modern History*, vol. 44 (1972), pp. 447–57, devoted to Fernand Braudel.

11 Among them were E. J. Hobsbawm, *The Age of Revolution 1789–1848* (London, 1962); E. J. Hobsbawm and George Rudé, *Captain Swing* (London, 1969); George Rudé, *The Crowd in History* (London, 1964); E. P. Thompson, *The Making of the English Working Class* (London, 1963); C. Hill, *Society and Puritanism in Pre-Revolutionary England* (London, 1964); Hill, *The Century of Revolution 1603–1714* (London, 1961).

12 I have tried to give a brief assessment of the History Workshop movement in my article 'Die "History Workshop"-Bewegung in England', in H. Heer and V. Ullrich (eds), *Geschichte entdecken: Erfahrungen und Projekte der neuen Geschichtsbewegung* (Reinbek bei Hamburg, 1985), pp. 37–45.

13 *The Feminist Movement in Germany, 1894–1933*, SAGE Studies in 20th Century History, Vol. 6 (London, 1976).

14 For a discussion of this point, see the introduction to my book *Comrades and Sisters: Feminism, Socialism and Pacifism in Europe 1890–1945* (London, 1987).

15 The book was reviewed in only one major West German historical periodical, the *Vierteljahrschrift für Sozial- und Wirtschaftsgeschichte*, vol. 65 (1978), pp. 567–9, by an associate of the editorial team who was himself researching in the same area. There were three other German-language reviews, one in a political magazine, one (just a mention) in a local history journal, and one in the main East German historical review, the *Zeitschrift für Geschichtswissenschaft*.

16 See my brief article 'Auch Deutschland hatte seine Suffragetten', *Frankfurter Allgemeine Zeitung*, 27 Apr. 1978, p. 11.

17 It is telling evidence of the present situation of history teaching and research in this country that of the ten contributors, two subsequently entered government service, two emigrated and only six are currently in full-time academic posts in the UK.

18 For general discussions of the work of younger British historians on the history of late 19th and early 20th century Germany, see R. G. Moeller, 'The Kaiserreich Recast? Continuity and Change in Modern German Historiography', *Journal of Social History*, vol. 17, no. 4 (1984), pp. 655–83; J. N. Retallack, 'Social History with a Vengeance? Some Reactions to H.-U. Wehler's "Das Deutsche Kaiserreich"', *German Studies Review*, vol. 7, no. 3 (1984), pp. 422–50; R. Fletcher, 'Recent Developments in West German Historiography: The Bielefeld School and its Critics', ibid., pp. 451–80; W. Mock, '"Manipulation von oben" oder Selbstorganisation an der Basis? Einige neuere Ansätze in der englischen Historiographie zur Geschichte des deutschen Kaiserreichs', *Historische Zeitschrift*, vol. 232 (1981), pp. 358–75; I. Veit-Brause, 'Zur Kritik an der "Kritischen Geschichtswissenschaft": Tendenzwende oder Paradigmawechsel?', *Geschichte in Wissenschaft und Unterricht*, vol. 35, no. 1 (1984), pp. 1–24. As Retallack remarks, 'It is no accident that the historiography of the Kaiserreich has

17

prompted recent reviewers to begin their discussions with a prominent question mark' ('Social History with a Vengeance', p. 423). See also the discussions in D. F. Crew, *Town in the Ruhr: A Social History of Bochum 1860–1914* (New York, 1979), pp. 1–7; R. Chickering, *'We Men Who Feel Most German': A Cultural Study of the Pan-German League 1886–1914* (London, 1984), pp. 12–15; I. V. Hull, *The Entourage of Kaiser Wilhelm II 1888–1918* (London, 1982), pp. 1–14.

19 R. Samuel, 'General Editor's Introduction: people's history', in R. Samuel (ed.), *Village Life and Labour* (London, 1975), pp. xiii–xxi.

20 D. Blackbourn, *Class, Religion and Local Politics in Wilhelmine Germany: The Centre Party in Württemberg before 1914* (London, 1980); G. Eley, *Reshaping the German Right: Radical Nationalism and Political Change After Bismarck* (London, 1980).

21 See H.-U. Wehler, '"Deutscher Sonderweg" oder allgemeine Probleme des westlichen Kapitalismus? Zur Kritik an einigen "Mythen deutscher Geschichtsschreibung"', *Merkur*, vol. 35 (1981), pp. 477–87; G. Eley, 'Antwort an Hans-Ulrich Wehler', ibid., pp. 757–9; H.-U. Wehler, 'Rückantwort an Geoff Eley', ibid., p. 760; H. A. Winkler, 'Der deutsche Sonderweg: Eine Nachlese', ibid., pp. 793–804; H.-J. Puhle, 'Deutscher Sonderweg: Kontroverse um eine vermeintliche Legende', *Journal für Geschichte*, vol. 3 (1981), pp. 44–5; J. Kocka, 'Der "deutsche Sonderweg" in der Diskussion', *German Studies Review*, vol. 5 (1982), pp. 365–79; D. Langewiesche, 'Entmythologisierung des "deutschen Sonderwegs" oder auf dem Wege zu neuen Mythen?', *Archiv für Sozialgeschichte*, vol. 21 (1981), pp. 527–32; and (more balanced, but still critical), D. Groh, 'Le "Sonderweg" de l'histoire allemande: mythe ou réalité?' *Annales ESC*, vol. 38 (1983), pp. 1166–87.

22 M. Wiener, *English Culture and the Decline of the Industrial Spirit* (Cambridge, 1981); E. P. Thompson, *The Poverty of Theory* (London, 1978).

23 G. Iggers, *The Social History of Politics: Critical Perspectives in West German Historical Writing since 1945* (Leamington Spa, 1985), pp. 34–5. As Iggers remarks, the work of Werner Conze and the Heidelberg circle, with its use of sociological models and (increasingly) quantitative techniques, went back further; but Conze's attempt to introduce the *Annales* school to a German audience in the 1950s fell flat, and it was not until 1976 that the first selection of their work appeared in German (C. Honegger (ed.), *Schrift und Materie der Geschichte: Vorschläge zur systematischen Aneignung historischer Prozesse* (Frankfurt, 1977). Much of the early work of the Heidelberg school was in labour movement history. A few individuals such as Wilhelm Abel pursued social history more seriously, but they remained untypical (see I. Farr, '"Tradition" and the Peasantry: On the Modern Historiography of Rural Germany', in R. J. Evans and W. R. Lee (eds.), *The German Peasantry: Conflict and Community in Rural Society from the Eighteenth to the Twentieth Centuries* (London, 1986), pp. 1–36).

24 Chapter 5 is taken from a longer essay, the rest of which forms the introduction to *The German Underworld* (London, 1988).

25 To which must be added, 'Religion and Society in Germany', special issue of *European Studies Review*, vol. 12, no. 3 (1982), from which Chapter 4 has been taken.

26 Evans and Lee, *German Peasantry*.

27 *Sozialdemokratie und Frauenemanzipation im Deutschen Kaiserreich* (Bonn and Berlin, 1979).

28 R. J. Evans, *Death in Hamburg: Society and Politics in the Cholera Years 1830–1910* (Oxford, 1987).

29 See the contributions collected in R. J. Evans (ed.), *The German Working Class 1888–1945: The Politics of Everyday Life* (London, 1982); and the discussion by G. Eley, 'Joining Two Histories: The SPD and the German Working Class, 1860–1914', in his *From Unification to Nazism: Reinterpreting the German Past* (London, 1986), pp. 171–99. Also Evans, 'Prostitution, State and Society in Imperial Germany', *Past and Present*, vol. 71 (1986), pp. 106–29.

30 G. Zang, *Die unaufhaltsame Annäherung an das Einzelne: Reflexionen über den theoretischen und praktischen Nutzen der Regional- und Alltagsgeschichte* (Konstanz, 1985); F. Brüggemeier and J. Kocka, *'Geschichte von unten – Geschichte von innen': Kontroversen um die Alltagsgeschichte* (Hagen, 1985).

31 For an outstanding example of this kind of work, see H.-M. Bock *et al.*, *Vorwärts– und*

nicht vergessen. Arbeiterkultur in Hamburg um 1930. Materialien zur Geschichte der Weimarer Republik (Berlin, 1982).

32 A. G. Frei, 'Die Zukunft beginnt in der Vergangenheit: Geschichtswerkstätten, Tendenzwende und demokratische Alternativen', *Moderne Zeiten*, vol. 4 (1984), pp. 3–6; Frei, 'Geschichtswerkstätten als Zukunftswerkstätten: Ein Plädoyer für aufklärerische Geschichtsarbeit', in G. Paul and B. Schossig (eds), *Die andere Geschichte: Geschichte von unten, Spurensicherung, ökologische Geschichte, Geschichtswerkstätten* (Cologne, 1985), pp. 258–80; Frei, 'Alltag – Region – Politik: Anmerkungen zur "neuen Geschichtsbewegung"', *Geschichtsdidaktik*, vol. 2 (1984), pp. 107–20; V. Ullrich, 'Geschichte von unten: Die neue Bewegung zur Erforschung des Alltags', *Journal für Geschichte*, vol. 2 (1984); H. Heer and V. Ullrich (eds), *Geschichte entdecken* (Reinbek bei Hamburg, 1985). Also 'Der Geschichtswerkstatt stellt sich vor', *Frankfurter Rundschau*, 4 Jan. 1984, p. 14; '"Ein kräftiger Schub für die Vergangenheit": Spiegel-Report über die neue Geschichtsbewegung in der Bundesrepublik', *Der Spiegel*, vol. 23 (1983), pp. 36–42. For two characteristic examples of the products of the movement, see *Hochlamarker Lesebuch: Kohle war nicht alles: 100 Jahre Ruhrgebietsgeschichte*, hrsg. von der Stadt Recklinghausen (Oberhausen, 1981), and Berliner Geschichtswerkstatt (ed.), *Projekt: Spurensicherung: Alltag und Widerstand im Berlin der 30er Jahre* (Berlin, 1983).

33 Linguistic and conceptual difficulties rule out a direct German equivalent of 'social history' as it is understood in Britain: *Sozialgeschichte* traditionally meant labour history (hence the *International Review of Social History* had as its main function early on the publication of studies and documents relating to Marx, Engels, Kautsky and other socialist theorists). *Gesellschaftsgeschichte* ('societal history') appears to mean a history based on an explicitly Weberian social theory, or at least has been appropriated as a term by those who want to write history in this way.

34 P. Borscheid and H. J. Teuteberg (eds), *Ehe, Liebe, Tod: Zum Wandel der Familie, der Geschlechts- und Generationsbeziehungen in der Neuzeit* (Münster, 1983); P. Borscheid, 'Plädoyer für eine Geschichte des Alltäglichen', ibid., pp. 1–14; and subsequent volumes in this series, e.g. C. Wischermann, *Wohnen in Hamburg vor dem Ersten Weltkrieg* (Münster, 1984). The later work of the Heidelberg school also shared some of these qualities: see e.g. H. Schomerus, *Die Arbeiter der Maschinenfabrik Esslingen: Forschungen zur Lage der Arbeiterschaft im 19. Jahrhundert* (Stuttgart, 1977); P. Borscheid, *Textilarbeiterschaft in der Industrialisierung* (Stuttgart, 1978); W. Conze and U. Engelhardt (eds), *Arbeiter im Industrialisierungsprozess* (Stuttgart, 1979). None of my comments should be allowed to detract from the fine quality of a great deal of this work in terms of empirical research, or from its frequently innovatory contribution to quantitative methodology.

35 There are particularly strong concentrations of these historians at the University of Konstanz and the Max Planck Institut für Geschichte, Göttingen. A representative sample of their work might include D. Sabean, *Power in the Blood* (Cambridge, 1984); H. Medick and D. Sabean (eds), *Emotion and Material Interest* (Cambridge, 1985); G. Zang et al., *Provinzialisierung einer Region* (Frankfurt, 1978); D. Schott and W. Trapp (eds), *Seegründe: Beiträge zur Geschichte des Bodenseeraumes* (Weingarten, 1984).

36 Brüggemeier and Kocka, 'Geschichte von unten – Geschichte von innen'; Zang, *Unaufhaltsame Annäherung*. See also L. Niethammer, 'Anmerkungen zur Alltagsgeschichte', *Geschichtsdidaktik*, vol. 5 (1980), pp. 231–42; and D. Peukert, 'Arbeiteralltag – Mode oder Methode?', in H. Haumann (ed.), *Arbeiteralltag in Stadt und Land* (Berlin, 1982), pp. 8–39. For criticisms, see H.-U. Wehler, 'Der Bauernbandit als neuer Heros', *Die Zeit*, 18 September 1981, reprinted in Wehler, *Preussen ist wieder chic* (Frankfurt, 1984); J. Kocka, 'Theory and Social History: Recent Developments in West Germany', *Social Research*, vol. 47 (1980), pp. 426–57; Kocka, 'Klassen oder Kultur? Durchbrüche und Sackgassen in der Alltagsgeschichte', *Merkur*, vol. 36, no. 10 (1982), pp. 955–65; Kocka, 'Historisch-anthropologische Fragestellungen – ein Defizit der Historischen Sozialwissenschaft? Thesen zur Diskussion', in H. Süssmuth (ed.), *Historische Anthropologie: Der Mensch in der Geschichte* (Göttingen, 1984), pp. 73–6; and G. Eley and K. Nield, 'Why does Social History Ignore Politics?', *Social History*, vol. 5 (1980), pp. 249–69. Replies include M. Broszat, 'Plädoyer für Alltagsgeschichte: Eine Replik auf

Jürgen Kocka', *Merkur*, vol. 36, no. 12 (1982), pp. ¡244–8; H. Medick, '"Missionäre im Ruderboot"? Ethnologische Erkenntnisweisen als Herausforderung an die Sozialgesschichte', *Geschichte und Gesellschaft*, vol. 10, no. 3 (1984), pp. 295–319; A. Lüdtke, '"Kolonisierung der Lebenswelten – oder: Geschichte als Einbahnstrasse?', *Das Argument*, vol. 140 (1983), pp. 536–41.

37 P. Schöttler, 'Historiker auf neuen Pfaden: "Spurensicherung" im Alltag', *Frankfurter Rundschau*, 4 January 1984, p. 14.

38 E. Le Roy Ladurie, *Montaillou: Cathars and Catholics in a French village 1294–1324* (London, 1978); N. Z. Davis, *The Return of Martin Guerre* (Cambridge, Mass., 1983); A. E. Imhof, *Die verlorenen Welten* (Munich, 1984). For the comments referred to, see Brüggemeier and Kocka, 'Geschichte von unten – Geschichte von innen'.

39 This applies not least to the essay by Medick, 'Missionäre im Ruderboot', but also to the contribution by Wehler in Brüggemeier and Kocka.

40 Zang, *Unaufhaltsame Annäherung*.

PART ONE

Historiographies

1

Wilhelm II's Germany and the Historians

In the early 1970s it became clear that there were quite a number of British historians of the same generation working on various aspects of the Wilhelmine Empire. It seemed a good idea, therefore, to put ourselves on the map by bringing together all our various work in a collection of original essays. Initially there was no thought that this would represent any kind of coherent view of German history, but conversations and discussions with a number of the contributors, especially Stephen Hickey, in Oxford, and David Blackbourn and Geoff Eley, in Cambridge, soon made it clear that a sufficient number of them were agreed on broad, central issues to make the book more than simply an eclectic collection of empirical studies. I had already been thinking about the problems and drawbacks of the kind of approach represented by Hans-Ulrich Wehler's *Das deutsche Kaiserreich* (1973) and other publications of the post-Fischer era, and writing the introduction to our collective volume, which took shape gradually in 1976–7 and was finally published under the title *Society and Politics in Wilhelmine Germany* (London, 1978; the introduction is on pp. 11–39), provided the opportunity to put down my thoughts in some kind of connected way. In retrospect, perhaps, the essay oversold the volume's coherence, but there can be no doubt that the book was widely regarded as adding up to much more than the sum of its parts, nor that it has subsequently come to stand for a fairly specific set of attitudes and approaches to recent German history. For this volume, the parts of the essay specifically devoted to introducing the subsequent contributions have been removed, while enough of the general argument has been retained to give a clear idea of their overall thrust. A conference on 'History and Politics in West Germany', held at the German Historical Institute in London by the Association for the Study of German Politics in December 1979, provided the opportunity to develop some aspects of this overall argument further. Parts of the paper, subsequently published as 'Rethinking the German Past', in a special German election issue of *West European Politics* (vol. 4, no. 2 (1981), pp. 134–48), have been incorporated into the chapter, above all in the opening section, to strengthen the historiographical aspects of the essay, which were

23

necessarily very abbreviated in the original, and the footnote references have been updated where necessary. In this, as in all chapters of this book, translations from the German are my own unless otherwise indicated.

articles written by Germans have been translated by him.

I

Today, more than forty years after the fall of the Third Reich, and more than half a century after the Nazi seizure of power, the shadow of the past still darkens the surface of German politics. It is not simply that the antics and outrages of neo-Nazis keep the memory of the Third Reich in the public eye; nor that there are still many former Nazis in high places, and that some of these, such as the former Minister-President of Baden-Württemberg, Hans Filbinger, have been at the centre of major controversies when unpleasant facts about their political past have been revealed: cases such as Filbinger's are likely to occur with increasing rarity as those who were adult before 1945 die out, while the neo-Nazi extremists seem to have even less support than the Baader–Meinhof group. History plays a less direct but more central role than this in West German politics. It was particularly in evidence during the 1979 federal election campaign. Voters were allegedly repelled by the unsuccessful opposition candidate Franz-Josef Strauss because, among other things, the violence of his invective and the alarmism of his foreign policies reminded them all too much of Adolf Hitler. And if this is going too far, then Strauss had certainly identified himself on a number of occasions with the long tradition of German nationalism, while his emphasis on discipline and order, his penchant for authoritarian state action, and his unbridled attacks on socialism, all called to mind, paradoxically in view of his Bavarian origins, the historical memory of the old Prussian state.[1] More generally, West German politicians have frequently addressed historical problems in a way that is unfamiliar in other countries. In 1971, for instance, President Heinemann urged West Germans, on the centenary of the founding of the Bismarckian Reich, to see themselves as the successors not of the Empire which the 'Iron Chancellor' created, and those who ruled it, but of Social Democrats such as Bebel and Liebknecht, who sat in gaol as it was being proclaimed, and of the other opponents of Bismarckian authoritarianism such as Eugen Richter, the left-wing liberal, or Ludwig Windthorst, the Catholic Centre party leader during the struggles of the *Kulturkampf*.

The connections between politics and historical (and other) scholarship in the Federal Republic are close. The political parties have their own educational committees which go as far as discussing school curricula in quite detailed terms; the state governments have to approve university appointments and frequently refuse to do so on political grounds;

examinations are also vetted by the state, which is also represented on the examining bodies. A major political party such as the Social Democratic Party of Germany (*Sozialdemokratische Partei Deutschlands*, or SPD) has its own research institute as part of the Friedrich Ebert Stiftung, which publishes a large quantity of historical literature, from general party histories to highly specialized monographs, and sponsors a large quantity of research. All these connections, while producing nothing like the rigid 'party line' familiar in East German historiography, do constitute a consistent set of pressures operating in the direction of the politicization of historical research, above all as it applies to the history of the last 150 years.

Since the end of the Second World War, German historians themselves have also been acutely conscious of the political relevance and importance of their discipline. In his opening address to the first postwar Congress of German Historians (*Deutscher Historikertag*) in 1949, entitled 'Present Situation and Future Tasks of German Historical Scholarship', Gerhard Ritter, the president of the Congress, laid particular stress on the sins of the past in this respect. In his view, the historians of previous generations had been all-too-characteristic examples of the 'unpolitical German':

> Since Ranke, German historical scholarship has always been especially proud of its objectivity. And certainly one may say in retrospective praise that its development was less closely connected with party-political tendencies than, for instance, English or even French historical scholarship was ... But frequently this objectivity was the result not of a real sense of truth and justice but rather of cautious or unworldly neutrality ... [This] also robbed it in many cases of political nerve and did not protect it from ... the intrusion of political prejudices in favour of Prussia and Germany, from the spirit of nationalistic arrogance.[2]

He called therefore for a stronger political engagement on the part of historians; for a sober and self-critical reappraisal of the German past and of the methods by which German historians had hitherto approached it. Similarly, many younger German historians in the early 1970s argued that history had an important role to play in the creation of a new, more securely rooted democratic consciousness among the citizens of the Federal Republic. History, as one of the most prominent of these historians remarked, should aim to contribute consciously to the development of 'a freer, more critical social consciousness', it should 'work out the consequences of decisions taken, or the social costs of decisions not taken, in the past, and thus increase the chances of a rational orientation of our behaviour and our lives, and embed them within the horizons of carefully-considered historical experiences.'[3]

German historians since the end of the Second World War, therefore, have addressed the recent past with very specific political questions in

25

mind. Chief among these has been the obvious one of how Germans can learn from their past in order to avoid repeating its mistakes. The questions which everyone wants to answer are: how can the Bonn republic survive where the Weimar Republic failed? What do Germans have to do to prevent the advent of another Hitler? Not surprisingly, the answers which historians have provided have differed widely according to their political position. A historian whose sympathies lie with the Christian Democrats, for instance, is likely to have a very different view of the past from one sympathetic to the Social Democrats or the Free Democrats. Correspondingly, any interpretation which an historian advances of the historical origins of the Nazi seizure of power is bound to have direct political implications for the present. Of course, the view that was put forward by Allied propaganda during the war, of the immutable wickedness of the 'German character', could only have the implication that never again could Germans be allowed to take charge of their own destinies.[4] Not surprisingly, therefore, for this if for no other reason, it has always been rejected by the Germans themselves. This posed the problem, however, of what should replace it. Ritter's main concern was to dissociate what he regarded as the central traditions of German history from what he argued were the novel and alien ideas and practices introduced by Hitler. In his essay on 'The Historical Foundations of the Rise of National-Socialism', written in the early 1950s, he therefore launched a strong attack on the 'continuity thesis':

> Up till the present there has been a strong tendency to seek the sources of National-Socialism in the dim past of German history. Attempts to do this were started in the Vansittart group's propaganda in the Second World War, when they tried to show that National-Socialist methods of violence existed among the Cimbri and the Teutons. More serious are the efforts of various foreign and German experts to explain the distinctly militarist nature of German nationalism by its origins at the time of the wars of liberation, and the glorification of war throughout the nineteenth century, which is shown by quotations from all kinds of authors. Others trace the prehistory of National-Socialism back to Frederick the Great, or even to the Reformation.[5]

Ritter objected strongly to such views, which he said were 'sterile if they are used to explain the rapid decline of the Weimar Republic and the triumphal ascent of the Hitlerian Party from 1930 to 1933' (p. 386). Indeed, at some considerable risk to himself, he had already objected publicly during the 1930s to the Nazis' own attempt to portray Luther in what appeared to them to be positive terms, as a predecessor of Hitler.[6]

Ritter countered these arguments by suggesting that the methods used by these historians were faulty. 'History', he wrote, 'can never be written by means of quotations from literature, since it is almost always possible to find such quotations contradicted elsewhere' (p. 386). Quotations illustrating nationalism, racism, militarism and anti-democratic criticism could be found in the literature of any European country. In Germany, moreover, literature was more than usually abstruse, personal, and 'not representative of real tendencies alive in the people.' More specifically, Ritter argued that historical experience showed that 'In general German people did not like political adventures' (p. 387). He also attacked the idea that Germans had no natural sense of liberty. 'Only a completely superficial study of German history can ignore the thousands of examples of a true sense of freedom, examples which are numerous since the early Middle Ages, and which frequently made the rulers of the German people think them unruly and difficult to govern' (p. 388). Enlightened despotism, liberalism, local autonomy and the Weimar Republic had all contributed to the political education of the Germans. The Weimar Republic failed not because it was a democracy but 'because it did not succeed in winning general confidence, in becoming genuinely popular through successes which could be appreciated from a distance' (p. 389).

For Ritter, the historical origins of National Socialism lay not in old-established traditions of German life and thought but in the destruction of those traditions after the First World War. That is not to say, of course, that he was entirely uncritical in his attitude towards those traditions; but he undoubtedly saw them, for all their faults, as an influence that might, under other circumstances, have prevented the rise of the Third Reich. The origins of the Hitler regime lay, first of all, he argued, in the destruction, during the First World War and the following inflation, of private incomes, and thus of the financial independence of the educated middle classes:

> Modern industrial society, a mass society of innumerable individuals united by common needs, has taken the place of the former *bourgeois* society, consisting of a layer of economically independent notables who were the great landowners and *bourgeois*. The First World War accelerated and intensified the process of economic and social levelling, by removing differences during wartime, especially in Germany. The whole of society was ground down to a uniform mass, grey as the soldiers; it was subjected to overall state control, to a totalitarian power which deeply affected even private life. (p. 390)

Universal suffrage meant the end of political parties composed of notables, of 'men who were socially and financially independent, who knew something about politics and were interested in them' (p. 391). Parties became bureaucratic machines; they abandoned 'political education, real discussion, individual thought', in the search for mass appeal. 'In order to

27

interest the masses, they must be attracted by sensationalism. He who is best is also the most popular. The most effective method is always the sermon of hatred, the least effective the voice of peaceable reason ...' Secondly, the struggle for liberty and national unity characteristic of the nineteenth century was replaced in the era of mass politics by 'the struggle for a higher standard of living'. 'Liberalism was attacked and discarded in favour of Socialism. Political thought became more and more materialistic' (p. 391). The material interests which replaced ideals in politics were irreconcilable, so parliaments became discredited and people became more and more discontented, using extra-parliamentary action (strikes, marches, pressure-groups, mass meetings) and searching for a 'strong man'. Thirdly, religious values declined. 'Christian teaching scarcely reached the populations of industrial towns.' Materialism, Social Darwinism, the glorification of power, and the Marxist idea that 'The only political reality was the conflict of material interests, and political ideals were only ideological camouflage' replaced it (pp. 392–3). Finally, new technical facilities for political propaganda made it far easier than before to mobilize the masses behind the new ideas.

For Ritter, then, the Third Reich represented the triumph of democratic radicalism over the principle of representative parliamentary liberalism, the triumph of direct popular sovereignty expressed through the rule of one man over 'political compromise reached by discussion, the just balancing of the opposing desires and interests of different classes, groups, and individuals'. Nazism was a revolutionary force directed against all the central traditions of German history:

Hitler himself never sought a restoration; he sought its opposite ... Hitler's propaganda was based not on the memory of 'our forefathers' deeds', but on an indomitable will for the future. His state was to be completely new, something that had never before been seen, contemporary and modern, a state that could be created only once. He poured criticism and scorn on the institutions which existed under a hereditary monarch under which the ultimate orders were made not by the most able, but by those in power on account of an accident of birth and of heredity, as he said in private ... It is a very great mistake to believe that the modern function of leader of the people is in any way the heritage and continuation of the old, monarchic power of the princes. Neither Frederick the Great, Bismarck, nor Wilhelm II were the historical precursors of Adolf Hitler. His precursors were the demagogues and Caesars of modern history, from Danton to Lenin and Mussolini. (pp. 298–9)

Thus Hitler's party was composed of 'uprooted individuals whose mentality was revolutionary', and its strongest attraction to the masses lay in 'the fact that it was contemporary' and in the fact that it was led not by one of the traditional notables but by 'a man of obscure, popular origins' (p 400).

It is easy to see the apologetic aspects of Ritter's arguments. He was, to begin with, concerned to spread the guilt well beyond the frontiers of Germany. 'It is difficult', he wrote, 'to understand how the Hohenzollern dynasty would have collapsed so quickly without foreign intervention (Wilson!), in spite of the serious moral uncertainty caused by the Wilhelmian regime and the disastrous result of the war' (p. 397). Similarly, the Treaty of Versailles united 'all German parties and groups' in violent opposition to it, then aggravated the conflicts between parties, 'since right and left each placed the responsibility for the disaster at the door of the other' (p. 406). Humiliation caused by foreign influence continued through the French occupation of the Ruhr in 1923 and the running sore of reparations. By the time things began to improve, with the Young Plan and after, it was too late: 'No government could survive without injury such serious and humiliating failures in foreign policy as did that of the Weimar Republic' (p. 407). Finally, Hitler himself was an outsider:

> The history of Hitler's intellectual background certainly bears little relation to the general intellectual history of Germany. It is more related to the history of his own country, Austria, [where] ... the 'cultural superiority' of Germanism in the face of Slavonic races was a battle-cry which was continually raised ... There were, no doubt, similar conflicts in the German states which bordered on Poland; but a nationalist born in the Reich would never turn his energies to these, instead of to the traditional rivalry with the West, with the hereditary enemy, France ... In this respect, therefore, the historical origins of Hitlerism are to be found outside the Reich. (pp. 413–15)

Moreover, Ritter argued, 'when the causes of Hitler's great electoral successes are examined, his racial doctrines cannot be regarded as very important', for the masses never understood them. Hitler's anti-Semitism was more influential, especially among the lower middle class, but when, under the Third Reich, he passed from words to action on a huge scale, 'it is true to say that his popularity diminished rather than increased' (p. 415). Most important was the doctrine of *Lebensraum*, which was 'not invented by Hitler, but came from Darwinian theories which had been influencing the political literature of Europe for many years, and which caused disturbing symptoms in the writings of other countries too'. None the less, this too had little influence in winning over the masses. 'It is certain', wrote Ritter, 'that Hitler would never have dared to make his warlike plans for conquest known to the public earlier than 1933, for fear of destroying all the electoral success of his party. A war of conquest was certainly not a slogan for elections.' In fact, he concluded, Nazi ideology 'never became really popular'. It was not Hitler's ideas and programmes

29

that won him support, but 'his gift of radiating confidence in the future', his personal appeal, and the sophisticated propaganda techniques used to project it (p. 416).

Ritter's apologetic and exculpatory intentions also had a more precise and specific thrust. He was concerned above all to provide a justification for the behaviour of his own class, the educated bourgeoisie, during and prior to the Nazi seizure of power. While politics remained the province of the financially independent and educated middle classes, he argued, Nazism was impossible. Representative liberal parliamentarianism, in which the masses took no direct part, was clearly Ritter's ideal. Even more striking than the explicit elitism of Ritter's arguments were the implicit assumptions which informed them. There was, for example, an implicit equation of the 'educated bourgeoisie' with 'the Germans':

> The Germans themselves were more surprised than anyone else by the rapid rise of the National-Socialist Party to a position in which overall power in the state was at its disposal. Up to 1930 the vast majority of educated Germans thought Hitler's disciples to be a group of loud-mouthed extremists and super-patriots without any practical import-ance. The theatricality of their processions and meetings, the strange-ness of their uniforms and of their bright red banners might awaken the curiosity of a tasteless crowd or seduce the more vulgar lower-middle-class members of the large towns; but it all seemed absurd to educated people ... (p. 381)

Ritter's account continued then to equate 'the Germans' with his own class by writing in the passive voice: the November 1923 *Putsch* '*was* generally *considered* to be' a piece of Bavarian comic opera; Hiter '*was regarded* as a man who had had his day'; after 1930, however, 'Hitler's movement *was taken* seriously' (my emphasis). Ritter did not say by whom it was taken seriously after 1930. Implicitly, however, he disqualified the 'masses' who supported it from being able to take anything seriously, and he went on to describe how, 'the majority of educated Germans – that part of the nation which was consciously aware of its historical traditions – was very distrustful of the Hitler propaganda' (p. 384). In other words, Ritter assumed an equation between being educated (i.e. with a university degree), being aware of Germany's historical traditions, and being German.

In advancing these views, Ritter believed that he was taking his stand on old, sound German traditions which had been perverted or overthrown by the Nazis. He was not entirely uncritical of these traditions. He pointed out, for example, that the men from the liberal professions who ran the civil service and ministries of the Empire were uninspiring people who made no attempt to win general popularity, administrators rather than politicians; that Wilhelm II was equally incapable of gaining the heart of the nation; and that while Bismarck's rule gave German people the feeling that their nation had in the world the status it deserved, this was no longer true under Wilhelm II, when

> the rivalry with England, the ambition to become a people of the world (*Weltvolk*) and a sea-power began. In this forced atmosphere, composed of the national consciousness of strength, of inferiority complex, and the fear of being cut off from other countries, was born the radical nationalism of the Pan-Germanists, whose writings contained many characteristics of National-Socialist propaganda. (p. 406)

Finally, Ritter thought that the conflict between bourgeoisie and proletariat which gave Hitler his chance to project himself as a unifying force was 'the old, fatal relic of Bismarck's Reich'; both sides were to blame, but Ritter was critical of 'Bismarck's efforts to suppress, by police methods, the Social Democratic Party' (p. 403). Despite these reservations, however, Ritter still believed that it was the destruction of the German Empire in 1918, and the overturning of its traditions, which was the decisive influence in opening the door to the alien demagoguery of Hitler. Ritter regarded the German Empire as a 'constitutional monarchy', whose stability offered the best guarantee of order and civilization (p. 388). Under this system, the rule of the notables, of educated, propertied and responsible men, had secured the best interests of all. Ritter did not say explicitly in this particular essay in what he thought German traditions consisted, but he was clear that 'Hitler's victory ... did not represent the culmination, but rather a contradiction, of tradition, particularly of the German, Prussian and Bismarckian tradition' (p. 384).

II

Gerhard Ritter's views were not wholly shared, of course, by every West German historian of his day. Others, notably Ludwig Dehio, took a more nuanced view, while those who had gone into exile, such as Hajo Holborn, Hans Kohn, Fritz Stern and George L. Mosse, continued to pursue the ideological origins of Nazism in ways that were certainly far more subtle and defensible than those adopted by the wartime Allies, but were still anathema to most of the historians who remained in, or returned to, the Federal Republic in the 1950s.[7] These were overwhelmingly trained in the Weimar Republic, and some of them, such as Hans Rothfels or Hans Herzfeld, had already had chairs before the Nazi seizure of power.[8] Although most of them drew back from the sympathies they had previously shown towards Nazism, or some aspects of it, during the Third

31

Reich, they were unable to free themselves from the views they had grown up with in the Weimar years, and, in his general tendency to reproduce the conservative attitudes shared by the majority of the German historical profession in the 1920s, Ritter was undoubtedly a representative figure. The few younger, more radical dissenters, such as Hans Rosenberg, Eckart Kehr and George Hallgarten, who had been forced to emigrate in 1933 did not return; Kehr indeed died in exile shortly after leaving Germany.[9] Ritter's position as spokesman for the West German historical profession was cemented by his election to the presidency of the Historians' Association.

If there was one dogma which united virtually every German historian active during the Weimar Republic, it was a belief in the iniquity of the 'war guilt' clause in the Treaty of Versailles and a rejection of the charge that the First World War was the result of German aggression.[10] Under Ritter's leadership, indeed, French and German historians met as part of Adenauer's Franco-German reconciliation policy and hammered out an agreed version of the origins of the First World War for use in school textbooks in the two countries.[11] Not surprisingly, perhaps, they agreed that no one was really responsible for the war; it broke out by a kind of automatic process, as the two great armed camps of Europe were drawn willy-nilly into the conflict between Serbia and the Habsburg monarchy. In 1961, however, the consensus that had been built up during the Weimar Republic and re-established in the Adenauer years was rudely shattered by the publication of Fritz Fischer's book *Griff nach der Weltmacht* (published in English in 1967 as *Germany's Aims in the First World War*). Fischer's book brought a mass of documentary evidence to light on the vast range and extent of German war aims in 1914–18. The most controversial part of the book was its claim not only that Germany had sought to annex much of Europe and dominate the rest *during* the war but that this had also been the intention of Wilhelm II and his advisers for some time *before* 1914 as well; indeed, they had deliberately launched the war in order to achieve this. Outside Germany these arguments had been familiar to historians for some time. But within the West German historical profession itself they were regarded as little better than treachery to the national cause. Moreover, some of the implications of Fischer's work were even more disturbing. If Wilhelm II's Germany deliberately launched a war of European conquest, then Hitler's Third Reich was perhaps not such a unique phenomenon as German historians had previously professed to believe. It was scarcely surprising, therefore, that Fischer's book aroused a storm of controversy within the German historical profession, particularly since it appeared at a time when the West German Federal Republic was trying hard to establish its credentials as a democratic and peaceful country before a sceptical and mistrustful international audience.[12]

32

The so-called 'Fischer controversy' was argued out largely within the confines of traditional methods of diplomatic history, with historians hurling newly discovered documents at one another in support of rival theses, and doing their best to discredit the reliability of the documentation presented by their opponents or to dispute the construction which they put on them.[13] As the controversy subsided, however, it had already become apparent to German historians younger than the chief participants in the debate (nearly all of whom, including Fischer himself, were in their fifties or sixties, and a few of whom, including Fischer's main critic, Gerhard Ritter, were even older) that these methods were of limited value in solving the profounder questions at issue. Moreover, as it became clear that Fischer's main points – the large measure of responsibility of Germany for the outbreak of the First World War and the far-reaching aims pursued by Germany during the war – had been substantiated beyond all reasonable doubt, several other implications emerged to strengthen this sense of methodological dissatisfaction among the younger West German historians.[14]

how the older hist view has been agreed by younger.

In the first place, if there really were some similarities between Hitler's foreign policy and that of Wilhelm II, then might there not also be some similarities in the *internal* political structure of Germany under Hitler and under the last Kaiser?[15] Indeed, could not some of the longer-term origins of the Third Reich – origins whose existence the older generation of historians had denied, ascribing the rise of Nazism largely to the demonic genius of Hitler[16] – lie precisely in developments that took place in Wilhelmine or even Bismarckian Germany? Furthermore, if Germany really did launch the First World War, then must there not have been powerful internal social and economic influences prompting her to do so – influences more profound that the mere incompetence of her diplomacy or the blinkered technical rigidity of her military men?[17] Finally, if it was admitted that Nazism had fairly deep roots in German history, and that the German government had borne the major responsibility for the terrible carnage of the First World War, what implications did this have for the role of historical study in Germany? Clearly the historical profession could no longer go on performing the role it had acquired during the nationalist era of the mid-nineteenth century and retained right up to the 1960s – that of helping Germans acquire a national identity through giving them a sense of pride in their past. At the end of the 1960s, therefore, West German historians found themselves searching for a new role.[18]

These considerations led the younger generation of West German historians to a radical break with the traditions of German historiography as they had been developed by the great historians of the past, from Ranke to Meinecke; and it is this, rather than the Fischer controversy itself, which constituted the real revolution in German historiography. Traditional German historical writing placed the state at the centre of the historical stage, and argued that its major policies were dictated by its position in the world of nation states.[19] The younger generation turned this thesis of the so-called 'primacy of foreign policy' (*Primat der Aussenpolitik*) on its head and argued instead for the 'primacy of internal policy' (*Primat der Innenpolitik*) in determining matters of war and peace. As they turned their attention in the wake of the Fischer controversy to the internal politics of Bismarckian and Wilhelmine Germany, they began to take a much more critical view of the German Empire than their predecessors had done. In this process of reassessment, the younger German historians began to discover neglected radical predecessors who had taken a similarly critical view in previous decades (and had been cold-shouldered by the historical profession for precisely this reason) – most notably, perhaps, Eckart Kehr and Hans Rosenberg.[20] More important still, they also began to reach out to the social sciences for new concepts and methods with which to make sense of the new past they were discovering: it was in social history, as they came to believe, that the key to the internal structure and development of Imperial Germany was to be found.[21]

It was here too that the new role of the historical profession could be carved out: in helping people to understand the need for formal democratic institutions to be underpinned by a genuine democratization of society,[22] as they had not been in the Weimar Republic. This need was dramatically revealed by the political crisis of the West German state in 1967–70, with neo-Nazism gaining ground in the elections and a massive student revolt taking place against traditionalist authoritarianism in the German university, a revolt with many features of which the younger generation of historians, as young lecturers or postgraduate students, undoubtedly sympathized. Not surprisingly, therefore, an element of 'New Left' Marxism was also added to the conceptual armoury of these younger historians, through the influence of philosophers and sociologists such as Jürgen Habermas. It informed their approach to problems such as the legitimation of rule by oppressive or undemocratic groups in society. But these elements of Marxism were harnessed, as we shall see, to a concentration on the responsibility of pre-industrial élites for the misfortunes of Germany in the nineteenth and twentieth centuries that was fundamentally alien to the main emphasis of more consistently Marxist work on the role of the capitalist system and big business in the origins of the First World War and the rise of fascism.

The reason for this peculiar slant given to Marxist concepts by the new German historiography lies in the fact that the general reorientation of German historiography of which it was a part was really a reflection of a seismic shift taking place in West German society as a whole, from the era of reconstruction under Adenauer in the 1950s to the period of stability and maturity that the Federal Republic came to experience under the Social Democratic–Liberal coalition governments of the 1970s. A major aspect of this shift has been the recognition of the existence of East Germany as a separate state; and the process of self-definition which this involved for West Germans also left its mark on the younger generation of West German historians, who had to come to terms with East German historiography as well as with the interpretations evolved by their own predecessors.[23] The explicit role played by Marxist–Leninist theory in East German history books provided an example to West German historians, helping to provoke them into giving theory a similar role in their own work. But it has also been a deterrent, forcing them – unlike their radical contemporaries in Britain and America – to give Marxist ideas a strictly subordinate role; the proximity of the East German model of Marxism to West German historians has meant that the latter have equated Marxism purely with East German Marxist–Leninism, and have virtually ignored other variants of it, rather as 'Eurocommunism' on the Italian model has been a non-starter in West Germany because of the identification there of Communism with the East German regime. As a result, West German historians have largely sealed themselves off from the influence of alternative models of Marxist theory and historiography as developed in Italy, France, or Great Britain. A certain theoretical parochialism has been the consequence, and West German historians have tried to mitigate this by turning to the USA, and to the disciplines of political and social science as they have evolved there, above all under the inspiration of the sociological theories of Max Weber, for concepts and approaches. It is not only in the physical aspect of its cities and in the structure and dynamism of its economy that West Germany is the most Americanized of European countries; its intellectual life, too, is more heavily influenced by America than that of any other European country. At the same time, as the historical paths of West and East Germany have slowly diverged, the proximity of the East German model has also ensured that historical monographs in West Germany have come more and more to resemble a kind of social-democratic mirror-image of their East German counterparts, with empirical material being sandwiched between two slices of theoretical discussion – and, as often as not, effectively unrelated to either of them.[24] Similarly, the West German historians' preoccupation with history as a form of political education can also be seen as a parallel to the explicitly didactic conception of historical writing favoured by the East Germans.

By the middle of the 1970s the historiographical revolution in West Germany had more or less run its course. Its major proponents had moved into senior academic posts, produced a long series of important monographic studies, founded their own historical journal – *Geschichte und Gesellschaft* ('History and Society', subtitled 'A Journal of Historical Social Science') – reprinted many of the works of rediscovered predecessors such as Eckart Kehr, issued many collections of essays and readings and begun to produce works of synthesis which summed up the views they had developed.[25] Perhaps the most important of these syntheses has been Hans-Ulrich Wehler's *Das deutsche Kaiserreich 1871–1918* (1973), a general history of the German Empire under Bismarck and Wilhelm II. Wehler's book, which has gone through several editions and recently been translated into English, may be taken as representative of what the American scholar James J. Sheehan termed the 'new orthodoxy' in German historiography.[26] In many ways, indeed, through his role as editor of an important series of monographs, the *Kritische Studien zur Geschichtswissenschaft*, as well as the journal *Geschichte und Gesellschaft*, and as a prolific author of books, articles and collections of essays himself, Wehler may be regarded as a representative figure of this 'new orthodoxy' of the 1970s, variously described as 'social-liberal' after its ties to the Social Democratic–Free Democratic coalition government of 1969–82, or 'Kehrite', after its (at least partial) allegiance to the views of Eckart Kehr, or 'the Bielefeld school', after the university where Wehler and his closest colleagues, such as Jürgen Kocka, are based.

Wehler's interpretation of the long-term origins of Nazism and the triumph of Hitler could hardly be more different from that advanced by Gerhard Ritter in the 1950s. In *Das deutsche Kaiserreich* Wehler, in total contrast to Ritter, was concerned above all to establish the links between the 'Prusso-German tradition' and the rise of Nazism. Wehler accepted the main thesis of the Allied propaganda which Ritter had so strongly objected to: the uniqueness of Germany's history, and its disastrous divergence from the path followed by the Anglo-Saxon nations. Hitler's seizure of power took place little more than twelve years after the end of the Empire: 'How could one manage to explain this without the historical dimension, which means the history of the Empire?'[27] Conservative historians such as Ritter, he charged, had stifled any self-critical discussion of the problem of continuity in German history, in order to defend their notion that all was well with the world before 1914. This, he said, was mere 'escapism', which sought to overcome the problem of National Socialism by presenting it as an illegitimate perversion of German history, 'instead of recognizing it as a result of deep-rooted continuities' (p. 16). The majority of the preconditions for radical fascism were present in German society under the Empire, or were the result of the Empire's policies.

None the less, Wehler realized that it was impossible to go back to the rather arbitrary procedures of intellectual history by which older writers on the Allied side had attempted to support the theory of continuity in German history, and which Ritter himself had so trenchantly criticized. Instead, Wehler argued, it was necessary to look more deeply into the socio-economic and political structures of German society in the late nineteenth and early twentieth centuries. In Wehler's analysis of these structures, almost all of Ritter's major arguments were sharply contra-

36

dicted. To begin with, the élite groups which Ritter regarded as the major guarantors of political rationality before 1914 were presented by Wehler as the groups with whom the primary responsibility for the catastrophe of 1933 lay.

While Ritter saw the old ruling class as preserving solid virtues and values against the vulgarity and materialism of the masses, Wehler alleged that the old ruling class, using modern propaganda methods, was stirring up nationalistic ambition, anti-Semitic hatreds and anti-democratic passions among the masses as a means of preserving its own traditional, privileged position. Ritter's own class was not immune from such criticism either, for Wehler argued that it shared the socio-political attitudes of the aristocracy, and hence its burden of historical responsibility for the rise of the Third Reich as well. Thus the exclusion of the masses from political equality was in this view a fundamental reason for the rise of Nazism, rather than the major factor preventing it. While Ritter saw the Empire as a constitutional, parliamentary system, Wehler saw it as arbitrary and authoritarian. While Ritter saw Christian values as an essential moral defence against the 'materialism' which he believed had so encouraged people to listen to Hitler's message, Wehler regarded religion as an 'ideology of legitimation' through which pre-industrial and anti-democratic, authoritarian values were purveyed: 'Precisely in order not to be outbid in his claim to be a loyal citizen, the Catholic became equally as subservient and circumspect a subject of the monarchical state power as did his Lutheran neighbour' (p. 122). Both churches offered effective opposition to the forces striving for freedom, emancipation and equality. In dealing with 'materialism' and 'idealism' on a more general level, the two historians were similarly at opposite ends of the interpretative spectrum. While Ritter implicitly suggested a contrast between the 'idealistic' élites and the 'materialistic' masses, Wehler explicitly argued that the élites' main concern was the preservation of their own economic position, and suggested that it was the masses who in their struggle for political equality, above all in Prussia, were idealistic.

Ritter directed his fire in particular against socialism and Marxism. In his view, they undermined political morality by portraying political ideals as mere camouflage for economic interests. In 1914–18 'the radical propaganda of socialists and Communists had weakened or destroyed the will to fight of many sections of the army' (p. 397) and so had assisted foreign powers in their destruction of the Empire. Wehler, by contrast, aimed his criticism at the employers' associations and industrialists' pressure-groups, which, he argued, financed and promoted radical nationalism as a means of winning new markets and new sources of raw materials abroad, and deliberately stymied the growth of democratic institutions which would have allowed more power to their employees. Wehler saw Bismarck and Wilhelm II as precursors of Hitler, not as statesmen who bore little or no resemblance to the later dictator. Bismarck, in Wehler's view, was himself a dictator, and he quotes a number of authorities, from the historian Friedrich Meinecke to the contemporary English ambassador Lord Ampthill, all of whom echo this view with phrases such as 'the German dictator', 'the all-powerful dictator' and so on, in their descriptions of the 'Iron Chancellor'. While Ritter presented racism as an alien importation into German culture, Wehler argued that before 1914 there was systematic discrimination against minorities such as the Poles, and above all there was a pervasive anti-Semitism on a 'massive' scale (p. 113). Bismarck and his aides, such as Minister of the Interior von Puttkamer, encouraged the radical and 'vulgar' anti-Semitism which was ultimately to triumph in the person of Adolf Hitler. In foreign policy, as well as in domestic affairs, Social Darwinism, militarism and a radically racist and expansionist pan-Germanism gained increasing acceptance among the 'opinion-forming upper and middle strata' of society and, even if only indirectly, had a powerful influence on the government (p. 181). In all these ways, therefore, contrary to what Ritter maintained, many of the central elements of Nazism were already present in the Bismarckian Empire; and Prussian traditions such as militarism, deference to authority, absolutism and autocracy, hostility to parliamentarism and democracy, joined with more novel techniques of rule such as Bonapartism, 'social imperialism' and the conscious manipulation of mass opinion, to lay the foundations of the Third Reich well before 1914.

III

How did the new view of Imperial Germany as a dress-rehearsal for the Third Reich work out in detail? Imperial Germany, in the view of this 'new orthodoxy', was dominated by the problem of

> the defence of inherited ruling positions by pre-industrial élites against the onslaught of new forces – a defensive struggle which not only became ever sharper with the erosion of the economic foundations of these privileged leading strata but also created ever more dangerous tensions because of the success it achieved, and stored up an evil heritage for the future.[28]

The dominant pre-industrial élite was the Prussian landed aristocracy, a feudal-military caste which controlled the destinies of Prussia through the bureaucracy, officer corps and Prussian parliament (particularly the House of Lords but also the Chamber of Deputies, whose electors were divided into three classes according to a property qualification, the two richest classes electing most of the deputies even though they constituted

38

only a small fraction of the population). The German Empire, founded through the defeat of Austria and the south German states in 1866 and the victory against France in 1870–1, represented in military reality as well as in political effect the conquest of Germany by Prussia. The position of German Emperor was always to be filled by the King of Prussia; the German Army was effectively under his command – formally so in time of war; the exiguous ministerial and administrative organs of the Empire were staffed by Prussian bureaucrats; the formal government of the Empire, the Bundesrat, representing the heads of state of the federated kingdoms, principalities, grand duchies and city republics of the Empire and alone possessing the right to initiate legislation in the Reichstag, the lower chamber of the imperial legislature, was dominated by Prussia, whose representatives could in practice always outvote the others. The pre-eminence of Prussia was underlined by the fact that in size and in economic strength it surpassed all the other states of the German Empire put together.[29]

Wehler and other historians of the 'new orthodoxy' argue that the feudal-military aristocracy which ruled Prussia, and, through Prussia, Germany, retained its power by a number of techniques of political and social control. The Empire was not a constitutional monarchy: it was, rather, a 'pseudo-constitutional semi-absolutism'.[30] The Reichstag's powers were strictly limited. Ministers were neither elected nor responsible to it. It could not initiate legislation. Governments were appointed by the Kaiser, who also had sole control over the declaration of peace and war. All that the Reichstag could do was to hold up the budget or the military estimates. Under Bismarck, the government got round even this limited power of delay by drumming up a foreign policy crisis every time the military estimates were due which was not very often. In order to gain the support of the masses and reduce the power of the liberal opponents of his policy, Bismarck had established the Reichstag elections on the basis of universal male suffrage. It is for these reasons that German historians have come to characterize Bismarckian Germany as a 'plebiscitary dictatorship' on the lines of Napoleon III's Second Empire in France; and to describe Bismarck's technique of rule as 'Bonapartism' or 'Caesarism'. No one, neither the erratic Kaiser Wilhelm II nor the Chancellors who succeeded Bismarck – the well-meaning Caprivi, the senile Hohenlohe, the pliant Bülow and the grey bureaucrat Bethmann Hollweg – could fill the gap left by Bismarck after his departure in 1890. Instead, the 'traditional oligarchies' ruled Germany through the 'anonymous forces of authoritarian polycracy', consisting of 'rival centres of power' in the bureaucracy, army, navy and court, and the growing number of nationalistic and economic pressure-groups which exerted an increasingly powerful influence on affairs in the era of Wilhelm II. Though there was no longer any German Caesar, the élites continued to rule through a 'Bonapartist

39

strategy' and to develop the techniques of control first elaborated by Bismarck.[31]

The most overt of these methods – according to these historians – was that of *repression*. Civil rights and freedoms were, they argue, drastically curtailed in the Germany of Wilhelm II. Even if oppositional political parties were not formally outlawed, as the Social Democrats were under Bismarck from 1878 to 1890, they were discriminated against by the exclusion of their members from political power and social influence. No Social Democrat could become a schoolteacher or university professor, no liberal or democrat could join the officer corps in the Prussian Army. An elaborate apparatus of police controls and censorship laws severely restricted freedom of expression. There were few Social Democratic newspaper or magazine editors who had not served several terms in prison for permitting seditious or anti-monarchical opinions to be printed; often prosecutions of this kind were made on the merest pretext. Policemen were in attendance at all public meetings, empowered to dissolve them should disloyal or 'immoral' phrases pass the lips of the speaker, or the suspicion be aroused that the meeting might degenerate into disorder. These powers were not used sparingly. Nor were judges, ultra-conservatives to a man, inclined to be lenient towards radicals or Social Democrats or indeed anyone accused of criticizing the authorities in any way. Strikes and industrial disputes almost invariably ended in arrests; lockouts and dismissals were commonplace; many industries – above all, those controlled by the government, such as the railways, or those closely connected with government interests, such as the armaments or iron and steel industries – dismissed union members and circulated blacklists of known 'agitators'. Beyond this system of 'class justice'[32] loomed the threat of martial law should the position of the ruling élites ever seem seriously endangered. The country was divided into areas, each under a military commander, with powers to suspend civil liberties, arrest 'troublemakers' and override civil government in times of 'emergency'. Detailed plans were actually drawn up for such an eventuality. The ultimate threat was that of a *Staatsstreich* or *coup d'état* from above, which was seriously and openly canvassed by Wilhelm II and his advisers at various critical junctures and hung over the constitution like the sword of Damocles, constituting a permanent reminder to opposition politicians of what would happen if they carried their opposition too far.[33]

In addition to repression, the ruling élite, it is argued, also employed the tactic of *manipulation*. The political parties, which posed perhaps the most serious threat to the continuation of the Bonapartist-dictatorial regime, were drawn through a skilful policy of manipulation away from political coalition on the basis of shared beliefs and reduced to mere vehicles of economic interests. A classic example of this was the way in which Bismarck split the liberals, perhaps his most dangerous political opponents in the 1860s and 1870s, by exposing the contradictions between nationalism and constitutionalism in liberal ideology through unifying Germany without liberalizing it (1866–71) and then (1878–9) through introducing protectionism combined with a further curtailment of civil liberties in the Anti-Socialist Law. By the 1890s the National Liberals, representing heavy industry, were at odds with the south German liberals, representing peasants and petty-bourgeois townsfolk, and various groups of north German left-liberals backed by professional men or light industrialists. Similarly, the conservatives were tied to the Agrarian League by the mid-1890s, the Social Democrats to the trade unions, and so on. This dissolution of political parties into competing pressure-groups, and their inability to emerge from their respective provincial or social milieux to combine, further enabled the government to manipulate the groups and prevent them from forming a viable majority in the Reichstag for constitutional reform.[34]

Another form of political manipulation practised by the ruling élite, it has been claimed, was that of the *diversion* of emancipatory and reformist impulses into enthusiasm for foreign conquest, empire and international prestige: the so-called technique of 'social imperialism'. With the encouragement of the government, organizations such as the Navy League, the Colonial Society and the Society for the Eastern Marches set about mobilizing the masses behind a programme of nationalist enthusiasm and political conservatism.[35] This tactic was backed up, particularly with reference to the working classes, by a policy of *compensation* for loyalty to the ruling élite in the form of social insurance and welfare policies.[36] The loyalty of the masses was further cemented through a concerted policy of *indoctrination*, through the encouragement of deferential modes of thought and traditionalist monarchism in the schools, the legitimation of the social and political status quo by the state-controlled Protestant Church, the formation of a wide range of voluntary organizations, such as the League Against Social Democracy, whose aim was to win the masses away from subversive ideas through counter-propaganda, and the provision of anti-democratic models of behaviour in the authoritarian father, the Prussian army officer or the social élite of the student duelling corps.[37]

Finally, the ruling élites themselves, it is alleged, were kept together despite their apparently divergent economic interests by the political device of *negative integration*, that is, by portraying certain groups in society – the socialist working classes, the Catholic south Germans, the Polish, Danish and French national minorities, the Jews – as so subversive and dangerous that the possessing classes had to close ranks in order to survive against the threat which they posed. The tactic of negative integration in turn isolated these groups and forced them to turn in on themselves, so that the Social Democrats, for example, were unable to pursue their radical policies with any success, and devoted their energies instead to building up their own compensatory organizational activities, which 'integrated' the workers into society negatively, by rendering them politically harmless.[38] The counterpart of negative integration was the so-called *Sammlungspolitik*, the policy of gathering together in one political camp all the social and political groups of the Right – the 'productive classes', in one formulation, or, more classically, the classes which were said to support the state (*staatserhaltend*). In the first place this meant the owners of heavy industry and the landed aristocrats. At the end of the 1890s the bargain between these two groups was sealed through the aristocracy's agreement to support industry's demand for a big navy, which meant lucrative contracts for armaments manufacturers and iron and steel producers, and a 'world policy' (*Weltpolitik*), which meant the diplomatic search for new markets in competition with the British Empire. Heavy industry in turn agreed to give the landed aristocracy a quid pro quo in the form of higher import tariffs on grain (to cushion them against foreign competition).[39] More generally they continued to acquiesce in the social and political status quo. The industrialists' support for the continued dominance of the landed aristocracy in state and society was facilitated by the phenomenon which German historians have dubbed the 'feudalization of the bourgeoisie' – the adherence of the middle classes, above all the 'barons' of heavy industry, to modes of thought and action that were pre-industrial rather than middle-class or liberal after the example of the English bourgeoisie. Industrialists such as Krupp behaved towards their employees much as a medieval baron might towards his serfs, with a mixture of paternalism and despotic ruthlessness; while the social prestige that attached to the position of an officer in the army reserve was so great that wealthy bourgeois gladly conformed to the feudal standards of behaviour expected of them in order to secure appointment.[40]

In sum, then, if these views are correct, it is clear that the techniques of rule through which the Wilhelmine élite hoped to stay in power were formidable in their range and effectiveness. Wehler and those whose views he has synthesized claim that they enabled the Prussian aristocracy, with the aid of the barons of heavy industry, to maintain the status quo intact not only until the Revolution of 1918 – though the situation had been desperate enough to cause them to launch the First World War as a last fling of social imperialism in 1914 – but even afterwards. Just as the élites had mobilized the petty-bourgeoisie behind their social-imperialist ideologies before 1914, so as things got worse for them during the Weimar Republic they eventually had recourse to the encouragement of the far more dangerous (but essentially similar) forces of National Socialism. It was through their agency that Hitler was brought to power in 1933. Only when it was too late did they realize that Nazism was a force they could not control. By the time they came to revolt, in 1944, their power was almost at an end; Hitler's savage reprisals after the failure of their plot

42

removed them once and for all from the historical scene. 1944–5 thus marks the real end of the élite's dominance, and constitutes therefore the only really major discontinuity in recent German history,[41] despite the superficial appearance of sharp breaks in 1871, 1918 and 1933. And seen in a wider perspective the élite's work lived on even longer; its manipulations had been responsible for preventing the spread of democratic ideas among the middle classes, and, perhaps even more decisively, for fatally weakening the determination to succeed of the one truly democratic force in the *Kaiserreich*, the Social Democrats.

Although the Social Democrats were, superficially at least, implacably opposed to the social and political status quo in the Wilhelmine Empire, in reality, as time went on, it is argued, they became progressively more reluctant to translate this opposition into action. Instead, frightened in case they would be outlawed altogether, and increasingly dominated by pragmatic trade unions who were even more terrified at the prospect of losing their assets and destroying years of hard organizational work by courting total repression in the form of a *Staatsstreich* or a revival of the Anti-Socialist Law, they became steadily more passive in their political tactics, encouraged by the inexorable growth of their electoral support to believe that one day they would secure a majority of seats in the Reichstag and so be able to assume the mantle of government. 'Negative integration', in other words, is seen as having affected not only the élite by keeping it together, but also the Social Democrats, by cowing them into sub-missiveness. Moreover, the conservative and nationalistic education through which the great majority of SPD members passed in the state primary schools was, it is argued, a further influence in weakening the allegiance of the party to peace and democracy. The result of these influences was not only full Social Democratic support for the war in 1915 but also a marked reluctance on the part of the SPD leaders to push through the revolution of 1918 to a more radical conclusion, and, finally, a legalistic passivity in the face of authoritarian and Nazi attacks in 1932–3 which finally proved the party's downfall.[42] In the long term, then, the policies of the ruling élite of Wilhelmine Germany not only weakened the commitment of the middle classes to democracy, it weakened the working classes' commitment to it as well; and it was in overcoming the effects of this legacy that many West German historians of the 1960s and 1970s saw their mission.[43]

IV

At the time of its first formulation, in the late 1960s and early 1970s, this interpretation provided a source of great intellectual stimulation and excitement in the study of modern German history. It was novel both in method and in content, and it seemed to offer a coherent explanation of why fascism happened in Germany in such an extreme form, while remaining relatively unimportant in Britain and the USA. As time went on, however, some limitations and problems became apparent. Viewed politically, it seemed to have a double-edged character. On the one hand, the new arguments amounted to a sharp attack on the conservative traditions of Prussia, a fierce critique of the old ruling classes whom Ritter was trying to defend, and a plea for a complete reassessment of the German past. The 'conquest of the past' by the Germans demanded the self-conscious rejection of a large part of their heritage, and the recognition that those aspects of German history formerly most admired, above all the nineteenth-century unification, should now be seen as ominous developments leading directly to the barbarism of the Third Reich. On the other hand, there is a positive side to these arguments which verges on the apologetic or exculpatory; for if pre-capitalist classes such as the Junkers and the *Mittelstand* were primarily responsible for the rise of the Third Reich, then present-day West Germans have little to feel guilty about, for in the meantime those classes have long since declined drastically in number and lost virtually all the power they once had.

Similarly, if the industrialists helped Hitler to power not because they were industrialists but because they were 'feudalized', then there is no necessary connection between capitalism and fascism; indeed, quite the reverse, since, as Wehler argues, what was wrong with the German Empire was that economic 'modernization', the triumph of capitalism, failed to bring with it its 'natural' consequence, the triumph of liberal democracy. Correspondingly, it was with the foundation of the Federal Republic that the process of 'modernization' was finally completed. Once again, it is easy to see how these arguments serve to legitimize the Federal Republic by dissociating it from the evils of the German past. Here, 1945 rather than 1918 marks the decisive discontinuity in the development of modern Germany; and everything that happened before 1945 is consigned to prehistory, having an increasingly tenuous connection with life in present-day West Germany.

Historians' research and writing is always stamped by their individual personalities, their intellectual idiosyncracies and their personal views. These interpretations in no sense have any official public endorsement from any of the political parties, nor were they written at any party's behest. None the less, no historian can remain immune from the surrounding political atmosphere, and no historian's writing is uninformed by political beliefs of some kind. In the Federal Republic, the surrounding political atmosphere is particularly thick, and historians tend to be a good deal more concerned about the political implications of their work than elsewhere. It is therefore justifiable to view historical interpretations as representative not merely of the very different eras in which they were developed but also of the major political tendencies in the Federal Republic. Such a political background can be glimpsed in many views of German history. For example, Ritter made little distinction between Hitler and Stalin (or Lenin), and drew explicit comparisons between the Third Reich and post-Revolutionary Russia. Indeed, he ended on a pessimistic note, criticizing the Western leaders of the day for weakness and lack of resolution in confronting the Communist menace. For Ritter, therefore, the danger of a renewed collapse into barbarism and dictatorship was only too close; in his view, it came once more from outside Germany, from the East. Writing as the cold war was at freezing-point, Ritter was clearly an adherent of the doctrine of totalitarianism, in which the rise of mass society was made responsible not only for the rise of Hitler but also for the rise of Stalin. Wehler, by contrast, writing at a time when, with Brandt's *Ostpolitik* in full swing, *détente* was at its warmest, presented Nazism as a variety of fascism, and located its predecessor, the 'Bonapartist dictatorship' of Bismarck, specifically within the context of the traditional social order. So theories of 'totalitarianism' were much less in evidence in this account. Again, while Ritter stressed the importance of Christian values in resisting the totalitarian urge, an emphasis reflected in the presence of the word 'Christian' in the names of the two major conservative parties, Wehler echoed long-standing liberal and Social Democratic tradition in voicing his suspicion of the role of organized religion in the *Kaiserreich*. Similar parallels and connections can be drawn from most of the rest of the two historians' arguments.

Yet at the same time the two approaches also had much in common. They may have been in conflict, but they still fought on the same battleground. The new approach to German history still concentrates on high politics. It claims to be 'historical social science'. But as Georg Iggers, perhaps the most authoritative external observer of the German historiographical scene,[44] has remarked it is not so much social history as it is understood in Britain, France or America, as the *social history of politics*.[45] Political processes, changes and influences are perceived as flowing downwards – though now from the élites who controlled the state, rather than from the socially vaguer entity of the state itself – not upwards from the people. The actions and beliefs of the masses are explained in terms of the influence exerted on them by manipulative élites at the top of society. The German Empire is presented as a puppet theatre, with Junkers and industrialists pulling the strings, and middle and lower classes dancing jerkily across the stage of history towards the final curtain of the Third Reich.[46]

While German historians continue to concentrate on high politics and 'history from above', the British historiographical tradition has been developing in quite a different direction. British historians have come increasingly to emphasize the importance of the grass roots of politics and the everyday life and experience of ordinary people. It is worth noting, perhaps, that this trend has taken place across a whole range of historical subjects, political opinions and methodological approaches and has been expressed in many different ways. It can be seen in the tendency over the last two decades for studies of the English Civil War of the seventeenth century to get away from events at the centre, in London, and reach a new understanding of the most profound of all political conflicts in British history through detailed study of provincial society, where the great majority of English people spent their lives – a tendency that has been explicitly developed in reaction against the Marxist interpretations of the 1950s.[47] It has also manifested itself in the development of a new school of 'people's history', written by working people and arising directly from their experience of work; the studies produced by this school, in their books and pamphlets and in their journal *History Workshop*, are enabling us to see the history of British society in the last 150 years in a new light.[48] Other students of nineteenth-century history have opened up very different perspectives on the Victorian political system by leaving Whitehall and Westminster and going into the country to look at the shaping of national politics at its most basic, fundamental level.[49] Nor has this approach been confined to students of British history: British historians such as George Rudé and Richard Cobb, though working in very different ways, have been instrumental in advancing our understanding of the French Revolution through detailed examinations of riots, protest, crime and other expressions of discontent among the common people.[50] 'History from below' in this very broad sense, encompassing a wide variety of methods and opinions, does not mean a history without theory, though it would be true to say that British historians tend to integrate theory with empirical study rather than separate it out and so make it more obvious and more explicit in the way that German historians do.[51] Nor does it mean 'history with the politics left out'. Rather, it means an enlargement of the definition of politics to include many areas of life which German historians, continuing to equate politics with high politics, tend to assign to the category of the 'unpolitical'.[52] In this widened concept of politics, social and political history find their meeting-place. When the history of Wilhemine Germany is approached from below, in this way, familiar features appear in an unfamiliar light. The picture that emerges is different from that portrayed by the 'new orthodoxy' among German historians. In some respects it contradicts it; in others it complements it through illuminating aspects of the Wilhelmine Empire which it has left obscure.

For example, one of the great strengths of British historiography lies in its tradition of local history, a subject which has little real equivalent in Germany, where local historical studies are still often antiquarian in character. Mainstream German historiography concentrates overwhelmingly on Prussia; indeed, one of the many terms which it uses to characterize the Wilhelmine Empire is 'Prussia-Germany', implying not simply the unassailable dominance of Prussia over the rest of the Empire but even the virtual identity of the two. This is certainly the way it looks at the top, in the Reichstag, the General Staff, the imperial court or the government ministries. But if we shift our focus down to the level of society, to the ordinary people, the picture changes. There was another Germany besides Prussia, south of the Main; indeed, Prussia itself was in many ways a composite, artificial entity, containing a wide variety of social and political formations. Germany was an even more variegated and diverse society than France, the richness of whose local and provincial traditions historians have long been engaged in exploring. Sweeping generalizations often made about state repression of intellectual freedom in the Wilhelmine Empire must be qualified by more specific reference to the great variety of local and regional conditions. In Munich, for instance, the authorities seem to have taken a relatively tolerant attitude towards the literary and artistic avant-garde, and the legal system seems to have favoured intellectual freedom to an extent that compared favourably with other countries.[53] In Hamburg, Germany's largest city after Berlin, state intervention in society was rejected as foreign to the local tradition of republican independence.[54] Germany in the 1870s and 1880s was united only in the most superficial sense; and even in the Wilhelmine period diversity and decentralization were far more marked than, say, in Britain at the same time.

Not only do the approaches of the 1960s and 1970s impose a false uniformity on German society in the past, they also fit it into a static mould that allows far too little room for historical change. In this respect, they resemble the old version of German history as the expression of an immutable 'German character'. By rejecting the narrative approach for a 'problem-oriented structural analysis', for example, Wehler conveys the impression that in their fundamentals the political and social structures of Germany hardly altered at all between 1871 and 1918. Yet this was a period in which Germany underwent cataclysmic social and economic changes and suffered the trauma of a rapid transition to industrial maturity. Given the nature and extent of this transformation the idea that the political superstructure of German society remained basically unchanged seems implausible, to say the least.[55] It is an opinion which can only be held if one allows one's view of German history to be structured by the perspective of 1933. During the Wilhelmine period, in fact, economic and social change was mobilizing new social groups *from below*; and the pressure on the political system exerted by the stage-by-stage process of the political self-mobilization of the petty-bourgeoisie played a major and much-neglected part in the progressive creation of a mass fascist movement.[56]

Even here, however, there is an important qualification to be made; for not all petty-bourgeois groups which mobilized themselves in this way contributed towards the development of National Socialism. As Ian Farr has shown, there is no doubt about the parallels between the political mobilization of the Bavarian farmer and the simultaneous creation of radical movements of the Right among petty-bourgeois groups in the north. Like the political awakening of the artisans or white-collar workers, the entry of the Bavarian peasantry on to the political scene was far more a response to economic pressures acting from below than a result of political manipulation acting from above. The influence of the major 'manipulative' group in agrarian politics, the Junker-dominated Agrarian League, was strictly limited in Bavaria, where it was largely restricted to Protestant enclaves in Swabia and Franconia. The bulk of Bavarian peasants, solidly Catholic in religion, rejected the Agrarian League as the representative of the Protestant Prussian aristocracy. They also rejected the militarism of the Agrarian League, because it meant that they would have to pay higher taxes. 'Social imperialism' cut little ice with tight-fisted Bavarian peasants. The formation of Peasant Leagues in the 1890s was as much as anything else a result of the lack of a sympathetic response to the peasants' economic plight by the Catholic Centre Party; and as soon as the Peasant Leagues began to make serious inroads into the party's electoral support, it responded by forming its own pressure-groups for small farmers, with a programme remarkably close to that of the Peasant Leagues themselves. The Catholic groups soon succeeded in reducing the influence of the Leagues and in winning back most of the support which the Centre Party had lost. In this way, the peasant populism of the 1890s – militant, stridently anti-Semitic and strongly opposed to the dominance of aristo-cratic élites – radicalized the Catholic Centre Party in Bavaria, just as the petty-bourgeois right was being radicalized in Protestant areas.[57]

Moreover, by approaching Wilhelmine Germany through the concept of continuity and treating it in terms of the prehistory of the Third Reich, a great deal of recent German historical writing not only tends to underesti-mate the social and political changes which took place between 1888 and 1918 but also slants our perspective on the *Kaiserreich* so as to draw our attention away from features of Wilhelmine society and politics that fit awkwardly into the model of historical continuity so constructed. On the political scene, perhaps the outstanding example of this distortion of perspective is the extraordinary neglect suffered by the Catholic Centre Party. The party's significance derived in the first place from the fact that it was the largest political group in the Reichstag until 1912. Without its support, it was virtually impossible to put together a workable Reichstag majority. No government in Wilhelmine Germany could hope to get its legislation through in the absence of such a majority to support its proposals. The one brief attempt to do so, the so-called 'Bülow Block' of 1906–9, ended in failure. Despite all this, however, the Catholic Centre

Party has been relatively neglected by historians of the period. The problem is that the Centre does not really fit most of the generalizations which have become commonplace about the Wilhelmine political system. It has not really been possible to portray it as the mere representative of some organized economic interest. It is not easily classifiable in terms of Right and Left. It was clearly not a political vehicle of the élites; but neither was it brought over to support the system by 'social imperialism' – on the contrary, it went into opposition in 1906 objecting violently to some of the more unpleasant features of Germany's imperial adventures. Theories about Wilhelmine politics which do not fit the most important political party are clearly in need of some revision.[58]

In the *Kulturkampf* of the 1870s, the Catholic Centre Party had been a political pariah, subject to the kind of official hostility and persecution that was reserved in the Wilhelmine period for the Social Democrats. Yet for more than two decades, from 1890 to 1914 – the exception being the period of the Bülow Block from 1906 to 1909 – it was the major support of the government in the Reichstag. Conventional explanations ascribing this to mere political opportunism are too vague and superficial to be convincing. David Blackbourn has shown that the changing political alignments of the Centre Party can only be understood by approaching the problem from below, through a study of the Catholic community's place in the social system of the *Kaiserreich*, and through a careful examination of the social and geographical distribution of the party's active and passive support. When this kind of study is carried out, it emerges that a number of important changes were taking place in the late Bismarckian and early Wilhelmine period which provide the clue to the party's move from an oppositional to a governmental position in the Reichstag. The party was rapidly losing its clerical character and becoming a middle-class party, led by lawyers and supported by the urban and rural petty-bourgeoisie of southern Germany. The emergence of these groups and their competitive striving for 'insider status' led them to try to prove their national reliability by supporting the government in the Reichstag. Peasants, petty-bourgeois and middle-class Catholics looked to the Centre Party to affirm their social worth. It was this, rather than manipulation from above, that kept the Centre away from the left-liberals and Social Democrats with whom it was ultimately to co-operate in the Weimar Republic.

Similarly, the radicalization of Catholic Centre politics through the emergence of peasant populism in Bavaria was also one of the influences in producing the decline of Munich as a cultural centre, a decline which was to give Berlin a virtual monopoly over avant-garde art in the Weimar Republic. Populist Catholicism was hostile to the moral libertarianism of Munich's artistic community. It was popular pressure from below that brought about the decline of artistic freedom, as much as manipulation or repression from above.[59] Again, when the German working class under

Wilhelm II is examined not through its political organizations but rather through its *social* components, the picture which the 'new orthodoxy' in German history has painted of a relatively passive, socially integrated proletariat, bought off by social insurance and cowed into submission by state repression, stands in need of some modification. Recent studies have shown the enormous diversity of experience and attitudes among the German working class, involving not only strong contrasts between formal organizations and the rank-and-file but also sharp differences between the workers of one trade and another, and wide variations between different regions and towns or even across different parts of the same city.[60] Indeed, this diversity of experience and attitudes, character-istic of many industrializing societies, can also be established for other social classes in Wilhelmine Germany, most notably perhaps the petty-bourgeoisie, whose political position could vary from radical liberalism to right-wing extremism. Wilhelmine Germany was a society of enormous complexity, a society in the throes of a very rapid transformation or series of transformations, where complicated cross-currents of social, economic and political change produced patterns of thought and action not easily comprehended in terms of a few simple formulae. It is this, indeed, that makes it such a fascinating subject for the historian. It is vital, therefore, to rehabilitate Wilhelmine society as an object of study in its own right, and not to treat it merely as a prelude to the Nazi era.[61]

NOTES

1 The issue of *Western European Politics* from which the present chapter is partly drawn (vol. 4, no. 2 (1981)) was devoted to analysis of the 1979 election.

2 'Gegenwärtige Lage und Zukunftsaufgaben deutscher Geschichtswissenschaft', *Historische Zeitschrift*, vol. 170 (1950) pp. 1–22, at p. 6.

3 H.-U. Wehler, *Das deutsche Kaiserreich 1870–1918* (Göttingen, 1973), p. 12.

4 There is a useful collection of extracts illustrating these views in J. C. G. Röhl (ed.), *From Bismarck to Hitler: The Problem of Continuity in German History* (London, 1970). For an account of the developing historiography of the subject, see P. Ayçoberry, *The Nazi Question: An Essay on the Interpretations of National Socialism (1922–1975)*, (New York, 1981). For the originals of these views, see R. Butler, *The Roots of National Socialism* (London 1941); A. J. P. Taylor, *The Course of German History: A Survey of the Development of German History since 1815* (London, 1945); and W. L. Shirer, *The Rise and Fall of the Third Reich: A History of Nazi Germany* (New York, 1960). See K. Epstein, 'Shirer's History of Nazi Germany', *Review of Politics*, vol. 23 (1961), pp. 230–45, for a classic statement of objections; also G. Barraclough, 'Mandarins and Nazis', *New York Review of Books*, 19 Oct. 1972; Barraclough, 'The Liberals and German History', ibid., 2 Nov. 1972; Barraclough, 'A New View of German History', ibid., 16 Nov. 1972. It is revealing to note Taylor's attempt to struggle with the implications of his view in his preface to the 1961 edition of *The Course of German History*, published in Methuen's University Paperbacks ('Maybe the Germans will forget their imperialist dreams so long as they remain prosperous. I have almost reached the point of believing that I shall not live to see a third German war; but events have an awkward trick of running in the wrong direction, just when you least expect it', p. x). The argument that the 'German character' has indeed changed since 1945 is advanced in

K. Baker, *Germany Transformed* (New York, 1982), but this rests on a rather shaky set of unexamined assumptions about German political culture in the preceding century, briefly summarized in less than a page of text.

5 G. Ritter, 'The Historical Foundations of the Rise of National-Socialism', in *The Third Reich* (International Council for Philosophy and Humanistic Studies, London, 1955), pp. 381–416, at pp. 385–6.

6 However, as Georg Iggers, *The Social History of Politics: Critical Perspectives in West German Historical Writing since 1945* (Leamington Spa, 1985), p. 21, points out, Ritter had asserted in a publication of 1936 that Frederick the Great *was* a precursor of Hitler, only in a positive sense!

7 Iggers, *Social History of Politics*, pp. 1–22. A fuller and more nuanced account would also discuss F. Meinecke, *The German Catastrophe: Reflections and Recollections* (trans. S. B. Fay; Cambridge, Mass., 1950), with its bewildered questioning and its appeal for a renewal of 'Western Christian traditions', and the more critical approach of L. Dehio, in a number of books, including *Germany and World Politics* (London, 1959; German edn. 1955).

8 Iggers, *Social History of Politics*.

9 Ibid.

10 The German foreign ministry financed a scholarly periodical in the 1920s devoted to refuting the 'war guilt' clause of the Treaty of Versailles: *Die Kriegsschuldfrage: Berliner Monatshefte für Internationale Aufklärung*. See W. Jäger, *Historische Forschung und Politische Kultur in Deutschland* (Göttingen, 1984). The German historians of the 1950s saw the Wilhelmine Empire as a kind of ideal society before the disasters of 1914–45. See e.g. the recollections of H. Rothfels quoted in the introduction to K. Saul, *Staat, Industrie, Arbeiterbewegung im deutschen Kaiserreich* (Düsseldorf, 1974).

11 Reprinted in D. E. Lee (ed.) *The Outbreak of the First World War: Who was responsible?* (Boston, Mass., 1963), pp. 64–6. There is a useful collection of articles, including analyses of Ritter and his work, in H. W. Koch (ed.), *The Origins of the First World War: Great Power Rivalry and German War Aims* (London, 1972).

12 For an account of the 'Fischer controversy' in English, see J. A. Moses, *The Politics of Illusion* (London, 1975). Perhaps the clearest German account is by I. Geiss, in his *Studien über Geschichte und Geschichtswissenschaft* (Frankfurt, 1972), pp. 108–98.

13 A. Sywottek, 'Die Fischer-Kontroverse', in I. Geiss and B.-J. Wendt (eds.), *Deutschland in der Weltpolitik des 19. und 20. Jahrhunderts* (Düsseldorf, 1973), pp. 19–74.

14 The most recent account of the controversy is in Jäger, *Historische Forschung*.

15 It is worth noting, perhaps, that not all historians who accepted the first argument went on to concur in the second; cf. the remark by J. Röhl, *From Bismarck to Hitler: The Problem of Continuity in German History* (London, 1971), p. xiii, that 'if precise comparisons [i.e. between Bismarckian, Wilhelmine, Weimar and Nazi Germany] are relatively easy to make when dealing with the foreign policy of German statesmen, they are virtually impossible in the field of ideas or social change'.

16 Cf. the discussion in Section I, above.

17 Fischer went on to explore these reasons in his second book, *Krieg der Illusionen* (Düsseldorf, 1969), published in England as *War of Illusions* (London, 1975).

18 This problem inspired a great many theoretical essays published during this period. They include I. Geiss, 'Kritischer Rückblick auf Friedrich Meinecke', in Geiss, *Studien über Geschichte*, pp. 89–107; W. J. Mommsen, *Die Geschichtswissenschaft jenseits des Historismus* (Düsseldorf, 1971); A. Sywottek, *Geschichtswissenschaft in der Legitimationskrise*, Archiv für Sozialgeschichte, supplement 1 (Bonn, 1974); V. Rittner, 'Zur Krise der westdeutschen Historiographie', in I. Geiss *et al.*, *Ansichten einer künftigen Geschichtswissenschaft* (Munich, 1974); R. Koselleck, 'Wozu noch Geschichte?', *Historische Zeitschrift*, vol. 212 (1971), pp. 1–18. This list is by no means exhaustive. The crisis came to a head in the debate over the proposal by the authorities in Hessen to abolish history as a separate subject in schools; see K. Bergmann and H.-J. Pandel (eds), *Geschichte und Zukunft* (Frankfurt, 1975).

19 For the history of German historiography, see G. Iggers, *The German Conception of History* (Middletown, Conn., 1968). For an interesting comparison between present-day English and German historical scholarship, see V. R. Berghahn, 'Looking Towards England', *The Times Literary Supplement*, 5 Nov. 1976, p. 1401.

20 E. Kehr, *Der Primat der Innenpolitik: Gesammelte Aufsätze zur preussisch-deutschen Sozialgeschichte im 19. und 20. Jahrhundert*, ed. H.-U. Wehler (2nd edn, Berlin, 1970).

21 H.-U. Wehler, *Geschichte als Historische Sozialwissenschaft* (Frankfurt, 1973); J. Kocka, 'Theorieprobleme der Sozial- und Wirtschaftsgeschichte', in H.-U. Wehler (ed.), *Geschichte und Soziologie* (Köln, 1972), pp. 305–30; Kocka, 'Theorien in der Sozial- und Gesellschaftsgeschichte: Vorschläge zur historischen Schichtungsanalyse', *Geschichte und Gesellschaft*, vol. 1, no. 1 (1975), pp. 9–42; also some of the works cited in n. 8 above, (e.g. Mommsen).

22 e.g. D. Groh, *Kritische Geschichtswissenschaft in emanzipatorischer Absicht* (Stuttgart, 1973); H.-U. Wehler, *Das deutsche Kaiserreich 1871–1918* (Göttingen, 1973), p. 12; Geiss, *Studien über Geschichte*.

23 East German historians have also been prolific critics of the German tradition of historiography: see for example J. Streisand (ed.), *Studien über die deutsche Geschichtswissenschaft*, 2 vols. (East Berlin, 1963–5).

24 For an example of this, cf. S. Mielke, *Der Hansa-Bund für Gewerbe, Handel und Industrie* (Göttingen, 1976), with East German research monographs on this period.

25 The earliest synthesis by a member of this school in English was V. R. Berghahn, *Germany and the Approach of War in 1914* (London, 1974); some essays have been printed in English translation in J. J. Sheehan (ed.), *Imperial Germany* (London, 1976).

26 *Journal of Modern History*, vol. 48, no. 3 (1976), pp. 566–7; Sheehan also comments in this review on the continuing concentration of German historians on the 'commanding heights' of politics.

27 H.-U. Wehler, *Das deutsche Kaiserreich 1871–1918* (Göttingen, 1973), pp. 12–15.

28 Wehler, *Das deutsche Kaiserreich*, p. 14.

29 See the summary in Berghahn, *Germany and the Approach of War*, chs 1–2; and M. Kitchen, *A Military History of Germany from the Eighteenth Century to the Present Day* (London, 1973).

30 Wehler, *Das deutsche Kaiserreich*, p. 60

31 Ibid., pp. 63–72.

32 See Saul, *Staat, Industrie, Arbeiterbewegung*, for a comprehensively detailed survey; in English, see A. Hall, *Scandal, Sensation and Social Democracy* (Cambridge, 1977).

33 There is a brief explanation of *Staatsstreichpolitik* in Berghahn, *Germany and the Approach of War*, ch. 1, esp. pp. 13, 18, 22.

34 For the idea of political 'milieux' in Wilhelmine society, see M. R. Lepsius, 'Parteien und Sozialstruktur: Zum Problem der Demokratisierung der deutschen Gesellschaft', in G. A. Ritter (ed.), *Deutsche Parteien vor 1918* (Köln, 1973), pp. 56–80. More generally, see Wehler, *Das deutsche Kaiserreich*, pp. 73–90.

35 Wehler, *Das deutsche Kaiserreich*, pp. 172–9.

36 cf. the account ibid., pp. 135–40, entitled 'Entschädigungsleistungen zur Loyalitätssicherung: Sozialversicherung statt Sozialreform'.

37 Ibid., pp. 118–35.

38 Ibid., pp. 105–18. See also Chapter 6, below.

39 The classic exposition of this interpretation is E. Kehr, *Battleship Building and Party Politics in Germany 1894–1901* (ed. and trans. P. R. and E. N. Anderson; Chicago, 1975).

40 See Kehr, *Primat der Innenpolitik*, pp. 53–63.

41 Wehler, *Das deutsche Kaiserreich*, pp. 227–39 ('Eine Bilanz').

42 Elements of a reinterpretation of SPD history along these lines may be found in H. Mommsen (ed.), *Sozialdemokratie zwischen Klassenbewegung und Volkspartei* (Frankfurt, 1974).

43 The views summarized here can be found, with varying accentuations and nuances, in innumerable publications of the 1960s and 1970s, for example M. Kitchen, *The Political Economy of Germany 1815–1914* (London, 1978); K. D. Barkin, 'Germany's Path to Industrial Maturity', in D. K. Buse (ed.), *Aspects of Imperial Germany, Laurentian Historical Review*, vol. 5, no. 3 (1973); R. Dahrendorf, *Society and Democracy in Germany* (London 1978); K. Holl and G. List (eds), *Liberalismus und imperialistischer Staat* (Göttingen, 1975), esp. the contributions by I. Geiss and P.-C. Witt; and the essays in C. Stern and H. A. Winkler (eds), *Wendepunkte deutscher Geschichte 1848–1945* (Frankfurt, 1979). See also the footnotes to Chapter 3, Section II, below. To avoid

misunderstanding, I should say that the necessarily brief summary given here is a selection of the most oft-repeated elements in this interpretation; it is not intended to convey all the many different versions of it. For critical discussions of these views, see T. Nipperdey, 'Wehlers Kaiserreich: Eine Kritische Auseinandersetzung', *Geschichte und Gesellschaft*, vol. 1 (1975), pp. 539–60; H. G. Zmarzlik, 'Das Kaiserreich in neuer Sicht?', *Historische Zeitschrift*, vol. 222 (1976), pp. 105–26. The methodological and theoretical background to the discussion, in which both the innovative intentions and the political thrust of the new interpretation come to the fore, forms the subject of another series of controversial articles. See especially K. Hildebrand, 'Geschichte oder "Gesellschaftsgeschichte"? Die Notwendigkeit einer politischen Geschichtsschreibung von den internationalen Beziehungen', *Historische Zeitschrift*, vol. 223 (1976), pp. 328–57; H.-U. Wehler, 'Kritik und Antikritische Kritik', *Historische Zeitschrift*, vol. 225 (1977), pp. 347–84. See also the defence of Wehler in V. R. Berghahn, 'Der Bericht der Preussischen Oberrechnungskammer: Wehlers "Kaiserreich" und seine Kritiker', *Geschichte und Gesellschaft*, vol. 2 (1976), pp. 125–36. For general summaries of the development of West German political history in this period, see K. D. Barkin, 'From Uniformity to Pluralism: German Historical Writing since World War I', *German Life and Letters*, vol. 34, no. 2 (1981), pp. 234–47; H.-U. Wehler, 'Historiography in Germany Today', in J. Habermas (ed.), *Observations on "The Spiritual Situation of the Age"* (Cambridge, Mass., 1984). G. Eley 'Memories of Underdevelopment: Social History in Germany', *Social History*, vol. 2, no. 3 (1977), pp. 985–91; G. Iggers, *New Directions in European History* (Middletown, Conn., 1975).

44 See esp. Iggers, *German Conception of History*.

45 G. Iggers, *New Directions in European History*.

46 This image was used by Zmarzlik, 'Das Kaiserreich in neuer Sicht?'.

47 For a synthesis of this research, see J. S. Morrill, *The Revolt of the Provinces* (London, 1976).

48 See the introduction to R. Samuel (ed.), *Village Life and Labour*, History Workshop Series, Vol. 1 (London, 1975).

49 E.g. the combination of local and national studies in J. R. Vincent, *The Formation of the Liberal Party 1857–1868* (London, 1966).

50 G. Rudé, *The Crowd in the French Revolution* (Oxford, 1961); R. Cobb, *The Police and the People: French Popular Protest 1789–1820* (Oxford, 1970).

51 E. H. Carr, *What is History?* (Harmondsworth, 1961), which has influenced the ideas of a whole generation of British historians, contains a useful discussion on the role of theory.

52 See e.g. the categorization of social history adopted in the various methodological articles by Kocka (see n. 21, above).

53 For legal and other constraints on art, writing etc. in Victorian England in the name of morality, see E. Trudgill, *Madonnas and Magdalens* (London, 1976).

54 See my *Death in Hamburg: Society and Politics in the Cholera Years 1830–1910* (Oxford, 1987).

55 However, for some further considerations on this point, see Chapter 3, below.

56 G. Eley, *Reshaping the German Right* (New Haven, Conn., 1980), pp. 231–53.

57 I. Farr, 'Populism in the Countryside: The Peasant Leagues in Bavaria in the 1890s', in R. J. Evans (ed.), *Society and Politics in Wilhelmine Germany* (London, 1978), pp. 136–59.

58 D. Blackbourn, *Class, Religion and Local Politics in Imperial Germany: The Centre Party in Württemberg* (London, 1980).

59 R. Lenman, 'Politics and Culture: The State and the Avant-Garde in Munich 1886–1914', in Evans, *Society and Politics*, pp. 90–111.

60 M. Nolan, *Social Democracy and Society: Working-class Radicalism in Düsseldorf, 1890–1920* (Cambridge, 1981); F. Boll, *Massenbewegungen in Niedersachsen 1906–1920* (Bonn-Bad Godesberg, 1981); E. Lucas, *Arbeiterradikalismus: Zwei Formen von Radikalismus in der deutschen Arbeiterbewegung* (Frankfurt, 1976); S. Hickey, *Workers in Imperial Germany. Miners in the Ruhr* (Oxford, 1985).

61 In addition, a number of more detailed points have emerged where particular aspects of the interpretation of Imperial Germany discussed in this chapter have been questioned. For example, the thesis of a 'conservative purge' of the bureaucracy in the 1880s has been

seriously undermined by M. L. Anderson and K. D. Barkin, 'The Myth of the Puttkamer Purge and the Reality of the *Kaiserreich*: Some Reflections on the Historiography of Imperial Germany', *Journal of Modern History* vol. 54, no. 4 (1982), pp. 268–284. The general approach to the history of the civil service is subjected to a more wide-ranging critique by J. Caplan, ' "The Imaginary Universality of Particular Interests": the "tradition" of the civil service in German history', *Social History*, vol. 4 (1979), pp. 299–317. The application of 'Bonapartism' as a concept to describe the alleged 'plebiscitory dictatorship' of Bismarck has been questioned by A. Mitchell, 'Bonapartism as a Model for Bismarckian Politics', *Journal of Modern History*, vol. 49, no. 2 (1977), pp. 181–99. The widely held belief that the Tariff Reform of 1902 was pushed through as a 'quid pro quo' for the Junkers in return for their acquiescence in the Navy Law of 1898 has been demonstrated to be without foundation by D. Bleyberg, 'Government and Legislative Process in Wilhelmine Germany: The Reorganisation of the Tariff Laws under Reich Chancellor von Bülow 1897–1902', PhD. thesis, University of East Anglia, 1980. The view of the peasantry as dupes of the big landowners has been subjected to criticism from various directions: see in particular J. C. Hunt, 'Peasants, Grain Tariffs, and Meat Quotas: Imperial German Protectionism Re-examined', *Central European History*, vol. 7, no. 4 (1974), pp. 311–31; D. Blackbourn, 'Peasants and Politics in Germany, 1871–1914', *European History Quarterly*, vol. 14 (1984), pp. 47–75. The application of the notions of *Sammlungspolitik* and 'social imperialism' to political processes in the *Kaiserreich* is criticized in two articles by G. Eley, '*Sammlungspolitik*, Social Imperialism and the Navy Law of 1898', *Militärgeschichtliche Mitteilungen*, vol. 15, no. 1, (1974), pp. 29–63; 'Defining Social Imperialism: Use and Abuse of an Idea', *Social History*, vol. 1, no. 3 (1976), pp. 265–90. The treatment of the *Mittelstand* as a united and conservative body is exposed as an ideologically laden oversimplification by D. Blackbourn. 'The *Mittelstand* in German Society and Politics 1871–1914', *Social History*, vol. 2 (1977), pp. 409–33.

From Hitler to Bismarck:
Third Reich and Kaiserreich in
Recent Historiography

This essay was originally written in response to a request from the Cambridge *Historical Journal* to review a number of books published at the end of the 1970s and the beginning of the 1980s. The sheer variety of approaches which these works adopted was a reminder that, however much the running is made by one particular interpretation at any given time, many if not most historians continue to labour in the archives and at their desks with the aim of producing solid monographic studies based on detailed empirical research. Yet from an examination of the twenty-odd books sent for review it became clear that many of them, consciously or unconsciously, suggested parallels between 1933 and 1914, between the Third Reich and the German Empire, not only in terms of what they found there but also in the concepts and methods with which they approached it. This seemed a point worth exploring, especially since it suggested that the notion of continuity had become so deep-rooted in the historiography of modern Germany since the 1960s that it was by now more a hidden assumption than a conscious theory. Beyond this, too, the books reviewed raised central questions about the role of personality in modern German history, the extent to which Bismarck, Wilhelm II, or Hitler were bound by their historical situation, or simply reacting to structural forces. In retrospect, perhaps, the essay was a little too hard on the biographical approach, and some polemical excesses which now seem unjustified have been removed. The essay has also been streamlined by the removal of comments on the less important books reviewed and the incorporation into it of a review first published in *History*, vol. 68 (1983), pp. 364–5, which does more justice to the work in question than the original brief remarks in the article. I remain to be convinced of the adequacy of an approach which is based on the assumption that a nation's fate is determined by a single individual, or even a small group of individuals. Particularly where this approach is proclaimed as an innovation, it is important to remind ourselves that it really represents the most traditional kind of political history 'from the top down'. The inadequacies of this approach have been widely recognized for decades. Attempts to shore it up with concepts and methods borrowed from psychoanalysis cause more problems than they solve, because of the inherent arbitrariness of the procedures they employ. Nor do questions derived from American sociological theory seem to get us much further when applied to German social history in a broader sense, although here too the last part of the essay has been amended to take account of second thoughts. Nevertheless, despite the critical nature of some of the comments in the essay, it remains the case that all the books it discusses are important contributions to our understanding of modern German history; if they were not, they would scarcely deserve the respect which a sustained critical engagement implies.

I

The score or so books reviewed in this chapter all appeared in 1979, 1980, 1981 or 1982; they represent only a fraction of the vast outpouring of work from university and commercial publishing houses of publications on German history in the period 1871–1945. Research on modern German history is conducted on an international scale, with significant contributions to the scholarly literature being produced in Britain, France and the USA as well as in Germany itself. The sheer volume of publications and the bewildering variety of approaches and interpretations makes any kind of general statement about current trends extremely hazardous. Yet it seems clear that many of the significant interpretations, the major controversies, the serious research orientations in the historiography of the Third Reich have their parallels in the historiography of the *Kaiserreich*. It is impossible to say with any certainty whether historians of both periods are responding in common to broader trends, or whether ideas and hypotheses first worked out with reference to Hitler's Germany are being imported back into the study of the Germany of Bismark and Wilhelm II; probably there is something to be said for both views. Both the timing of the debates in both fields, and the nature of the theses advanced, leads one to suspect that there is at least some element of importation from the historiography of the Nazi period back into the historiography of the Empire. That is why I have entitled this essay 'From Hitler to Bismarck'; for, whatever the reasons behind them, the parallels between recent work on the two periods are too striking to ignore.

To some extent, this remarkable feature of current scholarship on modern Germany is a reflection of the wide acceptance gained by the idea of continuity in German history (in its broadest sense) over the last two decades, since the publication of Fritz Fischer's work on Germany's aims in the First World War. If it has become generally accepted that there were at least some similarities between Hitler's Germany and Bismarck's or Wilhelm II's, then a consequence of this acceptance has been that similar theories and methods have been applied with increasing frequency to the study of both. Yet matters are not quite so simple as this; for even those historians who continue to insist on the uniqueness of Nazism, on its lack of historical roots, may find their methodological premisses shared by many who would violently object to such a view. Thus to emphasize the role of Hitler as sole dictator and arbiter of the Third Reich is only a denial of continuity in German history in so far as it is accompanied by a refusal to accept that any similar figures existed in the German past. Those who seek to portray Bismarck or Wilhelm II as dictators in their own time may share with the biographers of Hitler a common belief in the overwhelming importance of Great Men (though even this is not necessarily the case), but they are also – by implication – saying that, for whatever reason, Germany in the era 1871–1945 had an uncomfortably persistent tendency to throw them up and submit to their rule.

I have chosen to explore some of these parallels by dividing up the books under discussion according to the theoretical and methodological premisses on which they rest, rather than according to the periods or subjects with which they deal. In the next section, I examine two biographical studies, by John Röhl and Nicolaus Sombart, and by Margaret Anderson. These books are of major importance, and that edited by Röhl and Sombart in particular reproduces for the Wilhelmine period arguments already familiar from the Nazi era about the role and personality of the country's ruler; while Anderson's study illustrates the contribution that a broadly conceived political biography can make to historical understanding in a wider sense. In the third section, I go on to examine in more detail the controversy about Hitler's role in the Third Reich, on the basis of the works by Pierre Ayçoberry, Gerhard Hirschfeld and Lothar Kettenacker, and Martin Broszat. Opposed to the biographical emphasis is what I term a 'structuralist' approach, which lays stress on political and administrative structures and decision-making processes and their autonomous role in bringing about major decisions, above all in the field of foreign policy. This structuralist approach has also been applied to the history of the *Kaiserreich*. Two varieties can be distinguished: a radical-liberal, partly Weberian version, which concentrates on the role of 'traditional élites' (as in recent work by Wolfgang Mommsen and Paul Kennedy), and a Gramscian or neo-Marxist version, which emphasizes the shifting structures and alignments of the 'hegemonic bloc', as in a contribution by Geoff Eley, which is paralleled by the work of David Abraham on the collapse of the Weimar Republic, both discussed in the fourth section. Finally, I turn to the contribution of social history, and suggest ways in which a locally based approach, as in the *Institut für Zeitgeschichte* project on Bavaria in the Nazi period, the monograph on Germans in Prague by Gary Cohen, or the study of Bochum by David Crew, is beginning to undermine many of the conclusions reached by the biographical and structuralist approaches and is leading gradually to a redrawing of the map of modern German history at least as radical as that achieved in the wake of the Fischer controversy twenty years ago.

II

German historians have frequently and justifiably complained of the lack of a real tradition of political biography in their own country. There have been plenty of studies of Hitler, for example, but the majority of these have been by non-Germans. So it is too with Wilhelm II, who, Professor John Röhl complains, has become something of an 'unperson' in recent scholarship on the *Kaiserreich*.[1] For a number of years Röhl has been seeking to rehabilitate the idea, once advanced by the liberal scholar Erich Eyck, that Wilhelm II was the dominant figure in German politics before 1914. The basis of this view has been provided by the papers of Wilhelm's friend Philipp Eulenburg, which Röhl has edited with superb and meticulous scholarship.[2] Röhl's latest contribution is as joint editor with Nicolaus Sombart of a collection of essays on Wilhelm II by various hands.[3] They are the product of a conference on the monarch which, in a faintly ridiculous act of self-indulgence entirely appropriate to its subject, the contributors arranged in 1979 in the bedroom of the Kaiser's villa on the island of Corfu. In his two introductory papers to this well-produced and handsomely illustrated collection, Röhl seeks to rehabilitate Wilhelm II as the maker of German policy in his own time. Röhl is supported by his collaborator Thomas Kohut, who sees Wilhelm as having exerted 'a lasting and decisive influence' (p. 64) on German policy towards England. Kathy Lerman, too, in an essay on the Kaiser's most effective Chancellor, Bernhard von Bülow, asserts that Bülow's 'whole system' depended on his relationship with the Kaiser, whom he only 'seemingly manipulated' and whose will was only constrained by Bülow in relation to minor issues (p. 242). Röhl seeks to show that Germany before 1914 was personally ruled by the Kaiser, acting through an 'inner circle of some fifty men in control of the destiny of this mighty state in the heart of Europe' (p. 17). In this circle, which owed its existence almost entirely to the patronage of the Kaiser, social foibles and scandals could play a vital role in political advancement. The political history of Imperial Germany must in the first place, therefore, be researched by the 'traditional skills of the historian – of tracking down elusive documents and evaluating them with subtlety and sensitivity' (p. 10).

Much of this volume is devoted to uncovering the hidden life of Wilhelm and his courtiers, as if this were the determining influence in the making of German domestic and foreign policy in this period. New archival discoveries, however trivial, are given pride of place; and the documents most eagerly cited are those which previous historians, usually for reasons of propriety, have attempted to suppress. Petty court intrigues and family squabbles are recounted at vast length. Much is made of the homosexual tone of Wilhelm's immediate circle of friends. To such trivia great things are attributed. 'It is fascinating', writes Röhl, for example, 'to speculate what course German history might have taken if Bülow's and Eulenburg's infatuation with Wilhelm II had faded sooner (or for that matter if the Vienna bath-house keeper who started to blackmail Eulenburg for homosexuality in early 1876 had divulged his secrets there and then)' (p. 28). This is history as the butler saw it. But does the keyhole really afford the best perspective on the past? Contributions in the book written from this angle of vision suggest that it does not. For example, Thomas Kohut's essay on Wilhelm II's attitude to England makes no attempt to demonstrate the Kaiser's influence on policy-making but simply assumes it, and on this basis attributes the rise of Anglo-German antagonism up to 1914 to Wilhelm's desire to avenge his German father's subservience to his dominating English mother and to reconcile the 'English' and 'German' elements in himself. Throughout his essay, Kohut employs the flimsy inferential procedures so familiar in psychohistory. To begin with, one cannot help feeling that his definition of psychological normality is arbitrary; for instance Wilhelm's mother is described as 'possessive' on very thin grounds. Wilhelm is said to have been brought up by his mother in an attempt to make him an Englishman; at the same time, the ideal which she held out to him was evidently Prince Albert, her father, who was, of course, German (indeed the whole English royal family was widely regarded in England as 'German'). Wilhelm's education by the dominant figure of his childhood, his ferocious tutor Hinzpeter, is even described by Kohut as 'English' because Hinzpeter (a German) believed in constitutional monarchy! This is all very feeble stuff. Bismarck, after all, regarded the life of an English gentleman as ideal, and once remarked 'all my habits and tastes are English'; but this did not affect his political judgement any more than Edward VII's German connections did his.

A more sensitive level of analysis is provided by Isabel Hull's contribution on the Kaiser's homosexual friends in the 'Liebenberg circle', but she is unable to show that any of them apart from Eulenburg had any real political influence over Wilhelm. In her book on the subject (Isabel V. Hull, *The Entourage of Kaiser Wilhelm II, 1888–1918*, Cambridge 1982), Hull claims that the Kaiser's entourage was the institutional locus in which the personality of the Kaiser and the class and political and sexual make-up of his advisers acted as a decisive force in German history. The introduction argues that Wilhelm II's advisers were 'in an unparalleled position to imprint their peculiar vision of the world upon German policy' (p. 1). The first five chapters examine the Kaiser's relationship with Philipp Eulenburg and the Liebenberg circle, already familiar from the work of Professor Röhl. Eulenburg's political aims, which included opposition to imperialism and *Weltpolitik*, and uncompromising defence of the agrarian interest, bore little relation to those actually put into effect. The civilian entourage generally supported the policies advocated by Chancellors and ministers. They, too, spent much of their time trying to stop the Kaiser's impetuous interventions in policy-making, or in attempting to undo their worst effects. The Liebenberg circle is convicted of failing to alter Wilhelm's personality; this does not really amount to much, and its influence seems in general to have been small. Eulenburg was not very important after about 1897; the general conviction that he was at the head of a court camarilla a decade later may have caused his downfall, but its basis in reality was limited. For reasons which appear obscure, Hull then devotes a chapter to Krupp, Ballin and Fürstenberg, who were not very close to Wilhelm, and whose influence was even less.

Three more chapters argue that Wilhelm's military entourage was far more important, especially after the eclipse of Eulenberg. The younger Moltke in particular is convicted of spearheading the military entourage's successful campaign for a war of European conquest. But it is implausible to argue that Moltke represented the specific influence of Wilhelm's personal military entourage. What gave his opinion weight was the fact that he was the Chief of Staff and represented the army. Schlieffen, his predecessor, was not at all close to the Kaiser; he had advocated war unsuccessfully in 1905, but what made the difference in 1914 was not that Moltke had replaced Schlieffen, nor even – though this was clearly of some importance – that Bethmann had replaced Bülow, but rather that nine crisis-ridden, internationally humiliating years for the government had elapsed in the meantime, and that the domestic political constellation in 1914 was markedly different from what it had been in 1905. As Hull is forced to concede, the true feelings of the army were revealed on the outbreak of war, when it rapidly removed from the Kaiser any indepen-dent military power that remained to him.

Ultimately, in fact, when Hull moves from descriptions of court intrigues to considerations of real political questions, the entourage disappears and we are left with the alleged personal influence of two individuals – Eulenburg and Moltke. This is scarcely the novel approach to the history of Wilhelmine Germany advertised in the introduction. As we move – yet again – through the familiar story of court intrigues and scandals, with a detail added or corrected here and there, perhaps, but nothing fundamentally new, the political irrelevance of most of it becomes clear from the almost complete absence of any discussion of real political issues, at least in the domestic sphere. For these we have to look to the arenas in which such issues were actually decided – the vast Wilhelmine bureaucracy, the Reichstag, the federated states, the political parties, and the pressure-groups; and to understand what these issues were, and why they were decided in the way they were, we have to look even further afield, to the as yet barely researched economic and social history of the *Kaiserreich*. These are the subjects that really need research; Professor Hull's book, in contrast, adds little that is new or surprising to the sum of knowledge about Wilhelmine Germany, and her generalizations about the 'Junker ruling class' reveal a crude understanding of the overall socio-political structure of the Empire, which students should strongly resist.

If Hull's account, both in her book and in her contribution to the Röhl and Sombart volume, seems in the end rather inconsequential, despite its considerable psychological acumen, the same can be said *a fortiori* of Lamar Cecil's gossipy account, in his contribution to *Kaiser Wilhelm II*, of squabbles within the Anglo-German royal cousinhood, who certainly seem to have been a quarrelsome lot. At the end of it all, Cecil concludes disarmingly that none of his material is of any great importance (pp. 109–10). His assessment of the Kaiser, indeed, makes a nonsense of the wild claims for his importance advanced by Röhl and Kohut. 'The Kaiser himself', he remarks, 'was too easily manipulated and too spasmodic in effort to have capitalised on his autocratic prerogatives and thereby dictated German diplomacy'. He was 'lazy, capricious, prejudiced and indiscreet'. There were many forces, Cecil concludes, making for Anglo-German hostility, 'and even a more purposeful ruler than Wilhelm II would have had difficulty in controlling them' (p. 110).

More cold water is poured on by Paul Kennedy, in a characteristically commonsensical essay on foreign policy. Wilhelm II was widely held to be responsible for German foreign policy, he points out, but this was no more true than the general belief that Edward VII was the architect of the Anglo-French *entente*. The general direction of German foreign policy was set by more impersonal interests: by Germany's rapid economic growth, by the ideology of Germany's ruling élite, by the structural problems of Germany's domestic politics. Yet Kennedy spoils his case by trying to reconcile it with the notion that Wilhelm's personality and decisions *were* of crucial importance. Thus he asserts, for example, that the Kaiser's role in the formulation and adoption of operational war-plans was undoubtedly an important one (pp. 162–3). What was this role? Kennedy says that the generals showed Wilhelm all their plans and he never objected to any of them, however outrageous they were. But this is evidence of his unimportance, not of his importance. The same could be said of Kennedy's claim (p. 164) that Wilhelm was unable to choose between different and often mutually contradictory policies. Here again, vacillation and inaction seem to have been his contribution, rather than consistency and firmness of purpose.

The most persuasive contribution in the volume is that of Wilhelm Deist on the Kaiser's military entourage. Deist begins by noting that the Reichstag defeated or strongly modified most of Wilhelm II's pet political schemes in the 1890s. The Kaiser railed against the legislature in unbridled terms, but like so much of his talk it was empty and should not be taken seriously by historians. Wilhelm II jealously preserved his powers as supreme military commander (the *Kommandogewalt*); but he used it not on major matters of policy but rather on the trivia which so used to excite him – uniforms, titles, ceremonies, matters of honour and the like. Wilhelm's views on naval tactics and strategy were described by the head of his naval cabinet as 'amateurish nonsense'. Deist remarks that 'it cannot be said that Wilhelm II ever introduced any new leadership ideas, or influenced the development of military principles at all'. He was only concerned with the formal attributes of power, not with its substance – 'more interested in matters of decoration than in concrete realities', as Deist puts it (p. 185). Indeed he failed in his main duty as Supreme Commander – that of co-ordinating the strategic and operational plans of the two branches of the armed forces in the event of war. He surrounded himself with a military entourage selected by him for their personal compatibility and retained for long periods in office. Many of them were unqualified and incompetent. This gradually alienated the Kaiser from the real army and navy, of which these men were increasingly unrepresenta- tive. On the outbreak of war, Wilhelm was quickly robbed of any military role at all; the recognition that his claim to be Germany's sole ruler had long been a hollow one now spread very quickly. 'The fact is', as General von Einem remarked in 1915, 'we haven't had a working head of state for the last twenty-five years' (quoted on p. 187). This is a convincing corrective to the view, advanced by Isabel Hull, that the Kaiser's military entourage was a decisive influence on policy-making via its ties to the Kaiser.

Kathy Lerman also notes, in her well-documented contribution, that Wilhelm's only sustained intervention was in the realm of appointments, and here too his main concern was to appoint people he liked. In 1901, for example, he offered the finance ministry successively to Siemens, a pronounced liberal, and Henckel von Donnersmarck, a staunch agrarian! Chancellor von Bülow often had to contend with such interventions, but, as Lerman shows, his position was so strong that he could easily manipulate or dominate whoever was appointed. Moreover, 'when Bülow had a political reason for wanting to effect a personnel change, he generally seems to have been able to do so' (p. 234). Bülow also frequently asserted that he could contradict the Kaiser on matters of policy, or get him to change his mind, without difficulty, provided he did it carefully, and this indeed should not be surprising, given Wilhelm's known tendency to adopt the views of the last person he spoke to. Bülow worked hard to thwart Wilhelm's wilder demands, and on the whole he did this with success; the Kaiser himself confessed that he mainly left the business of government to his Chancellor. Almost every piece of evidence cited by Lerman demonstrates the strong hold that Bülow had over the Kaiser, and it is with some astonishment that one reads her conclusion, wholly unwarranted by the text, that Bülow only 'seemingly' manipulated him, and was only able to prevail in relation to 'minor issues' (p. 242). Nor does Lerman carry conviction in her assertion that Bülow's 'whole system' depended on his relationship with the Kaiser. The assessment provided by Terry Cole in his account of Bülow's role in the *Daily Telegraph* affair is much more realistic; and Cole, rose-tinted spectacles firmly in place, adds another thoroughly documented contribution to his attempted rehabilitation of Bülow as an independent, far-sighted and resourceful politician (pp. 249–68). His estrangement from the Kaiser, as Cole shows, went back as far as 1903, but it was only with the collapse of Bülow's majority 'Block' in the Reichstag in 1909 that Wilhelm was able to get rid of him.

What all this adds up to is a restatement of the well-known fact that the Kaiser was no dictator. Far from being the moving cog at the centre of the German governmental machine, Wilhelm II was usually a spanner in the works. It is unfortunate that the collection overstates its case so crudely, for elsewhere Röhl has taken a much more nuanced and contextualized approach to Wilhelm II's role in German politics.[4]

A model of what a political biography *can* achieve is provided by Margaret Lavinia Anderson's *Windthorst: A Political Biography* (Oxford, 1981). This substantial new study of the Catholic Centre Party leader, Ludwig Windthorst (1812–91), is the first biography since 1907 and the first to make use of the full range of printed and manuscript sources, some of which have only recently become available. This is not a biography after the English manner: there is not much attempt to plumb Windthorst's inner motives or gain any psychological insight into his character; he remains as personally impenetrable to the reader as he evidently was to contemporaries, an enigmatically imperturbable figure who gained his prominence through a mixture of tact, very hard work, a ready tongue and a mastery of parliamentary tactics. Anderson is concerned to use her study of his life to advance a series of important propositions about German politics in the period 1866–90, the years of Windthorst's national prominence, and she is not afraid of departing from the actual details of his life in order to do so. First, she uses his essentially parliamentary career to argue that the Reichstag was more important in this period than many historians have assumed. Anderson perhaps exaggerates Windthorst's dominance of that body, for this was surely the age of the great parliamentary debates and clashes between a number of dominant, oratorically gifted and charismatic political leaders, including not only Bismarck and Windthorst but also Bebel and Richter, to be succeeded gradually by a more bureaucratic, more highly organized style of mass politics during the 1890s. One could also put forward the caveat that anyone who researches for years on the career of a Reichstag politician is liable to come away with the impression that the Reichstag was at the centre of things, just as anyone

63

who is buried for decades in the private papers of the court camarilla is likely to come to the opposite conclusion.

Yet Anderson's book amounts, *inter alia*, to a sustained plea for historians to take the Reichstag seriously, not only for the 1870s but also for the 1880s. The *Kulturkampf*, she argues, was above all a struggle for civil liberties, in which the Centre Party filled the classical role of a liberal – indeed libertarian – opposition which had been so abjectly vacated by the National Liberals. As this book makes abundantly clear, the *Kulturkampf* did not abruptly cease in 1878 but was only gradually ended in a series of bitterly fought reforms in the succeeding decade. 'In the 1880s, the legislature was still the voice of the people, the focus of the national drama, the scene of Germany's great expectations ... By the 1890s, national attention had turned from legislation to *Weltpolitik*' (p. 406). The Centre Party, held artificially on a libertarian course by Windthorst, veered sharply towards the line taken by the government, while ambitious younger politicians increasingly sought to make their careers outside the parliament, above all in the new pressure-groups that sprang up everywhere during the 1890s.

Perhaps these arguments, once more, are overdone by Anderson, for among other things her study makes clear the close nature of the ties between the Centre Party and the Catholic Church, something that has been rather underplayed in recent studies. When Windthorst threatened to quit, it was after all to the pope that he intended to send his letter of resignation; and his involvement in clerical appointments was close and continuing. This surely was the Achilles' heel of the Catholic Centre. Windthorst's attempt to achieve a liberal solution of the *Kulturkampf* was undermined by Pope Leo XIII's negotiations with Bismarck in 1887; the effect on the Catholic Centre of Windthorst's betrayal by the pope in that year is compared by Anderson to that of Bismarck's Indemnity Bill of 1866 on the liberals. But this was not the only time that its clericalism led the Catholic Centre to abandon its commitment to civil liberties; indeed, the events of 1887 occurred again at the end of the Weimar Republic, when the pope's desire for a concordat with Hitler led him to persuade the Centre Party to vote for the Enabling Law and subsequently played an important part in bringing about the Catholic Centre's dissolution. To a degree, also, the Catholic Centre only functioned as the representative of a particular sector of the community. Anderson comments, for example, on its self-absorption and on the narrowness of its political focus; it rarely concerned itself with questions of foreign policy, for instance (p. 297). Moreover, Anderson's claims are further undermined by her admission that the Catholic Centre Reichstag deputies were noticeable throughout this period for their persistent absenteeism.

Yet on the whole Anderson's plea for a more positive assessment of the Reichstag in the 1880s, and of the Centre Party's role in its affairs, is persuasively made. It is all the more important because it involves a conscious downgrading of the significance of the policy changes of 1878–9. Anderson argues that the anti-socialist law of 1878 was a less important infringement of constitutional liberties than was the *Kulturkampf* because it involved a far smaller sector of the community. The tariffs of 1879 may have affected the National Liberals and encouraged them to move closer to the conservatives. But 'to see 1878–9 as a "radical transformation of German politics" and a "conservative reconstruction of the Reich" is to underestimate the Liberal–Conservative cooperation of the seventies; to overestimate the enthusiasm of Prussia's agrarian elite for Bismarck's new economic package; and erroneously to include the Catholic Centre in the "new political alignment" of Germany's anti-socialist, anti-parliamentary, plebiscitarian future' (pp. 234–5). Once more, therefore, Anderson lends weight to the argument that the 1890s rather than the late 1870s were the decisive years in the political history of the Empire; and in her use of Windthorst's career to advance these – and other – important theses, Anderson thus provides an outstanding example of what a political biography, if carefully handled, can achieve. Well written, spiced with waspish and combative footnotes from which scarcely a single historian of the period emerges unscathed, Anderson's study is not for the beginner, for it does assume a general conversance with the political history of the period. But it is a weighty and substantial study, a major contribution to our knowledge and understanding not only of political Catholicism in nineteenth-century Germany but also of the structure and development of German politics in the Bismarckian period as a whole. What it exemplifies above all is the elementary but none the less vital point that – to cite Marx – 'Men do make their own history, but they do not make it as they please, under conditions of their own choosing, but rather under circumstances which they find before them, under given and imposed conditions'.[5] Too often, biographers and those who would have us return to the days when history was all about Great Men, have ignored this dictum. But as the inadequacies of Röhl and Sombart's collection make clear, they have ignored it at their peril.

III

The view that Hitler himself was an all-powerful autocrat whose ideas and intentions are the key to an understanding of the Third Reich has for some years now been seriously questioned by a number of German historians. True, Hitler's dominance and total control of the Third Reich was for many decades treated as a generally accepted fact, as Pierre Ayçoberry's new account of the development of historical interpretations of Nazism usefully demonstrates.[6] Faced with the necessity of accepting the evidence of Nazi barbarism after 1945, conservative historians in Germany, led by Gerhard Ritter, tried to argue that the evils of Nazism were all imported from abroad: Darwinism from England, extreme nationalism from France, racism from Austria, and so on. The central place in this intrepretation was occupied by Hitler, the Nazi dictator, whose genius took advantage of the age of democracy that had arrived with the Weimar Republic, and mobilized the atomized masses in a movement that destroyed all independent institutions in Germany and reconstituted them into the totalitarian dictatorship of the Third Reich. This was also essentially the view of the totalitarianism theories of the 1950s. These placed the dictator in a wider context which did nothing to diminish his central importance to the interpretation. Totalitarianism theory emphasized Nazism's modernity, its dependence on the 'age of the masses' and its abolition of previously existing social forces. It stressed the total control exercised by the regime over its citizens – the all-embracing police powers, the destruction of all possibility of resistance, save at the very top, the standardization of society, the ubiquity of indoctrination, the monopolization of political power by a single party. But it also stressed the concentration of all these powers in the hands of a single individual and emphasized the key role played by the charismatic dictator. Both political science and traditional historical scholarship could thus agree on the centrality of the dictator to the phenomenon of Nazism. So the task of historical scholarship was to deduce Hitler's intentions from his writings, statements and actions, and to uncover the mechanisms by which he was able to put them into effect.

Ayçoberry's book deals with general interpretations of Nazism and the Third Reich; it does not, with few exceptions, go into detail on specific questions. By placing these interpretations in a chronological framework (the first eight chapters take us from 1922 to 1960 in short, self-contained periods), Ayçoberry is able to relate the interpretations intelligently to their political background. The coverage is broad, paying attention to Marxist views, East as well as West German scholarship, French as well as English and American historians. The interpretations discussed are also subjected to some acute criticism, which will be a boon to undergraduates seeking material for essays. But the book gets into a fearful muddle in the last four chapters, when it leaves the chronological path and opts instead for a part-thematic, part-methodological discussion. The problem here is that, while the study of Nazism and its origins developed along relatively clear lines until the end of the 1950s, since that date, with the massive expansion of universities everywhere, with the student movement of the 1960s, and with the development of new techniques and new ideas, there has been a veritable explosion of research, and it is no longer really possible for a single commentator either to keep track of every line of inquiry that has been developed, or to impose a coherent pattern of exposition on the bewildering variety of views that have been advanced. Thus the last four chapters of Ayçoberry's book jump from psychohistory to prosopography, from linguistics to phenomenology, from biographies and diplomatic histories to sociological theories that link Marxism to the broader question of the peculiarities of Germany's overall historical development; but there is no connecting thread visible, unless it is perhaps a rather naïve belief in the benefits of quantification.

One possible way through the maze is provided by Tim Mason's contribution to *The 'Führer State'*, a useful new collection of essays from the German Historical Institute in London, which under its director, Professor Wolfgang J. Mommsen, has become an indispensable centre for the exchange of views between British and German historians.[7] Mason launches a strong attack on what he calls 'intentionalist' historians of the Third Reich, represented in this book by Klaus Hildebrand. Historians such as Hildebrand or Karl Dietrich Bracher, he remarks,

> formulate the question: why did the Third Reich launch a murderous war of genocide and the destruction of human life on a hitherto unprecedented scale? They come in the end to the conclusion that the leaders of the Third Reich, above all Hitler, did this because they wanted to do it. This can be demonstrated by studying early manifestations of their *Weltanschauung*, which are wholly compatible with the worst atrocities which actually occurred in the years 1938–45. (p. 28)

Thus the goal of Nazism was genocide; and the Third Reich appears as a unique phenomenon, revolutionary and utopian, without real roots. Indeed, Klaus Hildebrand has even suggested that we should refer to 'Hitlerism' rather than 'National Socialism'. Hildebrand elaborates on this view in his contribution to the present volume, basing himself mainly on arguments first put forward by Karl Dietrich Bracher. He concedes that – as has long been known – the Third Reich was a chaos of competing institutions, but he suggests that this very competition only served to enhance the Führer's authority. He insists that the mass murder of the Jews was above all the result of Hitler's pathological ideology. To say otherwise, he remarks, is to sidestep the question of moral responsibility.

More recently, however, scholars such as Hans Mommsen and Martin Broszat have been engaged in a wholesale revision of this view. The effect of their work has been twofold; to downgrade the importance of Hitler, and to reconnect Nazism to the German past by upgrading the role of 'traditional élites' in the establishment and running of the Third Reich. In their contributions to the German Historical Institute's volume on *The 'Führer State'*, Tim Mason and Hans Mommsen argue that it is to the structural context of political decision-making that historians should turn their attention. 'The traits of systematization, regularity, calculability inherent in the construction of a comprehensive administrative base for the dictatorship, were perceived, particularly by Hitler, Himmler and Goebbels, as limiting factors, as constraints, actual or potential, on their power as they understood it' (p. 25). Thus the regime increasingly substituted propaganda for administration and evasions for policies. More and more it effected unprepared and drastic decisions which disrupted existing plans. To deal with special problems, it set up *ad hoc* institutions which quickly became permanent. Decision-making became fragmented, competences overlapped, conflict within the regime became sharper and more all-pervasive. Each separate decision carried with it unforeseen consequences which demanded further, often more far-reaching decisions. This process enhanced Hitler's power, but it did not take place as a result of any conscious decision on his part; indeed he was to a degree a prisoner of it, for his need to preserve his own popularity meant that he tended more and more to avoid associating himself with specific decisions, while at the same time encouraging the most national socialist (i.e. the most radical) policies advocated by his subordinates, however much these clashed with one another. Thus the effect of increasingly uncoordinated, unprepared, arbitrary and *ad hoc* decisions was to make the processes of policy-making 'cumulatively more arbitrary in their character, more violent and radical in their implementation, more conducive to competitive struggle among the executive organs of the régime' (p. 27). This process became self-generating and ultimately self-destructive. Once fully under way, it progressively narrowed Hitler's freedom of choice and circumscribed his field of action. Thus Hitler, in Hans Mommsen's controversial phrase, was a 'weak dictator'.[8]

The internal chaos of the Nazi regime has long been a familiar theme of historians; what is new about this 'structuralist' view is that it denies the ability of the leadership to keep this chaos in check. I use the term 'structuralist' to indicate that what these historians emphasize is the self-generating radicalism of political and administative *structures*, independent of the intentions of those operating within them or of social and economic forces acting upon them from outside. The first major attempt at a general exposition of this structuralist interpretation was Martin Broszat's *Der Staat Hitlers*, first published in 1969.[9] Broszat's book followed the unfolding of the radicalizing and disintegrative process of Nazi rule from beginning to end in considerable detail. The initial defeat of the revolutionary forces in 1934 was succeeded by a period of 'authoritarian rule' which was gradually undermined by the uncontrollable dynamism of the movement. Co-ordinating institutions such as the cabinet ceased to exist; the party gradually founded new institutions which by 1938 had effectively removed power from the parallel organs of the state. The arbitrarily created personal empires of the Nazi satraps proliferated, and the destructive elements in the system became paramount (thus in the conquest of the East, millions of Slavs were murdered, but very few German peasant settlements were founded). Crucial to this whole process, finally, as Broszat and Hans Mommsen argue with great force, was the collaboration and patronage of the 'traditional élites' from the 1920s up to 1938. Their final rebellion in the July Plot of 1944 appears in this version as no more than an attempt to restore the status quo of the 'authoritarian years' before 1938. Hitler, in this view, was certainly not at the mercy of events; but he was not wholly in control of them either.

Similar ideas have also been applied to the *Kaiserreich*. Some time ago, Wolfgang Mommsen advocated what he called a 'functional–structural approach' that took into account the institutional processes of decision-making involved in the decision to go to war in 1914;[10] he returns to this topic in a new contribution to a collection of essays presented to Professor Francis Carsten on his seventieth birthday.[11] This collection is as varied as *Festschriften* usually are, though unfortunately it provides little concrete reflection of Carsten's importance as an interpreter of the overall course of German history as well as a writer on the twentieth century. Mommsen's contribution focuses on the role of public opinion. It concentrates on the uncontrollable nationalist pressure-groups that emerged in the 1890s and had achieved enormous influence by the eve of the war, in persuading Bethmann Hollweg and others in the leadership of the Reich that war was inevitable. Mommsen is only one of a number of German scholars who have argued in recent years that the German decision to go to war was made in a desperate bid to escape the insoluble domestic problems which the Reich was facing by 1914. The political process seemed as paralysed in 1912–14 as it did in 1929–33. The forces blocking credible solutions to the various crises – financial, constitutional and diplomatic – which the Reich confronted seemed overwhelming. The gradual fragmentation of the decision-making process, with the Chancellor, the army, the navy and the foreign ministry all pursuing mutually contradictory policies, and the Kaiser completely unable to weld them all into a coherent whole, generated its own tension and dynamic. Finally, if the rulers of the Empire were to regain the initiative and prevent the Social Democrats from exploiting their election victory of 1912 to force major constitutional changes, then a war seemed the gamble most likely to pay off.

The view that the decision to go to war in 1914 was the result of cumulative political, economic and social pressures in Germany has now been given magisterial and comprehensive treatment in Paul Kennedy's massive new study, *The Rise of the Anglo-German Antagonism 1860–1914*.[12] The core of Kennedy's book is an old-style narrative diplomatic history, based on an impressive mastery not only of a wide range of printed material but also of unpublished sources in some sixty archives. This hard narrative core is surrounded by a softer pulp of analysis in which the author deals with broader influences on relations between the two countries. Finally, to round it all off, there is an attempt at a general comparison between the socio-economic and political structures of the two countries, the equivalent of a rather thin layer of pith and peel. Thus Kennedy's study is much more than a traditional diplomatic history; it also involves a highly ambitious attempt at a comparative history of two different nations. On one level, the work can be used simply as a handbook. If you want to find out what the *Sheffield Telegraph* thought of the prospects of an Anglo-German alliance, or why the Tübingen school of theology aroused such anger in England, or which British historians backed Bismarck in the Franco-Prussian War, or whether the German government's manipulation of the press was as subtle and gentlemanly as the methods used by the English, or who belonged to the Anglo-German Friendship Society, or whether the Catholic Centre Party approved of the Kruger telegram, then this is the place to look. The mass of detailed information, the comprehensive range of Kennedy's scholarship, the staggering industry of his researches, the sheer weight of his learning, are all tremendously impressive. Equally impressive is the clarity of structure and style with which all this information is presented. There can be no doubt that if anyone wants to start investigating the problem of Anglo-German relations before 1914, they must now start by reading this book.

Kennedy is essentially a synthesizer; his achievement – and it is a very considerable one – is to have combed the archives and libraries for every scrap of paper relevant to Anglo-German relations in this period and to have brought it all together in an orderly and readable form between the covers of one book. The central diplomatic narrative must surely now be regarded as definitive. Inevitably, however, weaknesses begin to creep in at the more general levels of analysis. Where Kennedy has real, first-hand expertise, as in the question of colonial rivalries, he is not afraid to engage with and criticize existing interpretations.[13] In dealing with non-diplomatic aspects of Anglo-German relations, and especially in questions of domestic affairs, he is more inclined to rely on the work of others. Thus he accepts virtually without question arguments about the 'refounding' of the Reich in 1878–9, the 'alliance of rye and iron', Wilhelm II's achievement of 'personal rule' by 1897 and many other theses of recent historiography. As we have already seen, these are the subject of sharp controversy, and should not simply be accepted. On occasion indeed he falls into error on such matters; for instance, he seems to think that Bavarian Peasant Leagues were part of the German Conservative Party (pp. 348–50), and his account of the German labour movement, which confuses revisionism with reformism and implies that collective bargaining was widespread in Germany before 1914, is frankly unsatisfactory. The broadest level of comparison, between the overall social and political structure and development of the two countries, is weak; it generally appears only in the margin, and has not been given the thought and attention accorded to the more detailed empirical research.

Moreover, despite the book's exemplary clarity of presentation, it is none the less dogged by serious structural problems. To begin with, it is hard to see why Kennedy devotes such lengthy attention to aspects of Anglo-German relations which he concludes were only of minor importance, such as the political parties up to 1880 or the development of cultural and religious contacts. The relatively even-handed treatment of all these various topics contributes in no small measure to the book's excessive length. Then again, Kennedy does not always relate his three levels of analysis to one another very well. It is all very fine to say that Germany's massive economic growth in the late nineteenth and twentieth centuries was the determining factor in the rise of the Anglo-German antagonism; but how or why it should have led to war with Britain requires more systematic analysis and explanation than it receives in this book. Many different explanations, embodying rival theories of the relationship of the economic and the political, have after all been advanced over the years; one would like to have seen them systematically assessed, even at the expense of some of the empirical material. Finally, the problem of how the war actually came about is sidestepped by the conclusion that it was more or less inevitable by 1906 anyway; indeed, the crucial years up to 1914 are relegated to a brief afterword. It may be true – as the author says – that there is little more to be discovered about international relations in these years. Yet one cannot suppress a certain feeling of disappointment that he has chosen not to extend to this final period – the outcome of which was surely a good deal less predictable than he claims – the comprehensively researched treatment which he has devoted to the earlier history of Anglo-German diplomacy.

All this amounts to the fact that although Kennedy's book revises previous accounts of his subject on innumerable secondary and minor issues, he has not used his prodigious archival labours to produce any really significant revision of our picture of Anglo-German relations in the crucial period of their estrangement (i.e. from about the turn of the century onwards). His account of the less well-known earlier period is more innovative; but of course, as he points out, this period was not particularly significant in the history of the rise of Anglo-German antagonism. In the account of the later period, the centrality of the naval building programme to Anglo-German antagonism is restated (its repercussions on diplomacy are persuasively dated a year or two earlier than convention usually agrees). The influence of public opinion on foreign policy – a commonplace of diplomatic history – is emphasized through a very thorough survey of the press, through a brief account of the rise of nationalist pressure-groups and through careful allusions to these in the course of the diplomatic narrative. Kennedy usefully notes that there was

71

much more cohesion in the 'collective mind' formed by Tirpitz, his junior staff, Reventlow, Schäfer, Bassermann, and the Pan-Germans – formed, that is, by people *in* and *out* of government – than there was in the perceptions of all those within that 'legally recognisable but politically mythical boundary which divided officialdom from everyone else' (p. 433). In the end, however, this insight leads him to reproduce the conventional wisdom that Germany's foreign aggressiveness was the outcome of 'domestic–political tensions, a flawed decision-making structure, undue deference to the military and excessive nationalism' (p. 454). Ultimately, he suggests, the rise of German economic power was the root of the antagonism, not because of the influence of capitalists on government (a topic to which he pays insufficient attention in the book) but because it made Germany the strongest state in Europe. The social consequences of economic growth, 'especially the growth of an industrial working class', and the mobilization of an increasingly discontented *Mittelstand* in extreme nationalist organizations which put pressure on the government to overturn the international status quo, Kennedy concludes,

> tempted beleaguered elites in Germany to seek a solution in overseas expansion and, when later frustrated by their failure to gain 'a place in the sun', to repeat the Bismarckian tactic of solving domestic questions by a foreign war: which, given the operational efficiency planning of the army, meant a westward military drive and a probable clash with the British. (p. 466)

Curiously, therefore, Kennedy's emphasis on the dynamic factor in the rise of the Anglo-German antagonism – the growth of German industrial power – conceals a deeper emphasis on the static factors which (he argues) translated that power into arms spending and foreign aggression: the persistence of pre-industrial élites, the tradition of Prussian militarism, the hankering after a repeat performance of Bismack's conquests of 1864–71, and the flawed decision-making structure of the German state.

IV

For all his concern to avoid controversy, Kennedy thus takes his stand with the many historians who have argued that Germany's political sins, from the launching of the First World War through the collapse of the Weimar Republic to the triumph of Hitler, can all be ascribed, in greater or lesser degree, to the struggle of outmoded ruling élites against the political consequences of industrial modernity, democracy and parliamentarism. In this struggle, it is often argued, the old élites (landowners, army officers, bureaucrats and Prussian nobility) co-opted and 'feudalized' the industrial bourgeoisie. They successfully manipulated the urban and rural petty-bourgeoisie into support for nationalist and backward-looking policies. And they weaned the proletariat away from an active policy of socialist democratization. In recent years, however, this argument has increasingly come under attack. Three major weaknesses have become apparent in it. First, it portrays too static a picture of German history and does not sufficiently allow for social and political change. Secondly, it ascribes too much to the manipulative wizardry of the political élites and neglects the independent effect on the political system of the allegedly manipulated groups in German society. Thirdly, it exaggerates the extent to which the ruling groups in late nineteenth- and early twentieth-century German society were 'feudal' or 'pre-industrial' or 'traditional' in their outlook at a time when Germany was already a highly industrialized capitalist economy.

As the discussion of Margaret Anderson's biography of Windthorst in Section II of this chapter indicated, the conventional view that Bismarck's turn to conservatism in 1878 set German politics in a mould which was not completely broken until 1945, has increasingly been challenged by the argument that it was the 1890s that witnessed the real turning-point of modern German history, with the entry of the masses on to the political scene. The political mobilization of the masses found its expression in the foundation of a staggering variety of new organizations. Many of these had a noticeable impact on the political parties or the Reichstag and ultimately on the whole process of political decision-making. Geoff Eley's *Reshaping the German Right* is ostensibly a study of one group of these new organizations, the radical nationalist societies.[14] But it is in reality far more than that. Eley uses his subject to launch a frontal attack on the whole range of orthodoxies in recent social-liberal German historiography, from the history of 'social imperialism' to the manipulative model of political mobilization. The book is bursting at the seams with ideas, packed with novel and arresting hypotheses; one comes away from it feeling intellectually punch-drunk. Eley has something new and surprising to say on almost everything he touches upon; he has written the kind of book to which one wants to return again and again. This makes it impossible to do the book justice in a brief space. More serious, perhaps, it is ultimately rather confusing, as in the maze of original ideas and interpretations one can too easily lose sight of the underlying argument. Matters are not helped by the book's complex language and abstract terminology, which make it difficult to recommend to students below graduate level. Moreover, the book's structure is rather chaotic; it should perhaps have been outlined in the preface and could have done with some reorganization. Unsettling and unfamiliar ideas demand particularly clear and ordered exposition. Eley has not really done enough to provide it.

Until the last decade of the century, argues Eley, Wilhelmine politics was dominated by a 'central contradiction':

namely the persistence of a state structure guaranteeing the historic privileges of a landowning interest, at a time when the capitalist transformation of German society, the diminishing role of agriculture in the economy and the antagonism of capital and labour were all demanding an adaptation of that state to an entirely novel situation. (p. 349)

In the 1890s the end of the Anti-Socialist Law, the growth of the SPD, the emergence of the mass media, the spread of local railway networks, and many other changes helped to bring about a broadening of the political nation, as peasants, *Mittelstand* and workers all in their different ways underwent a process of political mobilization. Simultaneously, from the end of the 'Great Depression' in 1896 the 'power bloc' of 'iron and rye' entered a long-term crisis as the Junkers' privileges in the Reich came under threat. A symptom of this crisis, and of the increasing need of the dominant classes to appeal to the newly mobilized masses, was the emergence of the nationalist pressure-groups. These showed clear populist, anti-governmental, radical, nationalist tendencies, though as yet such tendencies were held in check. The collapse of the Bülow Block over the refusal of landowners to tolerate the reform of the Reich's financial system, and the elections of 1912, were major defeats for the ruling 'power bloc'. They obliged the government to work more closely than ever with political parties in the Reichstag. In doing so, they forced the old right to join in a broader coalition with the radical nationalists, the 'national opposition' of the *Kartell der schaffenden Stände*. This was one of a series of increasingly broadly based and increasingly radical movements of the right. Via the Fatherland Party of 1917 and the German National People's Party (*Deutschnationale Volkspartei*) in the early Weimar years, these culminated in the emergence of National Socialism. All were attempts by one faction or group of factions within the 'power bloc' to ally with the radical nationalists. The aim was to reconstitute their dominance of the bloc and preserve, as far as possible, their fast-disappearing privileges. Where Eley is particularly original is in insisting that the alliance was concluded as much on the terms of the radical nationalists as it was on the terms of the 'power bloc'. The radicalization of right-wing politics which this complex process represented constituted, in Eley's view, a decisive break with the traditions of German conservatism. It played a major part in laying the foundations for the emergence of German fascism. Thus it was political change rather than political continuity which created the preconditions for the growth of National Socialism.

This overall argument is convincingly put and should command general assent. Many of those who have attempted to refute it have done so on rather flimsy grounds. The idea of the 'self-mobilization' of the masses, for example, has been ridiculed by some; but the concept surely does not prevent one from holding the view that the masses were structured, that village élites or other minority groups may have led the process of mobilization, or that independent agitators from a different social background may have played a role. There is now a considerable body of work to support the idea of the 1890s as the crucial decade of political mobilization in Germany, and to show that far from being deliberately engineered from above, by the government, the industrialists, or the Junkers, this process contained a powerful populist challenge to the political establishment, the government and the parties. Here again Eley has been criticized for abusing the notion of populism, but as his careful discussion of the term (pp. 184–91) indicates, the use of the concept is perfectly defensible in this context. By appealing to 'the people', the new pressure-groups of the 1890s forced the political establishment, sooner or later, to alter its ideology, its style and its methods if it was to recapture popular support.

Eley's conclusions, perhaps, do not all differ so radically as he would like to think from those of the structuralist historians whose views are constantly under attack throughout the book. But the intellectual route by which he reaches them certainly is different: a highly original, immensely thought-provoking, and carefully thought-out application of Gramscian neo-Marxism to Wilhelmine Germany. This is in itself a unique and considerable intellectual achievement. However, in some ways the book has distinct, discernible flaws. For one thing, it is very difficult to use it as a work of reference on the nationalist pressure-groups: it simply does not tell us with enough clarity or detail what were their ideas, what was their social composition, who were their leaders, or other basic facts of this kind. Obviously Eley did not set out to provide this kind of thing, but there are disadvantages involved in not doing so. For example, the development of the pressure-groups is not really related in the book to the development of the wider political problems to which they addressed themselves – indeed these barely get any discussion at all. So it is difficult to see how far the pressure-groups actually influenced government policy-making. The chapter on ideology, again, instead of outlining the programmes and major policies of the pressure-groups, mainly discusses their populist political style. This is perfectly justifiable in the overall terms of the book, though it rests on an unconvincingly broad definition of ideology; but it means that historians will not, on the whole, consult Eley's book for basic information, and this will enable some of them to avoid reading it or even discussing it altogether. This is all the more regrettable since the starting-point of Eley's work was his unpublished 1974 dissertation on the Navy League, which rested on a considerable body of archival research. In some ways it is a pity that Eley has chosen to cut down the presentation of this material in favour of extending the analysis to nationalist organizations. Here he is much more dependent on secondary work, and much of the book indeed concentrates on reinterpreting the kind of material already familiar from works such as Dirk Stegmann's *Die Erben Bismarcks* (Berlin and Cologne, 1970), rather than on presenting new results of primary research.

Nevertheless, the centrality of the Navy League to Eley's argument is abundantly clear. It was, after all, by far the largest of the nationalist pressure-groups. While the Colonial Society, the Society for the Eastern Marches and similar organizations never managed to get a membership much in excess of 30,000 or 40,000, the Navy League already had 250,000 members in 1904 and was nearing the million mark by the eve of the war. To some extent, this justifies the imbalance in the treatment accorded to these various groups. A heavy weight of interpretation rests on the empirical material which Eley presents in relation to the Navy League. In particular, his thesis that the pressure-groups were part of a 'self-mobilization' of the subordinate classes, and that their radical nationalism was forcing a far-reaching realignment of the Right, in opposition to the government, by 1909, rests heavily on the argument that the Navy League was not simply a creature of Tirpitz, the industrialists or the navy office. A convincing demonstration of this point would constitute an important revision of previous views, for example those presented by Wilhelm Deist in his *Flottenpolitik und Flottenpropaganda*.[15] But – strangely, in view of his combativeness on broader issues – Eley never engages Deist head-on, nor does he provide a detailed refutation of previous work on this point. In Eley's account, Tirpitz remains very much in the background, but an assessment of his role is really so crucial in the context of the overall argument that a sustained consideration of it is necessary. Moreover, at various critical points in the book (e.g. pp. 213–14) we are simply referred to Eley's unpublished doctoral dissertation for further details and references. This, when combined with the absence of a proper bibliography and list of archival sources, gives the book the appearance of a certain lack of empirical underpinning which, though misleading, has not helped its reception in Germany. Finally on this problem, a constant, central point of reference throughout the entire work is formed by the crisis of 1907–8 in the Navy League, in which the radical nationalists clashed with the old-style notables or *Honoratioren* backed by Tirpitz. It comes as something of a surprise to learn, therefore, that the *Honoratioren* were eventually victorious, and Eley's rather convoluted attempt to interpret the affair as a victory for the radicals is less than wholly convincing, partly perhaps because it is so compressed: the crisis deserved much more extended treatment in view of its crucial importance to the work as a whole.

The theoretical aspects of Eley's book are also not without their problems. The most serious of these is the tendency to reduce everything to politics, once the initial socio-economic stimuli of the 'self-mobilization' of the subordinate classes in the 1890s have been briefly listed. On a number of occasions Eley comes very close to suggesting that the political determines itself. Thus, for example, the central clash between the new radical nationalists and the old forces of *Honoratiorenpolitik* is defined not in sociological terms but in political terms: 'In many ways the attack on *Honoratiorenpolitik* came from persons who were themselves *Honoratioren* ... The radical nationalists were constituted as a distinctive political grouping not by their similar social origins, but by a shared political experience and its ideological formulation' (pp. 166–7). Eley is able to put forward this paradoxical idea because he defines the radical nationalists purely in terms of the most active elements in the leadership, and abolishes the significance of their constituency by arguing that ordinary members played no real part in the Navy League, whose activities he claims had little real meaning for them (pp. 137–9). This enables him to avoid having to provide detailed information on the social composition of the groups he is discussing. But it means that he portrays political activity once more as the affair of narrow élites. The Navy League's effects on a wider constituency are denied, despite the fact that a later section (pp. 218–20) reveals the vast scope and extent of its propaganda, with millions of leaflets and posters being distributed (some of them by the Ministry of Education), constant and energetic agitational speaking tours, and even a pioneering use of motion pictures. Eley's criteria for active political mobilization seem to me to be too strict in this case. Similarly, his criteria for judging the extent of industrialists' involvement in the Navy League are also unacceptably rigorous. He finds (pp. 142–5) that though donations from finance and industry kept the League going, these were made on an *ad hoc* rather than on a continuous basis, and concludes therefore that these links were only of secondary importance and that no manipulation by industrialists was involved! Eley's determination to rethink fundamentally every problem, every subject, with which he is confronted is deeply impressive; the gritty, sustained quality of the thinking that went into this book commands the reader's respect; but at moments such as these one is moved to protest that the author is perhaps trying a little too hard.

Similar things might be said of David Abraham's comparable attempt to apply a neo-Marxist structural approach to the parallel crisis of the later years of the Weimar Republic .[16] Both Eley and Abraham move within the same kind of theoretical universe, but Abraham, as much Althusserian as Gramscian, is more determined and more explicit in his political reductionism. Abraham defines class not by its relationship to the means of production but through 'practice in the political realm' (p. 19). Thus the crisis of Weimar is redefined not as the product of class antagonisms in the old Marxist sense but more as the outcome of conflicts within the 'ruling bloc'. Here we move once more in a familiar universe of political parties and pressure-groups (this time industrial and agrarian). Abraham's political definition of classes and fractions enables him to transform the crisis of Weimar into a sort of abstract quadrille in which agrarians, industrialists, petty-bourgeoisie and other groups advance, retreat, combine and change partners with increasingly bewildering frequency. Fundamentally he seems to me to be restating, in a very convoluted way, the familiar structuralist argument that the Nazis were put in power by the old alliance of iron and rye. Interestingly, Abraham notes that 'in examining the structures and trajectories of these various conflicts, and in analysing how they contributed to the demise of the Republic, one is struck by how much they had in common with the developments of the Empire's last decade. Pressure-groups, political parties and areas of contention all bore a remarkable similarity to their pre-war predecessors' (p. 4). Thus Abraham gives an Althusserian gloss to the structuralist view of continuity in German history in its most static form. He demonstrates little of the awareness which Eley shows of the regional and local diversity of German politics, or of the considerable problems involved in reconstructing the internal history of the *Verbände*. His book is difficult to read not least because the actors in it are not human beings for the most part but abstractions such as 'labour', 'capital', 'industry' and so on. At its most extreme this leads to statements such as 'the bourgeoisie saw no other way out of the crisis: it decided "consciously" in favour of the Nazis' (p. 323). It is difficult to know whether statements at this level of abstraction can be empirically validated at all. In this sense, it seems more sensible to regard Abraham's book as a work of political science than as a work of history.

Yet, for all this, Abraham's book is an important one not just for Marxist theorists or political scientists but also for historians of the Weimar Republic. It rests on a sustained attempt to link the effects of the economic crisis of 1929–33 on industry and agriculture with the shifting policies and alignments of the economic pressure-groups, and it makes clear why industrialists and agrarians had an interest in the destruction of civil liberties (though this is not the same as showing that they were responsible for bringing it about). It is an important contribution, therefore, to the continuing debate among historians on this subject.[17] Moreover, by moving questions of economic policy back into the centre of attention once more, it provides a salutary corrective to so much of the literature on the collapse of the Weimar Republic, which concentrates on questions of high politics, individual ambition, or anti-democratic political and ideological traditions. Finally, this is the first real attempt at a serious Marxist interpretation of these events that gets away from the sterilities of the 'Stamokap' approach, with its obsession with proving the guilt of individual capitalists, towards a more sophisticated structural approach. This has its costs, as I have briefly tried to suggest. However, for all these reasons, whatever reservations it may in the end inspire, Abraham's book demands to be taken seriously by anyone interested in explaining the collapse of the Weimar Republic.

V

It is striking that the work of Abraham and Eley, which together constitutes perhaps the most significant recent contribution of explicitly Marxist historiography to modern German history, is concerned not so much with the relations between classes as with changing alignments of class factions within the 'hegemonic bloc'. They are concerned to reinterpret a relatively familiar area of historical research. When we turn to a more broadly based view of the recent German past, we are confronted with a daunting lack of social and economic studies. Much older work concentrated on compiling a national picture based on aggregated statistics. But this obscured crucial questions of inequality and uneven development by region and class. A solution to these problems is increasingly being sought in Germany and elsewhere by a turn to local or regionally based social history. Recent work such as Ursula Büttner's highly informative study of Hamburg in the Depression of 1928–31 can contribute probably more to a precise answer to questions such as who suffered from the economic crisis, who voted Nazi, and what the economic interest groups were up to, than generalizing, nationally orientated work such as that of Abraham.[18] Only at a local or regional level can we obtain sufficiently detailed evidence to be able to test many of the general questions which historians have raised about the major features of modern German history, whether it is the extent to which the masses were manipulated by the élites or the degree to which the Third Reich commanded the assent of its subjects, or whether it is the cohesion and collective interest (if any) of the *Mittelstand* or the degree of acquiescence of workers in the capitalist socio-economic and political system. A local and regional social history which is aware of these larger questions has recently been making great progress in both East Germany and West. A striking example of what it can contribute to a reassessment of the German past is provided by the massive project of the Institute of Contemporary History in Munich, on Bavaria in the Nazi era.[19] The project, which makes substantial use of court records and of detailed local reports on the 'morale' and political behaviour of the population, long extracts from which make up the first volume of the series, originally began as a study of resistance and oppression. Historical scholarship in this area has gone through a number of stages over the past few decades. Initially, the Third Reich was portrayed as a complete and impregnable system of totalitarian rule and social atomization. Not long after its collapse, however, conservative historians in the Federal Republic began to recover the lost history of the oppositional movements that culminated in the Bomb Plot of 20 July 1944. The parallel East German recovery of the history of Communist opposition to the Third Reich was not followed until much later by a West German account of the workers' opposition, broadened to include Social Democratic groups as well. The problem with all this work, however, contends Martin Broszat, in his general account of the project, is that its analytical thrust is minimal. It exhausts itself 'in the outward form of the piety-filled payment of respect' (vol. 4, p. 692). The emphasis given to the all-embracing power of the regime throws the action of organized oppositional groups into stark, heroic relief. They stand out from their social context; their martyrdom and courage reinforces a simplistic and undifferentiated picture of the totalitarian power of their opponent. Such a view of the resistance, as Broszat notes, cannot mean very much to the younger generation of the present day. How are they to relate the image of heroic resistance fighter and the totalitarian state to their own experience of postwar West Germany? Indeed, he implies, the uncritical projection of this polarity on to the present can have disastrous political consequences. So the project aims to relativize the picture by showing that the regime was less 'totalitarian' than it might seem, and that resistance was a more complex, many-layered affair than previously suggested.

In reaching a moral judgement on those who resisted Nazism, Broszat argues, the student must bear in mind the context within which the individual had to operate, the degree of choice that was open to him or her. The motives and aims of those involved may be of only secondary importance in considering the moral significance of their actions. To judge an act of resistance by its results, and by its relation to the degree of opposition which the actor's situation allowed, is after all merely to judge it by the same criteria as are customarily applied to an act of collaboration. From this perspective the actions of army officers and higher civil servants, who enjoyed considerable social and institutional power and could bring into play values and standards of the pre-Nazi era, may appear of less moral significance than the less dramatic but perhaps, in their context, more successful actions of the socially disadvantaged, the dependent, the young, the powerless, or the isolated individual. The failure of active, illegal opposition, in almost every case doomed from the start, was no more tragic than the failure to take political advantage of the innumerable possibilities of effective partial resistance in the various stages of the regime's development. This view must of course be seen in the light of Broszat's overall interpretation of the self-generating, progressive radicalization of the Nazi political system outlined in Section III, above. Resistance should be measured against the real possibility of achieving something, not monumentalized into an heroic act of defiance against an invincible opponent. By analysing in detail the compromises and mixtures of conformity and deviance which characterized the behaviour of so many people and institutions in the Third Reich, the project demythologizes the problem of resistance and portrays it in all its human complexity.

The test of the value of this approach lies, of course, in the individual contributions. They range in subject from studies of the Bavarian nobility, the architectural profession, the civil service, the municipal authorities, the schools, the press and the theatre, to Catholic youth organizations, industrial entrepreneurs, the legal profession, women workers, Jehovah's Witnesses, deviant youth gangs and inmates of the concentration camps in Dachau and Flossenbürg (the later reserved for so-called 'asocial elements'). Not all of them fit in equally to the overall concept of the project, nor do they add up to a systematic or comprehensive picture. They are very varied in quality, and too many of them are institutional rather than socio-historical in orientation. The most substantial contribution, a study of the Upper Bavarian mining village of Penzberg by Klaus Tenfelde (vol. 4, pp. 1–382), is one of those that fits rather awkwardly into the overall project, since it deals with virtually the entire history of the village from its emergence as a mining centre at the turn of the century. Only after well over 200 pages, indeed, does Tenfelde get to the Third Reich itself, and perhaps it would have made more sense to have published it separately (it is, after all, nearly 400 pages long).[20] Tenfelde's massive study of nineteenth-century coalminers in the Ruhr is already a classic;[21] this new study is sure to become one. It is a superb example of what can be achieved by a social history of a single small community over a long period of time, if the right questions are asked and the political dimension is worked into the analysis. Penzberg was notorious as 'a red island in a brown sea'; the only convinced Nazis there before 1933, as Tenfelde shows, were a small group of office workers. By paying careful attention to the socio-economic determinants of the collective solidarity of the miners in this isolated industrial community, Tenfelde manages to present a convincing picture of the growth of the labour movement in all its aspects. This solidarity formed the essential social basis for the frequent acts of deviance and nonconformity which characterized the village throughout the Third Reich. They ranged from failure to give the 'Hitler greeting' – the subject of a splendidly revealing photograph on page 315 – to an uprising at the very end of the war, when the effort of former Penzberg Social Democrats and Communists to prevent further destruction was bloodily crushed by the 'Werewolf' organization in a final, brutal act of Nazi revenge.

Tenfelde's contribution also makes clear, however, how limited the possibilities of overt resistance really were. The isolated nature of the community and the pragmatic political orientation of its leaders prevented any acts of heroic but futile martyrdom. But even the mildest forms of disobedience or deviance could have the most appalling consequences for the perpetrators, as Peter Hüttenberger's exploration of cases brought before the special courts in Munich between 1933 and 1939 vividly illustrates (vol. 4, pp. 435–526). Many cases of anti-war jokes and rumours, critical remarks, symbolic disapproval and self-distancing from the regime were brought before the courts, and their meanings are subtly and carefully deciphered by the author to give a varied and nuanced picture of the discontents of the Germans under the Nazi regime. As Hüttenberger shows, if those who were found guilty were working class, poor or, above all, socially marginal, they were likely to incur savage punishments which contrasted strongly with the leniency or even tolerance with which such behaviour on the part of the middle and upper classes was often treated.

The fact that such cases mainly reached the courts through denunciations, which took place on a massive scale, also opens up the whole question of active collaboration, a question which is pursued further in Zdenek Zofka's contribution on rural society in the Gunzburg area (vol. 4, pp. 383–434). Zofka demonstrates convincingly that the Nazi regime, far from bringing the village *Lumpenproletariat* to power, compromised, perhaps out of necessity, with existing village élites. A further aspect of collaboration is examined in Ian Kershaw's discussion of the reactions of the non-Jewish majority of the population to the persecution of the Jews. As Kershaw demonstrates, the Nazis were able to build on the latent social anti-Semitism of the population to achieve a widespread toleration of the gradual removal of the (not very numerous) Jewish community from everyday social life in Bavaria; the many illustrations of village signs proclaiming 'Jews not wanted here' are a graphic reminder of the extent of this kind of prejudice. The mass murder of the Jews during the war, however, was an autonomous product of the Nazi system, not the result of an appeal to public opinion, let alone a response to public demand. Indeed, Kershaw argues that the Nazis came to power not because of their anti-Semitism but despite it; their increasing brutality towards the Jews caused them, if anything, to lose popularity, not to gain it. The Nazis' only attempt at a real outburst of nationwide anti-Semitic violence, the 'Night of Broken Glass', aroused so much adverse comment that it was never repeated. Yet while they were unable to turn the latent anti-Semitism of the population into a positive mass force, the Nazis were enabled by it to marginalize the Jews and to carry out their programme of destruction. In contrast to the 'euthanasia' programme, which was brought to a halt by the protests of the churches, the medical profession and the local population, the murder of the Jews went ahead without opposition, despite the fact that its existence was certainly not unknown to ordinary people in Germany. The contrast between the situation of the mentally ill and handicapped, with their multiple links with the rest of German society (friends, relatives, priests, doctors, etc.) and the increasingly isolated and marginalized Jewish community, its links cut off one by one, was decisive.

The lesson of all this is that where Nazi policy conflicted with deeply held local practices and beliefs, it failed to win support. Under some circumstances, indeed, it had to be abandoned or carried out in secret.

The major problem with this work, perhaps, is its tendency to expand the concept of resistance until it covers anything short of positive enthusiasm for the regime. Yet *Bayern in der NS-Zeit* demonstrates, none the less, that a regional or local social history can contribute to answering with a new subtlety and precision some of the most profound questions of German history.

The local case-study approach is now beginning to be applied to the Imperial period as well as to the Third Reich. A good example of this work is David Crew's study of Bochum, which is a pioneering attempt to apply the concepts and methods of the 'new urban history', as developed by Stephan Thernstrom and others in the USA, to the social structure of a German town in the age of industrialization.[22] Crew is critical of the structuralist approach to modern German history because 'by giving little weight to the experience and activities of the great mass of the German people it fails to provide us with a rounded social history of Germany during a critical period of transition' (p. 5). This is certainly true.

Bochum was a mining and steel town on the Ruhr. It experienced a staggeringly rapid population growth in the late nineteenth and early twentieth centuries. Though, curiously, Crew nowhere provides a table of basic gross population, it is clear that the town grew from the size of a village to the dimensions of a major industrial centre within a few decades. This overall growth concealed recurrent temporary migrations of even more impressive dimensions, and Crew's exposition of this point is one of the most valuable things in the book. Between 1880 and 1900 the net volume of population turnover amounted to thirteen times the total population in 1880; while the resident population rose from 32,798 to 64,702, some 232,092 people actually came to live in the town in this period while 194,836 left it. Few stayed there long, in other words. This makes any statistical analysis very hazardous, especially the kind attempted by Crew. He relies heavily on the city address books, which were annually issued and so missed out a lot of the temporary migrants, while also probably under-recording the poorest, most destitute elements in the population. (I once tried to trace a sample of several dozen people arrested in a riot in Hamburg through the city's address book; not surprisingly, perhaps, hardly any of them could be found.) At the other extreme, the richest people in the town, who might well have had country residences elsewhere, may also be under-recorded. All this causes a lot of difficulties for Crew's pioneering attempt, in chapters 3 and 4, to tackle the problem of whether society in Bochum was more highly stratified and less mobile than comparable societies in other industrializing nations, above all in the USA.

He concludes that the majority remained occupationally stable, but this may well reflect the fact that most of those who did not probably got jobs elsewhere and so disappeared from the record. The same goes for his conclusion that non-manual workers had an extremely low rate of downward mobility into manual work, and also for the conclusion that hardly any manual workers were able to move into the non-manual world. The high rate of geographical mobility, when added to deaths and retirements, means that Crew's random sample of 1,117 adult males found in the address book in 1880 is reduced to 484 by 1890 and 290 by 1901. Even within ten years, 57 per cent of the sample had disappeared and though out-migrants were mainly (though far from exclusively) unskilled, we do not know what they did after they left. A second problem is age, an important determinant of occupation in trades such as mining and steelwork where physical strength and control were paramount and industrial diseases and accidents frequent. Crew assumes that entering a non-manual occupation was a step up, but for a retired miner to have opened a small shop or bar may not have meant very much in terms of social mobility. Similarly, although Crew lists the occupations of 697 workers who married in 1900 and compares their jobs with those of their fathers, for the exercise to carry real conviction they have to be compared with the jobs their fathers had *at the same age*. The educational statistics (p. 94) are slightly more satisfactory in this respect, though they are still rather rough and ready, and they are valid only for the *Gymnasium*, a rather middle-class institution in any case. The statistics of savings and home-ownership are interesting, but their relation to social mobility is only loosely established, and needs to be buttressed by a study of the town's social geography.

Finally, women are virtually absent from this, as from the great majority of all social-mobility studies. After all this, Crew's conclusion that social mobility in Bochum was lower than it was in America appears less than wholly convincing. The whole chapter seems to be leading up to an endorsement of Dahrendorf's argument that the persistence of pre-industrial values in Germany inhibited the growth of individualism and the desire for personal advancement. Crew concludes, surprisingly, that the lack of social mobility reflected instead the insecurity and unpredictability of working-class life, which limited the worker's ambition to the acquisition of a steady job. This is plausible, but there are much better indications of working-class values and the problems of the worker's life than an index of social mobility, so the value of compiling it remains debatable.

The central chapter, on social stratification, is by far the longest in the book, and deals respectively with industrialists and the *Mittelstand*. There are some sketches of members of the 'urban élite', and an account of their relations with artisans, shopkeepers and small property-owners, but without a serious exploration of local politics it all remains very unclear: there is no systematic analysis of local political and municipal institutions and their social composition, for example. Moreover, where politics are mentioned there is too little attention paid to the dynamics of political change, with evidence from widely differing periods being lumped rather indiscriminately together. Next to nothing is said about election results or the relative strengths of the parties, though interestingly the Social Democrats did less well in Bochum than one might have expected. Crew is more concerned with sociological questions derived from American studies (especially Herbert Gutman's work on Paterson, New Jersey). Finally there are two substantial chapters on worker protest and strikes. These too are based on questions asked by American sociologists such as Neil Smelser and Charles Tilly. Crew concludes that miners were more liable to strike than metalworkers because they worked in gangs, and lived in the same neighbourhoods. They thus formed an 'occupational community', while metalworkers did not. This is a useful concept, but more needed to have been done in areas such as living standards, health and disease, family structures, religion, ethnicity, crime and social order if the roots of worker protest were really to have been laid bare; all these important features of working-class life are underplayed in Crew's book.[23]

Nevertheless, for all its weaknesses, many of them perhaps inevitable consequences of its pioneering status, Crew's work on Bochum does succeed in making a significant contribution to the debate on modern German history at a number of points. It presents a considerable quantity of evidence to suggest that the *Mittelstand* in the town was socially and politically divided and by no means successfully manipulated by the government and the big bourgeoisie (pp. 127–45). It contains an important discussion of employer paternalism, which Crew portrays – in detailed and convincing contrast to the commonly accepted thesis of the 'feudalized bourgeoisie' – as a consequence of the employers' need to attract and retain a steady workforce in a situation of high labour turnover, and to control labour costs as far as possible by preventing workers from organizing and striking. It contains an account of charitable voluntary associations (especially the Association Against Street and House Begging) that is all the more valuable because of the paucity of similar studies for other parts of Germany.

Above all, perhaps, Crew demonstrates that the questions suggested by the classics of American urban history and sociology may not be the right ones when approaching the history of German industrial towns. Much of the intellectual fascination of Crew's book derives not simply from its struggle to find an adequate methodology but also from the constant tension in it between the hypotheses applied and the results obtained. Crew seems to have started the book as an American sociologist and ended it as a British Marxist. The fact that he ends by concluding that comparisons between American and German experiences of industrialization are meaningless – thus throwing out of the window the whole premiss on which the book was originally based – only makes the process of argument and research by which he reaches this conclusion all the more interesting to follow. Bochum, with its relative absence of pre-industrial traditions, may not be the best local example on which to base an assessment of the importance of such traditions in German industrial society, but on a smaller scale and in more specific, partial questions Crew's book is a thought-provoking contribution to the current debate, and a reminder of the importance of a locally based social history as well as of the formidable difficulties of providing it with a satisfactory quantitative base.

These difficulties are solved rather more satisfactorily by Gary Cohen in his imaginatively researched study of Germans in Prague from 1861 to the First World War.[24] The quantitative skeleton on which Cohen builds his work is provided by samples from the manuscript census returns, which include among other things information on language of everyday use, occupation and status of employment, as well as basic demographic data. The resulting analysis is a significant contribution to the social history of nationalism. Cohen shows that there was little ethnic differentiation in mid-nineteenth-century Prague. Most people spoke both Czech and German and considered themselves Bohemian. By the 1850s, however, Czech nationalism was making important advances among artisans and craftworkers, and the upheavals of the 1860s led to a response in the form of the emergence of an organized German-speaking public life. This was expressed through a network of voluntary associations led by the German Casino and extending through the German Gymnastics Society and the foundation of German professional organizations such as the German Society of Practising Physicians, founded in 1862. Yet these associations were dominated by the local German notables, the *Honoratioren*, who were reluctant to give German-speaking artisans and workers a role. Deprived of a satisfactory group life, the lower classes gradually drifted away, stopped speaking German and changed their names to give them a Czech character. Moreover, as Prague industrialized, there was a massive influx of purely Czech-speaking immigrant labourers and their families to the city. From their base in the artisan community the Czechs moved on to an increasing extent to conquer the world of the small businessman or shopkeeper and the lower reaches of the state service. This was compounded by the shift in the ethnic loyalties of this part of the city's substantial Jewish community from German to Czech. This was not because the liberal German notables were anti-Semitic; in fact anti-Semitism was much stronger among the Czech nationalists. Jewish membership in the German Casino increased to 45 per cent by 1898–9, and there were several Jews among the directors. These bourgeois Jews retained their religious identity and were vigorous in opposing anti-Semitism. But as the liberal notables of the Casino proved increasingly unable to defend the German community, particularly among the lower classes, so new, more radical and *völkisch* German nationalist groups with a strongly anti-Semitic flavour emerged. At the same time radical Czech nationalists were also prone to violent outbursts of anti-Semitism. Faced with these pressures, a large part of the Jewish lower classes chose to submit to the stronger threat in the 1890s and switched their allegiance from German to Czech, hoping thereby to lessen the Czechs' identification of the Jews with the hated German community.

So Cohen's book is among other things a richly detailed study of the decline of *Honoratiorenpolitik* and the rise of radical nationalism which in some ways provides a useful socio-historical counterpart to Eley's broader study of the same phenomenon in Imperial Germany. Cohen's careful statistical procedures make his analysis convincing; but they are embedded in an insightful and sympathetic qualitative account that makes every effort – including the provision of many interesting contemporary photographs – to convey the flavour of German community life in late nineteenth-century Prague. His discussion makes it clear that while nationalist conflicts were played out in the public arena, in private life Czechs and Germans continued to live side by side and engage in daily business with one another as usual. This is a carefully nuanced, most instructive piece of work; what impresses most, however, is the way in which Cohen's statistical techniques have been carefully subordinated to a broader approach drawing on many other kinds of evidence in a way which Crew, for all the strengths of his work in some respects, largely fails to do.

VI

What conclusions can be drawn from the contributions to modern German history surveyed in this chapter? In the first place, surely, it is clear that there is no longer any real justification for talking of an 'orthodoxy' in German historiography, if indeed there ever was one. The moment at which the structuralist paradigm was built up, in the wake of the Fischer controversy and into the 1970s, has now passed. Different interpretations and methodologies, different schools of thought of the most varied kind exist side by side and continue to be developed. A second, fairly obvious feature of all this work is a heightened awareness – to put it no more strongly – of theory. This is found at its most extreme in the neo-Marxist work of Eley and Abraham, but it can also be detected even in the apparently most unreflective of the approaches surveyed here, the biographical approach, which owes at least something to élite theory (in so far as the Kaiser or the Führer is studied in the context of an élite group such as the Liebenberg circle or the top Nazi leadership) and

displays a detectable tendency to incorporate the concepts of psychoanalysis, sometimes (as in the work of Kohut, for example) on a fairly
systematic basis. Thirdly, there is an increasing diversity of research
methods. The detailed reconstruction of personalities, and relationships
and events, at the centre of politics continues, and the structural study of
economic and nationalist pressure-groups which was placed on the
research agenda in the 1960s and 1970s shows no sign of slackening off.
But these approaches have now been joined by others. The quantitative
study of economic and social history, both at a national and at a local or
regional level, has reached new levels of sophistication. In books such as
those of Cohen and Crew, it has shown – despite its problems – that it has a
major contribution to make at a number of points. There is also a growing
body of work on what the Germans call *Alltagsgeschichte*, often avowedly
non-quantitative in method, that is opening up new kinds of sources and
showing a new and welcome concern with the recovery of everyday
human experience in the past.

Fourthly, this work is being conducted internationally. It is not possible
to talk any more of a specific approach or interpretation being adopted by
German historians and to contrast it with that prevalent in the Anglo-
Saxon world. This is as true of style as it is of content. It has often been said
that British and American historians are more concise and more readable
than their German colleagues, but in reality authors such as Abraham and
Eley are no less dense and difficult than many of their German counterparts, while a book such as Kennedy's rivals any German dissertation in
length and is certainly far from unique in this respect in the Anglo-Saxon
literature. Anglo-American scholars are, of course, to some degree
detached from the German scene, and the vehemence with which their
work is attacked in the Federal Republic when – sometimes unexpectedly
– it strikes a raw nerve or upsets a cherished point of view, has often been
surprising. But the scholarly community is increasingly an international
one. Frequent conferences in Germany and elsewhere, generous research
scholarships offered by German government agencies and foundations,
easy international travel, and the establishment of foci of contact such
as the German Historical Institute in London, have built up a strong
network of relationships between British, German and American historians. Non-German historians of Germany are indeed taken seriously in
the Federal Republic, but only if they have done as much work in German
archives as their German counterparts. Sometimes, indeed, as in the case of
Ian Kershaw, this work is actually being carried on as part of a larger
research project organized in Germany itself. This international dimension of historical scholarship is reflected on almost every level. Neo-
Marxist theories are being applied to history in Germany as well as in the
USA – for example, in some of the work produced at the Max Planck
Institute in Göttingen, or at the University of Konstanz.[25] Structuralist

views of continuity are advanced by historians in America as well as in Germany. The biographical approach has its adherents in Britain as well as in Germany and across the Atlantic.

These are mostly welcome developments. But it would be wrong to suggest that the various approaches surveyed here are all part of a diverse but essentially collaborative effort. Historiography today is a fragmented discipline; not only are there innumerable subdisciplines and specialisms, but increasingly there are also competing theories and methodologies as well. Yet German history, more than most, is structured by a set of major questions, above all relating to the Third Reich and its short- and long-term origins. This means that, far from confining themselves to often unrelated specialist discourses, most historians of Germany are still to an unusual degree talking about the same things. Along with the political relevance of these questions, this makes for a lot of controversy, as each approach claims to get to the heart of the matter under discussion and relegates competing approaches to a category of useful but ultimately marginal knowledge. Faced with this situation, it seems appropriate to enter a plea for theoretical and methodological eclecticism, in which as many of the available theories and methods are used as are appropriate to the subject, provided that they are not mutually contradictory; and urge that historians bear in mind the broader context of their own particular work.

In the end, however, a choice of priorities in this area is unavoidable. To begin with, then, it seems to me that the biographical approach in its present form has reached the limits of its usefulness. Even where, as in the case of Anderson's biography of Windthorst, the subject's life is fully contextualized, the broader questions to which the biographer addressed herself might arguably have been better answered by focusing more sharply on them than on the life of one individual – by writing a monograph on the Catholic Centre Party, in other words. More traditional 'Great Men' biographies have little to offer. Michael Kater has recently commented that our understanding of Nazism has hardly been advanced at all by the recent spate of biographies of Hitler.[26] Little has so far been gained by trying to use psychohistorical techniques on the Führer. More important perhaps is to obtain a subtler understanding of the presentation of the individual in society, as Kershaw has attempted by contrasting what is known of Hitler's personality and actions with propagandistic projections of the 'Führer' image and popular responses to them.[27] Alternatively, as Kater has suggested, Hitler can be seen in his social context, and his social prejudices and incertitudes can be used to generate a new understanding of some of his policies. Finally, as the structuralists maintain, Hitler has also to be seen as one element among many in a complex decision-making structure, which influenced him as much as he influenced it. All these points are relevant to an understanding of Kaiser Wilhelm as well. If biography is to have a future, it needs to incorporate not a historiographically unattainable psychoanalytic understanding but a sociological or anthropological concept of the individual.

Secondly, what I have called the 'structuralist' approach, though less obviously and rather unevenly, is also coming up against the limits of its explanatory power. I suggest this perhaps rather tentatively, because clearly a great deal of work in this mode is still continuing to appear, and much of it is undoubtedly of the highest quality. Yet how far can the study of decision-making processes, of bureaucratic instances, legislative chambers, government ministers, economic and ideological pressure-groups and political parties, take us towards an understanding of the major questions of modern German history? A common feature of much of this work is to see politics in something of a vacuum, with economic and social structures and processes very much underplayed. As Mason remarks in his critique of the structuralist (or, as he terms it, 'functionalist') approach, 'What was permitted by conditions, or was possible, must be analysed, and it is here that Marxism offers a more comprehensive framework than an approach which concentrates heavily upon political institutions and decision-making processes'.[28] Yet Marxism nowadays is as fragmented as any 'bourgeois' discipline, and offers not one framework but many. In some cases, such as David Abraham's work, it seems to me to do some violence to the notorious regional, social and institutional diversity of pre-Nazi Germany and to present itself in a rigid and abstract form that goes some way towards justifying the criticisms that have traditionally been levelled at it. In the hands of a more subtle historian, such as Geoff Eley or indeed Mason himself, Marxist and neo-Marxist approaches (particularly of a Gramscian rather than an Althusserian variety, though no doubt the contrast between the two should not be overdrawn) do, however, clearly have much of value and originality to offer.

Even those studies, like Eley's, which make reference to local and regional socio-economic structures, suffer from the lack of available research monographs in this area. Local and regional history in Germany was long dominated by an antiquarian approach, while mainstream history had an unmistakably centralizing tendency, even to the extent of ignoring most of Germany other than Prussia. Historians are now beginning to be aware that the regional and local diversity of German society holds the key to a number of important general questions about the development of modern Germany. It is more than simply saying that things were more complicated than was previously supposed, or that there were regional variations on national themes. Germany was politically united only late in the day, and German society remained highly localized throughout the nineteenth century. The development of the German economy was uneven, and political groupings such as the liberals had their roots above all in local social structures. Here too the allegedly non-political elements of German public life were most strongly anchored: the distaste for politics which is supposed to have played such an important role in modern German history was to a degree based on local resentments.[29] The meaning and role of politics in everyday life and its relations to economic and social structures can really only be studied at a local or regional level, where the evidence is sufficiently thickly textured to facilitate a thorough exploration of these problems.

NOTES

1 J. C. G. Röhl and N. Sombart (eds.), *Kaiser Wilhelm II: New Interpretations* (Cambridge, 1982), pp. 2–6.
2 J. C. G. Röhl, *Germany without Bismarck* (London, 1968); Röhl (ed.), *Philipp Eulenburgs Politische Korrespondenz*, 3 vols (Boppard, 1973–83).
3 Röhl and Sombart, *Kaiser Wilhelm II*.
4 See e.g. J. C. G. Röhl, 'Kaiser Wilhelm II, Grossherzog Friedrich I und der "Königsmechanismus" im Kaiserreich: Unzeitgemässe Betrachtungen zu einer badischen Geschichtsquelle', *Historische Zeitschrift*, vol. 236 (1983), pp. 539–77.
5 *Marx–Engels Selected Works* (Moscow, 1956), p. 275, quoted both in P. M. Kennedy's contribution to *Kaiser Wilhelm II* (p. 143) and by T. Mason on p. 37 of the collection cited in n. 7, below.
6 P. Ayçoberry, *The Nazi Question: An Essay on the Interpretations of National Socialism 1922–1975* (London, 1981).
7 G. Hirschfeld and L. Kettenacker (eds), *The 'Führer State': Myth and Reality: Studies on the Structure and Politics of the Third Reich* (Stuttgart, 1981).
8 H. Mommsen, *Beamtentum im Dritten Reich* (Stuttgart, 1966), p. 98.
9 M. Broszat, *The Hitler State: The Foundation and Development of the Internal Structure of the Third Reich* (trans. J. W. Hiden; London, 1981). Unfortunately the translation is of poor quality: see the detailed critique in the original version of the present chapter, in the *Historical Journal*, vol. 26 (1983), pp. 485–97.
10 W. J. Mommsen, 'Domestic Factors in German Foreign Policy before 1914', *Central European History*, vol. 6 (1973), pp. 3–43.
11 V. R. Berghahn and M. Kitchen (eds.), *Germany in the Age of Total War: Essays in honour of Francis Carsten* (London, 1981).
12 P. M. Kennedy, *The Rise of the Anglo-German Antagonism, 1860–1914* (London, 1980).
13 P. M. Kennedy, *The Samoan Tangle: a Study in Anglo–German–American Relations 1878–1890* (Dublin, 1974).
14 G. Eley, *Reshaping the German Right: Radical Nationalism and Political Change after Bismarck* (New Haven, Conn., 1980).
15 W. Deist, *Flottenpolitik und Flottenpropaganda: Das Nachrichtenbureau des Reichsmarineamts 1897–1914* (Stuttgart, 1976).
16 D. Abraham, *The Collapse of the Weimar Republic: Political Economy and Crisis* (Princeton, NJ, 1981). Inaccuracies of detail in the book gave rise to a violent controversy, in which Abraham was (quite unjustly) accused of deliberately falsifying and fabricating evidence to support a theory which (in fact) he did not hold. See 'Debate: David Abraham's The Collapse of the Weimar Republic', *Central European History*, vol. 17 (1984), pp. 159–293.
17 cf. B. Weisbrod, *Schwerindustrie in der Weimarer Republik: Interessenpolitik zwischen Stabilisierung und Krise* (Wuppertal, 1978); R. Neebe, *Grossindustrie, Staat und NSDAP 1930–1933* (Göttingen, 1981); M. Grübler, *Die Spitzenverbände der Wirtschaft und das erste Kabinett Brüning* (Düsseldorf, 1982); and, most recently, H. A. Turner, *German Big Business and the Rise of Hitler* (New York, 1985).
18 U. Büttner, *Hamburg in der Staats- und Wirtschaftskrise 1928–31* (Hamburg, 1983).
19 Institut für Zeitgeschichte, *Bayern in der NS-Zeit*, Vol. 1, M. Broszat, E. Fröhlich and

F. Wiesemann (eds.), *Soziale Lage und politisches Verhalten der Bevölkerung im Spiegel vertraulicher Berichte* (Munich, 1977), Vol. 2, Broszat and Fröhlich (eds.), *Herrschaft und Gesellschaft im Konflikt*, pt. A. (Munich, 1979), Vol. 3, Broszat, Fröhlich and A. Grossmann (eds.), *Herrschaft und Gesellschaft im Konflikt*, pt. B. (Munich, 1981), Vol. 4, Broszat, Fröhlich and Grossman (eds.), *Herrschaft und Gesellschaft im Konflikt*, pt. C. (Munich, 1981).

20 It has in fact appeared subsequently in a revised form as *Proletarische Provinz: Radikalisierung und Widerstand in Penzberg/Oberbayern 1900–45* (Munich, 1982).

21 K. Tenfelde, *Sozialgeschichte der Bergarbeiterschaft an der Ruhr im 19. Jahrhundert* (Bonn, 1977).

22 D. F. Crew, *Town in the Ruhr: A Social History of Bochum 1860–1914* (New York, 1979).

23 For further work in this area, also dealing with Bochum, see S. Hickey, *Workers in Imperial Germany: Miners in the Ruhr* (Oxford, 1985); F. Brüggemeier, *Leben vor Ort* (Munich, 1983). See also H. G. Gutman, 'Class, Status and Community Power in Nineteenth Century American Industrial Cities. Paterson, New Jersey, a Case Study', in H. G. Gutman, *Work, Culture and Society in Industrializing America* (New York, 1977), pp. 234–59; Neil Smelser, *Social Change in the Industrial Revolution: An Application of Theory to the Lancashire Cotton Industry, 1700–1840* (London, 1967); C. L. and R. Tilly, *The Rebellious Century 1830–1930* (London, 1975).

24 G. Cohen, *The Politics of Ethnic Survival: Germans in Prague 1861–1914* (Princeton, NJ, 1981).

25 See e.g. P. Kriedte, H. Medick and J. Schlumbohm, *Industrialization before Industrial-ization: Rural Industry in the Genesis of Capitalism* (Cambridge, 1981); G. Zang (ed.), *Provinzialisierung einer Region* (Frankfurt, 1978).

26 M. Kater, 'Hitler in a Social Context', *Central European History*, Vol. 14 (1981), pp. 243–72.

27 I. Kershaw, *Der Hitler-Mythos: Volksmeinung und Propaganda im Dritten Reich* (Stuttgart, 1980).

28 Hirschfeld and Kettenacker, '*Führer State*' p. 32.

29 R. Koshar, 'Away from the Centre: Two Recent Local Studies of Nazism from the Federal Republic', *Social History*, Vol. 8, (1983), pp. 77–86.

3

The Myth of Germany's Missing Revolution

This essay began as an attempt to convey to an audience interested more in problems of Marxism than in the details of German history some of the main issues in the furious debate set off in West Germany by the publication in 1980 of David Blackbourn and Geoff Eley's book *Mythen deutscher Geschichtsschreibung*; the essay was substantially revised to take account of the revised English version, which appeared in 1984 as *The Peculiarities of German History*. It appeared in *New Left Review*, vol. 149 (Jan./Feb. 1985), pp. 67–94. Marxist interpretations have long been at the centre of debate on German history, and it seemed a good opportunity to stand back from the more detailed issues at stake and to look at their application in a wider sense. Marx and Engels both wrote a good deal about German society and its development from the 1840s, when they were actively involved in the German political scene, to the period of unification and after, by which time they had long since been obliged to observe it from their enforced exile in England. Their attempts to link economy, society and politics remain an endless source of fascination, and their theoretical and historical writings are full of implications, both implicit and explicit, for the study of German history.

The essay is printed here without alteration except for the removal of a passage (towards the end) which overlaps with part of Chapter 2, the restoration of a paragraph excised at the last minute by the editors on grounds of space, and the replacement of some quotations translated from the German edition of Blackbourn and Eley's book by corresponding quotations taken directly from the English one. It tries to suggest the power of Marxist ideas to open up central questions of German history. During the late 1960s and early 1970s Marxist concepts were used quite freely by many younger historians in West Germany, but in the more conservative intellectual climate of the 1980s they have gone out of fashion. It is important, therefore, to reaffirm their usefulness once more, and to show how wide of the mark are the accusations of crudity, dogmatism and disregard for the complexity of the historical process which so frequently greet any serious attempt to make use of them in historical research and debate. Fortunately most of the audiences to whom this chapter has been given as a lecture or paper, in various forms and at various stages, treated the subject unpolemically, even if they were fundamentally at odds with the whole approach, and many of their criticisms

93

and suggestions eventually found their way into the final version. In this connection thanks are especially owing to the audiences at seminars in the University of Edinburgh, Stanford University, the Sixth Annual Irvine Seminar on Social History and Theory (University of California at Irvine), the University of Southern California, the University of Pennsylvania, the University of California at San Diego, the Auckland Historical Society, the Goethe Society (New Zealand), the Victoria University of Wellington, the University of New England (Armidale), the University of Sydney, and Flinders University (Adelaide).

I

It is now more than half a century since Hitler came to power in Germany, inaugurating twelve years of bloodshed and destruction without parallel in human history. Throughout this period the Nazi phenomenon has posed a major challenge to human understanding. Why should fascism, in such an extreme, racist and destructive form, have taken power in Germany and not elsewhere? Why should German parliamentary democracy have collapsed so totally and so easily in the economic crisis of 1929–33 – a crisis which, after all, had a severe impact on other countries besides Germany? Those historians who have not seen the events of 1933 either as largely accidental, as German conservatives tended to do in the 1950s,[1] or as the product of some inbuilt weakness of the German 'national character', as Allied wartime propaganda was inclined to argue,[2] have looked to the peculiarities of Germany's political and social structures for an answer. In recent years the argument that these structures remained uniquely backward and overwhelmingly hostile to parliamentary democracy has gained a wide currency. It is an argument with a long pedigree. Harold Laski, writing in 1943, argued that Germany had never experienced a bourgeois revolution, and that its traditional ruling class had never adapted to the twentieth century.[3] Talcott Parsons, writing in 1942, referred to the persistence of feudalism, the power of the bureaucracy, the domination of organized interest groups over political parties and the bourgeois taste for titles as elements in a specifically German system of values. The crisis of these values in the Weimar Republic produced the desire to recover them through the institution of the Nazi dictatorship.[4] The growing influence of sociology over historical scholarship since the 1960s has contributed to the spread of this conception and at the same time has reformulated it, to a greater or lesser degree, in terms of 'modernization theory'.

Ralf Dahrendorf, writing in 1960, cited the verdict of Thorstein Veblen, published as early as 1915, that Germany had experienced a capitalist industrial revolution while retaining a feudal social tradition and a dynastic state; the bourgeoisie had adopted the values of the aristocracy, and the landowners continued to control the major institutions of the state – the army, the bureaucracy and the court.[5] Dahrendorf might have added that such a view found support in the writings of other, less theoretically minded contemporaries of Veblen. Winston Churchill described the German government in 1911 as 'a military and bureaucratic oligarchy supported by a powerful Junker landlord class', and Lord Northcliffe, writing in the same year, also saw a danger of war in 'the precarious position of German industry and the determination of the Prussian Junkers to force on, if possible, some foreign complication in order to prevent the destruction of their privileges by internal reform'.[6] Dahrendorf used these ideas to argue that Germany was a case of partial or unsuccessful modernization (economic but not political). For his part, Barrington Moore, writing in 1966, used the term 'conservative modernization' to describe essentially the same thing – an alliance between a dominant old ruling class and a weak, subordinate bourgeoisie through which the economy was transformed while the social and political power structure was not.[7]

II

Thus many recent historians have suggested, in Hans-Ulrich Wehler's phrase, that a 'central problem' of the history of modern Germany was 'the defence of inherited ruling positions by pre-industrial élites against the onslaught of new forces'.[8] Michael Stürmer has also written of 'pre-industrial élites' preventing the political consequences ('democratization') of the industrial revolution ('economic rationalization').[9] And Volker Berghahn has remarked that 'if one considers the history of the Bismarckian Empire, one encounters at every step the formative influence of social forces whose first aim – from the founding of the Empire to the collapse of the monarchy in 1918 – was to prevent an alteration of the political and social status quo, with every means at their disposal.'[10] Berghahn claims in the same passage that these 'forces' 'resisted every change'.

Likewise, in a brief exposition of the main features of the Imperial German political system, Peter-Christian Witt has written of its domination by the pre-industrial élite's 'aim of maintaining the political and social status quo ... at least insofar as the mass of the population, namely the industrial working class and the propertyless inhabitants of the countryside, were denied any participation in political decision-making and any social emancipation ... and the liberal bourgeoisie, at least insofar as it took liberal ideas seriously, was only allowed to play the role of a cheer-leader'.[11]

Immanuel Geiss has described 'the second German Empire among other things as an attempt – unsuccessful on the whole – to ward off the political consequences of the industrial revolution which had been in the making for some 200 years'.[12] The Empire stood, as Dieter Groh has argued, 'under the compromise formula of industrialization without political innovation' and was dominated by the continuing power of 'late-feudal, agrarian strata'.[13] Indeed, Siegfried Mielke actually entitled an introductory section of his book on the Hansa-Bund: 'The Political System: Maintenance of the Domination of the Feudal Aristocracy'.[14] Jürgen Kocka, too, has noted 'the importance of the landowning aristocracy and its socio-cultural values for the "feudalization" of the bourgeois upper classes and its concomitant illiberal and anti-democratic consequences'.[15] Kenneth Barkin has referred to Veblen in pointing out the 'anomaly' in Germany's development, that 'here was the major industrial power in Europe led by a Junker oligarchy whose economic base was declining and whose views on industrial capitalism belonged to an earlier era.' Barkin himself alludes to 'the "feudal" ethos that pervaded the German elites and institutions such as the army', and cites Baron von Stumm as 'the epitome of the "feudalized" industrialist' because he 'built a castle and ran his factories on the model of a Junker estate'.[16] There are many other examples of such statements.[17]

The most crucial point in the struggle for survival of the pre-industrial, feudal or semi-feudal aristocracy was, it is widely agreed, the 1848 Revolution. As Barkin notes, the peculiarities of the Germans in the second half of the nineteenth century and the first half of the twentieth originated above all in the fact that

> Germany modernized without experiencing a successful social or political revolution. Only Japan among the major industrial powers bears comparison in this respect. The Junker oligarchy remained extremely powerful nationally and almost omnipotent in the local politics of rural Prussia. Attempts to wrest power away from them by the commercial and professional classes failed in 1848 and again in 1862.[18]

In 1848, in A. J. P. Taylor's phrase, 'German history reached its turning-point and failed to turn':[19] it was the point at which the German bourgeoisie failed to displace the feudal aristocracy as its French counterpart had succeeded in doing in 1789. 'The bourgeoisie was the class that could have taken the leadership in 1848', remarks Kitchen, but 'the bourgeoisie of 1848 was not equal to the task of taking on this role. They had already made their historic compromise with the old order.'[20] The crucial question indeed, as Winkler put it from the perspective of the twentieth century, is: 'Why had the German bourgeoisie, unlike the French, not overcome the political domination of the aristocracy much earlier? Why the failure of the 1848 Revolution?'[21] Theodore Hamerow has even gone so far as to claim that 'the mistakes of 1848 had to be paid for not in 1849, but in 1918, 1933 and 1945.'[22] In this view, which I shall refer to as the 'structural continuity thesis', German history differed sharply from that of other nations which underwent a full bourgeois revolution, such as England or France or Holland or the Scandinavian countries. The rise of capitalism and the emergence of the bourgeoisie led in Germany as elsewhere to a confrontation with the feudal aristocracy; but in Germany, unlike in the other cases, the confrontation resulted in a victory for the old order. The defeat of the bourgeoisie set the pattern for the next century. While other countries trod the path from a pre-industrial economy, a hierarchical society and an authoritarian political system to an industrial economy, an open society and a parliamentary-democratic political system, Germany wandered off the path in 1848 and failed to return to it until placed there by force in 1945. Germany certainly acquired an industrial economy; but this was not accompanied by an open society or a parliamentary-democratic political system. The dominant feature of Germany's political development in this period was the determination of the pre-industrial, feudal or semi-feudal aristocracy to retain power at all costs. To this determination more than to any other single factor can be attributed the unification of Germany from above, by Bismarck; the combination of democratic and constitutional forms with the authoritarian, arbitrary realities of the Bismarckian Empire; the entrenched irresponsibility of the army; the pattern of foreign aggression, designed to draw the nation together and to frustrate the critics of the political order; the manipulation of the masses, above all of pre-capitalist groups such as the peasantry and the artisans, against democracy; and the political desperation of conservative groups in the Weimar Republic, when they put Hitler into the chancellery in a last effort to recoup their losses with the support of what they imagined to be an easily manipulable mass movement of the far Right.

The increasing popularity of this view during the last two decades clearly owes something to the political and intellectual dominance of Social Democracy and liberalism in West Germany. The German Social Democrats dropped the remnants of the old Marxist-oriented ideology from their programme in 1959, entered government for the first time since the war in 1966, and stayed there until their liberal partners deserted them in 1982. During this period a new generation of 'social-liberal' historians came to the fore and established themselves in the academic world.[23] They generated a vast outpouring of historical research: much of it has been first-rate, and the scholarly validity of this work is unaffected by any political implications which it might have. Nevertheless, it is hard not to see the 'structural continuity thesis' to which these historians, with support from colleagues in Britain and the USA, to a greater or lesser degree adhere, as an attempt to give historical legitimacy to the liberal, capitalist social and political order of the 1960s and 1970s in West Germany. On the one hand, the thesis inaugurated a new and more critical view of the German past, in sharp contrast to the apologetics of conservative German historians in the 1950s. On the other hand, it radically dissociated the German past from the West German present. The catastrophe of 1933 was ascribed not to capitalism but to the survival of feudal or pre-capitalist élites. If industrialists supported Hitler it was not because they were industrialists but because they were 'feudalized'. Nazism succeeded because capitalism failed in Germany to produce its 'normal' concomitants in the form of a liberal society and a parliamentary-democratic political system. Since 1945, however, West Germany has experienced capitalism restored to its essential qualities as the old élites were destroyed and the pre-capitalist sectors of society have shrunk to insignificance. All that remained in the 1960s and 1970s was to remove the last remnants of the 'pre-modern' order and to come to terms with the legacy of those pecularities of the German past which had largely ceased to exist in 1945.

III

The structural continuity thesis aroused bitter and sometimes heated opposition from conservative historians in West Germany. But for a number of reasons it was never subjected to a convincing critique by the Left. The capitalist system in post-1945 West Germany has its own peculiarities, and most notable of these in the intellectual sphere has been the lack of an independent undogmatic tradition of Marxist historiography. The presence across the border of an entrenched Marxist–Leninist orthodoxy led West Germans to equate Marxism with Leninism and the threat of Soviet domination. The West German Communist Party remains insignificant in size compared with its French and Italian counterparts; more to the point, it has never succeeded in escaping from the dominance of the 'Marxist–Leninists' on the other side of the Wall. There is no 'Euro-communism' in West Germany. *Berufsverbot* and other, more powerful informal modes of discrimination have made it difficult for avowed Marxists to obtain university posts in the Federal Republic. The influence of the Frankfurt school lived on in some departments of philosophy and sociology, but in general its ideas have not had the direct political relevance which inevitably attaches to interpretations of the German past. Only very recently has an explicitly Marxist historiography begun to emerge in West Germany; so far, however, it represents an assimilation of neo-Marxist historiography and theory from England, France and Italy rather than an independent development with its own particular roots.[24]

In any case, the structural continuity thesis itself incorporated some

Marxist concepts, and built in part on an existing tradition of dissident Marxist thinking about the origins of the Third Reich, exemplified in the writings of people such as Ernst Bloch and August Thalheimer. As early as 1932, for example, Franz Borkenau argued that the ineffectiveness of the Weimar state made it absurd to explain Nazism in terms of the big bourgeoisie's need to defend its political power against the imminent threat of a proletarian revolution. All classes, in his view, were equally frustrated by the political paralysis of the Weimar Republic. Its weaknesses went deep into German history. In general, Borkenau asserted, 'fascism becomes a problem first, where democratic norms precede the development of modern capitalism; secondly, where for a long time they have lagged behind in relation to economic development', Germany being in his view an example of the second case.[25] The liberal–Social Democratic interpretation of German history was thus able to integrate the radicalism of the student generation of the 1960s into its own struggle against entrenched conservative views and helped to cut off the possibility of an alternative interpretation.

It is hardly surprising, therefore, that the first really serious neo-Marxist critique of the structural continuity thesis has been launched from outside Germany. British historians, David Blackbourn and Geoff Eley, in a series of important and thought-provoking articles published since the mid-1970s, two major monographs, respectively on local politics and on national pressure-groups in Wilhelmine Germany,[27] and in a jointly authored book published in German in 1980 under the title *Mythen deutscher Geschichtsschreibung*.[28] Taken together, these works constitute a substantial intellectual achievement. The issues which the two historians raise in their various publications are of crucial importance to our understanding not only of the structural origins of Nazism but also of historical materialism itself. Blackbourn and Eley's intervention is remarkable for the sustained and cumulative development of their critique, starting with highly specific analyses of difficult empirical questions, building up through dissections of some of the central concepts with which historians have sought to elaborate the thesis of the structural pecularities of German history, and culminating in an all-out attack on the thesis itself, delivered with considerable verve and *panache*. Not surprisingly, their arguments have aroused most controversy in the Federal Republic of Germany, where their most general critique of the structural continuity thesis was first published. Much of the debate around their intervention has taken place in learned periodicals or obscure journals published only in German. In this respect, indeed, it is an encouraging sign of the growth of international intellectual exchanges among progressive historians. But there has so far been little discussion of their work in English. This is true above all of their most recent, jointly authored book, which has now been published in an extended and revised edition by

Oxford University Press under the title *The Peculiarities of German History*.[29] The book sums up and significantly extends their earlier work, and it is on the arguments presented in this particular study that I shall concentrate in this article. More than any of their previous work, it mounts an explicitly Marxist challenge to the thesis I have outlined above.

Blackbourn and Eley's critique falls into two parts, theoretical and empirical. The substance of their theoretical argument is that the structural continuity thesis rests on an inadequate theory of the nature of bourgeois revolutions. It is inadequate for a number of reasons. First, Eley argues, it is theoretically eclectic, drawing on two mutually incompatible sources – Marxism and modernization theory. This eclecticism, he seems to imply, involves a distortion of the concept of 'bourgeois revolution' to mean simply the establishment of parliamentary democracy. Secondly, Eley asserts that a successful bourgeois revolution of the sort which, it is argued, failed to occur in Germany in 1848, never took place anywhere. The idea that the bourgeois revolution was a single dramatic event such as happened in England in 1640 or in France in 1789 has been discredited in empirical historical research as well as in recent Marxist writing. Equally dubious, he suggests, is the assumption that a bourgeois revolution, however long it might take, is brought about by the bourgeoisie itself, acting according to its own interests and with full 'class consciousness' in direct opposition to the pre-industrial or feudal ruling class. Here again this view has been rendered untenable by detailed historical research in the classic cases of England and France, so it seems unreasonable to demand that it should hold good for the German case. A third questionable assumption is that the bourgeoisie, if fully class-conscious, is necessarily liberal in its political views. This involves the notion that ideologies have a specific class basis – for example, that liberal democracy is the ideology of the bourgeoisie, or anti-Semitism of the petty bourgeoisie, or authoritarianism of the feudal aristocracy. Such an approach defines classes according to their form of consciousness (if a bourgeoisie is not liberal then it must be 'feudalized', i.e. not a true bourgeoisie). This reduces ideologies to the social position of their representatives. Finally, he argues, these historians have confused two separate things in their concept of the bourgeois revolution – on the one hand the creation of a liberal parliamentary democracy, and on the other the creation of conditions under which the capitalist mode of production could develop unhindered. The concept 'bourgeois revolution' should, he states, be properly reserved for the latter, which is thus almost by definition a long-term process in no way brought about simply by the political actions of a class-conscious bourgeoisie. In conclusion Eley suggests that there is no reason why a bourgeois revolution, as he defines it, should require a liberal or democratic political system to ensure its successful completion.

Blackbourn's theoretical points are more oriented towards problems of historical methodology. The German version of his essay, entitled *Wie es eigentlich nicht gewesen*, turns Ranke's famous phrase on its head and argues that historians have spent too much time studying the German past 'as it really wasn't'. By this he means not only that historians have devoted too much attention to the alleged absence of a bourgeois revolution but also that this obsession with Germany's failure to follow the assumed path of other nations to modernity has produced a whole variety of futile efforts to explain why there was no 'Gladstone coalition' in nineteenth-century Germany or to account for the small size of the pacifist movement or the 'backwardness' of German feminism. He notes that other authors, especially Perry Anderson and Tom Nairn, have advanced for England similar arguments to those made by the 'social-liberal' historians for Germany; and one attempt at least has been made to apply them to the whole of Europe. Marx and Engels, Blackbourn points out in his contri-bution to *The Peculiarities of German History*, thought very little of the political abilities of the bourgeoisie, not just in Germany but everywhere in Europe. Finally, both authors argue that the Kaiserreich must be looked at on the basis of its own conditions, not as the arena of an interplay of pre-industrial continuities, nor as a simple curtain-raiser to the later Weimar period and the Third Reich.[30]

Having cleared away what, in their view, are the theoretical and methodological confusions of the structural continuity thesis, Eley and Blackbourn then turn to developing their own notion of the 'bourgeois revolution'. Blackbourn argues that it is time to abandon the idea that bourgeois revolution necessarily involved 'the transfer of political power to the bourgeoisie as a class' (p. 174):

> The bourgeoisie characteristically became the dominant class in Euro-pean countries, although seldom the ruling class and never the sole ruling class, through means other than the heroic, purposive conquest of power. Its real strength and power were anchored in the capitalist mode of production and articulated through dominance in civil society. This, rather than one specific state-form, is what deserves the label bourgeois revolution ... (p. 175).

The type of state that functioned as guarantor of civil society varied from country to country and cannot be explained by the triumph or otherwise of the bourgeoisie, but only by a wide variety of particular historical structures and circumstances. On the basis of these premises, Eley and Blackbourn go on to deal with the argument, central to the structural continuity thesis, that because of the failure of the bourgeois revolution the German political parties were never able to unite, as they did in England (for example, in the 'Gladstone coalition'), in broad coalitions of social forces in a way that would have constituted a far more effective pressure for parliamentarization than they were able in fact to provide. Instead, they tended to be representatives of relatively narrow class interests, and there is a considerable literature on the problem of why the Social Democrats failed to extend their support significantly beyond the industrial proletariat; why, in Engels's phrase, the Prussian Junkers were 'incapable of providing the basis for a great independent party with a historical role in the life of the nation, as the English landowners are in fact doing';[31] why the different Liberal parties failed to unite; and, more recently, why the Catholic Centre failed to join forces with other political parties until the 'Weimar coalition' (once again, a subject on which Blackbourn, despite the fact that it is a 'negative question', has written illuminatingly and at length in his own book). Clearly this situation was not simply created by Bismarckian manipulation; it was also an aspect of the lack of national integration in a state structure that was only formed in 1871. Nor were the parties, limited though their social support may have been, *merely* representatives of economic interests, or *merely* supported by one class or fraction of a class – not to mention the very broad base of the Catholic Centre. Nevertheless, the adherents of the structural continuity thesis commonly argue that the lack of ministerial responsibility and parliamentary power, added to the fragmentation of parties, led to a proliferation of economic and political pressure-groups which bypassed parties and dealt directly with the government. This development, it is claimed, led to even more irresponsibility in domestic and foreign politics and further retarded the emergence of a firm parliamentary system in which the political parties would have been elements of sufficient weight to dissuade people from supporting the fundamentally anti-parliamentary, anti-party-politics movement of National Socialism in the late 1920s and early 1930s.

One of the clearest lines of argument in Eley and Blackbourn's work is the attempt to reassert the importance of the political parties, though this comes somewhat surprisingly from Eley, who has so far devoted most of his scholarly work to the study of the nationalist pressure-groups. Blackbourn argues, in particular, that from 1890 or thereabouts a national political arena emerged, helped by the spread of railways and the rise of a nationally oriented press and communications network. It was in this arena that the political parties played out their rivalries, which played a dominant role in public political life in the two decades before the First World War. The bourgeoisie trod the political stage with all the confidence that its dominance of social and economic life had given it. Yet here it not only encountered rivals – notably the political movement of the organized working class – but also fell foul of regional, religious and other divisions within itself, which, unimportant in the quietness of local social life, acquired a devastating power once they were brought out into the open. Thus it was on the political level that the unitary culture of the German bourgeoisie was fractured. At a social level, however, all the evidence, Blackbourn suggests, points towards a widespread *embourgeoisement* of cultural and social norms in late-nineteenth-century Germany, not to a continued dominance of 'feudal' values.

IV

When this critique is added to all the other attacks that Blackbourn and Eley have launched against the structural continuity thesis, it all amounts to a formidable indictment. Nevertheless, it is not without its own theoretical problems. These problems are present above all in the critique's relation to contemporary historiography, its relation to Marxist theory and its relation to historicist methodology.

In the first place, the two authors – but especially Eley – have not been very careful in their discussion of current historiography. Perhaps it was unwise of them to entitle the German version of their book *Myths of German Historical Writing,* for clearly no one would argue that what the scholars under discussion are engaged in is myth-making on the lines pursued by the pseudo-scholarship of the Third Reich. More serious was the claim of the book to be a critique of myths of *German* historical writing. Many of the most important exponents of the structural continuity thesis of German peculiarity have been, and are, not German at all. Hans-Ulrich Wehler has complained that Eley misrepresents the view of a minority of historians as a new orthodoxy, while Hans-Jürgen Puhle has charged in similar vein that Eley and Blackbourn have no sense of realistic proportions in regarding those they criticize as powerful representatives of the dominant doctrine in German historiography.[32] In places Eley appears to recognize that the *German* historians that he is attacking *are* a minority by referring to the 'Kehrites', a term coined by Wolfgang J. Mommsen. In writing about the origins of the First World War, Mommsen mentioned in 1973:

> The "Kehrite" approach (if I may be allowed to coin a new phrase) which tends to explain developments in the political sphere as the outcome of the defensive strategies of the ruling classes against what may be called the process of democratization; at times this approach has rather strong Marxist undertones.[33]

Mommsen described this as a 'very influential' view, supported among others by Hans-Ulrich Wehler, Helmut Böhme, Dirk Stegmann and (with reservations) Volker R. Berghahn. Interestingly, he tried to distinguish it from a broader 'functional–structural' approach (exemplified by Hans-Jürgen Puhle, Gerhard A. Ritter and Gustav Schmidt), which saw the launching of the First World War as an act of desperation by a chaotic governmental system under severe strain from new social forces and the advent of mass politics. Subsequently this distinction has been more or less abandoned, not least by Eley. I am inclined to agree with Puhle that 'Kehrite' is not a very helpful label.[34] It suggests that the historians in question are disciples of the radical–liberal historian Eckart Kehr, whose iconoclastic essays, written during the Weimar Republic, were collected and republished in the 1960s by Wehler.[35] Their intellectual debts are really much wider and more varied. Eley is certainly on safer ground when he refers to the 'Kehrites' than he is when he talks about 'the German historians', and it seems to me a matter of secondary importance whether one calls these historians Kehrites or 'social–liberal historians' as Wehler does, or the 'progressive wing' of German bourgeois historians as the East Germans tend to do. What is important is that the views discussed should not be generally attributed to the entire German historical profession, or even to a majority of it. It has to be recognized that these views are currently under fierce attack from conservative historians in the Federal Republic who wish to deny the peculiarities of Germany's historical development in order to resurrect the theory that Hitler's rise to power was an accident, more the consequence of his own unique genius than of any deeper-rooted forces in German history.[36]

A second theoretical problem of the critique appears in its relation to Marxist theory. How persuasive are the authors' claims that the term 'bourgeois revolution' should refer solely to the triumph of the capitalist mode of production? Marx and Engels certainly used the term 'bourgeois revolution' to encompass *both* the change in relations of production which brought the bourgeoisie to a position where it displaced the feudal aristocracy as the dominant owner of property and labour power *and* the consequent political changes by which the bourgeoisie secured the adaptation of 'superstructural' elements to conform more closely to its interests (for example, the abolition of guilds, the establishment of a free market in property, the removal of restrictions on the labour supply such as serfdom, the ending of mercantilist restrictions on trade and manufacture, the creation of a political system that would be responsive to its needs, and so on). There is no doubt that they considered it necessary for the bourgeoisie, defined in its broadest sense, to act in some degree as the agent of the latter process, though usually in alliance with other classes. But it could, in Marx and Engels's view, bring it about by various means. The classic examples to which they referred were the English Revolution of 1640 and the French of 1789, but neither of these, in their view, resulted in a purely bourgeois political regime; nor were these revolutions anything more than the most crucial and decisive of a series of such events. Thus in England the changes of 1640–60 and 1688 were said to have produced a permanent alliance between the bourgeoisie and the greater part of the large landowners, which was further changed by the events of 1830–32. In France the events of 1789 were only the beginning of a long period, marked by subsequent upheavals in 1793–4, 1799–1801, 1815, 1830, and 1848–51, in which political structures underwent dramatic changes. At times – notably under the Second Empire – the French bourgeoisie indeed surrendered political power, previously exercised through parliament, to an autonomous state bureaucracy and a despotic leader, in order to maintain its position in the face of the proletarian threat. Neither in England nor in France, however, did these upheavals and shifting class alliances within the political sphere alter the fundamental fact that a transition to capitalism, accompanied by such changes in the 'super-structure' as were necessary to remove serious obstacles to the trans-formation of the relations of production, had begun long before the period in question, had reached its decisive point respectively in 1640 and 1789, and was continuing to be refined and completed throughout the following decades.

Since Germany was one of the major industrial nations of the world by 1914, it is obvious enough that according to these criteria the transition from feudal to capitalist relations of production had taken place; and it should not be necessary to review the economic history of nineteenth-century Germany in detail to point out that, since it had also been accompanied by a whole range of changes in the 'superstructure', from the emancipation of the serfs through the abolition of guilds and the creation of internal free trade, a bourgeois revolution had indeed taken place. There were indeed some revivals of feudal forms in this sphere, such as the renewal of guilds in the 1850s, but no one has seriously suggested that these posed a real obstacle to further capitalist development. Equally, however, while these general, long-term trends constituted the triumph of the bourgeois revolution in the overall context of German society, the precise nature of the political, institutional and ideological elements of the 'superstructure', and of the class distribution of political power, remains a subject for more detailed investigation. It was, as Eley points out, the outcome of specific political struggles, which can only be explained by empirical research.

It also follows from the account given above, however, that the bourgeoisie in Germany could easily have surrendered political power, or shared it, provided that this did not damage its dominance of property relations. This in fact is what Marx and Engels tended to believe happened. In *The Role of Force in History*, Engels argued that the Revolution of 1848 secured the bourgeoisie a 'modest share' in political power, which it used to help speed up the development of capitalism. Further economic growth became inhibited by the political and legal particularism of Germany. However, he went on to argue that large-scale industry, and with it the bourgeoisie and the proletariat, developed in Germany at a time when, almost simultaneously with the bourgeoisie, the proletariat was able to appear independently on the political stage, and when, consequently, the struggle between the two classes had begun before the bourgeoisie had acquired either exclusive or predominant political power.

To have acquired such power, Engels maintained, would have been the only way

to eliminate the numerous relics left over from the days of decaying feudalism, which permeated legislation and administration. Only in this way was it possible to transplant the full results of the great French Revolution in Germany; to put an end to the whole antiquated condition of Germany; to take the road of modern development consciously and definitively, and to adapt her political to her industrial condition.

The equilibrium of proletariat and bourgeoisie, however, gave unusual freedom to the state, which was enhanced by the fact that 'neither Junkers nor bourgeois possessed even the average amount of energy', the bourgeoisie in particular being afraid of 'the menace of the advancing working class' and 'tractable by its whole previous history'. Thus Bismarck satisfied the economic needs of the bourgeoisie by unifying Germany and introducing certain legislative reforms, mainly affecting economic life, but denied their political aspirations 'in so far as they still had any'.[37]

These views were in some ways developing Marx's earlier argument about the virtually simultaneous emergence of the bourgeoisie and proletariat in Germany and its consequence, the political timidity of the bourgeoisie, advanced in his introduction to the *Critique of Hegel's Philosophy of Right* (1844).[38] Arguments about the historic weakness of the German bourgeoisie, therefore, seem to have their origin in the work of Marx and Engels themselves, not in any 'theoretical eclecticism'. Engels's account of course has its own problems: it elevates Bismarck, for example, even more than conventional histories do, by making him into the supreme manipulator of German history, miraculously aware of what the true interests of bourgeoisie and aristocracy were and implementing them against the wishes of both. At least, however, it represents a consistent attempt to link the political and the economic. As Eley recognizes in the English edition of *The Peculiarities of German History*, the definition of 'bourgeois revolution' which he adopts leaves unsolved 'the fundamental difficulty of relating specific political events like the English or French Revolution to the longer-run processes of social change that are thought to precede, inform and largely determine them ... To the

106

extent that the stress on "bourgeois revolution in the epochal sense" involves a retreat from the problem of causality', he admits, 'it amounts to an important weakness' (p. 88). The problem is, of course, that this weakness is as present in relation to the 1848 Revolution in Germany and the political problems of German liberalism as it is in relation to the history of England and France.

A third theoretical difficulty of the critique lies in its historicist tendencies, which are, as much as anything else, perhaps, responsible for the welcome which it has received from German conservatives. The German edition of *The Peculiarities of German History* was widely regarded as a revival of *Historismus*, a specifically German theory of history and its study, according to which (among other things) a historical period can only be studied in its own terms, and may not be assessed according to external criteria; in Ranke's phrase, every era was 'immediate to God'. The implication, of course, is that the concept of historical continuity is inadmissible. Moreover, the school of *Historismus*, which dominated German historiography well into the twentieth century, also argued that political institutions were nationally specific, and that parliamentarism, for example, could not be imported into Germany – a reminder that the thesis of the peculiarities of the Germans was in fact first developed by nineteenth- and early-twentieth-century German conservatives, and what the social–liberal historians have done is simply to stand it on its head.[39] Thus comparative history was ruled out by the Rankeans. Eley's critique of modernization theory and various concepts drawn from the social sciences was seen to have a parallel in the fact that *Historismus* involved a sharp rejection of explicit theorizing and conceptualization. Finally, reviewers detected a strong resemblance between Eley's critique and that advanced by Thomas Nipperdey, who has explicitly acknowledged his indebtedness to the tradition of *Historismus*.[40]

Now I for one cannot believe that Eley and Blackbourn have been directly influenced by a reading of Ranke or the tradition of *Historismus*, both of which are rather remote from the world of present-day British historiography. I prefer to think that their stance is a consequence of the current situation of Western Marxism. Stalinism posited a logical development of human history, governed by ineluctable laws, leading up to the (Stalinist) present or near future. Thus in its version of Russian history everything that contributed to the Stalinist present was labelled 'progressive', everything that delayed its arrival 'reactionary', and history was written as a struggle between progressive and reactionary forces; periodically, as Stalin's policies (and those of his successors) changed, it was rewritten and the labels redistributed. This led to the kind of teleological distortions so chillingly caricatured in Orwell's *1984*. Western Marxism has understandably been concerned to get away from this approach. For British historians the 'Whig interpretation', in which the national history was written in similarly teleological terms as one of progress towards parliamentarianism, with everything in the past assessed in the light of its contribution to this progress, and bouquets and brickbats doled out accordingly, constitutes another influence that has to be discarded. The problem is, how are we to escape teleology without falling into historicism? How are we to argue against the assessment of the past in terms of the present without arguing that it has to be understood purely in its own terms?

There can be no denying that the German edition of Blackbourn and Eley's book did not really solve this problem. At a number of points it did indeed take up what appeared to be a historicist position, by suggesting that historians should avoid asking counterfactual questions, and by denying the legitimacy of problems such as 'why wasn't Germany England?' The English version of the book, however, is rather more satisfactory in these respects. In their joint introduction, the authors go out of their way to rebut the accusations of historicism, while reaffirming their intention (p. 33) 'to try and restore a sense of contingency – although not of accident – to modern German history' (a distinction which, however, is not further explained). The comparison between Germany and England – the question 'why was there no Gladstone coalition in Germany?' – permeates the new version as it did the old, but this time it is buttressed by a much more careful and nuanced set of arguments about the perils of comparative history. The authors no longer appear to deny its legitimacy; rather, they are content to point out that historians have too easily accepted the uniqueness of the German experience, and that the contrast with similar arguments about the failure, or at least only partial success, of the English bourgeois revolution advanced some time ago by Anderson and Nairn suggests that careful empirical research is needed before the real areas of difference can be properly delineated. In this they are surely right.

V

The long tradition of the Marxist thesis of the political weakness of the German bourgeoisie and its frequent recourse to strong state action to protect its interests has been able, theoretically and empirically, to include as a conditioning factor the notion of feudal survivals at the political level. There is no reason either in theory or in practice to deny the existence of continuities of social attitudes and institutions or political values and ideologies from the age of Prussian absolutism in the eighteenth century up to the parliamentary democracy of the Weimar Republic. What is at issue, surely, is the interpretive weight that should be placed on these continuities. The real problem with recent work on German history is that much of it has enlarged the weight of these 'feudal' continuities beyond the bounds of usefulness or plausibility, until they have come to dominate the whole explanatory procedure. The most significant achievement of the two authors has been their attack on this explanatory inflation of the concept of feudal (or 'pre-industrial' or 'pre-modern') survivals in twentieth-century German society and politics. In recent work, the attribution of epithets such as 'feudal' and 'bourgeois' to certain values has threatened to take on an absolute character cut off entirely from the classes and productive relations which determined their formation. It may seem politically useful to describe the values of the late-twentieth-century British Establishment as 'feudal',[41] for example, but such labelling robs the concepts of their historicity and turns them into timeless terms of abuse.

Nevertheless, there are certain key pieces of empirical evidence which historians have long used to support the thesis of the dominance of feudal *social* values as well as of authoritarian political structures in Imperial Germany. In the English version of the book, Blackbourn devotes some attention to the notorious Prussian Junkers. Was the landowning class, as Engels maintained, feudal right up to the late nineteenth century? Engels justified his use of the term with the argument that the Junkers' continued dominance of local and provincial government ensured that rural labourers still lived in semi-serfdom.[42] But there are problems with this assertion. Empirical studies of the Junkers have long since established that in economic terms they had become a class of capitalist farmers by the mid-nineteenth century, following on the emancipation of the serfs and the growth of the sugar-beet (and later the distilling) industry. There was a free market in land and free mobility of labour. The draconian and restrictive terms of the *Gesindeordnung*, which formally placed the labourers in a kind of serfdom, were in many respects inoperative, and could not disguise the fact that the relationship between the Junker and his farm servants was a wage nexus, and that the Junkers produced, as they had done for many years, for a national, even an international market. Nor could they prevent labourers deserting *en masse* for the towns when industry became sufficiently developed to exert a significant demand in the national labour market. Besides, in what ways can the values and attitudes of the Junkers be meaningfully described as 'feudal'? These were middling capitalist farmers with a predominantly Calvinist ethic and a sharp eye for profits. Prussian landowners had no hesitation about becoming industrial entrepreneurs if the opportunity arose, whether through the discovery of mineral reserves on their land or through a rise in world demand for potato schnapps. It is also analytically important to distinguish between landowners as a class and the aristocracy as a status group. The Prussian kings were not slow to ennoble successful industrialists or senior civil servants, but such people no more became feudal than do their counterparts in Britain today, especially since, as Blackbourn points out, the sale of titles was a well-known source of government income in nineteenth-century Prussia (one should add, however, that this was confined to specifically *bourgeois* titles such as 'commercial councillor'). In all these respects it is more precise to talk of the Junkers as the landowning faction of the bourgeoisie by the late nineteenth century than it is to base an entire historical interpretation on the existence of a mythical 'feudal aristocracy'.

Another important piece in the mosaic of empirical evidence offered in support of the thesis of a missing bourgeois revolution is the late arrival of the German bourgeoisie on the historical scene. Blackbourn attempts to overcome this by suggesting of the early nineteenth century that the 'economically progressive bureaucracy served almost as a kind of surrogate bourgeoisie' (p. 176). However, the idea of the state as the handmaiden of industry has long been questioned by economic historians. Many would argue that it was not until the state *withdrew* from the economy in the 1830s and 1840s that the industrial revolution in Germany could get under way. It is striking that most of Blackbourn's examples of allegedly successful state involvement, such as craftsmen's schools, industrial exhibitions and state-run railways, are drawn from states such as Baden, Bavaria and Hesse, which industrialized less rapidly and less successfully than Prussia. In this, the largest of the German states, the bureaucracy was lukewarm about railway building and similar projects, and industrialization took place, some historians would argue, partly in the face of considerable opposition from the state, partly as a consequence of the dismantling of state economic enterprises such as the *Seehandlung* and the removal of guild restrictions and similar state-guaranteed privileges. The idea of the archetypal bureaucracy, that of Prussia, acting as a surrogate bourgeoisie also tends to reinforce the traditional picture of the German bourgeoisie as lacking in initiative, in this case economic as well as political.

It is often argued that when an industrial and professional bourgeoisie did arrive on the German social scene in sufficient numbers to make its weight felt, it was imbued in many ways with a 'feudal' social consciousness. In support of this assertion, historians frequently cite the power of the Junker-dominated officer corps in Prussian society. Successful business and professional men often aspired to become officers of the reserve, but they could do so only if they adopted the feudal code of honour, with its rejection of political liberalism and its recourse to the duel whenever it was slighted.[43] That many joined the officer corps despite, rather than because of, its Junker qualities – an assertion for which Blackbourn offers no empirical evidence – did not make much odds: the point was, they joined it. If young bourgeois aspirants managed to retain their liberal convictions, it was as often as not because some accident of fate held them back from entering this world – as with Theodor Heuss, who was prevented by chance from following his brothers into a duelling corps at

Tübingen University, and subsequently became a leading left-wing liberal. (Blackbourn's account of this episode seems to me to miss the point, which is that had Heuss actually joined the duelling corps, he might well have lost the bourgeois values he had imbibed from his family and school.) Of course, Catholics like Adolf Gröber opposed duelling on religious grounds, and south German towns sometimes also disapproved of it as a 'Prussian' custom. The fact remains, however, that duelling continued to be practised on quite a substantial scale in Protestant Prussia, not only among students but also among army officers, officers of the reserve, civilian aristocrats and impeccably bourgeois professionals such as doctors, dentists and apothecaries, well into the twentieth century. The contrast with England, where duelling effectively died out in the middle of the nineteenth century, remains to be explained.[44] Blackbourn is on safer ground when he charts the decline of the aristocratic component in the officer corps and its gradual confinement to a few socially prestigious regiments such as the Guards, a process which had obvious English parallels. Nevertheless, one cannot help feeling that he does not in the end deal very successfully with this particular area of the debate, and the point he is making has still to be proven.

Not only do the two authors argue that the bourgeoisie was not feudalized; Blackbourn in particular turns the tables and suggests that there was a general *embourgeoisement* of social mores in nineteenth-century Germany. The public park and gallery came to rival the aristocratic park and gallery. Princely menageries gave way to bourgeois zoos (Blackbourn's obsession with zoos delivers some of the most entertaining passages in the book). Opera-lovers internalized the bourgeois value of deferred gratification and started clapping at the end of the whole performance instead of after every aria. Sumptuary regulations were relaxed and the bourgeois uniform of the top hat and frock coat was worn even by aristocrats as they abandoned breeches and stockings. Travel was democratized by the railway, and the princely carriage became an object of scorn. This *embourgeoisement* of Germany created a culturally and socially homogeneous bourgeois society, with rules to which the aristocrats subscribed just as much as their social inferiors. Thus the bourgeoisie in a socio-cultural sense was not weak and divided, but strong and united.

This thesis is undeniably a very attractive one. Not the least of its incidental virtues is the way in which it demonstrates the relevance of the social history of everyday life to wider historical arguments centring on the explicitly political. But the argument is advanced over notoriously difficult terrain. A long and inconclusive debate within Marxism on the extent to which culture in this sense is socially determined, stretching from the German Social Democrats of the 1890s through to the socialist realists of Stalin's era and beyond, has revealed little more than the danger of deducing class values and positions from artistic and cultural artefacts or

111

attitudes. Blackbourn generally assumes, or vaguely implies, that certain cultural pheonomena were 'bourgeois' without actually attempting any definition of why we should consider them bourgeois rather than something else. His argument here strikes me as bearing certain similarities to the suggestive but unsatisfactory attempt of Arno Mayer to use cultural and artistic evidence to demonstrate a very different thesis – the dominance of aristocratic values in the same period.[45] Moreover, nearly all the examples cited by Blackbourn in support of his thesis are open to one kind of objection or another. Hagenbeck's zoo was as unusual in its way as Wagner's Bayreuth; private rather than municipal, open rather than caged, as much scientific as entertaining, it marked a far clearer break with the noble menagerie than did the conventional zoo. Moreover, whatever the rules which Wagner might have enforced at Bayreuth, audiences at conventional operas continued to applaud at the end of arias, as they do today; I recall an opera performance in London in 1964 or 1965 where some arias were repeated two or even three times in response to audience demand before the action moved on. The spread of the frock coat was paralleled by a growing elaboration of court, military and ceremonial dress. Archaic modes of transport, as David Cannadine has recently reminded us, came to inspire awe more than ridicule.[46] Aristocratic patronage continued (as Mayer is at pains to point out) to play an important role in the arts well beyond the turn of the century. Wagner, who owed almost everything to the patronage of King Ludwig II of Bavaria, was a prime example. One could go on. Clearly this is an area which needs not only sharper conceptualization but also more empirical research. One could do worse than begin by asking why the great novels of bourgeois life, so prominent in English and French culture in the nineteenth century, had no real counterpart in Germany – with the occasional exception, such as Thomas Mann's *Buddenbrooks*, or perhaps some of Theodor Fontane's work.

More central to the argument than zoos and operas, perhaps, is the thesis that German industrial magnates behaved in a feudal manner. The assertion that German employers regarded themselves as patriarchs, as masters in their own houses in pre-industrial terms, has been accorded a central place in the empirical underpinning of the thesis that the German bourgeoisie was 'feudalized'. Eley and Blackbourn are both anxious to refute this hypothesis. It is clear that substantial sections of the German bourgeoisie were highly critical of such attitudes and gave considerable support, for example, to the strikes of 1905–6. Many big German employers did indeed combine social welfare measures for their workers with a harsh policy of lockouts, blacklisting and the sponsorship of 'yellow' company unions, all tactics aimed at cementing the loyalty of the worker to his employer and preventing the spread of collective wage agreements. But these were overwhelmingly very large employers, whose ability to engage in such policies rested on the heavy concentration of capital in certain sectors, above all metalwork, mining, the chemical and electrical industries, and some big engineering enterprises. Paternalist measures were initiated more by managers or second-generation employers than by the original entrepreneurs. They were introduced above all after the major strikes of 1904–6, and in periods of high labour turnover, acute labour shortage and increasing trade union power. Similar methods were used at about the same period by employers such as Carnegie in the USA and were also widespread in Britain and France. Collective wage agreements were certainly far more common in Britain than in Germany; in 1910 they covered 900,000 coalminers in the UK and only 82 in the whole of Germany. But most of this difference can be explained by the higher capital intensity and cartelization of German industry. What remains is the fact that since mid-nineteenth century the British labour movement had been moderately reformist – which encouraged employers to put their trust in 'orderly' collective bargaining agreements arrived at with 'sensible' union leaders – while the German labour movement, with its close ties between the unions and the strongly Marxist SPD, was much more frightening to the employers. There is thus no reason to look for the 'feudalization of the bourgeoisie' or the transference of cultural values from the feudal aristocracy to the big bourgeoisie as the key to the policies and attitudes of German capital. These are attributable mainly to capitalist rationality and opportunity but also to the given political structures which were themselves the result of earlier historical developments.[47] Eley and Blackbourn's arguments in this area are much more convincing, and deserve general support.

VI

Eley and Blackbourn go on to suggest, in an argument that is given considerably more weight and emphasis in the English edition of their book, that the cultural unity and economic success of the German bourgeoisie made the conquest of state power unnecessary: indeed, when the bourgeoisie actually did tread the political stage, it rapidly became divided and lost the unity it possessed at the socio-cultural level. This is an ingenious and provocative argument, but despite the refinements which the authors have added since they first advanced it in 1980, it is still open to a number of objections. To start with, anyone who has read a nineteenth-century German manual of social etiquette, or who recalls the extraordinary proliferation of titles among the German bourgeoisie, for example, will be aware of the fact that social hierarchies and barriers seem to have been elaborate and sharply defined in this social class, perhaps even more so than among its English or French counterpart. Religion, which

Blackbourn asserts was primarily a political division, was surely in reality one of the fundamental *social* forces dividing the bourgeoisie, as it did other classes as well. Such divisions were obvious enough in the small towns and larger urban centres of Wilhelmine Germany, and it did not need political rivalries to bring them out into the open. On the contrary, in so far as the national political arena was the scene of the rise of the SPD, it could actually serve to bring the bourgeois groups together. 'In the bourgeois notable politics of mid-century', Blackbourn argues, 'nationalism was more of a consensus than an issue.' (p. 263). This is a strange verdict on the violent quarrels that tore the mid-century bourgeoisie apart over issues such as states' rights and particularism, *kleindeutsch* versus *grossdeutsch* versions of German unity, and scores of lesser matters. Whatever else the national issue was, it was not above politics even in the heyday of nationalist triumph in the 1870s.

Capitalism's success may at times have displaced class antagonisms from the point of production to the political sphere. But capitalism did not look very successful in the mid-1870s, when the break between liberalism and Social Democracy was decisively concluded. The restrictions which were placed on trade union organization at plant level – blacklists, yellow company unions, tied housing and so on – were only successfully imposed decades later, above all in the years after 1905. Moreover, curiously enough for two historians who elsewhere have rightly stressed the need to look at German politics away from the centre as well as in Berlin, Eley and Blackbourn's talk of the displacement of class antagonisms into the political sphere is all based on the assumption that the political sphere was a nationwide entity. For them, 'politics' is implicitly 'national politics'. Yet this ignores one of the really crucial differences between the political system of the German Empire and those of England and France, namely the fact that Imperial Germany was a *federal* state, in which whole areas of political decision-making were controlled by the federated states, from education and religious affairs to policing, law and order and health services. The federated states alone could levy direct taxes and were charged with the collection of federal tolls and postage dues. In their hands lay the area of civil liberties. Each of the states had an elected legislative assembly which debated these matters, though its power to influence them was usually limited, and varied from state to state. If one looks carefully at the debates of these legislative assemblies, and at the government files of the federated states, it soon becomes clear that economic and social conflicts were more often resolved here than displaced on to political quarrels at the national level. The national political arena was occupied by demagogy and rhetoric precisely because so many political issues vital to the interests of capital and labour were resolved at the level of the federated states.

It has long been a favourite argument of conservative historians that the

German political system would have evolved peacefully along British lines, towards parliamentary democracy, had it not been for the chance disaster of the First World War and its unfortunate consequence, the November Revolution of 1918. In support of it, they argue that Imperial Germany was *de facto* becoming parliamentarized before 1914. David Blackbourn is at pains to emphasize that he does not intend to resurrect the *de facto* parliamentarization argument. Geoff Eley, on the other hand, boldly states that there was a '*de facto* existing parliamentary system' (p. 119) before 1914. He defines this in a footnote as 'a limited practical stabilization of public life within the available forms of Wilhelmine constitutionalism' (p. 119, n. 4). But this is not what historians usually mean by parliamentarization, and to talk of 'Wilhelmine constitutionalism' offers a further hostage to conservative historians whose argument that Wilhelm II's Germany *was* a constitutional monarchy is explicitly rebutted elsewhere in the book. Blackbourn, too, argues that the import-ance of the Reichstag, and especially its committees, and of nationally organized political parties in the decision-making process was becoming steadily greater between 1890 and 1914, and that this had a 'cumulative significance' (p. 277). Both authors accept, however, that there *was* a continuity of authoritarian, undemocratic or illiberal political structures in Germany from 1848 at least up to 1918, including the executive's freedom from parliamentary control, the irresponsible position of the Kaiser, the checks on popular participation in government, the entrenched privileges of the army, and so on. On a European scale, there was nothing very unusual or archaic about these features of the Imperial German consti-tution. Yet this is hardly the point, for it is the comparison with *England* that remains central.

The major problem that the two historians face in confronting the thesis of a specifically German political road to modernity is the failure of German liberals to form a large and united political party akin to the French Radicals or the English Liberals, and to win the support of the German working class. As they quite rightly point out, a careful distinc-tion must be made between liberalism and democracy. For most of the nineteenth and early twentieth centuries the majority of liberals in England as in Germany opposed democracy and supported a limited representative system on the basis of a property-qualified franchise of a highly restrictive kind. It was indeed the realization that liberal parties depended for their electoral support on the propertied elements of the population that persuaded Bismarck to introduce universal male suffrage, in the misguided hope of mobilizing what he imagined to be the loyal and conservative lower classes in support of his regime. Eley points out that liberal political movements and ideas were not 'bourgeois' but were supported by a variety of social forces, varying at one time and another from artisans and small producers to East Prussian landowners, and that they cannot be ascribed to the bourgeoisie alone. Finally, he notes that liberal ideas varied from time to time and from country to country, a fact which makes it unhistorical to demand of nineteenth-century German liberals that they conform to democratic standards.

There are a number of problems about these assertions. To begin with, while Eley is adamant that liberalism is historically variable and must be assessed in its context, he is quite prepared to employ rigid and unvarying criteria when it comes to judging the existence of democracy. These criteria include, for example, universal *female* as well as male suffrage, something which remained exceptional in Europe until 1945, and was supported only by a small minority of radical liberals and socialists in most countries before 1914. According to these criteria not even the urban artisanate and petty bourgeoisie whom Eley regards as the main supporters of democracy in the mid-nineteenth century were democratically inclined. On the other hand, as Hans-Jürgen Puhle has pointed out, the men of the Frankfurt Assembly in 1848 were famous for their espousal of radical, theoretical liberal principles which made them perhaps more democratic, if also less realistic, than most of their liberal contemporaries.

Moreover, it is arguable that there *was* a connection between liberalism and democracy. By supporting parliamentary rule, liberals in many countries helped willy-nilly to create the possibility of extending the franchise by Act of Parliament, while such extensions could be more easily resisted in states without ministerial responsibility; and they contributed towards increasing the electoral pressures in favour of suffrage reform. Once a parliamentary majority became the basis for government, the competition between rival parliamentary groups or parties for electoral support created a built-in pressure for the extension of the franchise. Thus, as the experience of Britain or the Scandinavian countries seems to indicate, parliamentarianism tended to lead to universal male suffrage. The process was clearly very complex and long-drawn-out. It certainly did not occur because liberals intended there to be universal suffrage all along. Nor was it, of course, the only means by which the franchise was extended, as the case of Bismarck indicates. Arguably, nevertheless, parliamentary rule favoured the realization of popular democratic aspirations. This would have been denied by those who fought for it in mid-nineteenth-century Germany, Sweden, or Denmark. By about 1890, however, this implication was clear enough, and it is worth bearing in mind Peter-Christian Witt's contention that in the industrial age, with a large working class, parliamentary rule was impossible without democratization, which is one reason why so few middle-class Germans were enthusiastic enough about it to support a large liberal party.[48]

Finally a problematical position in the argument is occupied by the law. Blackbourn devotes a good deal of space to maintaining that German law was gradually converted in the nineteenth century to conform with bourgeois legal ideology. Law, indeed, was one of the major areas of social and cultural *embourgeoisement* in the nineteenth century. To some extent this is a matter of emphasis. Where Engels, for example, accentuates the way in which the feudal reality of social relations on the land continued more or less unaffected by the veneer of bourgeois law imposed in the 1870s and 1880s, Blackbourn lays greater stress on the way in which the law was amended in a more general sense to conform to the requirements of capitalist reproduction in industry as well as on the land. Obviously since German capitalism reproduced itself with remarkable success in this period, German law must by definition have been amended in this manner. Still, this leaves some awkward problems. Blackbourn generally tends to overweight the conformity of German law to classic bourgeois principles. He stresses the guarantee of basic rights of assembly and association, for instance, in the *Reichsvereinsgesetz* of 1908 (itself passed remarkably late in the history of the Empire: up to then these rights had been governed by the federated states). But while the *Reichsvereinsgesetz* did give the rights of assembly and association to women (previously denied them in Prussia), it took them away from young people and linguistic minorities.

Again, Blackbourn argues that the principle of equality of citizens before the law was well established in Germany by the early nineteenth century, to be translated into practice by the emancipation of the Jews, the abolition of seigneurial jurisdictions and other reforms in succeeding decades. In some respects, however, it was never fully achieved. Duelling, once more, is a prime example of an offence which, because it was committed by the upper classes in defence of their honour, was never accorded more than token punishment save in the most exceptional circumstances. Whole classes of citizens such as prostitutes were denied basic civil liberties, even the right to go to the opera or visit a zoo.[49] The police could make laws and regulations without any real possibility of redress or appeal through the courts – in many ways they were indeed a law unto themselves. German labour law was notoriously biased against the employee, far more so than its English counterpart. The Civil Code which came into effect in 1900 was not the apotheosis of bourgeois individualism which conservative critics made it out to be. Blackbourn argues that Germany was a *Rechtsstaat* without making it clear that the German concept of *Rechtsstaat* did not necessarily mean a state bounded by the rule of law but rather a state which agreed of its own free will to justify its actions in legal terms. The state remained the sole source of law in this doctrine. It was precisely because German criminal law did not allow the citizen adequate means of redress that industrial employers found it so easy to prevent the advance of collective bargaining.[50] Once again, as with the question of cultural values, so with the law: what is 'bourgeois' is capable of many different definitions, and is by no means as obvious as Blackbourn seems to think.

VII

What, then, were the real peculiarities of German history? In Blackbourn and Eley's view, the German experience constituted a heightened version of what occurred elsewhere. All countries, as Blackbourn remarks, are peculiar, but some are more peculiar than others. Germany's capitalism was exceptionally dynamic and successful; Germany's bourgeoisie got the economic prosperity and class domination it wanted without having to fight for it in the political sphere. The threat from below, in the shape of the world's largest and most highly organized socialist party, the *Sozial-demokratische Partei Deutschlands* (SPD), and other less obvious sources of political instability, such as peasant populism and the radical politics of sections of the petty bourgeoisie, placed a premium on a strong state. This closed off certain avenues of reform, including the creation of a full parliamentary democracy. It encouraged, on the one hand, an increasing bourgeois emphasis on administrative means of lessening class antago-nisms (for example, by municipal reform) and, on the other, a growing recourse to the demagogic rhetoric of racism and nationalism in an attempt to harness the discontents of the working class and the urban and rural petty bourgeoisie. Nevertheless, these efforts to control the antagonisms which emerged in the political arena were counterpointed at this level by the exposure, indeed the magnification, of the political divisions of capital. Such divisions effectively undermined attempts at liberal reform.

These developments, argue the two authors, continued in an ever more extreme form after the First World War. The Revolution of 1918 and the Weimar Republic brought with them the participation of the SPD in government and the creation of an elaborate system of social welfare. The drastic economic rationalization that took place after the inflation of 1923 created an even more modern and efficient capitalist industrial system at the cost of permanent high unemployment and further alienation of the petty bourgeoisie. All these features of the Weimar years were accentuated yet again by the crash of 1929 and the following Depression, more severe in Germany than almost anywhere else. The SPD blocked the attempt to dismantle the welfare state, while the rapid rise of the German Communist Party threatened the bourgeoisie with something worse still. The petty bourgeoisie was radicalized still further and flocked to support the Nazi Party. In a situation of full parliamentary democracy, the different fractions of capital were less able than ever to reconcile their interests at the political level, though in economic terms they were all agreed on the policy of smashing welfarism and the need to destroy the Communist Party and curb the unions. In this situation, they found a solution in the destruction of the Weimar state and the creation of a dictatorship, eventually accom-plished, with their tolerance or support, by Hitler.

Blackbourn and Eley's critique of the myth of the missing bourgeois revolution, and their substantial body of empirical work, come together to offer the beginnings of a new Marxist approach to the central problems of modern German history. This new approach, drawing heavily on Gramsci and other neo-Marxist writers in theory and method, does much to get away from the old Comintern dogmas which have informed so much Marxist work in this field – dogmas whose empirical foundation historians of Germany have increasingly revealed to be extremely shaky. The virtues of this work are obvious. It shifts the ground of Marxist historiography from simple questions of agency to more complex questions of structure and interest. It offers a more sophisticated understanding of the nature of the German state than that provided either by the old Stamokap theory or by the newer social-liberal structuralist approach. In historiographical terms it is contributing to a refocusing of attention away from vague and arbitrarily defined values and beliefs to questions of material interest which by their nature can be delineated more precisely in empirical terms. It mounts a new and explicitly Marxist challenge to recently developed liberal interpretations. It opens up many questions which previously seemed to be more or less settled. All this makes the appearance of this work an exciting moment in the historiography of modern Germany.

The political relevance of these arguments is also clear. If fascism was the product of pre-industrial or feudal influence, then it cannot happen again. If, however, we concede that a bourgeoisie, or fractions of it, even when completely purged of feudal remnants, is not indissolubly wedded to parliamentary democracy but may in times of severe crisis abandon this system for the harsh authoritarianism and brutal dictatorship of a relatively independent force such as an army or a fascist regime or an irresponsible, technologically advanced bureaucracy, so long as this does not seriously threaten its own interests, then clearly it *can* happen again. The latter view – which must appear convincing not only to Marxists but to all those who are concerned about civil liberties in our own society, or who have, for instance, taken the lesson of the destruction of parliamentary democracy in Chile in 1973 – is in no way incompatible with the view that parliamentary democracy is the normal political system for a reasonably secure capitalist bourgeoisie. Germany's social formation in the nineteenth and early twentieth centuries was as complex as that of any other capitalist system: an amalgam of many different elements, feudal and capitalist, aristocratic and bourgeois, proletarian and peasant. Just as the capitalist mode of production slowly reduced the area of operation of economic feudalism to marginality over the century, so the balance of forces in the social formation gradually shifted in favour of the bourgeoisie and the proletariat, reducing the social and political power of the feudal aristocracy bit by bit. This process was uneven, but it was the major transformation that took place in nineteenth- and twentieth-century Germany, and Blackbourn and Eley are surely right to draw our attention to this fact.

Yet some reservations spring to mind as well. The two authors' account of the historiography is not always very careful, though the English edition is an improvement on the German one in this respect. The relationship between liberalism and democracy was more complex, and more positive, than the authors allow. The thesis that the early-nineteenth-century bureaucracy acted as a 'surrogate bourgeoisie' rests on a very selective, some would say outmoded view of the role of the state in industrialization, and depends too much on south German rather than Prussian evidence. Too many of the arguments depend on problematical assertions in the area of cultural values and again on the use of evidence drawn from Catholic south Germany. The case for the socio-cultural unity of the bourgeoisie remains to be made. The argument that the law underwent a bourgeois transformation is overdone and needs refining. The conceptualization of 'bourgeois revolution' as a transformation of economic and social relations with few implications for state structures does not seem to accord with classic Marxist usage, and the emphasis on the role of the 'conjuncture' in the determination of state forms threatens to introduce historical accident again by the back door unless it is more carefully defined. The thesis that class antagonisms were transported upwards into the political sphere underplays the importance in federal Germany of regional and provincial politics and implies a vision of the political sphere as an exclusively national entity, centred on Berlin. It would be a pity if the end result of Eley and Blackbourn's work was a return to organizational and institutional political history at the top. Yet the questions raised by the two authors ultimately redirect our attention not just to the details of the political conjunctures but to much broader questions of social and economic determination as well. Despite the reservations expressed in the course of this chapter, the work of Blackbourn and Eley has raised crucial questions about our understanding of the German past, and in a wider sense, about the relationship between economic structure and politics.

Moreover, they have contributed signally to focusing the debate on the reality of change: on economic and social change, on political change, on new historical developments in the late nineteenth and early twentieth-centuries, and on how and why these took place and what effects they had. For these and many other aspects of their work, we all owe them a considerable debt of gratitude.

NOTES

1 The *locus classicus* of this view is G. Ritter, 'The Historical Foundation of the Rise of National-Socialism', in *The Third Reich* (London, 1955). Other contemporaries were less certain, however, e.g. F. Meinecke, *The German Catastrophe: Reflections and Recollections* (Cambridge, Mass., 1950).

2   R. D'Olier Butler, *The Roots of National Socialism* (London, 1941); see also A. J. P. Taylor, *The Course of German History* (London, 1945).
3   H. J. Laski, *Reflections on the Revolution of our Time* (London, 1943).
4   T. Parsons, 'Democracy and Social Structure in Pre-Nazi Germany', in Parsons, *Essays in Sociological Theory* (Glencoe, Ill., 1954).
5   R. Dahrendorf, *Society and Democracy in Germany* (London, 1968); T. Veblen, *Imperial Germany and the Industrial Revolution* (London, 1915).
6   Cited in J. Steinberg, 'The Kaiser and the British: The State Visit to Windsor, November 1907', in J. C. G. Röhl and N. Sombart (eds), *Kaiser Wilhelm II: New Interpretations* (Cambridge, 1982), p. 132.
7   B. Moore, Jr, *Social Origins of Dictatorship and Democracy* (London, 1967).
8   H.-U. Wehler, *Das deutsche Kaiserreich 1871–1918* (Göttingen, 1973), p. 14.
9   M. Stürmer, *Regierung und Reichstag im Bismarckstaat 1871–1880* (Düsseldorf, 1974), pp. 298–9.
10   V. R. Berghahn, *Der Tirpitz-Plan* (Düsseldorf, 1977), p. 592. `
11   P.-C. Witt, 'Innenpolitik und Imperialismus in der Vorgeschichte des I. Weltkrieges', in K. Holl and G. List (eds), *Liberalismus und imperialistischer Staat* (Göttingen, 1975), p. 13.
12   I. Geiss, 'Sozialstruktur und imperialistische Dispositionen im Zweiten Deutschen Kaiserreich', ibid., p. 43.
13   D. Groh, *Negative Integration und revolutionärer Attentismus* (Frankfurt, 1974), p. 13.
14   S. Mielke, *Der Hansa-Bund für Gewerbe, Handel und Industrie 1909–1914* (Göttingen, 1976), p. 17.
15   J. Kocka, 'Vorindustrielle Faktoren in der deutschen Industrialisierung', in M. Stürmer (ed.), *Das Kaiserliche Deutschland* (Düsseldorf, 1970), pp. 265–6.
16   K. D. Barkin, 'Germany's Path to Industrial Maturity', in D. K. Buse (ed.), *Aspects of Imperial Germany, Laurentian Historical Review*, vol. 5, no. 3 (1973), p. 29.
17   For one of the most succinct and influential collective statements of this whole thesis, see C. Stern and H. A. Winkler (eds), *Wendepunkte deutscher Geschichte 1848–1945* (Frankfurt, 1979); 25,000 copies of this book, which originated in a radio series, had been printed by March 1980.
18   Barkin, 'Germany's Path to Industrial Maturity'.
19   Taylor, *Course of German History*, p. 82.
20   M. Kitchen, *The Political Economy of Germany 1815–1914* (London, 1978), p. 82.
21   Stern and Winkler, *Wendepunkte*, p. 9.
22   T. S. Hamerow, *Restoration, Revolution, Reaction* (Princeton, NJ, 1958), p. viii.
23   For a good account of this process, see H.-U. Wehler, 'Historiography in Germany Today', in J. Habermas (ed.), *Observations on the Spiritual Situation of the Age* (Cambridge, Mass., 1984).
24   Thus a number of the works of Hill, Hobsbawm, Thompson and other 'Anglo-Marxist' historians have recently been translated into German, often many years after their first appearance in English.
25   F. Borkenau, 'Zur Soziologie des Faschismus', quoted and translated in P. Ayçoberry, *The Nazi Question: An Essay on the Interpretations of National Socialism (1922–75)*, p. 59. See also more generally, M. Kitchen, *Fascism* (London, 1976).
26   See esp. D. Blackbourn, 'The *Mittelstand* in German Society and Politics, 1871–1914', *Social History*, vol. 2, no. 1 (1977), pp. 409–434; Blackbourn, 'Peasant and Politics in Germany, 1871–1914', *European History Quarterly*, vol. 14 (1984), pp. 47–75; G. Eley, 'Defining Social Imperialism', *Social History*, vol. I, no. 3 (1976), p. 265–90; Eley, 'Capitalism and the Wilhelmine State', *Historical Journal*, vol. 21, no. 3 (1970), pp. 737–50; Eley, 'What Produces Fascism: Preindustrial Traditions or a Crisis of the Capitalist State?', *Politics and Society*, vol. 12 (1983), pp. 53–82.
27   D. Blackbourn, *Class, Religion and Local Politics in Wilhelmine Germany* (London, 1980); G. Eley, *Reshaping the German Right* (London, 1980).
28   D. Blackbourn and G. Eley, *Mythen deutscher Geschichtsschreibung: die gescheiterte bürgerliche Revolution von 1848* (Frankfurt, 1980).
29   D. Blackbourn and G. Eley, *The Peculiarities of German History* (Oxford, 1984).
30   For comparable arguments applied to other countries, see P. Anderson, 'Origins of the Present Crisis', *New Left Review*, vol. 23 (1964), pp. 26–54; T. Nairn, 'The English

Working Class', *New Left Review*, vol. 24 (1964), pp. 45–57, and A. J. Mayer, *The Persistence of the Old Regime* (London, 1981). The books which Blackbourn criticizes for their study of the absence of liberal successes in Germany include R. Chickering, *Imperial Germany and a World Without War* (London, 1975), and R. J. Evans, *The Feminist Movement in Germany 1894–1933* (London, 1976).

31 F. Engels, *The Role of Force in History* (London, 1968 ed. and transl.).

32 The sharpest attacks on Blackbourn and Eley's work have been Wehler, '"Deutscher Sonderweg" oder allgemeine Probleme des westlichen Kapitalismus?', *Merkur*, vol. 35, no. 5 (1981), pp. 477–87 (regrettably personal in tone), with replies in *Merkur*, vol. 35, no. 7 (1981), pp. 757–60; H. A. Winkler, 'Der deutsche Sonderweg: Eine Nachlese', *Merkur*, vol. 35, no. 5 (1981), pp. 793–804; H.-J. Puhle, 'Deutscher Sonderweg: Kontroverse um eine vermeintliche Legende', *Journal für Geschichte* (1981–4), pp. 44–5; J. Kocka, 'Der "deutsche Sonderweg" in der Diskussion', *German Studies Review*, vol. 5, no. 3 (1982), pp. 365–79.

33 W. J. Mommsen, 'Domestic Factors in German Foreign Policy before 1914', *Central European History*, vol. 6, no. 7 (1973), pp. 3–43; quotation is from p. 8.

34 H.-J. Puhle, 'Der Legende von der "Kehrschen Schule"', *Geschichte und Gesellschaft*, vol. 4, (1978), pp. 108–19. On other points, however, Puhle's article seems to me more open to criticism.

35 E. Kehr, *Economic Interest, Militarism and Foreign Policy* (Berkeley, Calif., 1977).

36 The account of the historiography of modern Germany is considerably more careful in the English edition of Blackbourn and Eley than in the German. In particular there is an extended consideration of the role of German sociologists who emigrated to the USA in the 1930s and whose influence was particularly felt in West Germany in the 1960s. For further considerations on this point, see my essay 'The Sociological Interpretation of German Labour History' in R. J. Evans (ed.), *The German Working Class 1888–1933* (London, 1982) (repr. as chapter 6, below).

37 F. Engels, *The Role of Force in History* (London, 1968), pp. 31, 95–7, 101, 104–6.

38 See M. Löwy, *The Politics of Combined and Uneven Development* (London, 1981), pp. 10–11.

39 This is explicitly recognized in the English edition of *The Peculiarities of German History*.

40 T. Nipperdey, 'Wehlers "Kaiserreich": Eine kritische Auseinandersetzung', *Geschichte und Gesellschaft*, vol. 1 (1975), pp. 539–60.

41 J. Bellini, *Rule Britannia* (London, 1981).

42 Engels, *Role of Force in History*, p. 93.

43 M. Kitchen, *The German Officer Corps 1890–1918* (Oxford, 1968).

44 D. T. Andrew, 'The Code of Honour and its Critics: The Opposition to Duelling in England 1700–1850', *Social History*, vol. 5, no. 3 (1980), pp. 409–34.

45 Mayer, *Persistence of the Old Regime*.

46 D. Cannadine, 'The Context, Performance and Meaning of Ritual: The British Monarchy and the "Invention of Tradition", c. 1820–1977', in E. Hobsbawm and T. Ranger (eds), *The Invention of Tradition* (London, 1983), pp. 101–65.

47 See Eley, 'Capitalism and the Wilhelmine State'; D. Geary, 'Employer Policies towards Labour in the Kaiserreich, 1871–1914', SSRC Research Seminar on Modern German Social History, unpublished paper, University of East Anglia, 1981; D. F. Crew, *Town in the Ruhr: A Social History of Bochum 1860–1914* (New York, 1977).

48 P.-Christian Witt, reviewing M. Rauh, *Die Parlamentarisierung des deutschen Reichs* (Düsseldorf, 1977), in *Militärgeschichtliche Mitteilungen*, vol. 29 (1981), no. 1, pp. 196–202. Witt's review is a devastating attack on a conservative historian's attempt to revive the 'parliamentarization thesis'.

49 R. J. Evans, 'Prostitution, State and Society in Imperial Germany', *Past and Present*, vol. 70, (February, 1976), pp. 106–29, for this particular example.

50 For these points, see G. Jellinek, *Allgemeine Staatsrechtslehre* (3rd ed., Berlin, 1922); K. Saul, 'Der Staat und die "Mächte des Umsturzes"', *Archiv für Sozialgeschichte*, vol. 12 (1972), pp. 293–350; and K. Saul, *Staat, Industrie, Arbeiterbewegung im Kaiserreich* (Düsseldorf, 1974).

PART TWO

Mentalities

split into

Sections

goes on to
talk about
revision a
topic which wasn't
looked much
upon clears
Germanys
History.

4

Religion and Society in Modern Germany

This essay began as the introduction to a special issue of *European Studies Review* (now *European History Quarterly*) devoted to the social history of religion in a German context (vol. 12, no. 3 (1982), pp. 249–88). This was an unfamiliar subject, especially to an English-language readership, so the essay included a substantial amount of basic background information. The collection originated in the fifth meeting of the Social Science Research Council (later: Economic and Social Research Council) Research Seminar Group on Modern German Social History, held at the University of East Anglia, Norwich, in 1981, where it was also clear that the social history of religion was new territory for most of the participants. So the essay tried to summarize the discussion, particularly where the specialists present at the meeting made a contribution; and many of those present will doubtless recognize their own discussion points in what follows. The religious division of the country into Protestant and Catholic communities is a fundamental fact of modern German history, not least in a political sense; the *Kulturkampf* and the rise of the Catholic Centre Party are familiar features of the nineteenth century to every student. But behind the political expression of confessional loyalties lay a whole world of popular belief – and, increasingly, unbelief – that has only recently begun to be explored. This is one area in which Anglo-French contributions have been especially outstanding, and the essay tries to explain why the subject of popular religious belief has had less attraction for historians in Germany until very recently. Because there was so little in this field at the time of writing, the essay has been revised to include discussion of one or two important recent works in this still rather neglected field, as well as removing some of the material originally designed to provide a context to specific contributions to the journal number which the essay introduced, adding a few new references and changing the overall structure. The focus of the essay is on secularization and the decline of religious belief, but this has to be seen, of course, in the context of the nature of the beliefs that were declining, as well as of those that were moving in to take their place. A concluding consideration of whether or not socialism and Nazism can be regarded as *ersatz* religions, leads back to the vexed question of the continuity or otherwise of attitudes and beliefs in the century before the advent of Hitler's Third Reich.

I

In recent years, social historians have been turning their attention increasingly from social structure to social attitudes, beliefs and mores. Quantitative studies of social mobility, social classes, occupational groups, communities, and families and households, have begun to give way to a more rounded, less two-dimensional approach, in which a determined attempt is made to give an account of the less tangible aspects of the history of human society. To a large extent, this has been a logical step in the progress of social history, resulting from the questions which the social-structural history of the 1960s and 1970s has posed with increasing urgency as the limits of its explanatory power have gradually been reached. Thus the rise of demographic history since the Second World War has resulted in a flood of quantitative information about people in the past, and although the problems of establishing reliable indices in this area are considerable, and many questions remain to be answered despite the increasing sophistication of research techniques, we are now able to generalize with some degree of confidence on a whole range of subjects which only a generation ago were wrapped in obscurity. For the eighteenth and nineteenth centuries at least, it is possible to provide detailed quantitative information on birth and death rates, life expectancy, household and family size and composition, marriage patterns, illegitimacy and a host of other subjects. We are beginning to establish how these patterns varied from area to area, from time to time, and between town and country.

Yet all this information has in some ways only increased our puzzlement about past society. It has established the basis from which a whole new set of questions has emerged, urgently demanding answers. Did high infant mortality rates lead to, perhaps also reflect, a general indifference on the part of parents, especially of mothers, to the fate of their offspring? Did the prevalence of death and disease make people callous and unfeeling? Did the widespread practice of arranged marriages and the interference of the community imply the absence of romantic love? These and many other questions cannot be answered without the underlying basis of demographic data, but the few attempts that have been made to answer them purely on this basis have been characterized by unfortunate shortcuts in reasoning and inadmissable argumentative leaps. The same can be said for the quantitative study of crime and law-breaking in the past: even ignoring the problems of quantifying these phenomena, problems to which historians of crime have largely failed to devote the same care and scepticism that have characterized the research of the historians of population, it is difficult to say what a rising rate of theft, or a declining rate of violence, for example, can tell us, unless we know a great deal more about the nature of law enforcement, the process of prosecution, the social

126

context of crime, and the social meaning and role of various kinds and degrees of law-breaking within the community.[1]

Thus quantitative studies have begun to be supplemented by studies of consciousness and belief, a development pioneered in particular by historians in France, where the study of historical demography using sophisticated modern techniques mainly originated. There is an increasing interest in what the French call *l'histoire des mentalités*: a vague and rather unsatisfactory term which encompasses consciousness, values, beliefs and ideology, in so far as these are all expressed in the everyday life and culture of ordinary people. This kind of history concentrates above all on reconstructing the mentality of the common people, for which there is very little direct written evidence of the conventional kind – although other social classes are by no means left entirely out of account. Here too, therefore, historians have had their ingenuity exercised in looking for new sources and new ways of interpreting them. Studies of changing attitudes towards death have made use of graveyard inscriptions, funerary sculpture, funeral orations, sermons and rituals, ballads, wills and other unconventional kinds of evidence; sometimes they have subjected them to a rigorous quantitative analysis. Studies of childhood, old age, marriage and sexuality, literacy, carnivals and festivals, popular justice and attitudes to authority, the uneducated people's conception of the world, the place of ritual in everyday life in the past, and of even less tangible subjects such as the history of honour, or of fear, or of national character, have all been similarly inventive. One might almost view this whole development in terms of the emergence of a historical psychology, though one that has little in common with the Freudian variety of psychohistory that has gained some popularity in the USA.[2]

All these areas of historical study have a number of things in common. In the first place, they involve, in most cases, a conscious use of theories and concepts derived from sociology and social anthropology. Functionalist approaches have enjoyed particular influence: historians have tended to 'explain' popular beliefs, values and behaviour patterns in terms of some social or psychological pattern which they might be argued to have fulfilled. Secondly, the starting-point of these recent historical studies lies in a determination to take seriously beliefs or practices which have previously been dismissed as unworthy of serious consideration. One cannot study popular rituals, common attitudes to death, or forms of popular justice in the past without first rejecting the view, widely held among middle- and upper-class contemporaries and subsequent historians, that these were merely expressions of superstition, consequences of ignorance, or evidence of a failure of human reason. Here, obviously, the discipline of social anthropology with its continual drive, expressed in a succession of different theories, to provide a satisfactory explanation of seemingly bizarre rituals and beliefs has had a major influence on

127

historians. Thirdly, such an approach involves in many cases a determined attempt on the part of the historian to interpret the available evidence 'against the grain'. With few exceptions, the bulk of the conventional written evidence in these areas consists of descriptions and reports by educated middle-class contemporaries, such as travellers, government officials, teachers, priests, judges, or policemen. These people looked at the subordinate classes with a selective eye, and often interpreted what they saw in a very unfavourable light. When an eighteenth-century priest tells us that his parishioners were licentious, or a teacher that his pupils were ignorant, or a local police official that his charges were disorderly, the historian must resist the temptation to take such statements at face value, however richly they are decked out with concrete examples. In this sense, indeed, the history of the subordinate classes must always encompass the history of their interaction with their superiors, and demands at least some assessment of the attitudes and behaviour of the latter.

Fourthly, central to virtually all studies of popular consciousness and behaviour in the past is the problem of religion, or, in other words, the fact that concepts of the supernatural and the sacred played a major role in people's lives and in the value systems and beliefs which informed them. Here too there have been a number of recent studies which have followed the general pattern I have outlined. As R. W. Scribner has pointed out:

> In recent years the way in which historians have dealt with the theme of religion in pre-industrial Europe has undergone a quiet and largely unremarked revolution. Not only has there been a growing interest in the social history of religion; there has also been a wider use of social theory to inform and structure analysis. Some wide-ranging and stimulating interpretations have been advanced, on the scale of Weber's Protestant ethic thesis, which threaten to push that rather tired theory from the stage as the showpiece debate on the relationship between religion and social change.[3]

Particularly striking has been the use of theories derived from social anthropology in the analysis of witchcraft in early modern Europe, in works such as Keith Thomas's *Religion and the Decline of Magic* (1971); but historical studies of religion in industrial society have also made extensive use of theories and concepts derived from the considerable sociological literature of the nineteenth and early twentieth centuries on the phenomenon of secularization. Largely as a result of the growing concentration of social historians on attitudes and beliefs, then, the history of religion has increasingly been treated as the history of a belief system which in most respects was like any other, to be analysed in largely secular terms within a specific social contest.

While this exciting new development in historical scholarship has been going on for two decades or more in England, France and the USA, however, it was until the beginning of the 1980s conspicuously absent in Germany. A number of reasons are responsible for this situation. In the first place one can point to the late development of social history of all kinds in West and East Germany. Particularly in the Federal Republic, the long-established dominance of political history, understood as the history of the state, its internal structure and above all its relations with other states, and intellectual history, understood as the history of individual 'great thinkers' and their ideas, continued well into the 1960s, and it is only since then – above all since the mid-1970s – that social history has, for a variety of reasons, become acceptable. The same is true to a degree of the German Democratic Republic, though here there was a greater concentration on the institutional and ideological history of the socialist movement than in the West. Thus it is only in the last decade that German historians have begun to undertake the kind of quantitative social-structural history practised in France since the early 1950s or even earlier.[4] Secondly, there has been a particular reason why German historians have been reluctant to embark upon the study of the values and beliefs of the common people. Like so many other areas of social history (for example, demographic and family history), it has been seriously retarded in Germany by the legacy of Hitler's Third Reich. In this case, the damage was done by the Nazis' anti-intellectualism, their conscious appeal to a mythical 'racial consciousness', their claim to have resurrected deep-seated, eternally valid beliefs and practices embedded in the tribal soul of the German peasantry, their perversion of folklore studies and social anthropology to their own ideological ends, and their pseudo-revival of many of these supposed 'Germanic' rituals and beliefs. Understandably enough, the Nazi episode ended by giving the study of popular consciousness a very bad name.[5]

In the field of religion, for example, any attempt to study magic and superstition (leaving aside for the moment the problematical nature of these concepts) was so forcibly reminiscent of the Nazis' attempts to revive 'Germanic' religion in opposition to the churches that it was effectively impossible in the first two decades of the Federal Republic, especially since, under the dominance of Christian Democracy, Christianity was widely seen as a necessary ideological basis upon which to overcome the evil legacy of the Third Reich.[6] Finally, there are a number of aspects of the institutional structure of German universities which have militated powerfully against the development of the social history of religion as it has been practised in France, Britain and the USA. The strength of the theological faculties in German universities, their explicit confessional allegiances and the tight grip which they have exercised over ecclesiastical history have prevented the emergence of a confessionally neutral, sociologically informed history of religion.[7] Neither the entrenched institutional position of Catholic and Evangelical theology, nor the development of comparative religion, nor the emergence of a new sociology of religion in Germany, has done much to improve the prospects for a social history of religion in the Federal Republic.[8]

II

Superficially at least, the basic facts of the religious history of modern Germany are well enough known. After the initial turmoil of the Reformation, the Peace of Augsburg (1555) established the famous principle *cuius regio, eius religio*: that is, the prince or ruler of each of the many hundreds of states which made up the Holy Roman Empire of the German Nation was free to decide which confession would be officially recognized in his domains. Broadly speaking, there were three to choose from: Roman Catholicism, Lutheranism and Calvinism; despite a certain amount of friction, the Lutheran and Calvinist churches managed to unite in 1817 to form the Evangelical or Protestant church in Prussia, to be followed shortly in other states. The Peace of Augsburg did not, of course, settle the religious struggle in Germany, and the armed conflicts of the next two centuries and more did a great deal to redraw the country's religious map. What it did set the seal upon, however, was a significant increase in the power of state over church. Until 1918 the ruler of every Protestant state was simultaneously the head of its Protestant church (*summus episcopus* or Supreme Bishop). The church was administered by the ruler's functionaries and largely lacked the means to assert its independence. Rulers saw to it that the church supported as far as possible the actions of the state, and that pastors spent much of their time inculcating in their flock obedience and loyalty to the monarch. In Protestant states, therefore, the established church was customarily supported by a wide range of laws discriminating against religious minorities. These laws were only gradually dismantled during the eighteenth century, and the tradition which they represented was resurrected for a while in the 1870s with the so-called *Kulturkampf*, discussed briefly below.

The situation of the Catholic church was stronger up to the end of the eighteenth century, because it had a built-in ascendancy in the structure of the Holy Roman Empire, combined with a good deal of secular power.[9] But in 1803 the Emperor decreed its disestablishment,[10] an act which led to the enforced sale of a massive quantity of church lands, to the dissolution of monasteries and to a reorganization of the church's administration. With the end of the Holy Roman Empire, destroyed by Napoleon in 1806, came the end of the Imperial Estate of Lords Spiritual, while former ecclesiastical states such as the prince-bishopric of Münster now disappeared altogether. Within a relatively short space of time, therefore, the Catholic church was reduced to the status of a confession, like its

Protestant counterpart, subject to the control of the state, its status regulated by a series of concordats between the pope and the various secular rulers of the German states, rather along the lines of Napoleon's concordat of 1801. The territorial changes brought about by the Congress of Vienna completed the process by which the Catholic church's power was reduced. None the less, Catholics still formed a majority of the population within the German Confederation, amounting in 1855 to perhaps 53 per cent. It was only after the expulsion of Austria from Germany in 1866 that they were decisively reduced to the status of a religious minority in Germany as a whole.[11]

By the nineteenth century, therefore, the official religious map of Germany may have been relatively clear, but when we turn to the level of the confessional affiliation of ordinary people, it becomes a great deal more complicated. Successive territorial adjustments in the centuries after the Reformation had led to the creation of substantial religious minorities in a number of German states. The annexation of Silesia, the partition of Poland and the gains of Rhenish territory at the Congress of Vienna had added major Catholic areas to Prussia, while, in creating the enlarged Grand Duchy of Baden, the Congress created a state whose inhabitants were divided into Catholics and Protestants roughly in the proportions of two-thirds to one-third. In Württemberg these proportions were reversed, while strongly Catholic Bavaria received the addition of a pronouncedly Calvinist area in the Palatinate. Thus, although one can say, as a broad generalization, that northern, central and eastern German states were Protestant, southern and western states Catholic, the situation was in reality a good deal more complicated. For by this time, if not before, where the ruler's religious convictions differed from those of his subjects, it was effectively impossible for him to do anything about it.

Nevertheless, it has become conventional for historians of Germany to regard religion, above all Protestantism, mainly as an 'ideological state apparatus', serving above all the purpose of legitimizing the state and disciplining its subjects. A. J. P. Taylor, for example, has remarked that 'Luther gave to Germany ... the Divine Right of Kings, or rather the Divine Right of any established authority. Obedience was the first, and last, duty of the Christian man'.[12] Much recent work has emphasized the role of religion in inculcating in the common people the habits of order-liness, regularity and discipline which were a necessary prerequisite for their integration into industrial society. For example, in her work on peasant society in late-eighteenth- and nineteenth-century Württemberg, Christel Köhle-Hezinger has drawn attention to the tight control exercised by the church over the daily life of the village community.[13] Particularly in the areas of partible inheritance, where viticulture and non-agricultural employment made it possible for a family to subsist (though only just) off a landholding as small as 3 hectares, the Württemberg village was a compact, overcrowded and close-knit community. Köhle-Hezinger argues that 'from the physically cramped conditions of the village community, and on the basis of legally enforced as well as indirect social controls, there developed an almost unbelievably tight normative regulation of everyday village life' ('Religion', p. 5). It was crucial to the social control function of the church in this situation that the pastor was invariably an outsider, removed from the village community not simply by virtue of his superior education. All Württemberg pastors were moved about frequently from parish to parish by the consistory of the Protestant church, and while Catholic priests remained in their parishes for considerably longer than their Protestant counterparts, even they seldom stayed more than ten to twelve years in the same post, unless they were very old. Pastors were never appointed to the parishes in which they had grown up, though their secular counterparts, the village schoolteachers, sometimes were. Pastor and schoolteacher were in a very real sense the 'rulers of the village', especially since all other village officials, from the nightwatchman to the president of the village court, belonged to the local community.

The disciplining power of the pastor and the schoolteacher was exercised not simply through sermons in church and lessons in school but also through 'numerous village institutions, which complemented each other with an amazing perfection and in part overlapped in their competence and function. Thus they furthered the maintenance of general morality in the village, but they also brought the community fatally close to a situation of total order and control' ('Religion', p. 10). These institutions were various in kind. They included the *Ruggericht* or *Vogtgericht*, which – according to an official instruction issued in 1826 – had to investigate and improve the local secular administration. Its regular meetings were summoned by the tolling of the largest church bell, at the sound of which all adult males had to leave whatever they were doing and make their way to the churchyard, the usual place of assembly:

> The men placed themselves in a line, one after another, including the priest, the village mayor and the local councillors as equally entitled, went one by one to the senior official, and had their complaints and suggestions noted down. According to their seriousness these were either decided upon immediately or referred to a higher instance.[14]

In addition to the *Ruggericht* there was the *Dorfgericht*, which was concerned with civil lawsuits (for example, concerning inheritance and the division of property). But social control was exercised above all by ecclesiastical institutions. Two of these were especially important. First, the church visitation (*Kirchenvisitation*), in which the local pastor attended the village school once a week on his own, and twice a year in the company of the head of the village community (*Ortsvorsteher*), to examine

132

the pupils. This was no mere intrusion into an otherwise secular form of education. Up to 1796 all texts used for reading and writing lessons in Württemberg schools had to be of an explicitly religious character, and even after that date the only secular texts that could be used were for many years 'moral stories' intended to encourage discipline, obedience and piety. Once or twice a year the village was also visited by the pastor's immediate superior in the church hierarchy (the *Herr Spezial*), who examined not only the children but also their teacher, the pastor himself and the village officials down to the lowest level, on their 'mode of life, property, zeal, industriousness ... submission to higher authority, conduct of their business'.[15] Not content with this, he was also obliged to ask them what they thought of each other in these respects, and often simply stopped the villagers in the street to examine them and obtain their opinions of their superiors as well. The notes which these visitations produced on village life are a valuable source for the historian.

Even more striking than these visitations were the church conventions (*Kirchenkonvente*), introduced in 1644, extended to Catholic areas in 1803 and not abolished until 1891. Once a month, the convent, with the pastor in charge, met to investigate the moral failings of the village's inhabitants: 'transgressions such as failure to attend divine service, working on a Sunday, cursing, swearing, using the magic arts, drinking, fighting and marital quarrels were formally considered, and the guilty parties were summoned and punished'.[16] The church convents did not simply enable the pastor to involve himself in the most intimate details of the private lives of his parishioners; they virtually compelled him to do so. Local people were said to fear the dishonour of a citation or condemnation in the church convent more than anything else. Yet, not content with these means of control, the authorities in Württemberg, Köhle-Hezinger has reminded us, sought to encourage the villagers to spy on each other by issuing the so-called 'Evil House Decrees' (*Übelhäuser-Erlasse*), dating from the seventeenth and eighteenth centuries, which offered a financial reward to anyone who managed to convince them that a neighbour was immoral, lazy, or idle. If the neighbour in question was found guilty, and if he was a male under 40 years of age, he was generally drafted into the army, as often as not with the result that his property was sold off to the person who denounced him. Thus, concludes Köhle-Hezinger, a comprehensive network of social controls, overwhelmingly religious in character, ensured that the subordinate classes in rural Württemberg were well prepared for the discipline under which they would be placed when they entered the workshops and factories of the industrial revolution ('Religion', pp. 11–13).

The problems facing this argument are, however, the same as those which are involved in the use of the concept of social control in other contexts. It is clear enough that a comprehensive network of rules and regulations existed in Württemberg with the aim of enforcing obedience and discipline on the village community. Yet it is illegitimate to jump straight from the fact of their existence to the conclusion that they were effective. Köhle-Hezinger herself provides a number of points which suggest that the villagers' ability to resist or evade these controls should on no account be underestimated. To begin with, a close-knit village community such as was common in partible-inheritance areas of Württemberg had its own way of dealing with outsiders, as the work of the Institute for Empirical Cultural Studies at Tübingen University, with which Köhle-Hezinger herself has been associated, has shown in its studies of the village of Kiebingen.[17] Silence, uncooperativeness, deception and the whole arsenal of peasant cunning were brought to bear by the village community to defend itself against the unwelcome attentions of outsiders, who, as we have seen, included the pastor and other ecclesiastical agents. Such action was undoubtedly made easier by the social and educational gap between the priest or pastor and his parishioners. In rural areas, where highly individual dialects were spoken by the peasant community, the linguistic comprehensibility of sermons delivered in High German was doubtful, to say the least; and a commentator writing in the late eighteenth century in Catholic Bavaria noted that

> In the sermons, which are largely held for the people, one hears nothing but complaining and raging, today over the decadent, irresponsible times, tomorrow over free-thinkers and godless books ... and all this for an audience, among whom perhaps hardly three have ever held a book in their hands, and who do not know what the sermon is about ...[18]

Moreover, the village community had several levers of power which it could operate against an over-zealous pastor. The pastor frequently depended on the village community for a good deal of his material support, whether as a farmer himself and thus a participant in the three-field system and a user of communal agricultural labour and equipment, or as a collector of tithes, the submission of which again offered endless opportunities for the exercise of peasant cunning.

The tendency to view the village community as isolated, autonomous and totally cut off from the outside world, and hence all the more easily controlled by emissaries of church and state, has perhaps been overstressed in recent work. Marriage and kinship linked the village with other communities nearby; colporteurs, sellers of books, tracts and pamphlets, wandering pedlars and merchants, itinerant labourers, money-lending Jews, a whole gamut of 'travellers' (*fahrende Leute*) linked the village to the outside world, and such people, as Scribner has pointed out, were 'detached from settled communities, ... detached from the normal patterns of Christian life, and held to be "irreligious"'.[19] With little real power over the village, they posed no real threat and so are less likely to have met with suspicion and resistance than the formally appointed agents of church and state. Moreover, communities such as those discussed by Köhle-Hezinger, which were heavily dependent on viticulture, artisan production and proto-industrial outwork were – if comparable research on France is any guide – closely linked to wider market structures and in consequence unusually open to intellectual influences from the town.[20] Such links and possibilities of escape may well have made resistance or evasion of ecclesiastical controls easier: peasants may simply have done a good deal of their sinning when they went to market.

In addition to all this, the kind of evidence that the records of ecclesiastical courts and visitations has left us demands, as we saw earlier, careful interpretation, in which the historian often has to work against the grain. Thus the constant reissue of ordinances compelling children to attend school may suggest not that the state was successfully compelling children to do so but the reverse; while the multiplicity of institutions of social control may also suggest that, taken singly at least, they were found to be relatively ineffective. Even Köhle-Hezinger concedes that the church conventions, for example, became progressively less effective in the course of the eighteenth century, as earlier, more drastic punishments were replaced by fines ('Religion', pp. 12–13).

These considerations can be supported by evidence from recent studies of peasant life in Catholic Bavaria.[21] The records of parish visitations in the early nineteenth century are full of lamentations about the declining moral and religious standards of the peasantry. In the parish of Gremertshausen, for example, it was said in 1822 that 'morality and religiosity [were] on the whole in such a bad condition that deteriorations were daily visible'.[22] Yet such reports demand careful interpretation, for they were often made with a view to supporting the clergy's argument that the powers of law enforcement and moral supervision which it had lost in the disestablish-ment of 1803 had to be restored to it if the moral condition of the countryside was not to sink even lower than it had done since then. Outwardly at least, the peasantry continued to be assiduous in their attendance at church, and communion services continued to attract over 90 per cent of adult parishioners at least until the 1850s. Such religiosity was not, however, accompanied by a continuing conformity to the official morality of the church, for the area showed a sharp rise in illegitimacy from the beginning of the nineteenth century, increasing from 4.09 to 18.04 illegitimate births per 100 live births a year in Massenhausen between 1750–9 and 1820–9, and from 3.94 to 25.53 in Thalhausen in the same period. By 1840 one birth in five was illegitimate in Bavaria. The clergy fulminated against this development, which was indeed to some degree a consequence of the decline of legal sanctions against illegitimacy

135

such as public degradation or fines, the latter abolished in 1808. Yet the trend began well before the disestablishment of the church in 1803, and was certainly not seen by the peasantry as an example of moral decline. It was not accompanied by any significant increase in cases of adultery, rape or other sexual crimes. On the contrary, if one follows the arguments of Lee, the rise in illegitimacy did not reflect any fundamental changes in peasant attitudes; illegitimate children in Bavaria had always been happily accommodated within the structure of the rural community. What it did demonstrate was the fact that, as Lee concludes, 'if it came to a conflict between social norms, as recognized by the rural community, there was little doubt as to which would be adopted.... In the face of behavioural norms adopted by various strata of rural society, the church was ultimately powerless.'[23] Whether this was quite as true of Protestant areas as it was of Catholic remains perhaps to be investigated. Yet such evidence casts doubt on whether religion can really be seen simply as an instrument of social control. These doubts are strengthened when one considers the definition of religion upon which such arguments rest. In Köhle-Hezinger's view,

Religion is experienced by the villagers only through its expression in the state church. Whatever might be latently 'religious' beyond this, in the sense used by the old *Volkskunde* or the contemporary sociology of religion – 'superstition', 'religiosity' – cannot be comprehended by the historian [*wird für uns historisch nicht fassbar*]. 'Religion' at any rate is tied to the church, identical and interchangeable with it in a subjective and also in an objective sense. The object of our interest is, however, not the church as an institution, 'dogma' or 'teaching', but the cultural forms and institutionalization of religious behaviour, and the religious influences on social structures, processes and consciousness.[24]

This definition excludes, however, an enormous area of peasant beliefs and practices: perhaps the greater part of popular religion, indeed, may not have been encompassed by the formal doctrines and practices of the church.

III

It may well be the case that the Protestant church in Germany was not only more concerned to 'purify' religion by stamping out popular 'superstitions' and 'pagan' relics than was its Catholic counterpart but also more successful in doing so. Certainly, both Reformation and Counter-Reformation launched a determined attack on popular culture. Yet, although both Protestant and Catholic churches attempted to reform popular culture, 'we must not', Scribner has warned, 'leap from recognising the attempt to assuming its success', and he adds that 'when the process is studied at the popular level, it can be seen to have been singularly unsuccessful'.[25] The mass of handbooks and dictionaries of popular religious practices and beliefs compiled by nineteenth-century folklorists and summarized in Bächthold-Stäubli's *Dictionary of German Superstition* testifies eloquently enough to the fact that, as Scribner concludes, both in Protestant and in Catholic areas 'popular belief persisted in more or less the same forms that it had taken before the Reformation until well into the twentieth century'.[26]

The majority of Bächthold-Stäubli's volumes, the first of which appeared in 1927 and the last in 1942, were published in the Third Reich; and German folklorists and ethnographers are now hesitant about examining the 'hidden' aspects of peasant culture because this is what their forerunners in the field of *Volkskunde* used to do under the Nazis. One can understand, therefore, Köhle-Hezinger's exclusion of these aspects of peasant belief from her definition of religion. But the consequence of this decision is a certain foreshortening of perspective on popular culture in the past. This reluctance must surely be overcome if the study of popular beliefs in the past is to make the progress in Germany that it has in France, Britain or the USA. Simply because the traditional concerns of *Volkskunde* were closely bound up with German nationalism all the way up to, and including, their final, perverted incarnation in the ideology of National Socialism, does not mean that they should be abandoned altogether, or that they cannot be set in a different theoretical context, or even turned to other political purposes. The persistence of popular beliefs which were regarded by the church as reprehensible superstitions is a case in point: they can be taken easily enough as evidence that the church's campaign to reform popular culture was less than wholly successful, a conclusion which might well have been reached by Köhle-Hezinger had she considered them, without in any way necessarily implying that they were – as the Nazis asserted – part of a coherent, primitive, 'Germanic' religion that was in some way superior to organized Christianity.

A point that deserves emphasis in this context is that peasant religion did not simply consist of 'pagan superstitions' which existed alongside formal Christianity; formal Christian beliefs and practices themselves frequently seem to have been interpreted by the peasantry in a pragmatic, crypto-materialist sense. Peasants in the Lauenburg area were wont to call a pastor rather than a physician in cases of illness, since Holy Communion was believed to have a healing power and also, unlike the services of a physician, cost nothing to obtain. Other customs included feeding one's cattle immediately on one's return from taking Holy Communion, since it was thought that some of the power would then pass into the beasts; or wiping one's mouth, after taking the wine, with some object that would be used later for secular purposes. Similarly, great store was set by objects such as candles, palms, or bread, that were blessed by the priest and taken home to be used for protection against illness, storms and other dangers.[27] The clergy invested these objects with divine power; their use was then left to the laity. While such beliefs continued to play a role in the Catholic church, even if they were barely tolerated by the hierarchy, the more hostile attitude of the Protestant clergy seems to have ensured that by the nineteenth century 'magic', as Hugh McLeod has observed, 'had become largely detached from the Protestant church'. Thus in Protestant Saxony one observer, writing in 1902, observed that 'superstition can only be rightly evaluated if it is seen as the real religion of the people. Generally speaking it is the unofficial religion standing over agaı ıst the official church version of the Christian religion'. The peasants, he believed, saw in religion mainly a force which could help them in a material sense. 'They believe, pray, go to Church, in order to obtain God's protection and help in this earthly life.'[28] Thus peasant beliefs, whether they related to official Christianity or whether they were so distant from this as to invite the active hostility of the church, seem to have been characterized by a kind of crypto-materialism, in which sacred power was used for material purposes, as often as not against the wishes, and without the knowledge, of the clergy.

Indeed, there is a considerable quantity of evidence that indicates that the officially sanctioned religious beliefs and practices of the church coexisted with a great many other beliefs and practices, above all in rural areas. Many villages had a magician or sorcerer, to whom the villagers turned in cases of illness or misfortune, often in preference to trained physicians. Belief in witches continued to be a force in rural life well into the twentieth century. An investigation carried out in the Leipzig diocese in 1908 revealed some forty-five individuals, scattered over the various villages, who were generally regarded by the local inhabitants as witches; in 1905 a case of grievous bodily harm, and in 1912 even a murder, were shown in the courts to have been caused by the belief that the victim was a witch. More mundanely, the use of charms, amulets and other objects to ward off evil was widespread in the German countryside. Ploughs or parts of ploughs were used, for example, as a protection against theft, or to recover stolen goods; during epidemics it was common for the body of the first victim to be dug up and decapitated, to stop it from taking any more people with it, as happened during the cholera epidemic of 1866, or even later (the last recorded instances being in Pomerania in 1890 and Putzig in 1913); while major agricultural events such as the harvest provided the occasion for a wide variety of similar practices. As late as the 1860s people still took the opportunity of an execution to obtain handkerchiefs soaked in the blood of decapitated criminals, and the remains of executed malefactors found a wide variety of uses, from warding off the danger of fire to improving the strength of a landlord's beer.[29] Such practices and beliefs reflected the helplessness of peasants in the face of natural phenomena – death, disease, famine, drought – which they were unable to understand or control. If nothing else, they helped to relieve the feeling of insecurity and emotional stress which the ever-present threat of natural disaster created.

In support of this view one can point to the fact that there was a close correlation between the structure of peasant religious practice and belief on the one hand and the structure of the individual life of the peasant and the economic life of the peasant community on the other. Both the life-cycle of the individual and the calendrical cycle of peasant agriculture were marked by religious rituals and practices. Baptism, confirmation, marriage and funeral ceremonies not only provided 'rites of passage' to mark the progress of the individual from one state of being to another, but also affected the structure of relations within the community, and between generations and kin-groups. Religious rituals also marked the stages of the agricultural year, invoking divine aid for sowing, harvesting and numerous other vital activities. There was a complex system of links between rituals concerned with the fertility of the crops and those concerned with sexual relationships within the community; and the rhythm and spacing of religious festivals throughout the year closely followed the rhythm and spacing of agricultural activities. Yet such parallels should not be over-stressed. The fit between ritual and agrarian life was often inexact, and it is easily possible to point to religious ceremonies which served no obvious purpose beyond the purely religious. Such objections have led some scholars to question the wisdom of looking for a functional explanation of religious practices at all, and to argue that religious belief has to be studied as an autonomous system of thought explicable only in its own terms. It is certainly important that religion should be studied in this way, but it is equally important that the relation of religious systems of thought to social structures and processes should also be studied; and it is this latter problem which is of most interest to the social historian. Here there are many difficult questions to be answered. The more the social history of religion succeeds in uncovering the nature of popular belief, the more it becomes clear that the institutionalization of religion is the concluding point of a much more complex process of the formation of belief. The nature of religious beliefs may be easy enough to pinpoint when one is dealing with theological tracts or church dogma, but it becomes much more difficult when one turns to popular religion. Thus it is essential for the social historian not to take religion as something 'given'; a major task for the social history of religion lies in investigating how religion is constituted, how religious beliefs are generated, and how they change.

An attempt to do this has been made in the recent work of Werner Blessing on the influence of church and state on popular mentalities in nineteenth-century Bavaria.[30] Blessing shows quite successfully how the reforming, rationalist bureaucracy of the early nineteenth century

139

attacked popular 'superstitions', festivals, cults and the like, and how it was backed by an increasingly well-educated, liberal and 'enlightened' clergy which was similarly alienated from popular religiosity. However, this assault had not got very far before the rise of a new, Romantic, conservative and Catholic absolutism in the 1830s and 1840s displaced the bureaucratic rationalism of earlier government policy and opened a space for a revived Ultramontane Catholicism to reattach itself to surviving forms of popular ritual and belief. The clergy of this era, in Bavaria at least, was quite prepared to bless horses (several hundred at a time on special occasions), to tolerate horseracing, dancing and drinking on saints' day festivals, and in general to retreat from its earlier distaste for the mixing of sacred and profane. On this basis the post-1848 Catholic church in Bavaria built an expanded Catholic community, with the growth of lay associations, the increasing popularity of the Marian cult, and the general encouragement of popular religiosity. Against this the secularizing impulse of the primary-school system remained limited in its effects. Nevertheless, the church's efforts could not prevent a gradual secularization of the population, not only through urbanization and other forms of social change but also through the cultural and political pressures generated by the state as it returned to a 'modernizing' programme in the second half of the nineteenth century and gave way to a strongly liberal political orientation after 1870.

While Blessing paints quite a plausible picture of the policies and attitudes of church and state, he generally has little to say about popular religious beliefs, not least because, like Köhle-Hezinger, he also assumes that superstition and crypto-materialist practices 'to a large extent ... are beyond historical investigation'.[31] Having made this point – which, as we have seen, is an unduly pessimistic one, to say the least – he goes on to claim, necessarily without foundation, that 'the importance of "superstition" in daily life was less important as a rule than church religiosity'.[32] Moreover, Blessing has little to say about the relations between clerical moral precepts and popular moral practice, and makes virtually no attempt to take the dynamics of social and economic change in the countryside into account, although he correctly notes that secularization and the decline of religious practice cannot be equated simply with urbanization and industrialization. Thus his book ultimately only gives one side of the picture, and falls too often into a way of looking at the German past which regards traditional society as a kind of passive entity, a *carte blanche* on which 'modernizing' bureaucrats and educators write their own script with greater or lesser difficulty according to the given circumstances.

A more fruitful way of approaching the history of popular religious belief has been indicated recently by the work of Jonathan Sperber, whose study of the Rhineland-Westphalia district has argued that a religious revival occurred within the Catholic community in the 1850s and 1860s.[33]

In the first half of the century, he suggests, popular Catholicism was in a state of decay. Pilgrimages and processions became more worldly, as the elements of secular festivity within them increased in importance and clerical control over them was weakened. Illegitimacy rates were high, and church attendance was often low. Religious brotherhoods 'spent more time in the taverns than in the church' (p. 278). The clerical hierarchy was very critical of such developments, but because of the weakening of its position during the French Revolutionary wars, with their accompanying disruption of ecclesiastical administration and training; and the disestablishment of the church as a secular authority it was unable to prevent them. Prussian reforms such as the abolition of the guilds and of marriage restrictions added to these influences weakening the clergy's position, while economic growth brought an influx of middle-class Protestants into previously Catholic areas and encouraged secular associational life and the propagation of Enlightenment anticlericalism. As we have seen, this argument assumes too easily that the mixture of secular and sacred in religious festivals, high illegitimacy rates and the like indicated a decline of popular religiosity, and it takes the complaints of the clergy too much at face value. As Blessing has suggested, the failure of the clergy to change this situation may in the end have been to its benefit.

After the mid-century economic crisis, the situation changed dramatically, for, Sperber argues,

> The subsistence crisis of the years 1846 to 1855 had impressed upon the lower classes of the countryside and non-industrial small towns, the necessity for a more restricted and sober life-style. Their path to economic survival ran through delayed marriage, more frequent celibacy, prolonged economic dependence, thriftiness, and denial of pleasure. (p. 280)

They thus became responsive to the religious appeal of the clergy, who took over the control of popular festivities once more, and, with the aid of the Marian cult, were able to transform them into less secularized forms of religious celebration, although here perhaps Sperber underestimates the extent to which the clergy continued to compromise with popular belief, the degree to which new developments such as the Marian cult were successful precisely because they catered for the crypto-materialist attitude to religion described earlier. At the same time the growth of a Catholic proletariat in the new industrial towns of the area created a demand for social institutions to help immigrants adjust to urban–industrial life, and this too was supplied by the Catholic church, now freed from bureaucratic interference as the Prussian authorities, in contrast to the period before 1848, saw the clergy as a force for stability and order.

As Sperber points out, there are parallels here with the revival of popular

Catholicism in post-famine Ireland[34]; but the same pattern was present in other Catholic areas of Germany, though generally in a less clear-cut form, with areas of liberal support and religious heterodoxy remaining in Baden, for example, and a strong element of peasant anticlericalism emerging in Bavaria towards the end of the century.[35] The religious revival of the 1850s and 1860s provided the essential basis for the solidarity of the Catholic community in the subsequent period, reflected above all in the growth of popular support for the Centre Party, although here it is important to note, as Blessing points out, that the solidarity of the Catholic community was not invulnerable, and that a decline of religious practice began to occur from the 1890s here as well. Protestantism went in a different direction, as the church failed to maintain its hold on popular religion. The Protestant working class drifted off into Social Democracy. The Protestant middle classes became less religious and spearheaded the attack on religious 'obscurantism' in the 1870s. The Protestant petty-bourgeoisie eventually 'drifted off in a proto-fascist direction' (p. 296). However, as Sperber concludes, both Protestant and Catholic communities in the second half of the century were characterized by a growth of politically conservative associational life, and the fact that the Catholic religious revival took place 'independently of the state's authority ... is one more piece of evidence suggesting that the strength of conservative tendencies in German history is not simply a consequence of the application of state power but a reflection of underlying social processes' (p. 296).

IV

Ecclesiastical historians in particular seem to run the risk of regarding secularization as having originated in intellectual developments and having then spread gradually downwards through propaganda and education. Certainly Germany had its secularist ideologies in the nineteenth century as much as any country did. Beginning with Immanuel Kant, generations of German scholars enthusiastically applied the techniques of secular scholarship to subjects previously considered too sacred to be approached in any spirit other than that of unquestioning faith. David Strauss's *Life of Jesus* (1835) was only the most controversial example of this approach, which soon permeated not only the philosophical and historical faculties of many German universities but even, in the form of 'rational theology', theological faculties as well. A generation of Prussian and other bureaucrats, lawyers, teachers, doctors and intellectuals in general were thus trained in the spirit of Kantian rationalism, and the subsequent influence of Hegel was exercised in much the same direction. The biblical scholarship of men like Strauss created massive controversy, and may well have done much to undermine the religious faith of the educated classes.

Yet social historians cannot be content with an approach which concentrates on 'the secularization of the European mind in the nineteenth century'.[36] Secularization should be seen as a social as much as an intellectual process. Indeed, to a degree it already appeared to contemporaries as such. In 1844, for instance, the *Allgemeine Kirchen-Zeitung* (Darmstadt) reported of the inhabitants of the Magdeburger Börde, a predominantly rural but partially industrialized area in the province of Saxony, that the 'larger landowners, officials and factory-owners' were

> veritable enemies of the human race, for their God is Money, their temple is the brewery or distillery, or the factory with its incense-like smoke, their hymn is the roaring of the boilers and the throbbing of the machine.... If they think they can get away with it, they frequently break the law against Sunday working, which indeed cannot be enforced to the letter, and if they are forced to conform to the law, and thus talk of their own day of rest, then they often mean by this simply that they are spending one day indulging in even more sensual pleasures than usual. Hardly anyone talks of going to church, or communing quietly with himself, or of composing his mind in a religious sense and rousing his feelings to the contemplation of the Deity, neither on Sunday nor, it need hardly be said, on weekdays.[37]

The author considered that these landowners and industrialists exercised a bad influence over the rural labourers who made up the great majority of the area's inhabitants, both by forcing them to work on Sundays and by setting them a bad example in general.

The appointment of an energetic pastor or the imposition of stricter controls on the open expression of hostility to the church might have some small effect but was clearly unable to halt the decline in the long run. As the pastor in Alvensleben reported in 1836,

> Out of 800 souls a maximum of 420 attend Holy Communion. In this respect it is worthy of note that 15–20 years ago, when such outward aspects of religiosity were less strictly controlled by the authorities than they are now, the number of communicants stood at over 600, while the present Minister began with scarcely more than 200. People do not give voice openly to their low estimation of Church and Altar any more, but it is there all the same.[38]

Only the small class of independent peasants and small landowners remained pious. It was only in this class, it was alleged, that 'Father and Mother still stand at the head of the family and are a model for their children and servants in their blameless life, their fear of God, their strict, religious adherence to the law and their worthy observance of the Sabbath through diligent attendance at church services.'[39] Numerous other reports from the area made it clear that, as another general account of local religious practice, noting that only about 15 per cent of the parishioners had managed to attend Communion during the year, observed, 'the situation with regard to attendance at church has indeed only become really bad in the last 40–50 years'.[40] This was precisely the period since the rapid conversion of local agriculture to sugar-beet production and the growth of a locally based sugar-refining industry in the 1830s. While it was of course possible that local pastors, influenced by the theological rationalism prevalent in the nearby University of Halle, may have contributed to weakening the religious commitment of their flock, a far more important role was played by the intensification of work brought about by the transition to beet production, which obliged men to work on Sundays and also brought them into contact with migrant labourers who came into the area to assist in the construction and operation of the refineries and factories and the railways which connected them to the national market. After all, the piety of the independent peasants does not, at least according to contemporary reports, seem to have been adversely affected by the 'theologically rational' sermons to which they, as the churchgoing class, were regularly exposed.

The obvious conclusion to draw seems to be that the class on which religion exercised the strongest hold was precisely the class which depended most directly and exclusively upon farming for its subsistence, and thus was most likely to be harmed by natural catastrophes against which there were few adequate means of defence. Thus there is something in the view that as the areas of uncertainty in the securing of everyday existence were reduced, and means of minimizing the risk of natural disaster became more effective, so the role of the sacred in daily life was reduced as people found it less and less necessary to invoke its aid in explaining their lives. Or, as a Dutch saying puts it: 'artificial fertilizers make atheists'[41] – and not only artificial fertilizers but also the use of insurance companies, the improvement of medical techniques, the spread of hygiene, and many other developments which began in the eighteenth century but for the most part really exerted their influence only in the nineteenth.

Such factors may indeed help to account for the fact that secularization seems to have begun earlier, and progressed more rapidly, in the propertied middle classes than among the peasantry. As in the Magdeburg area, it seems to have been the lower middle class that clung most tenaciously to its religious beliefs, in both town and countryside. In Berlin, as Hugh McLeod has observed, 'the mainstay of most city parishes seems to have been the "little men" (*die kleinen Leute*): self-employed craftsmen, minor officials, clerks'.[42] Studies of the reading habits of nineteenth-century Germans seem to indicate that the lower middle class were more likely to possess religious books than were their social superiors, and other local studies – for example of Barmen – have tended to substantiate this point. For the educated professional and industrial middle class, on the other hand, studies of Berlin, Württemberg and other areas suggest that Nietzsche was altogether correct when he made his famous claim in 1882 that 'God is dead'.[43] The middle class was more likely to be influenced by literary and scientific attacks on religion, and it was here that most of the very large demand that made materialist and evolutionary tracts such as Ludwig Ernst Büchner's *Force and Matter* (1855) and Haeckel's *Riddle of the Universe* (1899) so enormously popular, existed. Moreover, it was also precisely this class that provided the major reservoir of support for German liberalism, and was thus further alienated from the church, above all from the Protestant church, by its explicit political conservatism. But above all it was this class whose members in their daily life experienced least of the uncontrollable natural disasters which so often drove the peasantry into the arms of religion. They lived an urbanized existence, made full use of mechanized transport facilities such as the railway and the steamship, could afford the latest benefits of medical science, and were beginning to create a network of leisure activities that left small room for churchgoing. The urban petty bourgeoisie, on the other hand, with its limited education, its dependence on family help in running the grocery or the artisan workshop, and its precarious, hard-working existence just above the margin of respectability, may still have required religion to stiffen its resolve to succeed, to hold together the paternalistic fabric of the family and the small workshop, and to console it in adversity.[44]

But, as the arguments discussed earlier in this essay have already indicated, it would be an exaggeration to reduce religious belief wholly to its psychological functions in this manner. They do not explain why, for example, Calvinism continued to be so popular among the Prussian aristocracy. Nor do such arguments take us very far towards understanding why secularization appears to have progressed more rapidly in Protestant than in Catholic rural areas, despite clear similarities of social structure and mode of production. Thus the percentage of Protestants taking Communion in Bavaria in 1906–8 was 63, while in 1912 the percentage of Catholics taking Easter Communion in the diocese of Regensburg (in Bavaria) was 75, and there was an average of seven communions during the year per church member. In the same year only 8.23 per cent of Protestants in Schleswig-Holstein attended Communion on Holy Day.[45] Of course, these figures need more detailed interpretation than can be supplied here; but they can be supported by others pointing in the same direction, and such data as are available do seem to suggest an earlier secularization among Protestants. Thus, in the Magdeburger Börde, Catholic rural labourers were noted for their high church attendance, often walking miles to Communion on Sundays, while Protestant labourers were notoriously indifferent by the 1880s, and, according to a contemporary report, even Protestant immigrants from more pious areas soon conformed to the local reluctance to go to church. When told by their pastor that they should be ashamed of themselves, and should follow instead the pious habits of the Catholics, they replied, 'they are Catholic people and have to go to church; we Protestants don't need it', or even 'they aren't as well-educated and advanced as we are'.[46]

A number of reasons may be adduced to account for these differences. In the first place, as we have seen, the Catholic church managed to keep open its lines to popular religious practices, while its Protestant counter-part had long since severed them. The result was that Catholic peasants still saw a material reason to go to church, take Communion and participate in official religious ceremonies, while Protestant peasants did not. Secondly there seems to have been a much wider social as well as intellectual gap between Protestant clergy and laity than between Catholic priests and their flock. For example, as Bormann has shown in his study of the Württemberg clergy, some 76 per cent of Catholic clergy in the kingdom came from rural backgrounds at the end of the nineteenth century, and a total of 37 per cent of students of Catholic theology were the sons of peasants. In the same period, however, only 22 per cent of Evangelical pastors in Württemberg were of rural origin, and only 3 per cent of the students of Evangelical theology were peasants' sons. Already by the eighteenth century, Bormann suggests, the Evangelical clergy had become to a remarkable extent a self-recruiting élite (unlike Catholic clergymen, of course, they were allowed to marry), with additions from the families of teachers and civil servants.[47] Whether this was true everywhere in Germany remains to be established. Württemberg was peculiar in the sense that the Protestant church was highly centralized, and in other areas, including Prussia, the church was often economically weaker and less independent and so relied far more on local patronage for the support of its pastors. Where there was a powerful landed nobility, rather than (as in Württemberg) a basically peasant society, the power of appointing pastors was often exercised locally by nobles, and this, combined with the lower social status of the clergy in such areas, may well have reduced the gap between the pastor and his flock.

V

However, one should not push these comparisons too far without recalling that, seen in broad perspective, the social and economic basis of Catholic Germany was very different from that of its Protestant counter-part by the end of the nineteenth century. Industrialization took place above all in Protestant areas, in the great Protestant cities of Berlin and Hamburg, each of which was in itself a major industrial centre, and in smaller industrial centres such as Chemnitz, Leipzig and Dresden. Heavy industrial concentrations in the Ruhr, around Dortmund and Essen, and in Silesia, at least in the north-western part, around Breslau, were also clearly, if less exclusively, Protestant. The strongest Catholic region – Bavaria – was overwhelmingly rural. Nevertheless, there were also important industrial developments in Catholic regions, for example in Prussian Poland and areas of Western Westphalia and the lower Rhine. What tipped the socio-economic balance in favour of the Protestants were essentially political factors. Catholicism tended to be strongest on the periphery of the German Empire founded in 1871: the expulsion of Catholic Austria from Germany in the war of 1866 and the creation of a 'small Germany' under Prussian domination had drastically altered the political balance of the confessions. This was followed by the so-called *Kulturkampf*, in which Bismarck attempted to limit the independence of the Catholic church, in which he saw the representative partly of a foreign power – the Vatican – and partly of regional or national minorities reluctant to admit the legitimacy of the new German Empire – above all, Poles, Alsatians and Bavarians. Moreover, Bismarck thought that the new Centre Party, which was backed by the Catholic church, threatened to bring all these forces together in a coalition that would threaten the existence of the Empire. During the 1870s laws were duly passed abolishing church supervision of schools, dissolving the Jesuit order and expelling its members from the country, making a university training in philosophy, history and German literature compulsory qualifications for aspirants to the priesthood, and giving disciplinary powers over the church to state-appointed bodies. From 1874 the Prussian government began to imprison and expel bishops and priests who resisted these laws. By 1876 over 1,400 parishes in Prussia were without priests, and the church was refusing to fill vacant bishoprics. The situation gradually returned to normal as the *Kulturkampf* came to an end in the late 1870s and early 1880s, but by then the damage had been done.[48]

Catholics felt themselves to be a persecuted minority in the new Empire: they quickly developed a complex network of social and political institutions with which they could preserve their identity and protect themselves against persecution. These included social clubs, leisure organizations, Peasant Leagues, workers' associations, women's societies, in short, a whole range of secular bodies which catered for the interests and needs of all categories of the Catholic laity. Perhaps the two most important such organizations were the Catholic Centre Party and the People's Association for Catholic Germany. As a focus of political resistance to the policies of the *Kulturkampf*, the Centre Party rapidly gained widespread support in the Catholic community, and by the end of the 1870s was the largest single party in the Reichstag, a position which it held until 1912, when it was superseded in this respect by the Social

Democrats. After 1890, indeed, as the National Liberals and Conservatives declined, the support of the Centre became crucial for every German government, and the only attempt to do without it – the Bülow Block of 1906–9 – was a failure. Particularly in the 1870s and 1880s, led by the energetic Ludwig Windthorst, the Centre gave political expression to the aspirations of Catholics and their outrage at the iniquities of the *Kulturkampf*.[49] It was in the 1890s, however, that the real proliferation of Catholic social organizations began, spearheaded by the People's Association for Catholic Germany, founded in that year. This organization, which combined social-welfare activities with efforts for social reform, education and propaganda to keep the Catholic working classes from defecting to the Social Democrats, had no fewer than 800,000 members by the eve of the First World War. With all these organizations, the Catholic community had succeeded by the 1870s in building up a social 'subculture', which was to a perceptible degree cut off from the main institutions of German society.[50]

This development was imitated in many respects by Protestantism, but without a great degree of success. For this a number of reasons can be adduced. Perhaps most important was the fact that Protestants were not persecuted as Catholics had been in the *Kulturkampf*, despite the effects of its legislation on the Evangelical church, and so they felt no such need to form a distinct social community. To this can be added the closer ties between clergy and laity among Catholics, already alluded to. In consequence, as Vernon Lidtke has pointed out,

> For many Catholic workers, industrialization and urbanization did not lead to estrangement from the larger religious community.... Within the social-cultural milieu of Catholicism, workers, as well as others, found not only religious worship, but most of the ingredients for a way of life.... Piety, sobriety and success were not preconditions for belonging; ritual observance, communal approval and even poverty would do.... Evangelicals, holding firmly to puritanical ethics, worked on the principle that all 'pleasure seeking' should be excluded. They were the only workers' clubs in all of Germany to ban dancing at festivals. They believed that a worker's confessional club should above all be religious. Within the context of German Protestantism that meant that they also had to be patriotic, monarchical and in favour of social harmony.[51]

This clearly limited their appeal to a relatively small section of workers, while, as Lidtke remarks, 'Catholic clubs could emphasise secular activities because their members lived within a milieu strongly influenced and held together by confessional consensus' (p. 33).

An important consequence of all this was the development of a strong

Christian trade union movement in Imperial Germany, which, although nominally interconfessional, was in practice dominated in every sense by Catholic workers. By 1912 there were more than 3,000 Catholic workers' clubs with a total membership approaching half a million; this contrasted strongly with Protestant workers' clubs, which at that date numbered only 644 with a total membership of just over 100,000, figures which appear even more striking when we remember that the great majority of workers in Germany were Protesants, not Catholics. By the eve of the First World War, too, Christian (that is, in effect, Catholic) trade unions had also emerged, numbering no fewer than 350,000 members in 1912. These were genuine trade unions which, as David Crew has remarked, 'presented a position which was neither strictly confessional nor *wirtschaftsfriedlich* (economically non-combative)'.[52] Christian trade unions were quite prepared to go on strike to further their members' interests, and frequently did. But, as Crew has shown in his interesting study of the Christian trade unions in action during the metalworkers' strike in Dortmund, they were reluctant to do so in conjunction with the Social Democratic party-dominated 'free' trade unions and so – given their considerable strength – exercised a divisive influence within the labour movement as a whole.

Attempts, such as the People's Association for Catholic Germany and the Christian trade unions, to come to terms with industrial society and to forge instruments with which the Catholic community could play a role in the new and rapidly evolving German Empire of the late nineteenth and early twentieth centuries, could not disguise the fact that Catholics were proportionately less well represented than Protestants in many of the major institutions of the new Germany, such as universities. By and large, they were poor, and lived in small towns or the countryside, and were under-represented in the population of the large cities. There were relatively few Catholics in the senior ranks of the civil service in Prussia, and discrimination in state employment went down to more humble levels. As David Blackbourn has noted, for example, 'in towns where Catholics made up a majority or a large minority of the population, professional employees in the municipal gas and electricity works, abattoir, hospital and architect's department were commonly non-Catholic.'[53] Even in Catholic Bavaria Catholics were under-represented in university posts. Socio-economic backwardness may well have helped slow down the process of secularization among Catholics, since secularization seems to have proceeded fastest among the population in the big cities and urban areas where Catholics were under-represented, and among the industrial and professional middle classes where they also failed to establish a presence commensurate with the overall size of the Catholic population in the country as a whole. Relative socio-economic backwardness also in the long run tended to make the Centre Party something of a spokesman for peasant, small-town and petty bourgeois interests; and the desire to achieve equality prodded the party ever more sharply into demonstrating that, whatever Bismarck might have claimed, it was more than loyal to the German empire and its policies in the world.

Despite all the efforts of the churches and the numerous secular organizations which they founded, however, their popularity gradually waned as Germany industrialized. Nominally, indeed, the overwhelming majority of Germans remained members of one or other church. But in view of the fact that church membership was legally enforced in most German states until the 1870s, and was legally difficult to repudiate even after then, it is hardly surprising that few took the complicated step of 'leaving the church', especially since this involved braving all kinds of social prejudice as well. Figures of church attendance in urban–industrial centres, however, tell a very different story. In 1906–8 as few as 8 per cent of Protestant church members in Hamburg took Communion, rising to about 15 per cent in Berlin, and few of these are likely to have belonged to the working class. When the social investigator Adolf Levenstein asked a large sample of German workers a few years before the First World War whether or not they believed in God, 62 per cent of the textile workers he questioned said they did not, 50 per cent of the metalworkers agreed with this view, and 44 per cent of the miners were also atheists. Most of the rest failed to answer the question, while the average in all three categories of those who did say they believed in God was only 13 per cent. No wonder a French investigator described the German cities in 1908 as 'spiritual cemeteries', observing that in Berlin only the 'official world, taking its cue from the Emperor, still went to Church'.[54]

The spread of secularization in the big cities and towns of industrial Germany was an uneven process. The intensity of religious practice varied from area to area in the countryside, not only between Catholics and Protestants, or between independent peasants and landless labourers working on sugar-beet cultivation on large estates, but also for historical reasons going back as far as the seventeenth century. Nevertheless, it seems clear that migration to the towns played a crucial role in the secularization of the urban and rural population. Rainer Marbach's study of a Protestant rural area near Göttingen between 1890 and 1915 shows a steady fall in church attendance in the poorer districts, where workers increasingly went to the town during the day, or for the week, or even for the whole summer, to find employment – a development facilitated by the construction of a local railway network towards the end of the century. In the better-off villages, where the richer soil could support a functioning peasant economy, church attendance fell more slowly. Similar processes were taking place in many parts of Germany at this time. As Marbach comments,

Many of those who lived on the land became subjected to processes of social and geographical mobility through taking up work outside the village where they dwelt and through the separation of residence and workplace which this involved. They accumulated impressions and experiences which relativized their accustomed, traditional norms and values, took them back to their local environment and spread them there. Outsiders who came to work on the land had a similar effect, but such an effect was also achieved by other developments such as changing and proliferating possibilities of communicating with the rest of the world, for example through improvements in transport facilities and the spread of information through newspapers.[55]

Thus the increasing geographical mobility of ordinary Germans in the late nineteenth century encouraged de-Christianization, not only in the rapidly growing towns and cities but also in the countryside.

This development took place particularly among men, for it was generally the women who remained behind to look after the smallholding or vegetable garden while their menfolk went to the town to look for work. It was not surprising, therefore, that the difference in church attendance between men and women in rural areas tended to be smaller in the winter, when the men were present in the community all the time, than in the summer, when they were not. In the area investigated by Marbach, some 60 per cent of the congregation attending Sunday service in the parish of Roringen in 1892 were women; by 1912 this figure had risen to 75 per cent. In roughly the same period the proportion of women among Sunday service congregations in the parish of Bischhausen rose from 54 per cent to 67 per cent (1896–1914) and in Kerstlingerode from 56 per cent to 67 per cent (1896–1914). In areas where the urban influence made itself felt directly in the daily life of the home, as in Geismar, which at the turn of the century was being transformed into a suburb of the expanding town of Göttingen, female participation in church services also began to decline. Already in 1910, for example, the clergy in Geismar were complaining that women were ceasing to attend the Sunday services and overall church attendance was 6.3 per cent below the average for the area, whereas it had only been 2.9 per cent below in 1902.[56] In his article in *European Studies Review*,[57] Hugh McLeod explored some of the reasons for the differential pattern of secularization between working-class men and women; what might perhaps be stressed here is that the question of gender is one that deserves investigation in many other areas of the social history of religion as well. Religion could be a source of oppression for women, an ideological apparatus of male domination confining women to certain roles, regulating their sexuality and restricting their freedom of action. For example, the church underlined the belief that women were 'unclean' after childbirth: a systematic analysis of such beliefs as this in the context of popular religion would certainly repay investigation. Pietism could console peasant women for the increasing burden of hard work and suffering which they had to endure in many parts of rural Germany during the nineteenth century and so stifle any thoughts of rebellion. Yet religion could also offer women opportunities they lacked in secular life, such as a legitimate means of meeting and acting together outside the home – though it is fair to say that the church also did its best to destroy secular institutions of this sort, such as village spinning evenings, which it saw as occasions for immorality; the absence of such institutions in an urban context may actually have increased women's allegiance to the church. Clearly there is a need for more systematic research into the relationship of religion and gender, the ways in which religious belief contributed to the definition of sex-roles and sexual identity, and the different ways in which religion was experienced by men and women.

As secularization took its course during the nineteenth century, and attendance at church declined in the great cities and industrial heartlands of Germany to negligible proportions, contemporaries began to note that the new mass ideologies of the age – nationalism, socialism, or even the belief in progress – were comparable in many ways to the Christian beliefs they were replacing. As Wolfgang Schieder notes, the cult of the early socialist leader Lassalle had noticeably religious overtones, while a large number of commentators have remarked upon the millenarian aspects of nineteenth-century socialism.[58] Yet some care has to be exercised before we start talking, as Schieder does, of such ideologies as *ersatz* religions. Religious eschatology, for example, is essentially outside human time, while the socialist ideology of the late nineteenth and early twentieth century envisaged a social revolution occurring within human society and involving a continuation of society for the foreseeable future, albeit in a different form. Similarly, while we approach religion as a form of knowledge, such an approach will only bring us so far. Following Michel Foucault, we can certainly look at knowledge as a kind of power relation, a view which in the context of religion is amply justified by the existence of the clergy (or, for that matter, of witches); but ultimately, religion cannot be portrayed simply as a form of knowledge, acquired through emotion; conversion, chiliasm and enthusiasm were its foundations; above all, it involved experience of the supernatural, something which was absent from even the most irrational of the ideologies which are commonly argued to have replaced it. One should also distinguish between similarities in the outward forms of certain aspects of socialism or nationalism and religion, and the profound differences in their content, which far outweighed such superficial similarities. Finally, the concept of political ideology as ersatz or surrogate religion ultimately rests on psychological assumptions about people's 'need' for religion, which have no empirical justification and which ultimately hinder the social historian in the attempt to study religion in its social context by making the social context irrelevant.[59]

Secularization was certainly an uneven, long-term process, but its existence cannot be doubted. Of course, its different aspects must be carefully distinguished. The decline in attendance at ordinary church services was not followed until much later by a decline in the popularity of church rituals marking the transition of the individual from one stage of life to the next, the rites of passage, such as baptisms, confirmations, weddings and funerals. Such ceremonies were evidently widely felt to be important long after everyday churchgoing had fallen to negligible levels. Among oppressed minorities in German society – notably Poles and Jews – religion continued to play a vital role in preserving communal identity. Absence from church did not mean an immediate abandonment of popular religious beliefs, which were in any case, above all in Protestant areas, only tied to official religion in the loosest way. Indeed, popular religious belief survives in an attenuated but recognizably crypto-materialist form in industrial society with horoscopes, fortune-telling and ritual avoidance of bad luck. It is also arguable that the small minority of practising Christians who remain are more deeply committed to their church than were their predecessors when they were in the majority. Nevertheless in the last analysis it seems undeniable that the role of the sacred and the supernatural in everyday life has been substantially reduced over the last two centuries or so.

NOTES

1 L. Stone, 'The Revival of Narrative', in Stone, *The Past and the Present* (London, 1981), pp. 74–96, provides a good introduction to these developments, though the word 'narrative' is not perhaps the correct one to use in this context, and the extent to which the new developments are a reaction against quantification is to my mind overdrawn.
2 For references to some of this work, see Stone, 'Revival of Narrative'.
3 R. W. Scribner, 'Sacred and Secular: Problems of the Social Study of Religion in Pre-industrial Europe', SSRC Research Seminar Group on Modern German Social History, unpublished paper, University of East Anglia, 1981, p 1.
4 See Introduction, above, for further details and references.
5 See e.g. the introductory chapters to R. J. Evans and W. R. Lee (eds.), *The German Family* (London, 1981); R. J. Evans and W. R. Lee (eds.) *The German Peasantry* (London, 1986), for further discussion of this point.
6 See Chapter 1, above.
7 cf. the contribution of W. Schieder to the special issue of *European Studies Review*, vol. 12, no. 3 (1982), from which the present chapter is drawn.
8 See W. Schieder, 'Kirche und Religion: Sozialgeschichtliche Aspekte der Trierer Wallfahrt von 1844', *Archiv für Sozialgeschichte*, vol. 14 (1974), pp. 419–54; the special issue on religion of *Geschichte und Gesellschaft*, vol. 3 (1977), pp. 219–405, for further comments on this situation. Also, from an early modernist, R. van Dülmen, 'Religions-geschichte in der Historischen Sozialforschung', *Geschichte und Gesellschaft*, vol. 6 (1980), pp. 36–59.
9 E.g. in the prince-bishoprics and ecclesiastical states.
10 Sometimes referred to confusingly as 'secularization'.

11 N. M. Hope, 'Some secular issues which worried German churchmen in the 19th century', unpublished MS. (Glasgow, 1981).
12 A. J. P. Taylor, *The Course of German History* (2nd ed., London, 1966), p. 9.
13 C. Köhle-Hezinger, 'Religion in bäuerlichen Gemeinden: Wegbereiter der Industrialisierung?', (SSRC Research Seminar in Modern German Social History, unpublished paper, University of East Anglia, 1981), pp. 6–7. For another, much more extensive, study of religion in rural society, see H. Hörger, *Kirche, Dorfreligion und Bäuerliche Gesellschaft* (Munich, 1978). Köhle-Hezinger has also written an important study of interconfessional rivalry, *Evangelisch–Katholisch: Untersuchungen zum konfessionellen Vorurteil und Konflikt im 19. und 20. Jahrhundert* (Tübingen, 1976). On this subject see also K.-S. Kramer, 'Protestantisches in der Volkskultur Frankens: Konfessionelle Rivalität und Nachbarschaft', *Hessische Blätter für Volkskunde*, vol. 60 (1969), pp. 77–92.
14 A. Bischoff-Luithlen, *Der Schwabe und die Obrigkeit* (Stuttgart, 1979), p. 68.
15 Ibid., p. 91.
16 Ibid., p. 99.
17 U. Jeggle, *Kiebingen – eine Heimatgeschichte*, Untersuchungen des Ludwig-Uhland-Instituts für empirische Kulturforschung (Tübingen, 1977), vol. 44; A. Ilien and U. Jeggle, *Leben auf dem Dorf* (Köln, 1978).
18 W. R. Lee, *Population Growth, Economic Development and Social Change in Bavaria 1750–1850* (New York, 1977), p. 299.
19 Scribner, 'Sacred and Secular', p. 26.
20 P. Bois, *Paysans de L'Ouest* (Le Mans, 1960).,
21 See Lee, *Population Growth, Economic Development and Social Change.*
22 Ibid., p. 299.
23 Ibid., pp. 295–300; cf. F. M. Phayer, *Religion und das gewöhnliche Volk in Bayern in der Zeit von 1750 bis 1850* (Munich, 1970).
24 Köhle-Hezinger, 'Religion in bäuerlichen Gemeinden', p. 6.
25 Scribner, 'Sacred and Secular', p. 21.
26 H. Bächthold-Stäubli (ed.), *Handwörterbuch des deutschen Abergulabene* (9 vols, (1928–42); Scribner, 'Sacred and Secular', p. 22. See also the interesting work of D. Sabean, *Power in the Blood* (Cambridge, 1984).
27 Bächthold-Staubli, *Handwörterbuch*, 'Abendmahl'. See also Scribner, 'Sacred and Secular', pp. 24–5; and, for a rare modern study, A. Hoffmann, 'Aberglaube und religiöse Schwärmerei in der Pfalz im 19. Jahrhundert', *Archiv für mittelrheinische Kirchengeschichte*, vol. 27 (1975), pp. 203–13.
28 H. McLeod, *Religion and the People of Western Europe 1789–1970* (Oxford, 1981), p. 63.
29 Bächthold-Stäubli, *Handwörterbuch*, 'Hexe', 'Pflug', 'Scharfrichter' etc.
30 W. K. Blessing, *Staat und Kirche in der Gesellschaft: Institutionelle Autorität und mentaler Wandel in Bayern während des 19. Jahrhunderts* (Göttingen, 1982). Pupils of Karl Bosl in Munich, such as Blessing and Phayer, have been in the forefront of the social history of religious belief in 19th century Germany (see also n.23, above).
31 Blessing, *Staat und Kirche in der Gesellschaft*, p. 21.
32 A good deal has been written on popular religiosity within the bounds of church religion, especially on pilgrimages: see for example R. Böck, 'Volksfrömmigkeit und Wallfahrtswesen im Gebiet des heutigen Landkreises Friedberg/Schwaben', *Bayerisches Jahrbuch für Volkskunde* (1969), pp. 22–79; W. Brückner, 'Volksfrömmigkeit – Aspekte religiöser Kultur', *Kölner Zeitschrift für Soziologie und Sozialpsychologie*, vol. 31 (1979), pp. 559–69; E. Gatz, *Rheinische Volksmission im 19. Jahrhundert* (Düsseldorf, 1963); M. Scharfe *et al.*, *Volksfrömmigkeit: Bildzeugnisse aus Vergangenheit und Gegenwart* (Stuttgart, 1967); K. Rahner *et al.* (eds), *Volksreligion – Religion des Volkes* (Stuttgart, 1979).
33 J. Sperber, *Popular Catholicism in Nineteenth-Century Germany* (Princeton, NJ, 1984).
34 Ibid., pp. 293–4. See also J. J. Lee, *The Modernization of Irish Society* (Dublin, 1976).
35 I. Farr, 'From Anti-Catholicism to Anticlericalism: Catholic Politics and the Peasantry in Bavaria, 1860–1900', *European Studies Review*, vol. 13 (1983), pp. 249–69.
36 O. Chadwick, *The Secularization of the European Mind in the Nineteenth Century* (Cambridge, 1975).
37 Quoted in H. Plaul, *Landarbeiterleben im 19. Jahrhundert* (East Berlin, 1979), pp. 299–300.

38 Ibid., p. 301.
39 Ibid., p. 299.
40 Ibid., p. 303.
41 Quoted in McLeod, *Religion and the People of Western Europe*, p. 71.
42 Ibid., p. 101.
43 Quoted ibid., p. 98.
44 cf. the general discussion of these points in McLeod, *Religion and the People of Western Europe*.
45 H. McLeod, 'Protestantism and the Working Class in Imperial Germany', *European Studies Review*, vol. 12, no. 3 (1982), pp. 323–44, and the same author's *Religion and the People of Western Europe*, p. 84.
46 Plaul, *Landarbeiterleben im 19. Jahrhundert*, p. 306.
47 G. Bormann, 'Studien zu Berufsbild und Berufswirklichkeit evangelischer Pfarrer in Württemberg', *Social Compass*, vol. 13, no. 2 (1966), pp. 95–137.
48 The literature on the *Kulturkampf* is vast. For a recent useful study, see C. Weber, *Kirchliche Politik zwischen Rom, Berlin und Trier 1876–1888* (Mainz, 1970); and Weber's more wide-ranging *Der Kulturkampf in Deutschland 1871–1890* (Göttingen, 1962). Sperber, *Popular Catholicism* ch. 5, has a useful account of the local dimensions and suggests further literature.
49 See, most recently, M. Anderson, *Windthorst: A Political Biography* (Oxford, 1981).
50 See D. Blackbourn, *Class, Religion and Local Politics in Wilhelmine Germany* (London, 1980) for an introduction to these problems.
51 V. L. Lidtke, 'Social Class and Secularisation in Imperial Germany: The Working Classes', *Yearbook of the Leo Baeck Institute*, vol. 25 (New York, 1980), pp. 21–40, esp. pp. 30–3.
52 D. Crew, 'Steel, Sabotage and Socialism: the Strike at the Dortmund "Union" Steel Works in 1911', in R. J. Evans (ed.), *The German Working Class* (London, 1982), pp. 108–41, at p. 125. See more generally W. Patch, *Christian Trade Unions in the Weimar Republic* (London, 1985); E. Dorn Brose, *Christian Labor and the Politics of Frustration in Imperial Germany* (Washington, DC, 1985).
53 D. Blackbourn, 'The Problems of Democratisation: German Catholics and the Role of the Centre Party', in R. J. Evans (ed.), *Society and Politics in Wilhelmine Germany* (London, 1978), pp. 160–85. The substantial literature on the Catholic Centre Party and its social milieu can be approached through the English-language publications of E. L. Evans, *The German Center Party 1870–1933* (Carbondale, Ill., 1981); and R. J. Ross, *Beleaguered Tower: The Dilemma of Political Catholicism in Wilhelmine Germany* (Notre Dame, Ind., 1976).
54 H. Lichtenberger, *L'Allemagne Moderne* (Paris, 1908), p. 281, quoted in G. Castellan, *L'Allemagne du Weimar* (Paris, 1972), p. 210.
55 R. Marbach, *Säkularisierung und sozialer Wandel im 19. Jahrhundert* (Göttingen, 1978), p. 31.
56 Ibid., pp. 49–50. For other assessments of Protestantism and the decline of religiosity, above all in urban areas, see K. Tenfelde, *Sozialgeschichte der Bergarbeiterschaft an der Ruhr im 19. Jahrhundert* (Bonn, 1977), pp. 369–87; W. Köllmann, *Sozialgeschichte der Stadt Barmen im 19. Jahrhundert* (Tübingen, 1960), pp. 198–211; A. Kraus, 'Gemeindeleben und Industrialisierung: Das Beispiel des evangelischen Kirchenkreises Bochum', in J. Reulecke and W. Weber (eds), *Fabrik, Familie, Feierabend* (Wuppertal, 1978), pp. 273–96.
57 Mcleod, 'Protestantism' (n. 45, above).
58 See H. Grote, *Sozialdemokratie und Religion* (Frankfurt, 1975), pp. 289–300.
59 I am following here the discussion at the seminar mentioned in the introduction to this chapter; but see also the sensible remarks on this point in V. L. Lidtke, *The Alternative Culture* (New York, 1984). Social Democratic attitudes to religion are also usefully discussed in J. Hunley, 'The Working Classes, Religion and Social Democracy in the Düsseldorf Area, 1867–1878', *Societas*, vol. 4 (1974), pp. 131–49; and the religious affiliations of workers are given a substantial chapter in S. H. F. Hickey, *Workers in Imperial Germany: Miners in the Ruhr* (Oxford, 1985). See also H. McLeod, 'Religion in the British and German labour movements c. 1890–1914: a comparison', *Bulletin of the Society for the Study of Labour History*, vol. 51, pt. 1 (1986), pp. 25–35.

5

In Pursuit of the Untertanengeist: Crime, Law and Social Order in German History

One of the aspects of the 'German mentality' most frequently commented on is the so-called 'spirit of submission' or *Untertanengeist*. An invitation to give a paper to the inaugural conference of the International Association for the History of Crime and Criminal Justice, held in Washington, DC, in 1980, seemed a good opportunity to gather some thoughts on the subject in a survey of the relevant literature. My studies of feminism and the labour movement had already raised some questions about authority and obedience in German history, and this led on to a new research project in the area of crime and punishment, which has eventually become concentrated on a social and political history of the death penalty since the eighteenth century, currently under preparation. The history of crime is an area of the German past which has received little attention until very recently, although there is a rich sociological and statistical literature available dating back to the nineteenth century itself. In 1985, therefore, when the research seminar on German Social History originally funded by the Social Science Research Council (now Economic and Social Research Council), and by this time running with the support of the University of East Anglia, came to consider this subject, I revised and extended the Washington paper to take account of more recent work. It appears here in a condensed version, with some of the detail removed, and stands, I hope, as a brief introduction to a rapidly growing field of research, as well as a general reflection on one of the most oft-repeated clichés of German history. Unlike the other chapters in this book, it has not been published before.

I

Germany has generally been regarded by historians as the paradigm of an orderly society. Obedience to authority and a spirit of submissiveness to superiors – the famous 'spirit of submission' (*Untertanengeist*) – have been

156

cited by generations of commentators as prime characteristics of the 'German frame of mind' from the eighteenth century to the twentieth. A. J. P. Taylor, in his influential book *The Course of German History* (1945), traced this element in the national character all the way back to Luther:

> Luther gave to Germany a consciousness of national existence and, through his translation of the Bible, a national tongue; but he also gave to Germany the Divine Right of Kings, or rather the Divine Right of any established authority. Obedience was the first, and last, duty of the Christian man. The State can do no wrong; therefore, whatever the State orders, that the Christian man can do without danger to his conscience.[1]

Of the eighteenth century, R. R. Palmer has observed that 'Both in Prussia and in the smaller states there was a great respect for authority, a disposition to trust the rulers and their expert advisers'.[2] William L. Shirer, in perhaps the most widely read of all books on German history, *The Rise and Fall of the Third Reich* (1960), wrote that 'acceptance of autocracy, of blind obedience to the petty tyrants who ruled as princes, became ingrained in the German mind ... [In Prussia] individuals were taught not only by the kings and the drill sergeants but by the philosophers that their role in life was one of obedience, work, sacrifice and duty'.[3] 'The abasement of the individual before the State' was described by yet another historian as an essential element in the German mentality.[4] In fact, the list of historians who have made similar assertions about the German attitude to state authority could be extended almost indefinitely.

The principal reason for such a wide-ranging historiographical consensus is obvious: it is part of an attempt by historians to explain the long-term origins of the catastrophes that have beset Germany in the twentieth century, above all the triumph of Hitler in 1933 and the comparative lack of internal opposition to his rule under the Third Reich. On this basis, a number of different historiographical tendencies have combined to embed the concept of the *Untertanengeist* in the scholarly literature. First, the older generation of conservative historians who had grown up in Germany before 1914 looked back with nostalgia to what seemed to them in the light of the turbulence of the Weimar Republic to have been a society of peace and order before the First World War. To this was added the influence of Allied wartime propaganda in 1939–45 which portrayed the German character in terms which have continued to dominate popular stereotypes of the German in Britain and elsewhere to the present day: it was depicted as immutably militaristic, disciplined, orderly and subservient. This line of argument was presented in many publications; among the most influential was Rohan Butler's *The Roots of National Socialism* (1941). Taylor's *The Course of German History*, which was also written during the Second World War, and had its origins in a piece written for inclusion in what the author later described as 'one of the many compilations which were being put together in order to explain to the conquerors what sort of country they were conquering',[5] belongs essentially to the same category. This tradition of writing about the German mind was updated during the cold war, when Anglo-American writers tried to identify servility and obedience to authority with the East and freedom and individualism with the West, and claimed that until the Marshall Plan Germany had belonged fundamentally to the former category.[6]

Another way of putting the same basic idea across was developed by the radical liberal historians of the 1960s and 1970s, who sought to enlist the aid of functionalist sociology in their critique of Germany's past and their championship of a theory of continuity from Frederick the Great to Hitler. Germany, they argued, was a classic case of partial or retarded modernization, in which the feudal–absolutist traditions of the eighteenth century lived on into the twentieth. Hans-Ulrich Wehler, for example, in a widely read history of Imperial Germany published in 1973 and now in its fourth edition, wrote that

> The spirit of submission ... allowed people to accept passively arbitrary acts and excesses of state power, to react with silent and exaggerated caution to the petty chicaneries of everyday life, to step aside with doffed cap for the army lieutenant on the pavement, to see the splendour of the state reflected even in the village policeman, and in general to submit rather than to protest.[7]

In this view, police, school, church, army, family – in short, a whole range of socialising institutions described by Wehler as 'the matrix of authoritarian society' – functioned to instil in the Germans of the pre-1914 era a timorous respect for state authority. Small wonder, then, that – as he went on to claim – this affected daily life as well as political attitudes and produced 'the high degree of security which the German big cities then enjoyed in comparison to their American counterparts ... There is no doubt that one could live in them without being perpetually afraid for one's safety' (p. 132). Even Marxist commentators have not been immune from such views. Alf Lüdtke, for instance, has recently argued that in the transition from feudalism to capitalism, Prussia enjoyed a uniquely potent mixture of overt and symbolic violence, of coercive and hegemonic authority, in the attempt to discipline the workforce, protect property and prevent revolution:

> In Prussia [the transition to capitalism] took place under the umbrella of a bureaucratic state machine. The rhetoric of [the] authoritarian control of society, the welfare and police aims of the State machine, [and] its

increasing [use of] legal norms, were well designed to legitimate [the] violent practice of police power. In contrast to England, [this] continually affected the entire daily life of [the king's subjects. The daily activities of] officials ... came in time to pervade [the whole of society. They] served to prevent, or, at least, to calm any efforts [by the dominated classes to develop an alternative social praxis, not only] on the streets and in the inns, but also in the factories, on the fields, and inside their homes ... [All this remained] at work long after the breakdown of the Kaiserreich, right into the fascist period, by disposing even the majority of the "immediate producers" to passivity in 1933.[8]

Here the emphasis is on capitalist strategies rather than on feudal survivals; yet the actual content of the argument is much the same.

Nor have such views been confined to the historians. Thoughtful contemporaries, too, were apt to comment on the orderliness of German society. The philosopher Friedrich Paulsen, for instance, remarked on a visit to England in 1904, that 'In Germany, far into the middle classes, people have the idea that the policeman's business is to order them about; in England, everyone regards him as a man who is there for everyone's safety and protection. In England, everybody is a citizen; in Germany, everybody is a subject.' After ascribing this to the militaristic and autocratic traditions of the state in Germany, he went on to concede, in a revealing aside, that 'our military discipline has its good side, too: it has been remarkably successful in instilling into our population a taste for good deportment, orderliness and cleanliness. In England I have heard my wife exclaim: "One would have to go a long way in Germany to see such slovenliness among both sexes of the lower classes!"'[9] Similarly, the great scientist Albert Einstein spoke in 1919 of the 'hereditary slave mentality' of the Germans. And the sociologist Max Weber wrote in comparable terms. In other countries, he commented,

> the rise or the continuation of that internalized surrender to authority which strikes foreign observers as so lacking in dignity, but which has remained in Germany a legacy of unlimited patrimonial princely rule which will be difficult to dispose of, has been prevented or destroyed. From a political point of view, the German was and is decidedly a "subject" in the most profound sense of the world.[10]

In a similar vein, the American observer Raymond Fosdick, in reporting the results of a study-tour of police forces in Britain, France, Germany, Austria-Hungary, Italy, Belgium and the Netherlands carried out on the eve of the First World War, used the German attitude to law and order as a typical example of the situation obtaining on the European continent, in contrast to the English popular mentality in this respect. Fosdick was working for the New York Bureau of Social Hygiene, which sought to achieve voluntary methods of curbing prostitution, and he had an interest, therefore, in proving that the social control of crime was more effective than the use of legal and coercive state sanctions. Still, his study was thorough, painstaking and full of shrewd observations. His general conclusion, therefore, is worth quoting at some length:

> England is frankly individualistic in her point of view. The Englishman wants to mind his own business, to look to his own safety, to safeguard his own rights, to use his own judgement – in a word, to be let alone. The German point of view, on the other hand, may fairly be called paternalistic. The State must care for its own. So far from resenting it the German seems to require constant direction; without it he gives the appearance of being unable to take care of himself. Orderliness in Germany is not born of individual self-control; it is a social habit enforced by the army of *"Verboten"* signs; the things forbidden cover almost every phase of human activity. In all public conveyances and in stations, on the streets and in the parks, the citizen is informed by sign and official warning not only as to actions prohibited but as to actions mandatory. To these symbols of order the law-abiding German invariably and instinctively submits. One gets the impression that the Englishman's respect for law is more basic, more a matter of principle than that of the German. The respect of the latter runs rather to correctness in outward form, according to the prescription of public authority.[11]

Thus whereas in Germany public places were spotlessly clean, vandalism unknown and public disorder infrequent, the same could not be said of England. 'The task of the English constable in maintaining order, if less varied, is frequently more difficult than that of his brother officer in Germany' (p. 9).

Other foreign contemporaries agreed that the orderliness of German society was the result of an intrusive police presence on the streets. 'German cities', remarked the American Ray Stannard Baker in 1900, 'are safer for strangers, perhaps, than any other in the world'; but Baker also found 'the wild west in me slowly suffocating' on his German visit, because of constant police supervision.[12] And when the heroes of Jerome K. Jerome's celebrated comic novel *Three Men in a Boat* went to Germany, they discovered much the same sort of thing. 'They are a law-abiding people, the Germans', remarked Jerome in the sequel *Three Men on the Bummel*, published in 1900;[13] and much of the novel's action consists of the heroes getting into tangles with German officialdom. England, complains one of his characters, 'affords but limited opportunity to the lover of the illegal'. London policemen did not seem to notice if they were being insulted; the common nocturnal habit of putting out the street-lamps for a lark simply resulted in a man coming round to light them again. But 'in Germany, on the other hand', reflected Jerome, 'trouble is to be had for the asking'.

> To any young Englishman yearning to get himself into a scrape, and finding himself hampered in his own country, I would advise a single ticket to Germany ... In the Police Guide to the Fatherland he will find set forth a list of the things the doing of which will bring to him interest and excitement. In Germany you must not hang your bed out of the window. He might begin with that. By waving his bed out of the window he could get into trouble before he had his breakfast. At home he might hang himself out of a window, and nobody would mind much, provided he did not obstruct any body's ancient lights or break away and injure any passer underneath.

After detailing a variety of possible ways of getting into a scrape – feeding a horse in the street, for instance, wearing a kilt ('fancy dress'), rambling about after dark 'in droves', or shooting with a crossbow in a public place, Jerome concluded, however, that perhaps the best 'piece of material for obtaining excitement in Germany is the simple domestic perambulator':

> What you may do with a *Kinderwagen*, as it is called, and what you may not, covers pages of German law ... You must not loiter with a perambulator, and you must not go too fast. You must not get in anybody's way with a perambulator, and if anybody gets in your way you must get out of their way ... You must not leave your perambulator anywhere, and only in certain places can you take it with you. I should say that in Germany you could go out with a perambulator and get into enough trouble in half an hour to last you for a month. Any young Englishman anxious for a row with the police could not do better than come over to Germany and bring his perambulator with him.

Jerome's conclusions were similar to Fosdick's. Germans, he said, lacked individual initiative: 'the German can rule others, and be ruled by others, but he cannot rule himself ... When his troubles will begin will be if by any chance something goes wrong with the governing machine'.

II

In pursuit of the historical origins of the orderly German, historians and commentators since the late nineteenth century have invariably turned their attention above all to the allied German traditions of state absolutism and legal positivism. Many features of the constitutions of German states and of the German Empire after 1871 derived from the absolutist practice of the eighteenth century. Thus ministerial responsibility and elected governments were unknown in Germany until 1918; government in Prussia and the Reich was carried out by bureaucrats appointed by the monarch and responsible to him alone, and in other constituent states of the federal Empire of 1871 and its predecessors, comparable arrangements obtained. Legislation through parliaments was limited in scope; a great many matters remained outside the purview of elected assemblies and were governed by decree or administrative order. Vital institutions such as the army and the police were virtually immune from parliamentary control. Moreover, the absolutist state was not simply a negative or neutral institution: it claimed the right to mould society, to control and direct it, to supervise its functions and to force it in any direction which it considered desirable. Far-reaching claims for the primacy of state power were made at all levels of theoretical abstraction and concrete action in the eighteenth and nineteenth centuries, from Hegel, who saw the state as 'mind on earth, consciously realising itself there' and based on 'the power of reason, actualising itself at will',[14] to the bureaucrats of the Prussian Reform Era, who argued that the state was duty bound to 'ensure that the general welfare is promoted and increased', and followed up this precept in practice through activities such as the state ownership and management of industrial, mining and trading enterprises in the first half of the nineteenth century.[15] In the absolutist tradition, law was seen as an aspect of the state, not as a separate institution, let alone a superior principle. Lawyers were simply state servants; and until the mid-nineteenth century, criminal trials in Prussia were held (except in areas such as the Rhineland, which had come under French rule) without juries, and in secret, without even the participation of the accused once the interrogation had been completed. German legal positivist terms theory said that the state ruled through law rather than arbitrarily; the only limits on its power were those to which it voluntarily submitted. This was the basis of the concept of the *Rechts-staat*, or state based on the rule of law. The idea that legal institutions were separate from the administration, or that they could act as a check upon its activities, was foreign to German legal traditions.[16] The consequences of this in terms of what activities were regarded as criminal were particularly striking: from 1878 to 1890, for instance, virtually all activities of the socialist movement were proscribed, and between 1890 and 1914, socialists were constantly being prosecuted for a variety of offences ranging from *lèse-majesté* to treason (which was given a wide definition in law). Socialists were criminal because the state decreed it, and prosecutions continued unabated even after the Social Democratic Party (SPD) had become the largest single party in the German legislature in 1912.[17]

These traditions had their practical expression in a whole host of provisions and regulations which gave the state far-reaching powers over every aspect of the citizen's life, while affording the citizen very few possibilities of protection and redress in return. State power could reach into the most intimate areas of a person's daily life. According to the Prussian law code of 1794 (the *Allgemeines Landrecht*, a comprehensive document which, among many other things, reflected the drive of the absolutist state to increase its population, and which was not finally replaced until 1900), it was an offence for a Prussian citizen not to report the fact that an unmarried woman of his or her acquaintance had had an illegitimate baby, on the ground that such cases, if unreported, carried the risk of infanticide. It was not only the law, however, which brought the state into the everyday life of its citizens. An essential difference between the German police force and its English counterpart lay in the absolutist origins of the former. *Polizei* originally denoted all the non-ecclesiastical functions of government. As government became more specialized in the seventeenth and eighteenth centuries, *Polizei* became a residual category including all state functions not transferred to specialist branches of the administration. Two consequences flowed from this fact. First, the German police enjoyed a very wide competence in the nineteenth century. As Fosdick pointed out:

> In Prussia there are Insurance Police, Mining Police, Water and Dike Police, Field and Forest Police, Cattle-Disease Police, Hunting Police, Fisheries Police, Trade Police, Fire Police, Political Police, Roads Police, Health Police, Building Police and a score of others ... In Berlin, the fire department, the health department, the prison department, the building department (including the condemnation of land for public purposes) and certain functions of the charity department are all branches of the huge police organization. The police supervise the markets and the sale of provisions; they pass judgment on the quality of foodstuffs; they exercise an oversight of public assemblies and meetings; they abate nuisances; they inspect lodging houses, cafés and places of amusement; they supervise druggists, veterinaries and the details of various professions; they prepare construction plans for street and river-front improvement; they keep a strict watch on certain classes of banking institutions; they frame regulations for the public conduct of citizens and mete out punishment for violations. A simple list of their functions covers forty-six pages of the official police handbook.[18]

Similarly, the Hamburg police's reports on its activities in the first half of the nineteenth century regularly included some 140 separate items, such as 'concealed birth of a child', 'unseemly behaviour of servants', 'hiring of servants without permission', 'playing of dance music without permission', 'contravention of the censorship', 'throwing snow off the roof in the morning after the permitted hour', 'holding of a masked ball without permission', 'failure to follow a police order *re* cleaning of chimneys' or simply 'causing a nuisance'.[19]

Such categories indicate a second peculiarity of the German police in the nineteenth century: not only was the area of the police's competence extremely wide, but the independence, unaccountability and general powers of the police were also greater than in England. The police had the right to frame rules and regulations with the force of law and to punish those who contravened them. These covered most of the areas of competence already mentioned and, though they could be overruled by superior administrative authorities or by the courts, they did not usually require the consent or approval of any body save the police authority itself. These orders were virtually without limitation on the activities which they covered. In Prussia, for example, there was a saving clause in the enabling law of 1850 allowing such orders to be made with regard to a whole range of subjects 'and all else which must be regulated through the police power in the interest of the communes and their members'.[20]

'On every side and at every turn', wrote Fosdick in 1914,

> the German citizen is confronted by newly adopted police regulations. Thus in Berlin, the Police President has recently issued ordinances regulating the colour of automobiles, the length of hatpins and the methods of purchasing fish and fowl ... In Stuttgart, a driver may not snap his whip as he guides his horses in the street; a customer may not fall asleep in a restaurant or a weary man on a park bench; a barber may not keep his official trade card in an inconspicuous place; a cab driver may not leave his position in front of the railway station during the hours in which the police decree he shall be on duty; a driver may not hold his reins improperly or go through the public streets without having the owner's name in a conspicuous place on his cart or carriage; a delivery boy may not coast on a hand-cart; a passenger may not alight from a train on the side away from the platform or while the train is in motion; children may not slide on a slippery sidewalk; a citizen may not be impertinent to a public official on duty nor offer any affront to his dignity. These regulations are not only negative, they are often positive; not only general, but particular and directed against specific parties. Thus a house owner *must* sprinkle his street in hot weather when ordered by the police or a certain striker *must* refrain from picketing when so directed or a given contractor *must* remove building encumbrances on demand. (pp. 27–8)

Each of these ordinances provided a specific penalty for violation. The police were empowered to imprison for up to fourteen days or impose a fine of up to 60 marks for infringement, without reference to the courts, without any trial procedure, and without the accused being heard in his or her defence. The fine was simply levied by post, as the result of a report from the officer concerned, by the police headquarters, and though there was a right of appeal to the courts, this was costly, cumbersome and time-consuming, and the evidence of the police was in any case granted a higher status than that of civilians in court procedure as a matter of policy. These powers were not sparingly used. In Stuttgart, for example, a city in liberal south Germany with about 300,000 inhabitants, 40,000 police penalties were imposed each year in the later Wilhelmine period, with fines totalling nearly 85,000 marks annually.[21] Earlier in the nineteenth century, as Alf Lüdtke has recently shown, police powers were even wider. For example, the Prussian police were obliged to place under observation, by laws dating from the immediate post-Napoleonic period, 'all those persons who, either on account of their previous way of life or of voluntary or involuntary lack of legal means of subsistence, endanger public safety', and in particular, 'all local inhabitants and strangers not in service and all unemployed journeymen'.[22] Supervision involved not only constant observation ('enquiries must be made in the public houses as to how much he consumes there, and how high the stakes are, if he plays cards', commented a police handbook of 1818), but also severe restrictions on the affected citizen's freedom of action ('The individual under police supervision must not be allowed to live outside the walls or in any place that renders observation difficult or impossible', declared the same handbook).[23] In addition, there were a large number of garrison towns in early-nineteenth-century Prussia, where the powers of the military authorities, and their tendency to intervene in the daily lives of civilians, were even more far-reaching. As the police gradually took over duties of maintaining order in the second half of the nineteenth century, so they took over many of these powers too.[24]

III

The orderliness and subservience of the German people thus appears to have been proverbial. Nineteenth-century Germany, it seems, was a society in which the traditions of the absolutist police state lived on to produce a docile, deferential and law-abiding population. Public deference to state authority was ensured by continual surveillance and control of everyday life by a police force equipped with wide and virtually untrammelled powers over a huge range of daily activities, and it was cemented by continual indoctrination from 'ideological state apparatuses' such as the school system, the conscript army and the official Protestant church. Clearly such a broad consensus of opinion cannot be entirely wrong. From the point of view of civil liberties and the rights of the individual citizen, there can be little doubt that the wide-ranging powers of the police created a considerable potential for arbitrary arrest and punishment against which the possibilities of redress were severely restricted. Of course, there were limits beyond which such arbitrary state power could not be exercised; and public opinion, the press and parliament (whether at national level or at the level of the federated states) constituted increasingly important pressures on the police and – where it too was involved in policing – the army, to stick to the rules, or at least not to violate them to excess. At the same time the law itself, the necessity for prosecution to go through the courts, the possibility of appeal against arbitrary condemnation, even the existence of police rulebooks, further limited the arbitrary exercise of power. Nor should one underestimate the extent to which the police in nineteenth-century England were accused of similar violations of civil liberties. Yet, with all these qualifications, the contrast with England remains valid enough, at least at the level of formal legal structures, practices and powers.

However, if we are to pursue the *Untertanengeist* any further, if we are to penetrate beyond the cliché of the submissive and orderly German character to the social and political realities of authority and obedience under the conditions of the nineteenth century, we need to ask whether the extensive legal and police powers of the state were really enforced in practice in the systematic and all-pervasive way in which the literature on German history implies they were. Strangely, however, this is a question which has received relatively little attention until recently, for historians have generally been content to approach the problem from the perspective of the state rather than from the perspective of society. That is to say, they have carefully examined state laws and constitutions, police powers, legal theory and so on, without very often going on to examine how all this was reflected in practice. The extent to which police powers were actually effective is generally treated as a matter of secondary importance, if indeed it is alluded to at all. Characteristic, for example, is Lüdtke's work, which deals with this problem in a mere aside: 'The insufficient numbers and the limited fitness of many police officers may well have put restrictions on the practical realization of such permanent regimentation', he reflects. 'None the less', he goes on, at least the authorities tried to regiment society, and that was what counted.[25] Yet in assessing the extent to which the 'spirit of submission' was actually embedded in the popular mentality, an examination of the actual effectiveness and incidence of state coercion is vitally necessary. From the uniformity of state authoritarianism, historians have deduced a uniformity of public submissiveness. This process has been reinforced recently by historians' tendency to turn to functionalist sociology and to view German society in the nineteenth century as a working system in which conflict was minimal and order guaranteed by the simple one-way operation of 'social control'.[26] Yet detailed research on the extent to which measures succeeded or failed has been as infrequent as comparable research on the actual operation of state coercion.

Like many other aspects of the theories of historical continuity recently dominant in German historiography, the stereotype of the orderly German rests on a contrast between the history of Germany and that of other countries which it has assumed rather than demonstrated. Many of the central assumptions on which it relies – about the nature of British society in the nineteenth century, for example – are highly questionable. In this case, such assumptions stand in stark contrast to the picture which is actually emerging of the changing relationships of crime, law and social order in countries such as Britain and France. As an example of this, the work of the leading historian of crime and the law in nineteenth-century Prussia, Dirk Blasius, is particularly illuminating. Blasius has situated his pioneering studies within the interpretative context of the currently dominant interpretation of Prussian and German history in the nineteenth century. According to this view, the feudal Junker aristocracy managed to retard the liberalization of the political system, and preserve the authoritarian state institutions and practices upon which their own hegemony depended, by co-opting substantial sections of the bourgeoisie into the ruling class without significantly changing that class's attitudes and behaviour, which thus remained feudal (or semi-feudal) in character. Thus in penal practice and law enforcement, Blasius argues, the Prussian nobility, through their domination of the eastern provincial diets and, more crucially, of the bureaucracy, frustrated attempts to liberalize the criminal code in the first half of the nineteenth century. Instead, they pushed through a new 'repressive strategy' with the support of the middle classes, who were alarmed at the increase of crime and social disorder in the period. As Blasius concludes,

Criminal law and penal practice demonstrate the importance of pre-bourgeois power élites in the 'solution' of the crime problem. The social distribution of power in the first half of the nineteenth century prevented the formulation of an alternative to a repressive battening down of the hatches. Such an alternative could have contained welfare-state arrangements for correction and security. But the bourgeois movement was on the whole too weak, and its political orientation too much geared to compromise, for it to be able to give rise to initiatives which transcended its own social sphere.... Thus in the area of criminal law and penal practice, patterns of behaviour became embedded which indicated the historical burden under which bourgeois society in Germany laboured – the weight of the pre-bourgeois, feudal and bureaucratic traditions with which it was stamped.[27]

Thus crime came to be judged, in Blasius's view, according to the feudal–aristocratic standards which obtained in the bureaucracy (p. 60). For example, it was seen as the consequence of poverty resulting from early marriage, drunkenness, immorality and excessive education of the masses. The remedy was seen as lying in a toughening up of the criminal law. The decline of the feudal patrimonial courts in the first half of the nineteenth century, and the gradual transfer of their powers and functions to state judicial institutions, was viewed by many as a major cause of the increase in crime, because it was removing the people from patriarchal institutions where the punishment was swift and firm, to remoter instances where retribution came only slowly and hesitantly, especially since many judges (it was alleged) saw in the accused merely unfortunate victims of circumstances rather than the wicked and ungodly criminals which they really were. Although they were unable to reactivate the patrimonial courts, which finally ceased to exist in 1872, bureaucrats and provincial nobles successfully pushed through stiffer penalties for theft in the law code of 1851 and frustrated attempts to turn prisons into rehabilitative institutions. Instead, prisons continued to concentrate on punishment; such work as was introduced for the inmates was in order to cover costs, not to train them for life in the outside world; no attempts were made to separate different types of offenders. Few new prisons were built, and serious overcrowding was the result. The aim of imprisonment was stated by the authorities in 1830 to be:

> through the removal of some of the free pleasures of life, through strenuous, even physically exhausting work, and through accustoming him to discipline and submission, to produce such an effect upon the sentiments of the criminal that when his period of imprisonment comes to an end, he will prefer a lawful and useful life in civil society to the state of incarceration and forced labour, and will recognise in penal institutions something harsher than a place of refuge for the poverty-stricken. It would only provide a fresh cause of even more frequent recidivism if, against the experience and principles of the governing authorities, the deterrent element were entirely removed from such institutions. (ibid., p. 92, quoted from a Potsdam Government report)

Deterrence, then, rather than rehabilitation, was, according to Blasius, the keynote of the 'repressive strategy' adopted by the pre-capitalist élite to deal with the problem of rising crime rates in the period before 1851.

This interpretation contrasts sharply with that advanced in comparable studies by scholars working on the relationship between crime and the state in England and France. Two points have been particularly stressed in this context. First it has been argued that in pre-industrial society the ineffectiveness of law-enforcement agencies gave rise to exemplary and symbolic forms of punishment. This remained true during the spread of the capitalist mode of production through rural society, though this seems to have shifted the emphasis of punishment from symbolic retribution towards actual deterrence. Thus Douglas Hay has pointed out that capital punishment came to be more widely used in England during the eighteenth century because other methods of law enforcement were ineffective (or undesirable).[28] In a well-known article in *Albion's Fatal Tree*, Hay argues that the English ruling class tolerated a great deal of disorder in town and countryside because it lacked the means of effective law enforcement, and feared the political consequences of attempting to remedy this situation by setting up of a professional police force. The spread of exemplary public execution, conceived of primarily as a deterrent, was the strategy adopted as a substitute (pp. 18, 41). Similarly, Michel Foucault, writing about France, has stressed the interdependence of ineffective law enforcement and exemplary punishment. Inefficient policing was also, it seems, despite the beliefs of the English squirearchy, a characteristic of eighteenth-century France.[29]

The second major point that has emerged from recent studies of crime, law and social order in England and France relates to changes in the relationship between crime and punishment in the first half of the nineteenth century. According to Foucault, with the bourgeois revolution of 1789 and the longer-term rise of the capitalist mode of production, the bourgeoisie mounted an increasingly furious attack on the illegalities of the popular classes, above all in order to defend its own property and to facilitate the orderly accumulation of capital. The old economy of power was redistributed: the ultimate result was a uniform and efficient system of law enforcement coupled with a shift in penal practice from symbolic punishment of the body to the real correction and disciplining of desires and instincts. It was the ambition of the bourgeoisie to exert a total control over the popular classes. Thus the growth of an effective police force, the rationalization of law enforcement, the rise of the prison system and the decline of public capital punishment all went together (pp. 82–3, 87–8). Michael Ignatieff has recently analysed the transition from punishment as public ritual, characteristic in England of the period before 1770, and the rise of the penitentiary. Reformers such as John Howard urged the replacement of punishment directed at the body with punishment directed at the mind. An increasing proportion of offenders received prison sentences, as the ideas of the penal reformers were gradually implemented. The reformers replaced the 'traditional view of crime as merely an immemorial form of human wickedness and sin' with a new view of criminals as the products of social crisis, and therefore, in principle, corrigible.[30] Ritual displays of terror were ineffective, they argued; social stability had to be founded on popular consent, maintained by guilt at the thought of wrongdoing, rather than by deference and fear (p. 211). In the penitentiary, therefore, solitary confinement, training in obedience to authority, a disciplinary regime of extreme physical and psychological harshness and severity, were the means by which the mind of the offender was to be reformed. The criminal will was to be broken by isolation, by heavy but meaningless labour – the treadmill, oakum-picking, turning heavy handcranks, and so on – and then remoulded by exhortation into that of a useful citizen. This change in penal practice was accompanied by a growing severity towards petty crime, and a sharp increase in the effectiveness of law enforcement, above all with the introduction of the new police in the 1820s.

As far as the thesis advanced by Blasius for comparable developments in Germany is concerned, these arguments have a number of important implications. First a repressive penal strategy as described by Blasius was little different from the reformatory strategies described by Foucault and Ignatieff for France and England. Increased penalties for theft were similarly evidence not of the persistence of authoritarian feudal élites but of the anxieties of a property-owning bourgeoisie. Blasius's own findings, therefore, seem in the light of comparative studies to indicate the opposite of what he claims them to show: namely, that penal policy and practice of nineteenth-century Germany reflected the rapidly growing power of the bourgeoisie. This is confirmed by his other findings, which indicate the establishment of important liberal principles in the Prussian criminal law code of 1851, in the wake of the 1848 revolution, above all, the equality of all citizens before the law and the introduction of public trials with something akin to a jury system.[31]

The second implication of work on England and France is that pre-industrial society was characterized above all by inefficient and hap-hazard law enforcement. The wide claims of the absolutist police state, as Foucault suggests, were advanced in a social context in which it was never really intended that they should be enforced; and even had the intention been there, the means were altogether lacking. Efficient polic-ing in England was a concomitant of industrialization, not a precursor of it. A similar argument might tentatively be put in the case of Germany. As Carsten Küther has shown, law enforcement in the eighteenth century left a great deal to be desired. 'The state', he has written recently,

> was still far short of achieving an inner consolidation in the late eighteenth century. It was unsuccessful in the struggle to suppress robber bands, and also had little success in controlling and integrating lower-class vagabond groups. Its whole comprehensive efforts to estab-lish its rule were regarded with deep suspicion by large parts of the population.[32]

Robber bands were able to traverse the countryside and commit their crimes with virtual impunity. The very large segment of the population which tramped the road in search of bread and work was able to continue its way of life despite the widespread fears and anxieties it aroused in the state and its manifold connections with illegal activities and crimes all the way up to highway robbery.[33] Banditry and vagabondage were, as Küther has shown, part of the same social world, the world of the outcasts, of the marginal poor, of itinerant labourers, of dishonourable groups such as skinners, shepherds, charcoal-burners and molecatchers. In the conditions of war and upheaval that obtained in Germany until the expulsion of Napoleon's armies in 1813–14, such groups were able to operate even more freely than before.[34]

IV

With the coming of peace, order was gradually restored. The territorial redistributions of 1815 gave bandits fewer borders to escape across. Judicial reform, the reorganization of criminal jurisdictions and the reconstitution of police forces, especially of the rural *gendarmerie*, gradually extended state controls over vagabonds. Banditry and vagabondage were primarily problems of rural policing, however. Either implicitly or explicitly, the focus of historians of policing in Germany (such as Lüdtke) has mainly been on the towns. Here it was that police controls over the population were perhaps at their most extensive, and easiest to enforce.[35] Yet in the conditions of the early nineteenth century urban policing everywhere was notoriously inefficient in practice. One good example was the police force of the city-state of Hamburg, the second-largest urban centre in Germany after Berlin. In the first half of the nineteenth century, the administrative chaos, inefficiency and corruption of the Hamburg police force were notorious. Only during the reaction following the 1848 Revolution did the situation in the city begin to change. In 1851–2 the various police departments were centralized in the 'night and police watch' and the uniforms, equipment and procedure of the force were demilitarized. In 1869 the reforms were completed with the institution of regular salaries for officers and the extension of police duties (especially with regard to the maintenance of public order) following the dissolution of the citizen militia in 1868. Finally in 1876 the night and police watch was replaced with a centralized 'corps of constables' along English lines, with rationally divided local responsibilities and local police stations. Further reforms, especially in 1892–3 (when the corps of constables was replaced by a police force organized more along Prussian lines) completed the process of centralization and professionalization. The decisive measures in creating a professional police force, in other words, took place above all in the second half of the nineteenth century.[36]

Measures such as these were to a large degree a response to urban growth and the coming of industrial capitalism. Yet in many ways they were by no means an adequate response. In the first place, while in some respects at least the numerical strength of the police force in major, well-established cities like Hamburg was increased more or less in line with the population, the same cannot be said of the new industrial towns which sprang up almost overnight in areas such as the Ruhr. In Hamborn, for example, an iron, coal and steel town in the Ruhr basin which grew from a population of 6,000 in 1895 to one of nearly 102,000 a mere fifteen years later, the police force was pathetically inadequate to deal with the major problems of violence and crime which this rapid urban growth brought with it: in 1900 it was a mere twenty-five strong; two years later it was increased to thirty. When one calls to mind the fact that coalminers in Hamborn returned from work, or even simply went for walks, in groups of forty to fifty, carrying coalpicks in their hands, it is hardly surprising that cases of the 'forcible release of prisoners' figure frequently in the criminal statistics for the town. In the absence of an adequate police force, employers took to hiring their own police forces to protect their property. Many foremen carried revolvers, and private citizens donated trained police dogs to the force. Detailed figures are not available for the later period, but if one goes on the basis of twelve policemen per station (there were two stations in 1900 with twenty-five men) then with eight stations in 1907 there would have been about a hundred policemen in the town. In 1913 a new central police station was built with thirty-seven cells; most of the local stations already had prisons. Hamborn, a town in which there were nearly three men for every woman in the age group 18–20 and nearly two men for every woman in the higher age groups, was a violent, aggressive society according to its historian Erhard Lucas. Crimes of violence made up to 22.5 per cent of the overall crime figures in 1900–1908. Parts of the city were described as resembling the Wild West. Immediately after the First World War Hamborn was the centre of a major workers' revolt, in which a violent strike escalated into a direct confrontation with the authorities, with regular battles being fought between the two sides, both armed with a variety of weapons, including machine-guns.[37]

Even in towns where the numerical strength of the police was more impressive, serious problems of adjustment to social change remained. Raymond Fosdick, the American observer cited earlier, was severely critical of the German police in the period before the First World War. He described the Berlin police, for example, as 'over-organized':

There are bureaus and sub-bureaus, specialities and sub-specialities, with an interminable line of reports and documents proceeding through official channels to the president's office. Every official method is carefully prescribed; every action, even to the smallest detail, is hedged about with minute rules and regulations. Police business is reduced to a methodical and, as far as possible, automatic routine, the rigidity of which is accentuated by the laborious formalities of official courtesy and the stiff respect paid to rank and position. It almost seems as if the German genius for organization had exhausted itself in perfecting a piece of machinery from which the human element has been completely eliminated, leaving no room for individual initiative or imagination. . . . As one surveys the entire organization of the Berlin department, the impression becomes firmly fixed that it is a huge, ponderous machine, impeded by its own mechanical intricacy and clogged with work.[38]

This rigidity and lack of initiative, according to Fosdick, was particularly evident in the detective service, which, he argued, relied to an excessive degree on the *Meldewesen* system, by which everyone was obliged to register with the police on arrival in or departure from a locality, or on changing residence. Combining the use of this system with the consultation of criminal records was the major method of detection used by police forces in Imperial Germany. Evasion of the system was allegedly very difficult and certainly severely punished, but in fact it took place on a large scale, and was only partially countered by police raids on lodging houses, bars and places of amusement. (pp. 350–5)

Fosdick considered that reliance on this bureaucratic method of detection hampered the development of individual initiative among German detectives, and he pointed out that the *Meldewesen* system was effective only when those wanted for crimes were known by name. Furthermore, German policemen were poorly trained. Five weeks was the maximum time in Berlin for training courses for new policemen, and there was no special building provided either. This was hardly enough time to master the vast array of laws and regulations which the German policeman was expected to enforce (p. 216). The reason for this poor training lay in the fact that, as in many other branches of the state administration, service in the German police force in the late nineteenth and early twentieth centuries was reserved for ex-soldiers. Anything from six to nine years' service in the army was a prerequisite; that is, policemen were former professional NCOs rather than former conscripted privates. Police rulebooks concentrated on this military aspect of police activities. The Berlin police regulations began with a reminder that 'members of the police force are under military discipline, and must mould their conduct while on duty in accordance with military forms'. This meant saluting superiors, and barking at civilians: 'the speech of the police must be short,

definite and clear, and should not be accompanied by explanatory ges-
tures, or motions of head or body'. The military nature of the German
police was also expressed in their equipment, which in Berlin included as a
matter of course pistols and swords, and in Dresden the same with the
addition of brass knuckles (pp. 231–2).

Yet the authoritarian and often brutal behaviour which the militarization of the police produced was more than offset by the rigidity with
which they approached their duties. A military appearance was the most
important quality of a German policeman in the eyes of his superiors. The
length of service required in the army before recruitment to the police
force meant that the average age of new recruits was quite high: in Berlin it
was 31, compared with 23 in London, and Fosdick noted that 'the young,
fresh, keen, vigorous look of the London "Bobby" is almost totally
lacking in the Berlin *Schutzmann*, who ... has a heavy, inactive appearance'. Even the Berlin police department itself admitted that the men were
too old; but nothing could be done to reduce the nine years' army service
requirement, since the army insisted on this length of service in order to
prevent good NCOs leaving too soon for better-paid jobs in the police
force. As the German police forces of the federal states (for example,
Hamburg) were gradually remodelled during the Imperial period along
Prussian lines, so they too came to share these defects (p. 211).

V

In 1976 Howard Zehr, in a pioneering work, argued that crimes of violence
declined in relation to theft in nineteenth-century Germany, and the
association of both trends with subsistence levels weakened. Closer study
showed up a transitional stage in which 'many social groups ... were being
exposed to city life for the first time' and the problems of adjustment were
expressed in a temporary rise in rates of violence to keep pace with theft
rates before declining once more as the new urban–industrial society
became established.[39] This final phase up to 1914 indeed saw a stabilization
or even a decline in criminality in general. Thus violence was ultimately
'traditional', and criminal violence was 'an index of social tensions', 'a
form of punitive, "unrealistic" protest against developments in society and
the economy' or a transfer of old-established village habits such as feuding
to an inappropriate urban setting. Theft on the other hand was modern:
'rising theft rates indicate rising expectations, the spread of "modern"
economic values'. (pp. 138, 141–2, 117.)

Zehr was concerned to refute several long-held views about the nature
of crime: that it is irrational or pathological, for example, or that it is the
product of social disorganization and breakdown. He also wanted to
dispose of the widely held view that urban society is more violent than

174

rural. He was well aware of many of the problems associated with criminal statistics, and properly tentative and cautious about many of his conclusions. He performed a real service by putting some central questions on to the agenda and by pioneering the revival of interest in the history of crime in Germany. In the decade since his book was published, however, his major theses have been subjected to some searching criticisms. The social history of criminality in West Germany was revived in the 1970s by the important work of Dirk Blasius, which is (among other things) remarkable for its breadth of conception and the variety of ways in which it approached its subject. A substantial part of Blasius's work is statistical, and by using unpublished material from the files of the Prussian Ministry of Justice, he was able to pursue the quantitative study of crime in more detail and depth than was possible with the mainly printed sources on which Zehr had relied.

Blasius was able to establish close correlations between theft rates and rye prices in the first half of the nineteenth century, at least up to the middle of the 1860s (r = +0.90 or higher). A rise in theft rates in the 1830s and 1840s was above all the expression of the increasing pauperization of large parts of the population in the wake of the rapid population growth and nascent industrialization of the period (although Blasius was not able to identify precisely which groups were most involved in criminal acts). In the period 1836–1850 the general trend of both theft and violence was upwards; but in the years 1852–66 theft declined while violence rose even more sharply. This corresponds roughly to the transitional period identified by Zehr, who found that assault rates rose from 1852 to about 1895 before levelling out and declining slightly up to 1910 ('violence became more frequent but less serious'). In relation to theft, Zehr found that violence increased up to the turn of the century before beginning to decline. Blasius disagreed with Zehr's overall thesis, but in the end was unable to shake it because he was looking at an earlier period; indeed, if anything his figures tended to support Zehr's. The real problem with all these figures is that the evidence for 'modernization' in the form of a rising incidence of theft compared with violence is located only in a brief period from about the turn of the century to the First World War: the most obvious long-term trend across the whole of the second half of the nineteenth century is in fact a rise in crimes of violence, and it is this that needs explaining rather than the reversal of this trend from 1895–1900 on.[40]

More recently, the quantitative history of crime in Germany has been taken up by the American historian Eric A. Johnson and his collaborators. In a number of articles, and in a forthcoming book by Johnson, they have confirmed the findings of Zehr and Blasius that theft declined and criminal violence increased in the second half of the nineteenth century, but they have also gone beyond this work to present a more differentiated analysis that questions a number of Zehr's central theses. As Johnson has pointed out, time-series and highly aggregated data are of limited use,[41] and he has gone a long way towards examining differential patterns of criminality by region, by age and by sex. These patterns, he argues, show that the degree of urbanization in Germany (by region) was not on the whole a determinant of criminality. Towns were not notably more crime-ridden than rural society. Rather, crime and delinquency reflected the degree of social tension, whether this was caused by ethnic conflicts and economic hardship leading to mass emigration, as in the demonstrably violent areas of the far eastern provinces of Prussia in the 1880s, or by rapid industrialization in the Prussian 'Wild West', in Arnsberg and Düsseldorf, around and after the turn of century. Property offences were increasing in the towns and declining in rural areas, but this reflected economic hardship rather than a higher value placed on property and growing aspirations, for the correlations between economic indicators (such as mortality rates) and crime levels remained high up to 1914 and did not decline as significantly as Zehr claimed they did. Finally the growth in crimes of violence over time also reflected growing social tension. For example, offences against the person, libel and homicide all increased when Bismarck left office, 'because with him gone Germany turned towards a more violent foreign policy which possibly reflected a more disorderly, discordant, and violent internal culture'.[42]

Many nineteenth-century observers saw criminal acts as evidence of a growing rebelliousness on the part of the lower classes. Engels, for example, wrote that 'the clearest indication of the unbounded contempt of the workers for the existing social order is the wholesale manner in which they break its laws'.[43] Conservative commentators frequently echoed this point of view, though naturally from a very different standpoint. In Prussia in the mid-1830s a major inquiry was launched into the general increase in crime which the Ministry of Justice believed it had detected across the country. Provincial governors and local officials complained in their responses of a general decline in religion and morality, of the failure of the educational system to instil a proper respect for authority, and above all of a catastrophic rise in drunkenness with its concomitant threat to the maintenance of law and order. Some complained that disorder was following inevitably from the decline of the old feudal order, in which a 'patriarchal, to some extent familial relationship of the landowner with the villagers' (to quote a district official from Silesia) had acted as a guarantee of good conduct. More subtle observers noted that landowners had formerly acted outside the law to defend their rights. Another official writing in the mid-1830s remembered what he described as a typical incident when a feudal landowner had caught a peasant stealing his apples and had simply marched his men to the peasant's own land and harvested all the fruit in sight as compensation. The fact that patrimonial justice remained in force allowed landowners in East-Elbian Prussia to impose such informal sanctions with impunity.[44]

During the first half of the nineteenth century informal sanctions gave way in the countryside to a growing tendency – or necessity – to use formal, legal methods of prosecution for minor offences such as these. The effect which this must have had on the criminal statistics was already pointed out by contemporaries. It was compounded by the sharp increase in the enclosure of common land that followed the agrarian reforms of the first two decades of the century. As compensation for the loss of obligatory labour services and other dues, the feudal landlords received not only substantial amounts of peasant property but also common land as well. Their response to the increase in demand for cereal crops caused by the rapid population growth of these decades was to bring vast new areas of formerly waste land into their possession with a view to putting it to cultivation. As a result, a vast acreage of woodland now fell into private hands. The rural poor depended on wood, of course, for a whole variety of things, from heating in the cold north German winter to tools and utensils, furniture buildings and machinery. As the population grew, so the demand for wood grew, and prices of commercial wood became too much for the poor to afford. Consequently, there were huge numbers of wood thefts in these years. More than half of all thefts in Prussia in the 1830s were wood thefts. Since thefts in general made up 85 per cent of all recorded crime, this meant that wood theft was by far the largest category of crime at this period.[45]

But as Blasius shows, wood theft was not simply the outcome of popular desperation in the face of the declining availability of an essential product. It was also the expression of a set of popular beliefs which Edward Thompson, in a celebrated article, called the 'moral economy'.[46] Officials reported a 'traditional opinion' among the people that there was a difference 'between such property as is created by human effort and such as nature has brought forth without human aid': the second was free for all to use, and many people regarded wood theft simply as the reassertion of a traditional right.[47] The clash of this belief with the increasing commercialization of agriculture by the Junker landlords brought with it, argues Blasius, an increasing tendency on the part of the mass of the rural poor to assert their interests by opposing or ignoring the enforcement of the law. The lower classes were emerging from their feudal passivity and engaging in a historic offensive. Solidarity, courage and a sense of dignity emerged from the experience of resisting the claims of the rural entrepreneur on the woodlands and the practice of the state in enforcing these claims. These achievements, Blasius suggests, played their part in providing the basis for the emergence of the labour movement later on.[48] Wood theft can thus be classified as an aspect of 'social criminality';[49] like poaching, smuggling or arson, it expressed a collective consciousness of injustice and constituted a collective form of resistance to authority.[50]

It would be wrong, however, to draw too sharp a line between 'social' crime and individual crime. Josef Mooser has recently carried the social history of wood theft a step further by undertaking a detailed local study. Here a more complex story is revealed. Wood theft certainly appears as an aspect of an 'offensive' by the rural poor in defence of their existence at a time of rapid impoverishment. But the growing class of landless labourers stole from peasant farmers as much as from larger, noble landowners (who were in any case not very numerous in the Westphalian districts investigated by Mooser). The peasants opted for self-defence by both legal methods and illegal, and there were numerous cases not only of charivaris against the suspected culprits but also of physical attacks and even lynchings and murders carried out by peasants acting in groups of up to fifty or more. The ending of serfdom had brought the creation of a class of landless labourers and speeded the transformation of the landowning nobility into a class of capitalist farmers. But it also created an intermediate class of property-owning peasants, who proved even more determined in their resistance against popular rebellion (up to and including the revolutionary uprisings of 1848) than were the larger landowners and the state. Thus wood thefts did not reveal a simple bourgeois–proletarian polarization in the countryside, but rather a more complex picture, in which there was little evidence of a general solidarity among the subordinate classes.[51]

Moreover, Blasius's thesis appears to assume that the subordinate classes were entirely passive under feudalism. Peter Blickle has recently pleaded for a new view of the common people in medieval and early modern Germany which restores the subject (*Untertan*) to his – or her – proper place as an agent of history, not simply as an object. A period of political emancipation from 1300 to 1550 was succeeded, he argues, by a process (completed by 1800) in which the *Untertanen* found themselves 'on the road to inferiority'. 'Servility and a reluctance to assume responsibilities are comparatively recent phenomena in German history'.[52] Even in the late feudal system in the second half of the eighteenth century, however, the researches of William Hagen and others are uncovering a widespread preparedness on the part of the subordinate classes to resist authority and a successful defence of their rights against the attempts of ambitious noble landlords to encroach upon them.[53] It is difficult, therefore, to accept the rising wood-theft rate as evidence for the emergence of any fundamentally new insubordinate consciousness on the part of the subordinate classes. Even more problematical is the thesis that this new consciousness was transferred from the rural poor to the urban proletariat. As Mooser points out, when they succeeded in gaining property by themselves, the peasants stopped stealing wood from the large landowners and – like poachers turned gamekeepers – began prosecuting wood thefts themselves. Those who continued to steal wood – the growing class of landless labourers – were not concerned to challenge the distribution of wealth and power in society, they merely wanted to protect what they regarded as their rights and to secure the continued existence of the family economy. And in any case it was on the whole not former rural labourers who found their way into the labour movement but former urban artisans.[54]

However, the idea that rebellious impulses in the first half of the nineteenth century were eventually channelled into labour-movement organization in the second half has found its way into research on collective violence as well as work on individual criminality. In recent years there has been a substantial volume of work carried out on rioting in modern German history.[55] Collective violence is generally given the term 'social protest' in German work, presumably as a contrast to the 'social movement' (or labour movement) of the second half of the nineteenth century. The underlying thesis seems to be that there was a rapid growth of social protest in the 1820s and 1830s, culminating in the widespread popular uprisings which formed such an important element in the 1848 Revolution. After this, however, social protest diminished, indeed eventually it virtually disappeared, as the rebellious impulses that had fed it were channelled into the emerging socialist movement. Social protest by its very nature was violent, spontaneous and without clear goals, a form of 'primitive rebellion'; the social movement, by contrast, was non-violent, highly organized and equipped with a clear set of aims. If collective violence resurfaced in the Weimar period, this did not denote a revival of social protest but rather signified the increasing willingness of political parties, particularly at the extremes of the political spectrum, to use *organized* violence to achieve their ends.

The general distribution of historical research within this frame of reference has tended to produce a pre-programmed confirmation of its overall thesis. Nearly everyone who has worked in this field has concentrated on the period 1815–48; there has been virtually no work on the decades after 1848. The initial impression that protest was transformed into organization is greatly strengthened by this fact. Similarly, research into a wide variety of incidents in which the only common denominator was the occurrence of collective violence has, not surprisingly, come up with the conclusion that no clear set of goals existed among those involved in social protest. Moreover, the tendency in a great deal of this work to regard social protest as progressive (not least because it is supposed to have been channelled eventually into labour organization) has come up against serious problems when researchers have had to confront the fact that many of the riots which occurred in the first half of the nineteenth century were anti-Semitic in orientation. Some have simply ignored this problem,[56] while others have tried to get round it by suggesting that anti-Semitic riots were actually inspired, or at least encouraged, by the authorities.[57] Neither of these arguments is really convincing. Finally, of course, there have in fact been a good many popular disturbances since 1848 which were demonstrably not organized by political parties.[58] Current research is also beginning to reveal that even in the Weimar Republic it would be too simple to say that collective violence was universally inspired by political organizations in pursuit of clearly formulated goals.[59]

The quantitative study of social protest has proved even more problematical than the quantitative study of criminality. Richard Tilly and his collaborators argued, on the basis of a collection from a newspaper of all reports of violent incidents involving more than twenty people during the nineteenth century and all the way up to 1933, that social protest was frequent in the first half of the nineteenth century, but less so in the second half. 'Rapid urbanisation and industrialisation *reduced* the level of collective violence, because they moved masses of the potentially violent from familiar contexts and thus destroyed their means of collective action.'[60] Rising living standards caused a real decline in social protest, while such protest potential as continued to exist was channelled into new political movements. In the Weimar period, however, economic instability and crisis increased protest potential, which this time was channelled by the political movements into violent forms of action once more (pp. 234–7).

The basic finding that collective violence declined after the mid-nineteenth century is sound enough, though as we have already seen subsequent research has tended to exaggerate it by concentrating almost exclusively on the *Vormärz* period. There are of course problems of an empirical kind about the research methods used. Reliance on a daily paper from an urban area may have led to an under-recording of disturbances in the countryside, while the figure of twenty chosen as a minimum is, to say the least, somewhat arbitrary. But the real problems lie in the theory that the level of recorded violence reflected the level of social tension. Aggregating acts of collective violence in this way detaches each one from its historical context, and in many ways involves comparing quite different actions with very different motives. Non-violent protest does not enter the picture, so we cannot discover why some protestors become violent while others did not. A decline in collective violence may also be a result of improved state repression, as indeed Tilly's remarks about the poor state of policing in 1815–48 suggest. On the other hand, acts of crowd violence were frequently themselves provoked by police or military action, and so their occurrence may mainly be an outcome of the degree of official anxiety about disorder.[61] Other historians, as we have seen, have argued that the rise in *individual* acts of criminal violence in the second half of the nineteenth century shows that social tension was in fact *rising* during this period. Similarly, as Mooser has remarked, wood theft and other property crimes constitute a 'hidden form of social protest' through which 'tensions and conflicts in the nineteenth-century rural society become apparent which easily fall through the net of the researcher looking for public disturbances (with the exception of the revolutionary period of 1848/49)'.[62]

VI

Gareth Stedman Jones once remarked that historians often tend to see their own chosen period as one of dramatic transition between a time of stability before and the emergence of a new order afterwards.[63] This certainly seems to apply to historians in search of social tension in the German past. Blickle views the period 1300–1550 as one of popular protest and the period 1550–1800 as one of increasing popular quiescence and the creation of the *Untertanengeist*. Tilly sees the period 1800–1848 as one of popular protest and self-assertion and the period 1848–1914 as one of decreasing violence, growing repression and the establishment of a high degree of public order. Johnson on the other hand sees the decline of theft and the rise of violence in the second half of the nineteenth century as indicating a rise in social tension, as urbanization took hold on German society. Many historians, finally, have seen the Weimar Republic as a period of high social tension in comparison to the relative calm of the decades before the First World War. All seem agreed, however, that social tension expressed itself in popular self-assertion, in disrespect for the law and in the committing of illegal acts.

The *Untertanengeist* is so far turning out to be a rather elusive quarry. Perhaps the first step towards clearing up some of the confusion is to look more closely at the term 'social tension'. The trouble is, nobody has really bothered to define this concept. The assumption seems to be that when people get unsettled by some kind of crisis – whether it is a bad harvest, a move away from familiar surroundings, or an economic depression – they react by committing crimes. At the root of the concept, therefore, lies a psychological view of illegality rather than a more strictly historical one. It is difficult to show that any one given period or circumstance is more psychologically disturbing than another, or indeed that any one era is particularly stable. The concept of 'social tension' seems to be a mirror-image of the concept of 'social control', and a low level of recorded crime might just as easily be explained by the absence of the one as by the presence of the other.

This is not to say, however, that we should simply throw these concepts out of the window. In any new area of social history it seems inevitable that an initial period of bold theorizing is succeeded by a period of cautious empiricism. The social history of crime, as David Philips has complained in a recent survey of English work in the field, is no exception to this general rule.[64] Yet the turn towards local studies in German work in this area has not, so far at least, been a turn away from theory. There is a continued search for the broad determination of crime, and a refusal to regard it merely as the product of random factors. By locating criminal activity firmly in its local social context, historians have been able to illuminate far more than the criminal act itself. Here indeed, as in Regina Schulte's study of arson in rural Bavaria, violent acts can be seen as expressions of the real social tensions engendered by employment and inheritance structures and patterns of sociability in a peasant society; while the attitudes of the control agencies – psychiatrists and judicial and penal institutions – towards the criminals shows the startling gap that existed between the rationality of urban professionals and the alternative rationalities of the rural world.[65] Similarly, infanticide can also be seen as the outcome of structural determinants, although in this case the use of the notion of 'social tension' would appear to be rather less appropriate.

What this kind of research is beginning to reveal is that obedience was not indivisible: the *Untertanengeist* was a composite and fragmented being. It seems reasonably well established that the pattern of public order and law enforcement changed from the middle of the nineteenth century onwards. Inquisitorial justice and secret trials in which the confession was the only conclusive demonstration of guilt gave way to trial in open court and an increasing weight placed on independent witnesses and evidence; and the police began to take over law enforcement and investigation from other authorities such as the military or the public prosecutor's office. As Hans-Otto Hügel has shown in his analysis of the lost tradition of the German detective novel, these changes paved the way for a change in popular attitudes towards crime and law enforcement, in which detection by means of discovering clues became possible, and the rational and verifiable identifiction of the real culprit became the norm.[66] In the early German criminal novel, witnesses often had to flee the authorities and remain in hiding until the culprit confessed; the triumph of the true detective novel in the hands of writers like Adolph Streckfuss signified the triumph of a greater measure of security for the innocent suspect in reality as well as in fiction. Thus the second half of the nineteenth century may well have seen growing public acceptance of the legitimacy of the law-enforcement agencies in Germany.

At the same time, this period also witnessed a decline in collective violence and public disorder and a gradual increase in the effectiveness and efficiency of the police. However, these processes occurred with great unevenness. On the one hand, the foreign traveller walking the main streets of a major city such as Berlin or Hamburg could not fail to be impressed by the degree of order and security that it exhibited, or by the pervasive presence of the police, or indeed by the extent and elaboration or the regulations by which this order and security were enforced. But there were places where foreign travellers did not go: the 'Wild West' of the Ruhr, for example; or the *Gängeviertel* (rookeries) of Hamburg, where even the police only ventured to patrol in twos, and the lawlessness of the inhabitants was proverbial. Whole areas of German society lived outside the bounds of the well-ordered police state despite all efforts to bring them under control. Prostitution, for example, can be seen as a form of deviance from bourgeois norms which frustrated all official attempts to regulate it, perhaps because its relation to bourgeois society was an ambivalent and symbiotic one in which official repression operated within real if vaguely defined limits.[67] Another lawless area of society was that of the vagrants.

Vagabondism, it seems generally agreed, was an integral aspect of pre-industrial society. Not least as a defence mechanism against official hostility, vagabonds developed their own social mechanisms, their own argot, even their own sign language, largely invisible to the outside world, which regarded them with profound suspicion. The world of vagabonds was widely seen as a source of criminal activities, and from the Middle Ages to the twentieth century the authorities were unremitting in their efforts to bring it under control.[68] Industrialization brought new sources of vagabondism with it, as journeymen fell into destitution and increasing numbers of people tramped the streets from town to town in search of work. The spread of capitalist methods of farming after the agrarian reforms of the early nineteenth century also encouraged landowners in the north and east to employ temporary migrant labour, which further added to the population of the itinerant world.[69] The old-style itinerant trades-people, entertainers, journeymen, beggars and other wanderers of the pre-industrial world may have slowly ceased to exist as the roads became more effectively policed and the railways extended their tentacles across the land, but the vagabonds' subculture survived at least into the 1920s, when attempts to give it political organization culminated in the famous *Vagabundentreffen* at Stuttgart in 1929.[70] Other areas of German society were also to a large extent outside the law: the people who lived on and worked the thousands of cargo-boats and barges that plied Germany's rivers and inland waterways, for example, were notorious for their complete independence from society on the dry land.[71]

Yet more widespread were those broad sections of the working class which refused to conform to bourgeois notions of an orderly life in certain specific respects; the dock labourers who regularly pilfered from the cargoes they handled, the unmarried women who lived with their lovers despite attempts by the police to stop them, or the gangs of youths whose depredations caused so much anxiety in the 1920s. Yet all these groups – including the vagrants and the denizens of the *Gängeviertel* – had their own codes of conduct, their own notions of honesty and honour among themselves, and their willingness to break the law in certain respects cannot be taken as evidence of a generalized rebelliousness. Crime could, as Michael Grüttner has suggested, provide an alternative for workers when collective industrial action was difficult; yet crime and politics were not simple alternatives, as the persistent political radicalism of the *Gänge-viertel*, all the way up to their Communist commitment in the 1920s, and the interconnections between the youthful *Cliquen* of interwar Berlin and the Communist Party would seem to suggest.[72]

In the end, perhaps we need to make two broad distinctions in our attempt to pin down the *Untertanengeist*. The first is a distinction between classes. Like so many of the clichés of German history, the notion of the *Untertanengeist* may well have been developed with the middle class in mind. What surprised foreign observers more often was not the deference paid to uniformed officials even by the most distinguished and prominent bourgeois man on the street. White-collar crime was undoubtedly widespread (although it has been largely ignored by historians); but it was carried on behind closed doors. Working-class deference, but also perhaps a degree of working-class criminality, tended rather to be taken for granted. The second distinction to make is between society and politics. The *Untertanengeist* was first and foremost a political animal. Whatever the habits and attitudes of the working-class individual, observers frequently pointed to the exemplary orderliness of the working-class party, the SPD: and indeed there is no denying the emphasis the party laid, ultimately to its own detriment, on keeping strictly within the bounds of legality in its own behaviour, as far as the authorities allowed it to. Collective, public attitudes to authority may then have been different from private, individual ones. All recent researchers in the history of German crime have turned up evidence that, to quote Howard Zehr, 'flies in the face of national stereotypes of the docile, law-abiding German'.[73] Ultimately, therefore, the pursuit of the *Untertanengeist* would seem to lead inevitably to the conclusion that short-term political developments do not necessarily have to be explained by hypothesizing long-term mental attitudes or social norms.

NOTES

1 A. J. P. Taylor, *The Course of German History* (2nd edn., London, 1961), p. 9.
2 R. R. Palmer, *The World of the French Revolution* (London, 1971), p. 236.
3 W. L. Shirer, *The Rise and Fall of the Third Reich: A History of Nazi Germany* (London, 1960), p. 91.
4 R. d'O. Butler, *The Roots of National Socialism* (London, 1941), p. 276.
5 Taylor, *Course of German History*, p. vii.
6 See the comments in G. Eley, 'The Wilhelmine Right: How it Changed', in R. J. Evans (ed.), *Society and Politics in Wilhelmine Germany* (London, 1978), pp. 112–35, now reprinted in Eley, *From Unification to Nazism: Reinterpreting the German Past* (London, 1986).

7   H.-U. Wehler, *Das deutsche Kaiserreich 1871–1918* (Göttingen, 1973), pp. 133–4.
8   A. Lüdtke, 'The Role of State Violence in the Period of Transition to Industrial Capitalism: the example of Prussia from 1815 to 1848', *Social History*, vol. 4, no. 2 (1979), p. 221. I have rephrased the quotation in order to try to make it more comprehensible than it is in the original.
9   Quoted in H. Kohn, *The Mind of Germany: The Education of a Nation* (London, 1961), p. 266.
10 Wehler, *Das deutsche Kaiserreich*, p. 133, for both the Einstein and Weber quotations.
11 R. B. Fosdick, *European Police Systems* (New York, 1915), p. 9.
12 R. S. Baker, *Seen in Germany* (New York, 1901), p. 8, quoted in E. A. Johnson, 'The Roots of Crime in Imperial Germany', *Central European History*, vol. 16, no. 4 (1982), pp. 351–74, at p. 362.
13 J. K. Jerome, *Three Men on the Bummel* (Everyman edn., London, 1918), pp. 105–15. I am indebted to David Philips for drawing my attention to this book.
14 G. W. F. Hegel, *Philosophy of Right* (Oxford, 1942), p. 279.
15 W. O. Henderson, *The State and the Industrial Revolution in Prussia 1740–1870)* (London, 1958). The quotation is from the General Ordinance of 1808, cited in B. Chapman, *Police State* (London, 1970), p. 19.
16 For legal positivism, see G. Jellinek, *Allgemeine Staatsrechtslehre* (3rd edn, Berlin, 1922).
17 K. Saul, *Staat, Industrie, Arbeiterbewegung im Kaiserreich* (Düsseldorf, 1974).
18 Fosdick, *European Police Systems*, pp. 21–2.
19 Staatsarchiv Hamburg, Senat, Cl. VIII, Lit. Lb, No. 28a 2, Vol. 4: Polizei – Monatliche Tätigkeitsberichte.
20 Fosdick, *European Police Systems*, p. 26.
21 Ibid., pp. 27–8.
22 Lüdtke, 'Role of State Violence', p. 191.
23 Quoted ibid., p. 191.
24 Ibid., p. 191.
25 Ibid., p. 197.
26 See Chapter 1, above.
27 D. Blasius, *Bürgerliche Gesellschaft und Kriminalität: Zur Sozialgeschichte Preussens im Vormärz* (Göttingen, 1975), pp. 137–8.
28 D. Hay, 'Property, Authority and the Criminal Law', in Hay *et al.* (eds), *Albion's Fatal Tree: Crime and Society in 18th-century England* (London, 1975).
29 M. Foucault, *Discipline and Punish: The Birth of the Prison* (London, 1977), pp. 82–3, 87–8.
30 M. Ignatieff, *A Just Measure of Pain: The Penitentiary in the Industrial Revolution 1750–1850* (London, 1978), p. 210.
31 Blasius, *Bürgerliche Gesellschaft und Kriminalität*, pp. 231–6. However, in practice substantial inequalities remained, of course.
32 C. Küther, 'Räuber, Volk und Obrigkeit: Zur Wirkungsweise und Funktion Staatlicher Strafverfolgung im 18. Jahrhundert', in H. Reif (ed.) *Räuber, Volk und Obrigkeit: Studien zur Geschichte der Kriminalität in Deutschland seit dem 18. Jahrhundert* (Frankfurt, 1984), pp. 17–42, at p. 37.
33 C. Küther, *Menschen auf der Strasse: Vagierende Unterschichten in Bayern, Franken und Schwaben in der zweiten Hälfte des 18. Jahrhunderts* (Göttingen, 1983); Küther, *Räuber und Gauner in Deutschland; Das organisierte Bandenwesen im 18. und frühen 19. Jahrhundert* (Göttingen, 1976).
34 T. C. W. Blanning, *The French Revolution in Germany: Occupation and Resistance in the Rhineland 1792–1802* (Oxford, 1983).
35 A. Lüdtke, *'Gemeinwohl', Polizei und 'Festungspraxis': Staatliche Gewaltsamkeit und innere Verwaltung in Preussen, 1815–1850* (Göttingen, 1982); M. Walker, *German Home Towns: Community, State and General Estate 1648–1871* (Ithaca, NY, 1971).
36 *150 Jahre Hamburger Polizei* (Hamburg, 1964).
37 E. Lucas, *Zwei Formen von Radikalismus in der deutschen Arbeiterbewegung* (Frankfurt, 1976).
38 Fosdick, *European Police Systems*, p. 142.
39 H. Zehr, *Crime and the Development of Modern Society: Patterns of Criminality in Nineteenth-century Germany and France* (London, 1976), pp. 114–20.

40 D. Blasius, *Kriminalität und Alltag* (Göttingen, 1980).
41 E. A. Johnson, 'The Roots of Crime in Imperial Germany', *Central European History*, vol. 15 (1982), pp. 351–76, at p. 361. See also V. E. McHale and Johnson, 'Urbanization, Industrialization, and Crime in Imperial Germany', *Social Science History*, vol. 1, no. 1 (1976), pp. 45–78; ibid., vol. 1, no. 2 (1977), pp. 216–47; Johnson and McHale, 'Socioeconomic Aspects of the Delinquency Rate in Imperial Germany, 1882–1914', *Journal of Social History*, vol. 13, no. 3 (1980), pp. 384–402; R. E. Bergstrom and Johnson, 'The Female Victim: Homicide and women in Imperial Germany', in John C. Fout (ed.), *German Women in the Nineteenth Century: A Social History* (New York, 1984), pp. 345–67. Johnson, 'Longitudinal and Periodic Trends in Nineteenth and Twentieth-Century German Criminality, from Vormärz to late Weimar', unpublished paper, 9th UEA Research Seminar on German Social History, Norwich, 1985; Johnson, *The Rechtsstaat: Crime and Criminal Justice in Imperial Germany* (forthcoming).
42 Johnson, 'Longitudinal and Periodic Trends', p. 40.
43 F. Engels, *The Condition of the Working Class in England* (1844; trans. and ed. W. O. Henderson and W. H. Chaloner, Oxford, 1958), pp. 145–6, quoted in D. Philips, *Crime and Authority in Victorian England: The Black Country 1835–1860* (London, 1979), p. 13.
44 Blasius, *Kriminalität und Alltag*, pp. 27–9. Feudal rights and obligations were mostly abrogated in the decade or so from 1807, but a residue remained until 1848, and patrimonial courts continued in existence, though with an increasing loss of function, until 1872.
45 Blasius, *Bürgerliche Gesellschaft und Kriminalität*, pp. 39–52.
46 E. P. Thompson, 'The Moral Economy of the English Crowd in the 18th Century', *Past and Present*, vol. 50 (Feb. 1971), pp. 76–136.
47 Blasius, *Kriminalität und Alltag*, p. 56.
48 Ibid., pp. 77–8.
49 E. J. Hobsbawm, 'Social Criminality', *Bulletin of the Society for the Study of Labour History*, vol. 25 (1972), pp. 5–6.
50 For the classic collection of articles arguing along these lines see Hay *et al.*, *Albion's Fatal Tree*.
51 J. Mooser, '"Furcht bewahrt das Holz": Holzdiebstahl und sozialer Konflikt in der ländlichen Gesellschaft 1800–1850 an Westfälischen Beispielen', in Reif, *Räuber, Volk und Obrigkeit*, pp. 43–99.
52 P. Blickle, *Deutsche Untertanen: Ein Widerspruch* (Munich, 1981).
53 W. Hagen, 'The Junkers' Faithless Servants', in R. J. Evans and W. R. Lee (eds), *The German Peasantry: Conflict and Community in Rural Society from the 18th to the 20th Centuries* (London, 1986).
54 Mooser, 'Furcht bewahrt das Holz', pp. 43–99.
55 See esp. J. Bergmann and H. Volkmann (eds), *Sozialer Protest: Studien zu traditionaler Resistenz und Kollektiver Gewalt in Deutschland vom Vormärz bis zur Reichsgründung* (Opladen, 1984); R. Wirtz, *'Widersetzlichkeiten, Excesse, Crawalle, Tumulte und Skandale': Soziale Bewegung und gewalthafter sozialer Protest in Baden 1815–1848* (Frankfurt, 1981); H.-G. Husung, *Protest und Repression im Vormärz: Norddeutschland zwischen Restauration und Revolution* (Göttingen, 1983).
56 H.-G. Stühmke, '"Wo nix ist, het der Kaiser sien Recht verlor'n", oder "Der Stein auf dem Sofa der Frau Senatorin": Die Hamburger Unruhen vom 31. August bis zum 5. September 1830', in J. Berlin (ed.), *Das andere Hamburg* (Frankfurt, 1981), pp. 45–68. This analysis of anti-Semitic disturbances appears in a book devoted to 'democratic and libertarian movements' in Hamburg since the late Middle Ages.
57 Wirtz, *'Widersetzlichkeiten, Excesse, Crawalle, Tumulte und Skandale'*.
58 See Chapter 8 below; and M. Gailus (ed.), *Pöbelexcesse und Volkstumulte in Berlin: Zur Sozialgeschichte der Strasse (1850–1980)* (Berlin, 1984).
59 cf. A. McElligott, 'Mobilising the Unemployed: The KPD and the Unemployed Workers' Movement in Hamburg-Altona during the Weimar Republic', in R. J. Evans and R. J. Geary (eds), *The German Unemployed* (London, 1987), pp. 228–60.
60 R. Tilly, 'Germany', in C., L. and R. Tilly, *The Rebellious Century 1830–1930* (London, 1975), p. 216.

61 See Chapter 8, below, for an example of this.
62 Mooser, 'Furcht bewahrt des Holz', p. 45.
63 G. S. Jones, 'Class Expression versus Social Control? A critique of Recent Trends in the Social History of "Leisure"', in S. Cohen and A. Scull (eds), *Social Control and the State: Historical and Comparative Essays* (Oxford, 1983), pp. 39–49.
64 See D. Philips, 'A Just Measure of Crime, Authority, Hunters and Blue Locusts: The 'Revisionist' Social History of Crime and the Law in Britain, 1780–1850', in Cohen and Scull, *Social Control*, pp. 50–74, here pp. 67–8.
65 R. Schulte, 'Feuer im Dorf', in Reif, *Räuber, Volk und Obrigkeit*, pp. 100–52.
66 H.-O. Hügel, *Untersuchungsrichter – Diebsfänger – Detektive: Theorie und Geschichte der deutschen Detektiverzählung im 19. Jahrhundert* (Stuttgart, 1978).
67 See R. J. Evans, 'Prostitution, State and Society in Imperial Germany', *Past and Present*, vol. 70 (February, 1976), pp. 106–29.
68 See e.g. A. Kopecny, *Fahrende und Vagabunden: Ihre Geschichte, Überlebenskünste, Zeichen und Strassen* (Berlin, 1980); and esp. *Wohnsitz: Nirgendwo: Vom Leben und Überleben auf der Strasse* (Hg. vom Künstlerhaus Bethanien, Berlin, 1982).
69 K. J. Bade, '"Preussengänger" und "Abwehrpolitik": Ausländerbeschäftigung, Ausländerpolitik und Ausländerkontrolle auf dem Arbeitsmarkt in Preussen vor dem Ersten Weltkrieg', *Archiv für Sozialgeschichte*, vol. 24 (1984), pp. 90–162; Bade, 'Massenwanderung und Arbeitsmarkt im deutschen Nordosten von 1880 bis zum Ersten Weltkrieg', *Archiv für Sozialgeschichte*, vol. 20 (1980), pp. 265–323; H. Plaul, 'The Rural Proletariat: The Everyday Life of Rural Labourers in the Magdeburg Region, 1830–1880', in Evans and Lee, *The German Peasantry*, pp. 102–28; and G. Griepentrog, 'Peasants, Poverty and Population: Economic and Political Factors in the Family Structure of the Working Village People in the Magdeburg Region, 1900–39, in ibid., pp. 205–23.
70 See *Wohnsitz: Nirgendwo*.
71 See R. J. Evans, *Death in Hamburg* (Oxford, 1987).
72 See the contributions to R. J. Evans (ed.), *The German Working Class* (London, 1982).
73 Zehr, *Crime and the Development of Modern Society*, p. 89.

PART THREE

Movements

6

The Sociological Interpretation of German Labour History

This chapter began as an attempt to present in a more systematic form some of the ideas developed in a book on the German Social Democratic women's movement before and during the First World War. Study of this movement confirmed the usefulness of the notion of a 'Social Democratic subculture' in tackling the question of why the Social Democratic Party (*Sozialdemokratische Partei Deutschlands*, or SPD) wanted to recruit women, despite the absence of female suffrage before 1918; but its explanatory limitations became increasingly obvious as the research revealed both the untypicality of the women so recruited – they were mostly the non-working wives of SPD activists – and the conflicts which flared up within the SPD once a vigorous, independent and in no way subservient women's movement had been established. The following considerations derive therefore from a dissatisfaction with the idea of a coherent, harmonious and somehow politically harmless subculture that so many historians, following the lead of Günther Roth's fascinating and pioneering work in the field, had considered the organizational infrastructure of the SPD – the largest and most powerful socialist movement of its time – to be. The title of this chapter is not intended to imply that all sociological influences on historical interpretation should be rejected; indeed, the argument makes conscious use of the sociology of deviance as represented by the 'radical criminology' school in Britain during the 1960s and early 1970s. The chapter does not argue, either, for a notion of history 'with the politics left out', as some critics maintained when it first appeared as a conference paper; rather, it is intended as a plea that historians should study politics in a social context. The argument refers mainly to the Wilhelmine period, on which work had been concentrated at the time of writing; until recently, relatively little research had been carried out by modern historians on the period before, though there was already a mass of scholarly work available on the Revolution of 1918. In the course of the 1980s, there has been a steady growth of research in the directions suggested by the chapter, best represented by books such as Michael Grüttner's *Arbeitswelt an der Wasserkante* (Göttingen, 1984), Franz Brüggemeier's *Leben vor Ort* (Munich, 1984), and Stephen Hickey's *Workers in Imperial Germany* (Oxford, 1985). Were I to write the essay now, I should certainly want to take account of these recent developments and perhaps to soften some of the sometimes intentionally provocative formulations which betray its original existence as a conference paper. Different versions were read to the Social History Society conference on 'Peasants and Proletarians' held in Bristol in January 1979, to the second meeting of the SSRC Research Seminar Group on Modern German Social History held at the University of East Anglia, Norwich, later the same month, and to a student audience at the University of Warwick in 1981; I am grateful to the participants on these occasions for their comments, and also to Dieter Dowe, Dick Geary, Michael Grüttner and James Wickham for further critical observations. Some of the arguments advanced aroused hostile comment; for an initial critical reaction, see Geoff Eley and Keith Nield, 'Why Does Social History Ignore Politics?', *Social History*, vol. 5 (1980), pp. 249–71. Some of the points made were taken account of in the first publication of the essay, as the introduction to *The German Working Class 1888–1933: The Politics of Everyday Life* (London, 1982), pp. 15–53: I have not sought to develop them here, but have left the original intact, apart from excising some overlaps with other chapters, and removing or condensing passages which were explicitly devoted to introducing the subsequent contributions to the book.

I

The historiography of the labour movement in Germany has been dominated not by historians but by sociologists. The formative interpretations, the major theoretical initiatives, the seminal works, all owe more to the sociological profession than to its historical counterpart. Moreover, German labour history has not merely been strongly influenced by sociology *per se* – in itself no bad thing – but in particular a decisive role has been played by one specific theoretical tradition within the field of sociology – the functionalist or neo-Weberian approach. There are three main reasons for this unusual state of affairs. In the first place, academic historiography in Germany has been more reluctant to admit the legitimacy of labour history than it has elsewhere. Not only has it until recently been politically very conservative, it has also been able to use the highly organized character of the German historical profession – often compared by its critics to a medieval guild (*Zunft*) – to exclude unwelcome outsiders and political radicals.[1] This political conservatism and relative ideological homogeneity has been compounded by an overwhelming concentration on problems of foreign policy, a feature of traditional German historiography which began with the identification of historians with the nationalist movement of the nineteenth century, was strengthened by the widespread opposition in Germany, on largely historical grounds, to the Treaty of Versailles after 1918, and only ended with the final abandonment of the nationalist legacy in the mid-1960s.[2] In Britain, by contrast, even if labour history began within the labour movement itself, it was able to gain a place in the historical profession because universities were less ideologically homogeneous, and because historians were more prepared to admit the legitimacy of other subjects of historical inquiry apart from the central policies of the state.

Secondly, labour history in Germany tended at first, naturally enough, to be written by intellectuals within the labour movement itself, by members of the SPD. It formed part of the Social Democratic subculture, isolated from institutions of the dominant culture, such as universities, historical societies and learned journals, in a way that had few parallels in other countries. Here the dominant intellectual tone was strongly Marxist; and the major historical accounts to emerge from the labour movement were repudiated or ignored by the historical profession, and suppressed, along with the labour movement itself, in the Third Reich.[3] After 1945, in the cold war, in which the front line ran through the middle of Germany, this tradition was taken up by the German Communist Party and its successors in East Germany, who produced a large body of work from the early 1950s onwards, all designed more or less consciously to provide a historical legitimation for the East German regime.[4] This made labour history even more suspect in the West, where the Federal Republic was regarded as the heir not of German Social Democracy but of the regimes established by Bismarck and his successors.

Thirdly, these two features of the German historical tradition combined to create a vacuum which was largely filled by sociologists. The reason for this lay initially in the fact that sociology enjoyed a strong tradition in Germany before 1933, beginning in the late nineteenth and early twentieth centuries with such powerful figures as Weber, Michels, Tönnies, Sombart and Schmoller. All of these figures interested themselves at one time or another in the nature of German Social Democracy and its place in the German political system; indeed, with some of them, it formed a basic and central intellectual concern.[5] The German sociologists never established themselves securely in the German academic world, and this tradition too, like that of labour history, was submerged after 1933 and did not fully resurface until the end of the Adenauer era. But instead of migrating to the East, the German sociological tradition found a new home in the USA, where many of its leading exponents lived during the Third Reich. Here indeed it gained new strength, partly through the personal influence of its representatives in American universities, partly through its more general affinities with American liberalism and its consequent intellectual influence on American sociology. From here it was re-imported into West Germany during the 1960s and early 1970s, as part of the Americanization of West German intellectual life during this period. The influence of sociology increased as the West German historiographical tradition became discredited because of its associations with Germany's nationalist past,[6] and it moved in to fill the intellectual vacuum left by Germany's lack of a non-dogmatic Marxism of the kind which contributed so significantly to the reinvigoration of historical studies in England, France and the USA.[7] The prestige of American sociology in West Germany was completed by its scientific credentials, increasingly necessary in a society where science was coming to provide the major source of intellectual legitimacy.[8]

For all these reasons, the influence of the German–American sociological tradition, already considerable in most areas of historical scholarship in West Germany, has been overwhelming in the field of labour history.[9] The great founders of German sociology were concerned with the problem of the German labour movement because they were, as far as their political beliefs were concerned, middle-class liberals trying to seek an explanation for, and a way out of, their own political impotence. The political system in which the great German sociologists of the pre-1914 era lived was not one in which liberalism was able to enjoy as much direct political power as it did in contemporary England, America, France or Italy. Government was conducted by the emperor and his ministers, who lacked all formal accountability to the parliament, the Reichstag. Direct parliamentary pressure for reforms was extremely difficult; the most the Reichstag could hope to do was to exert a negative influence by blocking the government's measures. A great deal of legislative responsibility lay with the parliaments of the federated member states of the Empire, the *Länder*. This was especially true of areas of central concern to social reformers (for example, education). These assemblies were mainly elected on property franchises and were often conservative in complexion. Most important of all, however, was the fact that a vast area of the control of social and political life lay in the hands not of legislatures but of administrative authorities who were not in any way accountable to parliaments. The police were a particularly striking example, for their powers and competence, far wider than in, say, England, included many areas subject across the North Sea to Acts of Parliament. In a very real sense, Germany before 1914 was administered rather than governed.[10]

If liberals like Weber, Tönnies and Michels, therefore, found themselves blocked from this side, they were unable to turn to any mass support to help them change the situation. For, unlike their counterparts in Britain or Italy, they had no large or united liberal political party on which they could rely. German liberalism in the late nineteenth and early twentieth centuries was represented by no less than four different political parties, all of them relatively small and ineffectual to an increasing degree on a provincial as well as a national level. Even more serious, German liberalism had been unable to strike any kind of alliance with the labour movement. Almost from the very beginning, the German labour

194

movement had rejected all ideas of an alliance with middle-class liberalism; least of all was it prepared, on the British model, to allow itself to be absorbed by it.[11] In the 1880s the influence of Marxist ideology on the labour movement became paramount. The SPD adopted an attitude of uncompromising hostility not only to the state itself but also to all 'bourgeois' political parties, including the liberals. It demonstrated its unwillingness to co-operate by consistently voting against state budgets, and by refusing to join in ceremonies of the Reichstag which implied a recognition of the legitimacy of the Empire (such as the traditional 'cheer for the Kaiser'). It made no secret of the fact that it shortly expected a revolution which would sweep away the entire administrative and political structure of the German empire. And the SPD was no mere left-wing sect: by the turn of the century it was well on the way to becoming a mass party; by 1914 its membership had topped the million mark; by 1912 it had gained more seats in the Reichstag than any other party despite a gerrymandered electoral system which left urban areas seriously under-represented.[12] With the Social Democrats there was no compromise, no room for 'fellow travellers'; either one belonged, and submitted oneself to party discipline, including its explicit rejection of co-operation with liberals, or one was condemned out of hand as a 'class enemy'.

Thoughtful liberal reformists were naturally deeply worried by this situation. Some, like Michels, tried to move the SPD towards a more flexible position from within;[13] others, like Weber, attempted to persuade liberals, and perhaps themselves, that the SPD was by no means as radical as it seemed. While Michels eventually gave up in disgust, and sought an explanation for the party's continued adherence to a rigidly radical ideology in its gradual bureaucratization, Weber came to see bureaucratization as a source of what was for him a positive development – the growth of reformism.[14] These views could, of course, be reconciled by arguing – as has since become conventional – that the SPD remained radical in theory but became increasingly reformist in practice; for the bureaucratic leadership of the party was unwilling openly to challenge the party's radical ideology, enshrined in the Erfurt Programme of 1891, for fear of promoting a divisive internal debate, and it adopted the solution of continuing ' ᴕ pay it lip-service while increasingly ignoring it in day-to-day political affairs.

II

This interpretation was taken up in the 1950s by the sociologist Günther Roth, who had been brought up in Germany but had been teaching in the USA for some years by the time his book *The Social Democrats in Imperial Germany* came to be published.[15] Indebted particularly to the neo-

Weberian sociologists Reinhard Bendix and Seymour Martin Lipset,[16] Roth advanced the existing sociological interpretation in a number of ways.[17] First he pointed out that the SPD's isolationism went much further than a mere refusal to co-operate with bourgeois parties. It involved, he said, the creation of a Social Democratic subculture, by which he meant both 'a normative system of sub-societies' and the norms which governed the system (p. 159, n. 2).

> The labour movement came to offer to masses of workers a way of life which was significantly different from that of other groups, especially those explicitly supporting the prevailing political and social system. The vehicle for this way of life was a proliferating network of political, economic and cultural organizations. (p. 159)

As the SPD became a mass movement, so these organizations came to include almost the whole of social life. A member of the party could read Social Democratic newspapers and borrow from a Social Democratic library books which covered every aspect of life from a Social Democratic point of view; he could spend his leisure in Social Democratic pubs or gymnastic clubs, choirs or cycling societies; he could enrich his life through Social Democratic cultural and artistic associations; his wife could enlist in the Social Democratic women's movement and his son in the Social Democratic youth movement; if he was injured or ill, he could call upon the Working Men's Samaritan Federation to help him; if he died, there were Social Democratic burial clubs to see he received a decent funeral.[18]

Roth pointed out that the values which governed this subculture were strongly influenced by Marxism, though it was a Marxism attenuated by Social Darwinist evolutionary determinism, for the Social Democrats argued that since the course of history would inevitably lead to a proletarian revolution in Germany, it was not necessary for them to do anything to help bring it about: all they had to do was sit tight and wait (pp. 159–92). Nevertheless, it was clear that the Social Democrats regarded the subculture as a nucleus of the future socialist society; and they constantly emphasized the detachment of its organizations from parallel institutions in the dominant culture. A second point made by Roth about the Social Democratic subculture, however, was that it was by no means as isolated from the dominant culture as it appeared to be. To start with, many if not most party members either failed to understand Marxism or failed to take it seriously. At best, they believed in a series of vulgar Marxist dogmas – class struggle, the progressively increasing misery of the proletariat, the labour theory of value, the increasing concentration of the means of production, the inevitability of the social revolution, and so on – without understanding the connections between them (p. 201). At worst, they echoed the views of one active Social Democrat who told the social investigator Paul Göhre that, although he supported the SPD because it was the only party to champion the cause of the workers, he scarcely ever read a Social Democratic newspaper or book and added that he did not 'want to be equal to the rich and distinguished people. There must always be rich and poor' (p. 196). Analyses of books borrowed from Social Democratic libraries or read by individual Social Democrats, Roth argued, showed that the preferred reading of Social Democrats was 'bourgeois' in character, varying from penny-dreadfuls to the classics of German literature, and taking in popular works on Darwinism, history and religion on the way (p. 242, n. 63). Even the party press, which included many daily papers, was according to Roth, 'an organ for the declaration of faith and for intra-party communications ... The party press remained unable to attract those readers who fell under the influence of the *Generalanzeiger* press,[19] or to interest intellectuals who were looking for good news coverage' (p. 246).[20] And in its debates and policy on art and literature, the party demonstrated with particular clarity its inability to escape from bourgeois values, a feature of party attitudes which became stronger with the progressive *embourgeoisement* of the growing corps of paid party functionaries. (pp. 259–60). In a highly influential analysis of social divisions within the party, Roth asserted that

> there seems to be no significant evidence that the embourgeoisement of the leaders created any mass conflict between leaders and led. In contrast, there was sometimes conflict between proletarian functionaries and Social Democratic intellectuals. The intellectuals were often as doctrinaire as they were unsuitable for the routine tasks of lower-ranking positions ... (p. 261).

In other words, the fundamental division within the party was not between an *embourgeoisé* bureaucracy and a proletarian membership, but between the 'doctrinaire' (i.e. Marxist) intellectuals and the rest of the party, bureaucracy and membership together.

The point was, Roth argued, that while intellectuals may have been able to escape the influence of the dominant culture, ordinary workers, even if (or especially if) they ended up as full-time party functionaries, were not. Religion, education, popular literature and commercial newspapers, the official cult of the monarchy and the pervasive influence of militarism, all combined in his view to dilute the commitment of ordinary Social Democrats to a socialist revolution with a strong dose of allegiance to the existing structure of state and society. Citing the radical liberal historian of Imperial Germany, Eckart Kehr, Roth suggested that the authorities, led by Bismarck's reactionary Minister von Puttkamer and later by Wilhelm II, consciously used church, religion and education to cement the people's loyalty to the German state. This was not without its effects on the labour movement: many Social Democratic workers had a 'dual loyalty' (pp. 214–17), some of the SPD's cultural activities 'reinforced the workers' adherence to significant components of the dominant culture' (pp. 309–10), others failed to replace the existing culture in the lives of Social Democratic members, so that bourgeois literature was read side by side with socialist, Bismarck and Wilhelm II were venerated as much as Bebel and Liebknecht, and petty-bourgeois morality dominated personal relations and home life (pp. 212–48). Beyond this limitation, the Social Democratic subculture, by sealing itself off from the rest of society, effectively prevented the SPD from expanding its constituency into the middle classes. Finally, argued Roth

> The subculture was 'negatively' integrated into the dominant system because by its very existence it provided an important means for the controlled expression and dissipation of conflict and thus contributed, for decades of peacetime, to the stability of the Empire. Specifically, the Social Democratic subculture furthered political moderation and industrial discipline in the following way: (a) It gave the workers the political and social recognition which the dominant system denied them (b) Radicalism was greatly weakened because both the individual Social Democrat in his industrial job and the party as a whole had to be careful not to provoke retaliatory measures or an intensification of repressive policies. Because of the permissive aspects of the dominant system, party and unions had an overriding interest in legality and therefore strove to protect themselves against complete suppression by fighting Blanquist and anarchist tendencies (c) With the expansion of the labour movement, more and more workers were taught by their own representatives to accept the necessity of authority, discipline, skill and good work performance. Social Democratic workers endeavoured to prove to themselves and to others that radical political aims and personal respectability were not mutually exclusive (d) Indirectly the Social Democratic labour movement enforced better living and working conditions by its mere presence and thus promoted reformist moderation and industrial peace, even though the unions could not negotiate with big business and even though the Social Democrats did not cooperate on welfare legislation (pp. 315–16)

In these ways, then, the Social Democratic subculture not only failed to create a viable alternative to the dominant culture, but even contributed to the stability of the dominant culture rather than hastening its downfall.

Recent historiography has, in one respect, gone even further than Roth in exposing the limitations of the Social Democratic subculture, by arguing that it reproduced within itself many of the features of the dominant culture, even where it was apparently successful in constructing an alternative. In this view, the construction of an elaborate and increasingly independent and unpolitical party bureaucracy was a reflection of the nature and the place of the state bureaucracy in German society. The dominance, frequently expressed in the rough, authoritarian behaviour towards subordinates, of the party leader Bebel, was a Social Democratic expression of Bismarck or Wilhelm II's role in Germany itself; the growing impotence of the party congress, where more and more issues were decided not in debate but outside, in committee-room intrigues, was a reproduction of the impotence of the Reichstag and the dominance of personal intrigue in national politics; the tendency of the same leading figures, not only Bebel and Liebknecht but other lesser-known leaders both on a national and on a provincial or local level, to remain in power for decades, showed that the SPD shared the dominant culture's emphasis on respect for authority, age and hierarchy; the party's constant insistence on discipline, its perfectly organized street marches and demonstrations, the orderly structure of promotion within its ranks – usually on the basis of seniority – even the militaristic language which the party commonly used in describing its activities: all these made the SPD into a caricature of the Prussian army.[21]

With this exception, however, subsequent studies have mostly contented themselves with filling out the details of the picture painted with such ingenuity and pervasiveness by Roth. Thus Hans-Ulrich Wehler has traced the SPD's attitudes to German nationalism and found it by no means so hostile as its formal commitment to internationalism might lead one to suppose;[22] Peter Domann has done the same with the party's view of the monarchy, which, he argues, it was formally committed to abolishing but gradually came to accept in practice;[23] Hans-Josef Steinberg, Klaus Schönhoven and Dieter Langwiesche have shown the weakness of the membership's commitment to Marxism, above all by closely examining the borrowing records of a large number of workers' libraries;[24] Dieter Groh has taken the concept of 'negative integration' and studied its use by, and impact on, the imperial government and administration;[25] Dieter Dowe has shown that the workers' choral movement sang bourgeois songs as well as proletarian ones;[26] Horst Ueberhorst and others have examined workers' sports and gymnastic clubs and argued that they helped lessen class antagonisms and integrated workers into society;[27] studies of workers' festivals and theatres have argued that these mainly served the function of transmitting traditional or bourgeois culture;[28] and recent work on SPD attitudes to marriage, sex, women, children and the family has consistently argued in the same direction.[29] Major monographic studies arguing against these views have been almost entirely absent in West Germany. The few general surveys of labour history that have appeared, on the other hand, have endorsed them almost without comment.[30]

Clearly this remarkable unanimity is not coincidental; nor can it be ascribed to mere unoriginality or mediocrity on the part of the recent scholarship on German labour history, for many of the works which I have mentioned are remarkable for the high quality of their research. Nor do the scholars concerned all come from the same university background or training. The main reason for the wide acceptance of the interpretation developed by Roth and his sociological predecessors lies in the evident sympathy of most established labour historians in West Germany with the SPD in the Federal Republic of Germany. Here there is a tendency consciously or unconsciously to facilitate the historical legitimation of the present-day SPD by playing down its radicalism and its commitment to Marxism in the past, and by arguing that its adherence to the Erfurt Programme and its use of Marxist language – highly embarrassing to present-day Social Democrats – was forced on it from outside, by the negative attitude of the state. The SPD is portrayed in this interpretation as having been a predominantly non-revolutionary party from the beginning. This in itself indeed is a reasonable enough line to take; what is more open to question is the way in which this has been interpreted. What prevented the SPD from realizing its potential as a broadly based movement of social reform, it is often argued, was above all the hostility of the authorities. By subjecting the party to constant police harassment and by preventing Social Democrats from occupying socially prestigious positions such as those of army officer or university professor, the authorities manoeuvred the SPD into a ghetto. It was thus impossible for the party to make the politically crucial transition from a labour movement (*Arbeiterbewegung*) to a broadly based democratic party (*Volkspartei*). The verbal radicalism of the party, taken seriously only by its intellectuals, served as a rhetorical fig-leaf for its political impotence. Had the state offered the SPD full participation, the pseudo-Marxism of the party's programme would soon have been dispensed with. In this way, therefore, the Social Democrats' tradition is linked to the present-day SPD, and the blame for what is portrayed as its radical alienation under the Empire is placed on the 'pre-industrial' authoritarian Prussian state.[31]

It is for these political reasons, then, that Roth's hypotheses have been accepted in the West German historical profession with such striking unanimity, a process made easier by the fact that Roth's approach carries with it the scientific legitimation of the German–American sociological tradition. In the 1960s and early 1970s it undoubtedly exercised an intellectually liberating influence on German labour history, first by making the serious study of the subject academically respectable and by integrating it fully into the German historical profession for the first time,[32] secondly, in conjunction with the increasingly negative view of the Empire which followed in the wake of the celebrated Fischer controversy of the 1960s, by inspiring a great deal of important work on the repressive policies of state and employers towards the labour movement and thus illuminating the context in which the SPD had to operate,[33] and finally by drawing the attention of historians away from ideologies and institutions and towards the cultural and moral values of the party and its working-class constituency.[34] However, as monograph after monograph appears in which the author is forced to confess that he is doing little more than filling out the details of an already well-established interpretation,[35] it is becoming clear that the functionalist sociological approach is offering rapidly diminishing returns.

III

At the most general level, then, many of the most widely accepted hypotheses in current West German writing on labour history are consciously derived from functionalist sociology, and they share the limitations of this brand of sociological theory. The idea that society is a functioning system whose interlocking parts all contribute to its 'stabilization' (in a favourite phrase of German historians, are *systemstabilisierend*) allows *any* social institution or process to be portrayed as contributing to the social and political status quo. By explaining everything, it explains nothing. And it completely fails to account for or (characteristically, in the *general* context of West German historiography) drastically underestimates the extent and significance of the social and political changes that a moment's consideration indicates were taking place in Imperial Germany.[36] Using the functionalist model, for example, it is possible, as Roth demonstrates, to argue that the Social Democrats were on the whole a stabilizing factor in the Imperial 'system' because they diverted the workers' revolutionary potential into cultural activities which in themselves were a reflection of the dominant culture; or, as Groh and others have suggested, because the more they grew in number, the more reason they gave the ruling élites of industrialists and landowners to bury or paper over their differences and join together in an ever-fiercer defence of the status quo.[37] Using these models, there is no reason why we should not explain strikes, street demonstrations and revolutionary speeches as *systemstabilisierend* as well. When it comes to events which it is impossible even in this interpretation to portray as contributing to the maintenance of the status quo – notably the Revolution of 1918 – its exponents are reduced to using the metaphor of a temporary breakdown in the social order, occasioned by psychological factors (for example, war-weariness), and give the impression that the system was soon stabilized once more, above all by the actions of the SPD leadership itself.[38] Not only does this view ignore the increasingly deep and violent social antagonisms of the Weimar Republic itself, culminating in a virtual state of civil war during the Depression and ending, of course, with the collapse of the republic and the Nazi seizure of power, it also neglects, or fails to explain, the continuing periodic outbreaks of mass protest that occurred before 1914 as well, not to mention the progressive radicalization of the political right and the growth of anti-Semitism;[39] for there is nothing in the functionalist view which offers an explanation for conflict and change, except in terms of individual psychology; its whole attention is directed towards stability, which, not surprisingly in view of its theoretical premisses, it drastically overestimates.

The functionalist or neo-Weberian sociological interpretation of German labour history also adopts a highly simplistic view of the process of the formation of consciousness. The working classes are portrayed as passive receptacles waiting to be filled with ideas poured down from above; with ideologies formulated by intellectuals, attitudes propagated by church and school, or social values and practices developed by the bourgeoisie. This is particularly true of the view which sees the SPD as a caricature of the Wilhelmine state, Bebel as a radical but equally authoritarian version of Bismarck, the SPD's emphasis on discipline as a derivative of Prussian militarism and so on; but it is equally true of the thesis, almost universally accepted by present-day labour historians in West Germany, that the SPD's verbal radicalism, its isolationism, indeed the very existence of its self-enclosed subculture, were all basically consequences of the hostility of the state towards the labour movement and of the state's refusal to allow the SPD and its members to participate in the dominant institutions of the political and social system. Not only are the mass of SPD members (and the mass of the people in general) seen as mere ciphers without any specific historical tradition of their own, but – in a way highly characteristic of the dominant intellectual culture in Germany – the state is seen as active, society as passive. Little attempt is made to relate the ideas and actions of the labour movement to the specific situation of workers, where, more often than not, the most obvious explanation of the movement's behaviour is to be found. All that has been done is to incorporate the study of labour movement *institutions* into the study of German political history; their relation to *society* has been left largely untouched.

Moreover, while recent labour historians in Germany have paid close attention to tracing bourgeois or reformist elements in the SPD's theory and practice on a wide range of issues, from the monarchy and the nation state at one extreme to gymnastics and poetry at the other, few have paused to ask precisely the significance of the issues they examine, either for the formation of working-class consciousness or for determining whether the labour movement was radical or reformist. Much, if not most, work on the Social Democratic subculture has concentrated on leisure activities. This is most obvious in the case of the recent proliferation of studies of workers' singing clubs, football teams, bicycling associations, cultural societies and so on, but it is equally true of many studies of more directly political subjects. Thus a recent (generally excellent) examination of anti-Semitism in the pre-1914 SPD has used the party's satirical weekly magazine as one of its main sources,[40] and, more generally, studies of ideology (and particularly Marxist ideology) rely heavily on figures culled from workers' libraries demonstrating the popularity of romantic novels.[41] It is arguable, however, whether leisure activities are the right thing to look at when trying to gauge the extent of the Social Democrats' commitment to socialism and revolution.

Many of the studies carried out in the sociological tradition seem to take as their starting-point an image (perhaps 'ideal type' would be a more appropriate expression) of a revolutionary worker who has never existed outside the fantasies of Lukács,[42] dedicated wholly and exclusively to the cause of revolutionary socialism every waking hour, and presumably dreaming about it as well, since his or her consciousness has been entirely purged of all 'bourgeois' elements. Such an individual has never existed in reality of course; to start at the top, for example, Marx's own wide knowledge of 'bourgeois' literature is well attested, while Lenin's fondness for the ideologically ambiguous adventure stories of Jack London is also well known.[43] No one has ever suggested, however, that any of this impeded their revolutionary thinking or activity, nor is there any reason to suppose anything similar in the case of their followers. More seriously, any individual's consciousness is surely made up of a number of different elements, and it does not really amount to much to show that not all of these were socialist or Marxist.

The categorization of attitudes and activities into 'bourgeois' on the one hand and 'socialist' on the other is in any case a considerable oversimplification. The quality of being 'bourgeois' is not necessarily inherent in books, recreations, institutions or even ideas and beliefs; they also acquire this quality, or lose it, from the context in which they are placed. The same thing can have a different meaning for different individuals, groups or social classes. The SPD's insistence on the value and importance of the family as an institution, for example, has been seen by some historians as an example of its *embourgeoisement*, of conformity to the bourgeois cult of the family prevalent in Wilhelmine Germany.[44] Equally, however, it is clear that the Social Democrats saw the working-class family, united in its support of the party's beliefs, as an important focus of resistance to the dominant culture purveyed through school, church and army; and that the party also argued for, and in some ways gave practical support to, equality within the family as an alternative to the exclusive domination of the paterfamilias propagated by official ideology.[45] Similarly, though workers' libraries, choirs and so on have often been seen as little more than a means of transmitting bourgeois culture to the proletariat, they can also be seen in a quite different light: as Dieter Dowe has remarked, 'working people's embrace of the best cultural achievements of the past, whether feudal or bourgeois in origin, can ... be interpreted more meaningfully as a desire to appropriate to themselves the "national culture." '[46] The fact that this was done through *workers'* libraries, *workers'* choral societies and *workers'* clubs was surely a crucial element in defining the meaning of the cultural products involved.

There is a similar one-sidedness in the way in which recent German historiography has approached the dominant cultural institutions of Imperial Germany. School, church and army are generally portrayed as 'socializing agents' whose main function was to imprint the dominant social values on those who passed through them, a view which has been backed up in research mainly through evidence of political conservatism in textbooks and curricula.[47] Here again, quite apart from the failure to perceive that those who entered the primary school, the church congregation or the army barracks already brought values with them in the light of which they would interpret what was offered to them, there is an insufficient awareness of the fact that education, religion and military training were profoundly ambiguous in their potential effects: education enabled workers to read Marx and Bebel as well as Treitschke and Riehl, religion helped them to express moral repugnance at the hypocrisy of the ruling class, and military training taught them how to use weapons and proved an invaluable experience in insurrections such as that of the 'Red Army' in the Ruhr at the beginning of the 1920s.[48] Moreover, it is still by no means clear precisely in what degree these institutions affected the beliefs of those who passed through them; at the most basic level, for example, we do not yet know how often children were absent from school, working illegally or simply playing truant, nor do there appear to be any serious studies of attendance at church or of the social composition of army conscripts.

Finally, recent research, above all on a local level, has begun to reveal – often almost despite itself – that the functionalist sociological interpretation of German labour history is open to question on more detailed empirical grounds. Returning to these theses advanced by Roth, there are in particular two specific points on which some doubt can now be thrown. First, the role of the labour movement in stabilizing the social system. This claim rests on three assertions,[49] which I shall deal with in turn:

(1) *The movement gave the workers political and social recognition and instilled in them a belief in the need for discipline, skill and good work performance.* It must be remembered, however, that this recognition was based specifically on a denial of the legitimacy of the existing political and social system; that discipline was essential for the organization of revolutionary outbreaks, or even of successful

strikes; and that the skilled workers were among the most militant in the workforce, particularly during the First World War.[50]

(2) *The movement's growth frightened the ruling classes into ever-greater efforts to stabilize the political system.* Here, however, it has long been well known that these efforts met with little success; indeed, if we accept the view that they culminated in the launching of the First World War, then it is clear that they ended in total disaster.

(3) *The labour movement promoted moderation by helping to enforce better living and working conditions.* Here again one can refer to the militancy of skilled workers; but there are also more specific examples which can be offered. In Hamburg the minimum qualification for voting in state elections was an annual income of 1,200 marks sustained over a period of five years. Rising real wages, whether or not they were to some degree a result of pressure from the SPD and the unions, brought an increasing number of working men above this boundary, a process which gave the SPD its first seat on the city council in 1901, and twelve more in 1904. As a result, the city government felt obliged to forestall a further growth in the party's electoral strength by revising the franchise qualifications sharply upwards in 1906, thereby provoking the local SPD into mounting Germany's first-ever political general strike, which was followed by violent riots which the Hamburg police likened to the events of the 1905 Revolution in Russia. All this throws some doubt on the simple equation between the growth of working-class prosperity and the spread of political moderation and reconciliation to the status quo.

Secondly, Roth asserts the identity of party functionaries with ordinary party members, in opposition to the intellectuals in the labour movement. Although it has become conventional, following Roth, to minimize the effects of the bureaucratization of the labour movement, and to assert that reformist functionaries were only expressing the moderate views of ordinary party or union members against the intransigent and purely theoretical revolutionism of a small and increasingly isolated body of party intellectuals, local studies suggest that it is time that the political importance of the bureaucratization of the labour movement, first brought to the attention of students by Weber and Michels, was reasserted. Ralf Lützen-kirchen's study of Dortmund, for example, has shown quite clearly how in the disputes within the local SPD over the budget question in 1908–9, all the speakers who took the reformist line (save two) were middle- or high-ranking party or union functionaries, while most of the speakers who opposed them held party posts at the lowest level, the level, in other words, that was nearest to the ordinary member. A struggle followed in which local branches of the Dortmund party attempted – without success – to curtail the freedom of action of the functionaries by forcing party-congress resolutions to be put to a ballot of all party members and by depriving the party executive and Reichstag deputies of the right to vote at party congresses.[51]

The functionalist sociological interpretation of German labour history, then, is open to criticism on a number of counts. It tends to portray society as a self-regulating system in which every element plays a functional part and in which the possibilities of real change are minimal; it assumes that values are transmitted downwards from active state institutions on to a passive proletariat; it takes its evidence from cultural and leisure activities whose role in the formation of political consciousness is exaggerated; it overplays the significance of 'bourgeois' elements in workers' culture, which it presents as politically important deviations from a purely imaginary construct of permanent and total revolutionary socialist acti-vism; it ignores the fact that 'bourgeois' cultural artefacts, educational activities or social institutions can be given quite different meanings and uses according to the situation of the recipient; it fails to note the contradictory effects of improvements in working-class living standards and of the labour movement's imposition of discipline on its members; and it overestimates the success of ruling-class strategies of containment. This catalogue by no means deals with all the many facets of what is beyond doubt a very rich and highly stimulating interpretative tradition, or with the many ways in which its insights have become embedded in the literature; I have reserved one or two of the most important aspects for later in the discussion. Before they can be brought into focus, however, it is necessary to turn to the question of how one might begin to construct an alternative framework of interpretation.

IV

The first step necessary in order to transcend the functionalist sociological interpretation of German labour history is to make a distinction between Social Democratic (or labour movement) culture and working-class culture. Roth, for example, claimed that 'the labour movement came to offer to masses of workers a way of life which was significantly different from that of other groups'.[52] Yet it seems unlikely that the labour movement and its subculture played such a central role in working-class life. It is an obvious point that though it contained over a million members by 1914, the SPD contained only a minority of the working class as a whole. The same is true of the successor parties (Communists, Independ-ent Social Democrats) in the Weimar Republic. Similarly with the trade unions. Even among miners, often thought of as an exceptionally militant group, only a minority belonged to trade unions of any description, and in general only a minority of trade unionists actually belonged to the SPD.[53]

206

The numbers involved in the labour movement's cultural associations, however large, by no means encompassed a majority of the working class. The relationship of many of these associations with the political parties of the labour movement may have been loose or informal, but it is clear that there was a very substantial overlap in membership, and even without this the basic distinction, between labour movement and working class, still holds good. Recognition of this point is spreading among German labour historians: a good deal of work is being carried out on non-socialist labour organizations, and historians are beginning to explore regions of working-class life and experience not encompassed within the labour movement.[54] Yet these beginnings are very slow, as a recent book of essays on workers' culture edited by Gerhard A. Ritter indicates;[55] despite the editor's plea for more study of working-class as distinct from socialist culture, the great majority of the studies in the volume deal with socialist cultural organizations. Even major socialist festivals such as May Day did not play a particularly significant role in the life of the working class as a whole, though this seems to be assumed by the essay on it in the book.[56] Certainly, a number of primarily quantitative studies of the labour force in various nineteenth-century factories and towns in Germany have recently been undertaken, and these are rapidly transforming our knowledge of the German proletariat during the industrial revolution. Yet these studies are proceeding in a manner that is largely empirical in character, and in most respects are divorced from the existing historiographical debate about the nature of the German labour movement.[57]

The same is the case for another very interesting development in German labour history since the end of the 1970s: the turn to the 'history of everyday life' (*Alltagsgeschichte*) of the working class. A recent collection of essays on the 'social history of everyday life in the industrial age', edited by Jürgen Reulecke and Wolfhard Weber, gives some indication of the direction which historical inquiry is taking: there are contributions on miners and metalworkers, on housing and food, on primary schools, religion and sports.[58] The editors see their enterprise as an attempt to recapture 'the various hopes, fears and desires of "ordinary people"', which, they argue, run the risk of being neglected in 'technocratically congealed pluralistic societies, when an arrogant bureaucracy, contemptuous of ordinary human beings, seeks to determine everyday life' (p. 10). The influence of the French *Annales* school is acknowledged; and so too is that of contemporary social science. It follows from this that one of the major weaknesses of the collection lies in the way in which everyday experience is frequently dissolved into categories such as 'norm structures', 'conditions of socialization', 'need satisfaction', 'behavioural patterns', 'communication networks', etc., etc., thus reproducing static categories of sociology in a context (history) for which many of them are inappropriate. Moreover, although one of the impulses behind *Alltagsges-*

207

chichte is evidently the belief that the development of the labour movement cannot be properly understood without knowledge of the conditions of life and the everyday thought and action of its members and supporters, the development of *Alltagsgeschichte* as a specific area of historical investigation none the less runs the risk of separating social history from political history and of presenting itself as a mere *addition* to labour history, rather than a different way of looking at it.[59] In addition to this, there is a continuing tendency to present the working class as passive rather than active even in its daily experience of life: to write *Alltagsgeschichte*, in the words of Reulecke and Weber, as the history of 'how individual human beings *lived under the conditions* of the spectacular political events and social change processes of modern times, and how *these made themselves felt* in the daily life of the many individual and small groups [of people]' (my emphasis)[60]. Finally, 'the history of everyday life', at least as it has been developed so far, seems to fragment working-class experience, not only to divorce political from social life but to separate work from leisure, family from factory, and one occupation from another. The sense of what links these things, or what in the way of working-class culture or consciousness might transcend them, is lost.[61] The problem remains, therefore, of constituting the *working class* and its culture and values as objects of historical study, and of investigating the relationship between these and the institutions, culture and values of the *labour movement*.

A second step by which we might go beyond the functionalist socio-logical interpretation of German labour history is to move the focus away from leisure. As I have suggested, the sociological interpretation relies heavily for its evidence on investigations of socialist leisure organizations. More recently, historians have begun to move beyond this to examine patterns of working-class leisure in a more general way, including activi-ties and institutions unconnected with the socialist movement, such as football clubs.[62] Implicit in this new approach is still the view that working-class culture means what workers do or think when they are not working. But this was only a small part of the working-class experience. In an era when the working day was far longer than it is now, work stood at the centre of life for most people; through it, the employee was brought into daily contact with the dominant culture (again using the word in its broadest sense, meaning the attitudes and practices of the ruling classes). The centrality and intensity of this experience far outweighed any influ-ence exerted by bicycling clubs and male-voice choirs on the one hand or by school and military service on the other. It is to work, therefore, that we should be directing our attention; to the structure and conditions of employment and unemployment, to their economic meaning and social or personal significance.[63] Our starting-point should be the relations of employer and employed, the nature of work, and the conditions under which people laboured to secure their existence. It is from this perspective that we should then look to the social structure and function of leisure activities; from a study of work and leisure, and from their relations with one another, and with the labour movement, its ideology and its institutions, that we can begin to construct a picture of working-class attitudes to state and society more satisfying than that provided by the functionalist sociological interpretation. What is necessary is not only the penetration of historical investigation beneath the level of socialist organization and labour-movement culture to the reality of working-class life and attitudes underneath but, rather, the investigation of the relationship between these two levels. For working-class experience is no more real or authentic than the experience of activists in socialist political or cultural organizations; it possesses, certainly, its own autonomy and its own creative drive, but it does not, and cannot, remain unaffected by the ideology and politics of the labour movement itself.[64]

It is necessary at this point, therefore, to return to the specifics of the functionalist sociological interpretation of German labour history. According to Günther Roth, the German labour movement insisted on legal tactics and fought revolutionary activism within its own ranks. More generally,

> with the expansion of the labour movement, more and more workers were taught by their own representatives to accept the necessity of authority ... Social Democratic workers endeavoured to prove to themselves and to others that radical political aims and personal respectability were not mutually exclusive.[65]

The recent trends in historical scholarship discussed above have tended to reinforce this view. The investigation of the labour movement and the working class in Germany has produced a picture of proletarian culture that has highlighted its integrative aspects and the extent to which it (allegedly) diverted political energies into harmless, even 'bourgeois', leisure pursuits. Football teams, singing clubs, gymnastic associations, libraries, or even political festivals such as May Day were relatively respectable, generally innocuous activities, and if this is what the working class of Wilhelmine and Weimar Germany spent its time doing, it is scarcely surprising that it lost the taste for revolution, if indeed it had ever possessed it. The Social Democrats, it is argued, taught the proletariat to be law-abiding; but even more than this, the 'traditional' components of working-class culture (miners' festivals, guild practices and the like), which exerted a strong influence on the formation of the Social Democratic subculture, were themselves, it is suggested, profoundly addicted to the observation of rules and conformity to authority.[66] Much of the work that has been carried out on working-class culture has been motivated not least by a desire to establish its authenticity as part of the national culture and the value of its contribution to cultural life in general, by an urge to counteract the élitist view of the working class as a collection of ignorant, untutored savages with no authentic cultural life of their own.[67] It is this approach, with its narrow definition of 'culture'[68] as the artistic and creative life of a society or group within it, which helps explain why so much attention has been paid by historians to singing clubs, popular festivals, organized sports and the like; though there remains in this a refusal to look at more widespread but perhaps less elevating manifestations of popular culture (in this narrow sense of the word) such as the German equivalent of the music hall (*Variétés* and *Tingeltangels*).[69] Finally, of course, work on German labour history has been indubitably structured by hindsight; by the capitulations of 1914 and 1933, by the need to explain why the seemingly radical socialist Left first supported the German government at the outbreak of the First World War, then failed to mount any effective opposition to the Nazi seizure of power.[70] All these various influences, together with the elements of the functionalist sociological interpretation discussed in the earlier parts of this essay, have come together to produce a picture of working-class culture and working-class life in Wilhelmine and Weimar Germany that suppresses almost completely its rough, law-breaking and undisciplined aspects. The result is a drastically distorted view of working-class habits, manners and values which in turn leads to serious misunderstandings about the nature of working-class culture and politics.

V

Increasingly, historians are beginning to uncover evidence that working-class culture was far from being generally worthy, self-improving, respectable, law-abiding and harmless. A necessary premiss is of course a redefinition of the concept of culture – such as has already been proposed, though as yet scarcely carried out, by West German students of the subject – to include 'the social history of day-to-day experiences',[71] the whole package of values and practices which informed everyday proletarian life. In the particular case with which we are concerned – working-class culture in Germany – the question at the top of the historical agenda is (as it has always been) the extent to which it rested on either an acceptance or a denial of the legitimacy of the capitalist social order. The everyday life of the working class, at work and at leisure, involved constant deviations from the attitudes and patterns of conduct which the bourgeoisie laid down for the attainment of 'respectability'. Working-class culture contained many elements of which the ruling classes disapproved: heavy drinking, for instance, or, later, dancing, cinema-going and adolescent sexuality.[72] These deviations were also frequently necessitated by the economic and social situation of the working class: for example, small-time crime was built into the structure of work in the Hamburg dockland in the late nineteenth and early twentieth centuries. Dockers considered in effect that they had a right to appropriate part of the wares which they were required to load and unload from ships; and the casual, precarious nature of their employment encouraged them to maximize earnings in any way possible at the times when they were actually working. At moments of tension and conflict too, some workers could again feel few qualms about breaking the law and engaging in what were regarded as crimes of some seriousness and magnitude.

The question of 'deviance' leads on naturally to the problem of working-class attitudes towards the law. Many historians have pointed out that the law in Wilhelmine Germany (and to a lesser extent in the Weimar Republic as well) discriminated massively against the labour movement. Even though the Social Democratic party was no longer formally illegal after 1890, its activities were still constantly supervised by the political police, who arrested its members on the slightest pretexts. Few indeed by 1914 were the Social Democratic newspaper and magazine editors who had not spent some time in gaol on a charge of *lèse-majesté* or libel on the police, or as the result of some piece of legal chicanery engineered by the authorities. And countless were the SPD meetings that were broken up and dissolved by the police on one pretext or another, such as constituting a danger to public order. Strikes and union activities were similarly circumscribed by a whole set of legal restrictions and limitations.[73] This system of judicial bias and persecution, conventionally dubbed both by socialists at the time and by subsequent historians as a system of 'class justice' (*Klassenjustiz*), would not, it is generally argued, have existed in a society more liberal or politically 'modern' in its nature.

Yet this argument obscures the real nature of 'class justice' in late-nineteenth- and early-twentieth-century Germany. For the law was structured so as to constitute a massive interference not simply in labour movement activities but also in the daily life of the working class.[74] The policing of everyday life in Wilhelmine Germany extended even into the most intimate spheres of personal life; the police attempted, for instance, to prevent men and women living together and having sexual relations without being married, or even to prevent such people from getting married if they were adjudged to be 'immoral' characters.[75] Similarly, police control of prostitution in Imperial Germany involved a degree of interference in the lives of those concerned that was unknown in England even under the (short-lived) regime of the Contagious Diseases Acts. A special branch of the police existed in every German state to deal with prostitution – the 'morals police' (*Sittenpolizei*). These were empowered to arrest and subject to a medical examination any woman suspected of being a prostitute; those convicted were liable to be inscribed on the official list and subject to the morals police regulations. These were formidable in their scope and extent. Apart from the obligatory medical examinations, there were also provisions confining prostitutes to certain buildings or streets, regulating the hours at which they could go out, and prohibiting them from frequenting at any time a whole range of different, named streets, parks, cafés and other places in the various towns for which these regulations obtained. As has recently been written:

> they present such a close net of possibilities of contravention and prosecution that if she [i.e. the prostitute] is for a moment inattentive, she will then fall foul of them; on the other hand, if she lives according to these rules, she exists within an invisible but ever-present prison.[76]

It is important, however, to bear in mind that such attempts to control everyday life met with only limited success. As Stefan Bajohr points out, most couples living in *wilden Ehen* ('wild marriages') were able to circumvent police restrictions; if they really wanted to marry, they commonly went to London to do so. Similarly, in the case of prostitution, the strength of the morals police was altogether inadequate to deal with the scale of the problem which they (of their own choice) confronted, or to enforce even a tithe of the regulations which they had drawn up. The morals police were complaining by the end of the nineteenth century that prostitution was being increasingly carried on by women 'who for part of the time do a regular job, but who also from time to time sell themselves to men for money, in order to improve their financial situation'.[77] In such circumstances the police themselves became increasingly unwilling to enforce the regulation too vigorously, because the more unpleasant they made the situation of controlled prostitutes, the more prostitutes would be inclined to evade control altogether. None the less, by the early 1900s only a tiny proportion of German prostitutes were inscribed at all. In 1909 in Munich, for instance, less than 9 per cent of the prostitutes actually known to the police were inscribed and regulated; and even these were only part of the whole. The truth was, as one prostitute told the American investigator Abraham Flexner on the eve of the First World War, 'only the stupid are inscribed'.[78]

But working-class resistance to, or evasion of, the policing of everyday life extended well beyond the domestic sphere; it took place even at the workplace itself, and confronted police measures that, unlike the prevention of concubinage or the regulation of prostitution, would not have been considered unfamiliar or excessive in other countries. In the new industrial communities, working-class resistance to, or evasion of, police attempts to enforce the law were considerable.[79] Michael Grüttner's study of pilfering in the Hamburg docks shows clearly how workers defied the law at the workplace as well as on the streets or in their leisure hours.[80]

Being working-class in Wilhelmine and Weimar Germany meant, therefore, not only constant contraventions of bourgeois moral and social norms; it also meant continual evasion, defiance and disregard of the law and of those whose job it was to enforce it. Law-breaking was woven into the fabric of the everyday life of the working class.[81] Of course it is necessary to distinguish between different elements of the proletariat in this, as in other, contexts. Work in the docks provided more opportunities for pilferage than did some other kinds of employment, and the structure of employment in the docks was also of a kind to encourage illicit ways of supplementing income. Among working-class youth in Berlin during the 1920s, only a minority engaged in gang violence, though a great many more must, if they were like working-class adolescent gangs elsewhere, have constantly engaged in petty violations of the law.[82] And steelworkers in Dortmund only resorted to sabotage, if they did at all, at moments of extreme tension between workers and employers.

So it would be wrong to conclude that a hard and fast line should be drawn between those elements of the working class who broke the law and defied bourgeois morality and those who did not. Marxist theory has conventionally drawn a distinction between the working class, to whom are ascribed a set of functioning moral, social and political values, and the *Lumpenproletariat*, the 'proletariat of rags', 'a residuum drawn from all social classes, of society's outcasts, whose conduct no political or moral principles can be said to govern'.[83] Certainly Marx tended to use this term as a means of abuse in his writing: Louis Napoleon, for example, appears in the *Eighteenth Brumaire* as a member of the French *Lumpenproletariat*.[84] But more commonly, the term corresponded to what French writers in the nineteenth century called the 'dangerous class', in contrast to the honest 'labouring class'; the one lived off its wits, the other from its work.[85] Such a distinction may in certain circumstances be a useful one. But it has its dangers too, particularly if it is used in the polemical way in which it came to be employed by the labour movement in the late nineteenth century. It must not be taken to imply, as it was by Social Democrats in Imperial Germany, that the 'working class proper' never had any occasion to break the law or defy accepted moral standards. More useful may be a distinction between proletariat and sub-proletariat (the residuum of casually employed or structurally unemployed and under-employed, the poorest and most precarious sectors of the working class).[86] In the conditions of employment which obtained in the industrializing economy of Wilhelmine Germany, or the crisis-ridden economy of the Weimar era, the boundary lines between proletariat and sub-proletariat, between stable and unstable, solvent and insolvent, employed and unemployed, permanently engaged and casually hired, were fluid, shifting and hard to discern. Workers changed jobs frequently; sudden lay-offs, dismissals and lockouts were common. The extent of casual employment was far greater than in more mature capitalist societies.[87] Welfare provisions were inadequate to save a family from destitution when illness, accident or death incapacitated the main breadwinner. In such circumstances recourse to additional, illegal sources of income was common. But even in the higher-earning sectors of the working-class, as with lightermen in the Hamburg docks, such recourse was equally common. Nor do concubinage or heavy drinking seem solely to have been pursuits of the destitute. And sabotage in the Dortmund steel strike of 1912 was probably carried out by workers who were among the most highly and regularly paid in Germany. Certainly it would be exaggerated to suggest that all of the working class were breaking the law and contravening bourgeois morality all of the time, at least in so dramatic a way. But it would be equally erroneous to attempt to maintain any sharp dividing line between those who conformed and those who did not.

Working-class contravention of bourgeois norms did not necessarily constitute a repudiation of morality and law *per se*.[88] For example, although dock workers constantly stole from their employers, they did not steal from each other; those who did rob their workmates were ostracized, while the dockers felt no qualms about entrusting the funds of their organizations to fellow workers with previous convictions for stealing from cargoes. Similarly, although the Berlin *Cliquen* (a sort of cross between street gangs and hiking clubs) in the 1920s constantly engaged in violence, vandalism and theft, a member who made off with the funds of a *Clique* was an exception, and instantly stigmatized as a 'bad character'. And one of the ironies of police attempts to control 'concubinage' was the fact that many of the couples concerned actually wanted to live together in stable marriages and were only prevented from doing so by the law. Working-class culture involved its own sets of values and norms, its own codes of conduct, even though frightened conservatives frequently thought of the working class as a part of society that still existed in a state of nature, without morality, honour or law.[89]

Even before the First World War, the SPD did make some attempt to crack down on those aspects of working-class culture it disapproved of, at least within its own ranks. These were seldom successful. A Social Democratic campaign to stop party members drinking Junker-produced schnapps was a failure; so too were the efforts of the trade unions in the First World War and the early Weimar Republic to stop their members among the Hamburg dockers from pilfering cargoes. The party and the unions commonly asserted that those engaged in 'rough' or deviant behaviour were not organized workers but members of the *Lumpenproletariat*.[90] Yet this was patently untrue, as they themselves were well aware. To some extent such denials were a defensive mechanism against attempts by the authorities, employers and the right-wing press to assert that the labour movement encouraged such activities; that it was the creation of a demoralized, violent, drunken, lazy, thieving and fornicating working class, and that its main aim was to create more room for its members to indulge their base lusts and appetites instead of doing an honest day's work. The conservative press in particular portrayed the labour movement as subversive of all social and moral order.[91] It was necessary to refute such accusations if the movement was to remain credible as a political force or achieve some recognition at the bargaining table. Refuted, therefore, they were, even when – as in the case of dock pilferage, or drink, or participation in suffrage disturbances – the labour movement knew that, on a superficial level at least, they were true.

Implicit in such refutations was surely the knowledge that – as I argued earlier in this essay – the working class had its own system of values, that because dockers habitually stole from ship's cargoes, this did not mean that they were congenitally dishonest, that because workers drank large quantities of beer and schnapps in their leisure hours, this did not mean that they were depraved, that because proletarian women had illegitimate children, this did not mean that they were sexually promiscuous. Indeed, as in the case of the relations between the Communist Party and the violent juvenile *Cliquen* in Berlin in the Weimar Republic, the labour movement could put this insight to positive use in the struggle against its opponents. Yet such an insight, such tactics, depended on the labour movement's retention of a radical socialist ideology which had as one of its premisses a sharp distinction between proletarian and bourgeois morality and behaviour, and a recognition of the social relativity of the latter. As time went on, the Social Democrats, and the 'free' trade unions with which they were associated, gradually seem to have lost this way of looking at working-class culture, as they retreated from the socialist radicalism of the Wilhelmine era. By 1918–19 the trade unions no longer denied that there was a pilferage problem in the Hamburg docks, but actively urged the most extreme measures to combat it. James Wickham has suggested that the reluctance of the labour movement to adapt to new working-class cultural forms during the Weimar Republic was a major reason for its failure to attract the young.[92] Certainly after 1918 we see a much-reduced tolerance for working-class attitudes being displayed by the SPD. Only the Communists could be said to have tried to overcome it, and even in their case there were still ambivalences, problems and failures, while the attempt itself cut them off still further from the SPD and so divided labour movement culture ever more deeply within itself.

By 1930, in many ways, the SPD had ceased to recognize that working-class culture did possess its own authenticity. This culture involved a widespread deviance from bourgeois values, which a concentration on *organized* leisure and a concomitant neglect of informal, spare-time activities caused the SPD, like many historians who have followed in its footsteps, to neglect or misunderstand.

NOTES

1 See Chapter 1, above.
2 For a striking example of how this tradition affects even a historian who has previously devoted a whole monograph to the history of the SPD when it comes to writing a *general* account of Wilhelmine Germany, see H.-U. Wehler, *Das deutsche Kaiserreich 1871–1918* (Göttingen, 1973), in which 29 pages are devoted to foreign policy, over 70 to government and only 3 to the labour movement.
3 These include both general histories by authors such as F. Mehring and local studies (of particular importance in Germany) by writers such as E. Bernstein, H. Laufenberg, and others.
4 See esp. *Geschichte der deutschen Arbeiterbewegung*, 8 vols (East Berlin, 1966).
5 Among innumerable studies, see e.g. A. Mitzman, *Sociology and Estrangement: Three Sociologists of Imperial Germany* (New York, 1973), on Tönnies, Sombart and Michels; W. J. Mommsen, *Max Weber und die deutsche Politik 1890–1920* (2nd edn., Tübingen, 1974), on Weber.
6 A crucial role here was played by the 'Fischer controversy' of the 1960s: see the account in J. A. Moses, *The Politics of Illusion* (London, 1975).
7 The reasons for (and some consequences of) this crucial absence are outlined briefly in Chapter 1 above.
8 cf. my review of R. Rürup (ed.), *Historische Sozialwissenschaft* (Göttingen, 1977), in *Social History*, vol. 4 (1979), pp. 367–9.
9 Indeed, the functionalist sociological interpretation has become something of an orthodoxy. A parallel situation exists in the wider field of German political history as a whole: see the discussion in G. Eley, 'Defining Social Imperialism: Use and Abuse of an Idea', *Social History*, vol. 3 (1976), pp. 265–90.
10 The standard account of the constitution is E. R. Huber, *Deutsche Verfassungsgeschichte seit 1789*, Vol. 4, *Struktur und Krisen des Kaiserreichs* (Stuttgart, 1969).
11 W. Schieder, 'Das Scheitern des bürgerlichen Radikalismus und die sozialistische Parteibildung in Deutschland' in H. Mommsen (ed.), *Sozialdemokratie zwischen Klassenbewegung und Volkspartei* (Frankfurt am Main, 1974), pp. 17–34.
12 The standard account in English is still C. E. Schorske, *German Social Democracy 1905–1917: the Development of the Great Schism* (Cambridge, Mass., 1955).
13 For Michels's association with the revisionists see Mitzman, *Sociology and Estrangement*, p. 285. Michels's political evolution after his disillusion with the SPD eventually took him close to Italian fascism.
14 For Weber, see Mommsen, *Max Weber*, pp. 109–23. In this paragraph I am of course necessarily giving a selective and simplified account of the interpretations advanced by Weber and Michels.
15 G. Roth, *The Social Democrats in Imperial Germany: A Study in Working-class Isolation and National Integration* (Totowa, NJ, 1963).
16 Ibid., p. vii and preface (by R. Bendix), pp. xii–xiv.
17 It is worth noting that Roth declared himself, with commendable frankness, to be personally 'more sympathetic to the right and center of the Social Democratic movement than to the left' (ibid., p. 324).
18 Roth took only some of the multifarious aspects of the subculture as examples; the picture has been filled out by subsequent research (discussed later in this chapter).
19 Local (bourgeois) dailies which grew in popularity from c. 1900.
20 It should be added that this is an extremely unfair remark; in fact the news coverage of the SPD daily press (in newspapers such as *Vorwärts*, the *Hamburger Echo* and the *Leipziger Volkszeitung*) was broad and comprehensive, though of course the news stories covered were presented and interpreted from a Social Democratic point of view.
21 See esp. J. P. Nettl, 'The German Social Democrats 1890–1914 as a Political Model', *Past*

and Present, vol. 3 (Apr. 1965), pp. 65–95; P. Lösche, 'Arbeiterbewegung und Wilhelminismus: Sozialdemokratie zwischen Anpassung und Spaltung', *Geschichte in Wissenschaft und Unterricht*, vol. 20 (1969), pp. 519–33.

22 H.-U. Wehler, *Sozialdemokratie und Nationalstaat* (2nd edn, Göttingen, 1972).

23 P. Domann, *Sozialdemokratie und Kaisertum unter Wilhelm II: Die Auseinandersetzung der Partei mit dem monarchischen System, seine gesellschaftlichen und verfassungspolitischen Voraussetzungen* (Wiesbaden, 1974). See also W. K. Blessing, 'The Cult of Monarchy: Political Loyalty and the Workers' Movement in Imperial Germany', *Journal of Contemporary History*, vol. 13, no. 2 (1978), pp. 357–76.

24 H.-J. Steinberg, *Sozialismus und deutsche Sozialdemokratie: Zur Ideologie der Partei vor dem Ersten Weltkrieg* (Bonn-Bad Godesberg, 1972), pp. 129–42; D. Langewiesche and K. Schönhoven, 'Arbeiterbibliotheken und Arbeiterlektüre im Wilhelminischen Deutschland', *Archiv für Sozialgeschichte*, vol. 16 (1976), pp. 135–204.

25 D. Groh, *Negative Integration und revolutionärer Attentismus: Die deutsche Sozialdemokratie am Vorabend des Ersten Weltkrieges* (Berlin and Frankfurt, 1973).

26 D. Dowe, 'The Workers' Choral Movement before the First World War', *Journal of Contemporary History*, vol. 13, no. 2 (1978), pp. 269–76.

27 H. Ueberhorst, *Frisch, frei, stark und treu: Die Arbeitersportbewegung in Deutschland 1893–1933* (Düsseldorf, 1973).

28 K. Tenfelde, 'Mining Festivals in the Nineteenth Century', *Journal of Contemporary History*, vol. 13, no. 2 (1978), pp. 377–412; G. A. Ritter, 'Workers' Culture in Imperial Germany: Problems and Points of Departure for Research', ibid., pp. 175–6.

29 U. Linse, 'Arbeiterschaft und Geburtenentwicklung im Deutschen Kaiserreich von 1871', *Archiv für Sozialgeschichte*, vol. 12 (1972), pp. 205–71; R. P. Neuman, 'The Sexual Question and Social Democracy in Imperial Germany', *Journal of Social History*, vol. 7, no. 3 (1974), pp. 271–86; J. Quataert, 'Feminist Tactics in German Social Democracy: A Dilemma', *Internationale Wissenschaftliche Korrespondenz zur Geschichte der Deutschen Arbeiterbewegung*, no. 1 (1977), pp. 48–65.

30 Thus even authors critical of the present-day SPD conform to the general pattern, e.g. G. Fülberth, *Proletarische Partei und bürgerliche Literatur: Auseinandersetzungen in der deutschen Sozialdemokratie der II. Internationale über Möglichkeiten und Grenzen einer sozialistischen Literaturpolitik* (Neuwied, 1972). General surveys include H. Grebing, *Geschichte der deutschen Arbeiterbewegung: Ein Überblick* (Munich, 1966); W. Eichler, *Hundert Jahre Sozialdemokratie* (Bielefeld, 1963); H. Mommsen (ed.), *Sozialdemokratie zwischen Klassenbewegung und Volkspartei* (Frankfurt, 1974); H. Potthoff, *Die Sozialdemokratie von den Anfängen bis 1945*, Kleine Geschichte der SPD, Vol. I, Bonn-Bad Godesberg, 1974).

31 cf. the critique advanced in G. Fülberth and J. Harrer, *Kritik der sozialdemokratischen Hausgeschichtsschreibung*, Pahl-Rugenstein Hefte zu politischen Gegenwartsfragen, Vol. 22 (Frankfurt am Main, 1975). Unfortunately the same authors' attempt to provide a general account of Social Democratic history in no way fulfils the promise of their critique of other historians' work: see Fülberth and Harrer, *Arbeiterbewegung und SPD*, Vol. 1, *Die deutsche Sozialdemokratie 1890–1933* (Darmstadt, 1974).

32 H. Mommsen (ed.), *Sozialdemokratie zwischen Klassenbewegung und Volkspartei* (Frankfurt, 1975), p. 7.

33 See esp. K. Saul, *Staat, Industrie, Arbeiterbewegung im Kaiserreich: Zur Innen- und Sozialpolitik des Wilhelminischen Deutschland 1903–1914* (Düsseldorf, 1974).

34 G. A. Ritter, 'Workers' Culture in Imperial Germany: Problems and Points of Departure for Research', *Journal of Contemporary History*, vol. 13, no. 2 (1978), pp. 165–89.

35 cf., for example, J. Loreck, *Wie man früher Sozialdemokrat wurde: Das Kommunikationsverhalten in der deutschen Arbeiterbewegung und die Konzeption der sozialistischen Parteipublizistik durch August Bebel*, Schriftenreihe des Forschungsinstituts der Friedrich-Ebert-Stiftung, Vol. 130 (Bonn-Bad Godesberg, 1977), a study of worker autobiographies which explicitly regards itself as providing no more than further illustrations of Roth's theses.

36 The classic example of this is of course the almost entirely static picture of society in Imperial Germany portrayed by Wehler, *Das Deutsche Kaiserreich*.

37 This theory of 'negative integration' indeed is the main respect in which the SPD features in overall characterizations of the social and political system of Imperial Germany by present-day West German historians. See e.g. not only Groh, *Negative Integration*, and Wehler, *Kaiserreich*, but also, for a particularly clear formation ('artificially whipped-up fear of socialism ... [as] a relatively effective means of ... uniting all non-socialist forces'), P. C. Witt, 'Innenpolitik und Imperialismus in der Vorgeschichte des 1. Weltkrieges', in K. Holl and G. List (eds), *Liberalismus und imperialistischer Staat* (Göttingen, 1975), p. 16. cf. also S. Mielke, *Der Hansa-Bund für Gewerbe, Handel und Industrie 1909–1914* (Göttingen, 1976), p. 20. All of these general characterizations of the Wilhelmine state conform to this rule.

38 See F. L. Carsten, *Revolution in Central Europe 1918–19* (London, 1972); G. A. Ritter and S. Miller (eds), *Die deutsche Revolution 1918–1919 – Dokumente* (Frankfurt am Main, 1968); see also the critique by B. Peterson, 'Workers' Councils in Germany 1918–19: Recent Literature on the Rätebewegung', *New German Critique*, vol. 4 (1975), pp. 113–23.

39 For this see G. Eley, 'The Wilhelmine Right: How it Changed', in R. J. Evans (ed.), *Society and Politics in Wilhelmine Germany* (London, 1978), pp. 112–35.

40 R. Leuschen-Seppel, *Sozialdemokratie und Antisemitismus im Kaiserreich* (Bonn-Bad Godesberg, 1978), a study which concludes that 'the workers' culture of the nineteenth century, despite its emancipatory claims, was helplessly at the mercy of the dominant culture in both form and content'.

41 See n. 24, above; also Roth, *Social Democrats*, pp. 232–43.

42 G. Lukács, *History and Class Consciousness: Studies in Marxist Dialectics* (London, 1971).

43 S. S. Prawer, *Karl Marx and World Literature* (Oxford, 1977).

44 Quataert, 'Feminist Tactics', p. 48, n.1; on the general question of *embourgeoisement*, see H. Bausinger, 'Verbürgerlichung – Folgen eines Interpretaments', in G. Wiegelmann (ed.), *Kultureller Wandel im 19. Jahrhundert: Verhandlungen des 18. Deutschen Volkskunde-Kongresses in Trier vom 13. bis 18. September 1971*, Studien zum Wandel von Gesellschaft und Bildung im Neunzehnten Jahrhundert, Vol. 5 (Göttingen, 1973), pp. 24–49.

45 So, at least, I have attempted to argue in my book *Sozialdemokratie und Frauenemanzipation im Deutschen Kaiserreich* (Bonn-Bad Godesberg, 1979).

46 Dowe, 'Workers' Choral Movement', p. 273.

47 cf. Wehler, *Sozialdemokratie*, pp. 124–31; C. Berg, *Die Okkupation der Schule: Eine Studie zur Aufhellung gegenwärtiger Schulprobleme an der Volksschule Preussens (1872 bis 1900)* (Heidelberg, 1973); F. Meyer, *Schule der Untertanen: Lehrer und Politik in Preussen 1848–1900* (Hamburg, 1976).

48 E. Lucas, *Märzrevolution 1921*, Vol. 2, *Der bewaffnete Arbeiteraufstand im Ruhrgebiet in seiner inneren Struktur und in seinem Verhältnis zu den Klassenkämpfen in den Regionen des Reiches* (Frankfurt am Main, 1973), pp. 63–95.

49 See the quotations in Section II, above, for these assertions.

50 See E. Lucas, *Zwei Formen von Radikalismus in der deutschen Arbeiterbewegung* (Frankfurt am Main, 1976); D. Geary, 'Radicalism and the Worker: Metal-workers and Revolution 1914–23' in Evans, *Society and Politics in Wilhelmine Germany*, pp. 267–86.

51 R. Lützenkirchen, *Der sozialdemokratische Verein für den Reichstagswahlkreis Dortmund-Hörde* (Dortmund, 1970), pp. 51–70. In this case, of course, the stress laid by the functionalist sociological tradition's originators on bureaucratization was correct and is certainly much more helpful than the attempt by Roth to stress instead the isolated position of the party's intellectuals. However, the formation of a reformist party bureaucracy should be seen not as the mere expression of an 'iron law' of sociology, valid at all times and in all places, as Michels asserted, but rather in the context of wider social changes taking place within the working class, and as a response to specific historical circumstances. Again, the role of the bureaucracy in the German Communist Party in the 1920s was clearly very different from that of its counterpart in the pre-1914 SPD: see H. Weber, *Die Wandlung des deutschen Kommunismus – Die Stalinisierung der KPD* (Frankfurt am Main, 1969).

52 See Section II, above.

53 S. Hickey, 'The Shaping of the German Labour Movement: Miners in the Ruhr' in Evans, *Society and Politics in Wilhelmine Germany*, pp. 215–40, at p. 236.

54 See e.g. the essays collected in J. Reulecke and W. Weber (eds), *Fabrik, Familie, Feierabend: Beiträge zur Sozialgeschichte des Alltags im Industriezeitalter* (Wuppertal, 1978).

55 'Workers' Culture', special issue of *Journal of Contemporary History*, vol. 13, no. 2 (1978); expanded versions and additional contributions in G. A. Ritter (ed.), *Arbeiterkultur* (Königstein, 1979). A shorter but similar collection is to be found in J. Kocka (ed.), 'Arbeiterkultur im 19. Jahrhundert', *Geschichte und Gesellschaft*, vol. 5, no. 1 (1979).

56 D. F. Crew, 'The Constitution of "Working-Class Culture" as a Historical Object' (SSRC Research Seminar Group on Modern German Social History, University of East Anglia, July 1980).

57 e.g. H. Schomerus, *Die Arbeiter der Maschinenfabrik Esslingen: Forschungen zur Lage der Arbeiterschaft im 19. Jahrhundert* (Stuttgart, 1977); P. Borscheid, *Textilarbeiterschaft in der Industrialisierung* (Stuttgart, 1978). An exception is H. Zwahr, *Zur Konstituierung der deutschen Arbeiterklasse* (East Berlin, 1978).

58 See n. 54, above.

59 More promising in this respect are the essays in *Sozialwissenschaftliche Informationen für Unterricht und Studium*, vol. 6, no. 44 (1977); e.g. F. Brüggemeier, 'Bedürfnisse, gesellschaftliche Erfahrung und politisches Verhalten: Das Beispiel der Bergarbeiter im nördlichen Ruhrgebiet gegen Ende des 19. Jahrhunderts', pp. 152–9.

60 Reulecke and Weber, *Fabrik, Familie, Feierabend*, p. 7.

61 See the extended critique of *Alltagsgeschichte* along these lines in Crew, 'The Constitution of "Working-Class Culture"'.

62 See esp. G. Huck (ed.), *Sozialgeschichte der Freizeit* (Wuppertal, 1980).

63 See in this context the remarks of G. Stedman Jones, 'Class Expression versus Social Control? A Critique of Recent Trends in the Social History of "Leisure"', *History Workshop: A Journal of Socialist Historians*, no. 4 (1977), pp. 163–70.

64 These remarks are conceived as a response to G. Eley and K. Nield, 'Why does Social History Ignore Politics?', *Social History*, vol. 5, no. 2 (1980), pp. 249–71, criticizing an earlier version of the present essay.

65 Quoted in Section II, above.

66 Particularly strong emphasis is laid on the 'traditional' aspects of working-class culture in K. Tenfelde, *Sozialgeschichte der Bergarbeiter an der Ruhr in 19. Jahrhundert* (Bonn-Bad Godesberg, 1977), and Tenfelde's contributions to the various collections cited above, n. 55.

67 cf. the discussion of this point in Crew 'The Constitution of "Working-Class Culture"'.

68 For some of the complexities of this term, see R. Williams, *Keywords* (London, 1977), 'Culture'.

69 cf. the essay on similar institutions in Britain by G. Stedman Jones, 'Working-class Culture and Working-class Politics in London, 1870–1900: Notes on the Remaking of a Working Class', *Journal of Social History*, vol. 7 (1973–4), pp. 460–505.

70 For the argument that the history of the Wilhelmine period as a whole has been structured too much by the perspective of '1933', see G. Eley, 'The Wilhelmine Right: How it Changed' in Evans, *Society and Politics in Wilhelmine Germany*, pp. 112–35.

71 Ritter, introduction to 'Workers' Culture', special issue of *Journals of Contemporary History*, vol. 13, no. 2, pp. 165–90.

72 J. Wickham, 'Working-class Movement and Working-class Life', paper delivered to the 4th meeting of the SSRC Research Seminar Group in Modern German Social History, University of East Anglia, July 1980.

73 Saul, *Staat, Industrie*; Saul, 'Der Staat und die "Mächte des Umsturzes"', *Archiv für Sozialgeschichte*, vol. 12 (1972), pp. 293–350; A. Hall, *Scandal, Sensation and Social Democracy* (Cambridge, 1978); Hall, 'The War of Words: Anti-Socialist Offensives and Counter-propaganda in Wilhelmine Germany 1890–1900', *Historical Journal*, vol. 17, no. 2 (1974), pp. 365–86.

74 R. B. Fosdick, *European Police Systems* (New York, 1915), pp. 27–8.

75 See S. Bajohr, 'Illegitimacy and the Working Class: Illegitimate Mothers in Brunswick,

1900–1933', in R. J. Evans (ed.), *The German Working Class 1880–1933: The Politics of Everyday Life* (London, 1982).

76 R. Schulte, *Sperrbezirke: Tugendhaftigkeit und Prostitution in der bürgerlichen Welt* (Frankfurt am Main, 1979), pp. 181–2. More generally, see my article, 'Prostitution, State and Society in Imperial Germany', *Past and Present*, vol. 70 (Feb. 1976), pp. 106–29; A. Flexner, *Prostitution in Europe* (New York, 1914).

77 A. Urban, *Staat und Prostitution in Hamburg vom Beginn der Reglementierung bis zur Aufhebung der Kasernierung* (Hamburg, 1927), pp. 34–40.

78 Flexner, *Prostitution in Europe*, pp. 147–57.

79 Lucas, *Zwei Formen von Radikalismus* (Frankfurt am Main, 1976), pp. 109–18.

80 M. Grüttner, 'Working-class Crime and the Labour Movement: Pilfering in the Hamburg Docks, 1888–1923', in Evans, *The German Working Class*, pp. 54–79.

81 See R. Roberts, *The Classic Slum* (Manchester, 1971), pp. 75–7, for vivid details of the role of the police in an English working-class community before the First World War.

82 There is a large sociological literature on street gangs; see e.g. H. A. Block, *The Gang: A Study in Adolescent Behaviour* (Westport, Conn., 1976); A. K. Cohen, *Delinquent Boys: The Culture of the Gang* (Glencoe, Ill., 1976); E. Rosenhaft, 'Organising the "Lumpenproletariat", Cliques and Communists in Berlin during the Weimar Republic', in Evans, *The German Working Class*, pp. 174–219.

83 K. Marx and F. Engels, *The Communist Manifesto* (Seabury Press edn., New York 1967), p. 146.

84 K. Marx, *The Eighteenth Brumaire of Louis Bonaparte* (International Publications edn., New York, 1951), p. 65.

85 L. Chevalier, *Labouring Classes and Dangerous Classes in Paris during the First Half of the Nineteenth Century* (London, 1973).

86 See Chapter 8, below.

87 See e.g. S. Hickey, 'The Shaping of the German Labour Movement: Miners in the Ruhr', in Evans, *Society and Politics in Wilhelmine Germany*, pp. 215–40.

88 Fritz Lang's celebrated film *M*, made under the Weimar Republic, with its portrayal of a criminal underworld outraged by a child murderer, tracking him down and trying him in a 'court of thieves', is perhaps the best-known illustration of this point.

89 cf. the contributions by Grüttner, Rosenhaft, and Bajohr to Evans, *The German Working Class*.

90 ibid., contributions by Robert and Grüttner.

91 For illustrations of this, see my essay, 'Politics and the Family: Social Democracy and the Working-Class Family 1891–1914' in R. J. Evans and W. R. Lee (eds), *The German Family: Essays in the Social History of the Family in Ninetenth and Twentieth Century Germany* (London, 1981).

92 Wickham, 'Working-class Movement'; Wickham, 'Social Fascism and the Division of the Working Class Movement: Workers and Political Parties in the Frankfurt Area 1929/30', *Capital and Class*, no. 7 (1979), pp. 1–34.

7

Liberalism and Society: the Feminist Movement and Social Change

The emergence since the mid-1970s of women's history and, more recently still, of a generalizing feminist history, has been one of the most striking features in the transformation of the West German historiographical scene over the past decade. No historian today can afford to ignore the tremendous intellectual ferment that is going on in this field. Nor can anyone remain unaware of the implications for interpretations of German history as a whole when it is seen from the viewpoint of the female majority of the population. This chapter grew out of my early work on German feminism, discussed briefly in the Introduction. It is not, as some critics have assumed, merely a summary of my book *The Feminist Movement in Germany 1894–1933* (London, 1976); in fact it presents new material not published in the book and puts forward arguments that in some respects represent second thoughts. The essay was written not least in order to demonstrate the relevance of the history of feminism to a general understanding of the German past. When it was first presented, in a much shortened version, as part of a joint panel with David Blackbourn and Geoff Eley at a major conference on Imperial Germany organized by Wolfgang Mommsen in Mannheim in 1977, it encountered a mixed reaction from the audience, some of whom dismissed its relevance to broader historical problems out of hand. Subsequently its arguments have met with a similarly mixed reception from feminist historians, some of whom dispute the relevance of categories such as liberalism and conservatism to the history of feminism. Gertrud Bäumer's cult of motherhood has even been taken up by at least one wing of contemporary West German feminism, which correspondingly views the developments described in this chapter in a generally positive light. The essay's use of the term 'radical feminism' has also caused some misunderstanding among contemporary feminists, who use the phrase in a quite different sense; the term was applied to themselves by those German feminists who opposed what they referred to as the 'moderate' feminist leadership of the late 1890s, and is not an invention of later historians. In reprinting the chapter here exactly as it first appeared in published form, in my *Society and Politics in Wilhelmine Germany* (London, 1978), pp. 186–214, I do not mean to imply that there is nothing in it that could now be put rather differently, though it does go further towards explaining the history of German feminism in categories relating to the social history of women than previous attempts did. At the time of writing, feminist histories of German women had hardly begun to be written, and the comments in the essay on the historiography of German women are no longer valid today. There are many other ways in which the history of feminism can be approached apart from the one represented here. But given the direction taken by at least some contemporary feminists in reassessing the relationship between feminism and Nazism, it is more important than ever to reassert the interconnectedness of feminist politics and national politics, to reaffirm, for example, that imperialism and the cult of motherhood went together, to reiterate that the German feminists moved rightwards in 1908–14 *both* in national political *and* in feminist terms, and to recognize that these developments can neither be separated from one another nor detached from their culmination in 1933.

I

The social history of Wilhelmine Germany is only just beginning to be written; but already the battle-lines between rival interpretations are being drawn. The most recent attempt to analyse Wilhelmine society as a totality, Hans-Ulrich Wehler's *Das deutsche Kaiserreich 1871–1918* (1973), takes a pessimistic view. It portrays the social structure and political constitution of the German Empire under Bismarck and Wilhelm II as fundamentally illiberal and authoritarian in character. Germany was ruled by an anachronistic power élite composed of feudal aristocrats and big industrialists; their attempts to preserve the social and political status quo in the face of the growing demands of new social classes thrown up in the rapid expansion of Germany's industrial economy reduced the political system of the empire to a state of permanent crisis. The means the élite used to retain power varied from the threat of a military coup and the perversion of justice to more subtle strategies such as 'secondary integration' (cementing the élite together by stigmatizing groups such as Catholics or Social Democrats as dangerous enemies of state and society), 'social imperialism' (diverting the masses' demand for social emancipation and political reform into nationalist and imperialist enthusiasm), the provision of 'social insurance instead of social reform', and the employment of the church, the educational system and other social institutions as means of indoctrinating the middle and lower classes into habits of deference and mistrust of democracy. These policies, claims Wehler, were by and large successful. The power élite remained in charge, despite the disaster of its foreign policy, the Revolution of 1918 and the advent of the Weimar

Republic, to continue its policy of political manipulation through the crisis of 1933, when it brought Hitler into power, up to its final breakdown in the Second World War, when it was finally destroyed after the failure of the July Plot of 1944. Already by 1918 the adherence of the bourgeoisie and proletariat to emancipatory ideals and democratic beliefs had been fatally weakened by these strategies of political domination. In both these respects, the German Empire laid the foundations for the Nazi tyranny.[1]

This interpretation has not found universal acceptance. Two of Wehler's recent critics, Thomas Nipperdey and Hans-Günter Zmarzlik, have accused him of painting too black a picture. They argue that Wehler's model of continuity from Bismarck to Hitler is simplistic and one-dimensional. Not only does it ignore the major discontinuities that occurred within the period 1871–1933, it also neglects the alternative, positive continuities which made Wilhelmine Germany in particular something more than a historical one-way street leading straight to the Third Reich. The possibilities of reforming the social and political structure of Wilhelmine Germany, it is argued, are underestimated.[2] Wehler's account misses the significance of the growth and development of the Social Democrats or the liberal revival which took place after the turn of the century. A number of progressive social movements emerged at this period, at the same time as the right-wing pressure-groups on which Wehler concentrates, and (argues Zmarzlik in particular) they constituted a 'movement of renewal ... which structured the pre-political area of society'. In the long run, according to Zmarzlik, these movements were far more significant than the more immediately successful associations of the far right; and the concept of continuity in German history, he suggests, should be extended beyond the attempt to locate the prehistory of Nazism in Wilhelmine society to embrace a longer-term view. Wilhelmine Germany should be seen as the decisive phase in the prehistory of the post-1945 Federal Republic and the Social Democratic–liberal coalition of the 1970s.[3] Only in this way can full justice be done to every aspect of the historical potentialities inherent in German society under Bismarck and, especially, under Wilhelm II.

It is obviously impossible within the brief compass of a short essay to discuss these arguments in their full range and complexity. What I want to do, rather, is to test some of them by looking at one aspect of social change that is given particular prominence by Zmarzlik in his critique of Wehler's views: the emancipation of women and the rise of feminism. According to Zmarzlik:

It was in the *Kaiserreich* that women's position in society, accepted for millennia, became a critically formulated 'woman question' for the first time. Between 1890 and 1914 more than half a million women were organized – with socially important demands, which to some extent have still to be caught up with today. However limited and restricted by their own time the bulk of these women must appear to the retrospective observer, their emergence nevertheless marks a turning-point ... Before 1870 the only public places for women were in soup kitchens, charity bazaars and similar charitable positions on the margin of public life. It was in the *Kaiserreich* that women became for the first time an indispensable factor in industrial production and service industries, as workers. And for the 'young ladies' of the middle classes, the way was opened to the educational system, parts of the professions, and finally the party-political scene.[4]

Here is a phenomenon, it is suggested, which gives the lie to Wehler's portrait of Imperial Germany as an illiberal and restrictive society, undermines his contention that 'emancipatory urges' were diverted into imperialist enthusiasm and points forward to the democratization of German society under the Social Democratic–liberal coalition of the 1970s.

Zmarzlik's citation of the women's movement and the emancipation of the female sex itself implies a considerable revision of our historical perspective on the *Kaiserreich*. For the great majority of German historians, if they pay any attention to the feminist movement at all, regard it as a marginal phenomenon in German history. There are many reasons for this. Most important, perhaps, has been the long confinement of German historiography to a narrow and exclusive concern with high politics. There has also been a persistent inability on the part of historians of all varieties to link feminist movements and changes in women's status in the past to their historical context. Instead, they have usually treated these subjects in isolation, dealing with them simply in terms of a crude, linear continuity of progress and improvement unrelated to other aspects of historical change (except, in a very general and unreflective way, to industrialization). Finally, knowledge of the radical and advanced nature of the early and middle phases of Wilhelmine feminism was suppressed by the conservative women who wrote the history of the German women's movement from the vantage-point of the Weimar Republic and whose works remained standard right into the 1970s. Despite all this, however, the feminist movement and the 'woman question' did not seem marginal to contemporaries before 1914. Women's emancipation was one of the great social issues of the day; the women's movement was bracketed with the youth movement and the labour movement as one of the major emancipatory trends of the era – or, by extreme conservatives, as one of the greatest and most dangerous threats to the civilization and social order of their time. Politicians of all varieties, from August Bebel, the Social Democratic leader, whose book, *Woman and Socialism* (1879), was by far the most widely read of all Social Democratic texts, to Kaiser Wilhelm II himself, who devoted part of a speech delivered in 1910 to warning women to stay clear of feminism and remain at home far from all subversive movements of this kind, paid it far more than mere political lip-service. The prominence of the woman question in all European countries forced politicians to take notice of it; the example of the English suffragettes showed just how explosive an issue it could become. In the longer run, too, the political significance of the feminist movement was indisputable. German women were given the vote in 1918, and throughout the Weimar Republic they constituted by a considerable margin the majority of the German electorate.[5] How the Protestant middle-class women who formed the overwhelming mass of the supporters and members of the women's movement used their voting power after 1918 was thus a matter of some importance; and they cannot but have been affected in their views on society and politics to at least some degree by the feminist movement, whether they belonged to it or not. For all these reasons, therefore, the feminist movement lends itself well as a yardstick for measuring the persuasiveness and utility of the rival theories of continuity advanced by Wehler and Zmarzlik.

II

There were a number of women's organizations in Germany in the 1870s and 1880s, chief of them the General German Women's Association (*Allgemeiner Deutscher Frauenverein*), numbering about 12,000 members. But all of them were mainly charitable in orientation, steered well clear of politics, and entered the public arena only to petition cautiously for the admission of women to the medical profession and for the improvement of girls' education. Both these demands were based on the desire to defend the femininity of middle-class women, which (it was argued) was misunderstood by male physicians and distorted by male-oriented education.[6] In 1894, however, the women's movement took on a new lease of life, with the foundation of the Federation of German Women's Associations (*Bund Deutscher Frauenvereine*, or BDF). Initially, under the leadership of the General German Women's Association, the BDF aimed simply to co-ordinate women's welfare work, gathering under its aegis some 70,000 members and 137 associations by 1901, and claiming a total membership of half a million by 1914.[7] But after the death or retirement of the founding generation of BDF leaders around the turn of the century, a new generation, headed by Marie Stritt (1856–1928), perhaps the most important German feminist of the Wilhelmine period, took the BDF rapidly towards a more clearly defined feminist stance. In 1902 the BDF officially endorsed the principle of votes for women, and (in a hotly contested reversal of policies pursued since 1894) condemned the police regulation of prostitutes, which international feminism had long opposed as giving official sanction to sexual immorality on the part of men while condemning and punishing it in women.[8] In 1907 the BDF, overcoming the objections of its more conservative members, who thought that it should not venture on to such controversial terrain, issued a lengthy declaration of the 'principles and demands of the women's movement', to which all member associations were supposed to subscribe. These demands included full legal equality for women within marriage, the reform of the bastardy law to include legal responsibility of the father for the support of his illegitimate child and its mother, equal education for girls, including full co-education at secondary level, equal pay for equal work, equal status in all professions including the civil service and the law, and the right to vote and stand for election for all representative bodies up to and including the Reichstag.[9] Finally, at its general assembly in 1908, the BDF devoted most of its energies to debating a proposal by its legal commission that it should campaign for the repeal of paragraph 218 of the criminal law code and for the legalization of abortion which this would entail.[10]

Up to this point, then, the development of the German feminist movement seems to support Zmarzlik's view that it formed an example of the beginning of a *progressive* continuity in German history. Yet this is by no means the whole story. For after 1908 this process of historical change went into reverse. The proposal to support the legalization of abortion was rejected by the BDF general assembly in 1908, and the proponents of sexual liberation were effectively excluded from the movement.[11] A series of behind-the-scenes manoeuvres within the BDF's executive committee brought about the resignation of the BDF president Marie Stritt, whom the bulk of committee members now found 'one-sidedly radical', in 1910.[12] She was replaced by Gertrud Bäumer (1873–1954), under whose leadership the movement abandoned the idea of the equality of the sexes and adopted the view that women were fundamentally different in character and abilities from men. Rather than compete with men, it was now argued, women should simply seek out the 'female sphere' in life and develop their 'specifically female qualities' there. This doctrine, propounded on innumerable occasions by BDF leaders after 1908, and ultimately enshrined in the organization's revised programme of 1919, registered the abandonment by the feminist movement of any attempt to carve out new roles for the German woman outside her traditional sphere of the home and its extension into public life via social welfare activities. 'If she limits herself to house and family', wrote Gertrud Bäumer, 'she is under certain circumstances acting in this way more in accordance with the ideals of the women's movement than if she goes into any male profession.'[13] The movement's retreat from the emancipatory tenets of feminism was sealed by its adoption of an increasingly authoritarian Social Darwinist ideology, its commitment to 'racial hygiene' and 'population policy' (*Bevölkerungs-politik*), and its support of attempts to stop the decline in the German birth-rate, which it came to see as a danger to the long-term future of the German race.[14] Discussion of these matters was suppressed within the BDF; the general assembly ceased to be a forum for democratic debate and became instead a passive audience for edifying speeches.[15] Finally, the radical wing of the feminist movement, which had made all the running in the years up to 1908, underwent a process of rapid decline and disintegration from 1908 to 1914. The female suffrage movement, which stood to the left of the left-wing liberal political parties up to 1908, opposing for example their participation in the governmental Reichstag coalition known as the Bülow Block and lending their full support to the principle of universal suffrage at all levels of the constitution, was by 1914 split into three different factions, the two largest of which were associated with the Left-Liberal and National Liberal parties and supported merely *equal* suffrage for women, thus accepting the existence of property franchises in Prussia and other German states.[16] A similar process of collapse occurred in the sexual liberation movement, the *Bund für Mutterschutz*, in the period 1908–1914, as it broke up into mutually hostile groups, shifted ideologically away from liberal individualism and was abandoned by the most influential of its supporters, both within the women's movement and without.[17]

Here we have, then, a liberal movement of social emancipation which before 1908 certainly came close to advancing demands that are still controversial today, and which mobilized large numbers of previously politically inactive people and drew them into the political system, preparing them for the advent of democracy in the Weimar Republic. At the same time it is clear that an assessment of the feminist movement – such as Zmarzlik's – which went no further than this would be very partial indeed, just as partial in fact as an account of Wilhelmine society – such as Wehler's – which ignored the emergence of liberal reform movements altogether. It is evident from the foregoing brief sketch that the feminist movement abandoned liberalism, at least in the generally understood sense of the word, after 1908. The search for the causes of this abandonment brings us to the heart of the current debate about the nature of Wilhelmine society. Many historians have tried to explain the weakness of liberalism among the German middle classes; and in the feminist movement's shift to the Right we have an example of middle-class abandonment of an emancipatory ideology which may serve as a means of putting some of these historical generalizations to the test.

The most widely accepted of these explanations has been the theory of 'social imperialism', that is (in its current usage among German historians), the idea that German governments and conservative politicians diverted the reformist impulses of the middle classes into nationalist and imperialist enthusiasm. How far does the case of the feminist movement bear this out?[18] At first sight, it seems to provide an almost ideal illustration. The movement's swing to the right was accompanied by a growth of nationalist sentiment among its leaders and members. Gertrud Bäumer, who became BDF president in 1910, declared liberal opposition to imperialism 'outmoded' and argued that 'military power is ... simply a necessity of national self-preservation'. Under her leadership the BDF supported the development of German 'national identity' (*Volkstum*), opposed what she called 'cosmopolitan aims and international policies' and became very reluctant to co-operate with the International Council of Women in its efforts to develop a common policy for the preservation of peace.[19] The 'radical' feminists who dominated the BDF up to 1908, including Bäumer's predecessor Marie Stritt, were by contrast, to a greater or lesser degree, supporters of the pacifist movement.[20] The adoption of Social Darwinist ideas by the feminist movement after 1908, and its growing obsession with racial purity and the birth rate, can be seen as further evidence of a conversion to the nationalist and imperialist creed. These ideas certainly played a role in persuading the BDF general assembly to reject the legalization of abortion. Finally, there was no shortage of anti-feminist propagandists on the far Right to accuse the women's movement of being an internationalist, pacifist conspiracy to subvert the German family and thereby destroy the German race. Such accusations – raised by pan-Germans, *völkisch* nationalists and other right-wing extremists – undoubtedly had an effect on the feminist movement, forcing it to defend itself by asserting its commitment to family, nation and race.[21]

Yet the theory that the liberalism of the middle-class women who formed the feminist movement was the victim of a classic social imperialist strategy, diverting its emancipatory impulses into nationalist enthusiasm, will not really stand up to close examination. In the first place, direct social-imperialist pressure on the feminist movement did not really amount to very much until the formation of the German League for the Prevention of the Emancipation of Women (*Deutscher Bund zur Bekämpfung der Frauenemanzipation*) by right-wing nationalists (including August Keim, Dietrich Schäfer, Ludwig Schemann and Otto Schmidt-Gibichenfels) in 1912. By this time, the feminist movement was already firmly committed to nationalism and in full retreat from liberal values and liberal policies, a process that had begun some four years previously.[22] Secondly, though Social Darwinism certainly played a role in the movement's rejection of legal abortion and sexual emancipation, and encouraged a collectivist rather than an individualist attitude to politics, the main influence here was, in fact, religious, the main opposition from the German-evangelical Women's League and from women (such as Gertrud Bäumer) associated with the Evangelical–Social Congress. In any case, Social Darwinism itself, despite its ideas about the 'survival of the fittest' and the 'struggle for existence' could be a strongly reformist doctrine, encouraging the 'improvement of the race' through the provision of better housing, better medical care and better social welfare. In fact, nationalism was really given a place in the women's movement by disciples of the influential liberal politician and theorist Friedrich Naumann, who explicitly linked imperialism with social reform, arguing that the two were mutually interdependent, rather than offering Empire as an alternative to reform. Gertrud Bäumer herself was a close collaborator of Naumann's and worked with him in the editorship of his magazine *Die Hilfe*. Nationalism as such, however, played no real part in the internal disputes of the women's movement until the First World War.[23] And, most important of all, there were other significant, indeed decisive reasons for the movement's abandonment of liberalism which had nothing at all to do with social imperialism as it is conventionally understood by historians of Wilhelmine Germany.

It was not by chance that 1908 formed the watershed between the liberal and illiberal phases of German feminism's historical development. For it was on 15 May of that year that the single most significant legislative improvement in the position of women to be enacted in Wilhelmine Germany came into force: the Imperial Law of Association (*Reichsvereinsgesetz*), which replaced a variety of local laws existing previously.[24] Under these local laws, women in most parts of Germany (including Prussia) were forbidden by law from joining political associations or attending political meetings. These laws, which were mainly used by the police as a pretext for dissolving Social Democratic meetings where women were present, but were also on occasion used against the feminist movement itself, acted as a powerful deterrent to the great mass of law-abiding middle-class women from participating in the less charitable and more political organizations of the women's movement.[25] The principal sufferer was the women's suffrage movement, which in 1908, six years after its foundation, still had less than 2,500 members;[26] but the BDF itself, whose 1907 programme was undeniably political and whose general assemblies from 1902 onwards always included debate on political subjects, was also affected; in early 1908 it probably comprised little more than 100,000 women all told – a considerable number, but, as the next few years were to show, far below the number of women that the organization was potentially capable of reaching.[27] The new Imperial Law of Association changed all this. It made female participation in politics possible all over the Empire, above all in Prussia. Membership in women's associations no longer carried the stigma of illegality. Consequently the floodgates were opened and large numbers of more conservative women streamed in. The German-evangelical Women's League, 8,000 strong in 1908, with close ties to the conservative party, joined the BDF in September 1908. Its first act was to use its massive voting strength (50 votes) to help defeat the proposal to legalize abortion at the BDF General Assembly the following month, and to frustrate a reorganization of the BDF which would have had the effect of giving the radical feminists more voting power. Under its leader Paula Müller, who later sat in the Reichstag during the Weimar Republic as a deputy for the right-wing German-national People's Party or DNVP, it opposed female suffrage outright and played a major part in weakening the BDF's commitment to votes for women.[28] By 1914 the entry of many other right-wing groups into the BDF, including the German Women's League (*Deutscher Frauenbund*), which began life as the women's section of the Imperial League Against Social Democracy,[29] had increased the BDF's size enormously; from uniting perhaps 120,000 women in 1910 it grew so fast that by 1914 its total female membership was probably not far short of a quarter of a million.[30]

The female suffrage movement was also swollen to an unprecedented size with the entry of more conservative women into its ranks after 1908; from a total membership of 2,500 in 1908 it grew to a membership of at least 14,000 in 1914.[31] Before 1908 the suffragists had been on the extreme Left of left-wing liberalism. Many of their leaders were associated with the Democratic Alliance (*Demokratische Vereinigung*), a radical splinter-group which broke away from the Bülow Block liberals in that year.[32] But by 1914 the bulk of the suffragists were associated rather with the mainstream left-liberals (the Progressives), and not a few owed their allegiance to the National Liberals, who were even further to the Right. The Progressives were lukewarm about women's suffrage; the National Liberals indeed were actively hostile to the idea.[33] In this case, then, as with that of the BDF as a whole, expansion of membership, in the case of the BDF growth into a mass movement, was the major development underlying the retreat of liberalism. The women's movement proved unable to combine liberal ideology with mass support. The terms on which the great mass of the middle-class women who joined the BDF in the Wilhelmine period entered the public arena thus had little to do with either liberalism or women's emancipation. Nor did they have much to do with what were to become the demands of the women's liberation movement in the 1960s and 1970s. And they did not relate in any obvious way to the real problems faced by women in post-1945 Germany and the society presided over by the Social Democratic–liberal coalition of 1969. The feminist ideas and demands of which these statements could – at least to a limited degree – be made, had ceased to be the creed of the women's movement in Germany by the time that it came to have mass appeal.

The catalyst for the feminist movement's abandonment of liberalism was thus provided not by the diversionary tactic of social imperialism but by the emancipatory reform of 1908, the Imperial Law of Association, which allowed women to take part in politics without fear of legal reprisal. Other reforms came to fruition in 1908 as well: in particular in that year

Prussia admitted women to its universities as full-time students – the last of the German states to do so – and promulgated an important educational reform establishing a system of state secondary education for girls. Already, by the turn of the century, indeed, women had been admitted to the medical profession. And since the mid-1890s the feminist movement, previously ridiculed or ignored, had found increasing acceptance in public life.[34] While this series of reforms failed to bring the status of German women up to that of women in America or the Scandinavian countries, where for the most part reforms such as these had long since taken place, they did mark a significant advance over the situation of German women in the 1890s.[35] Moreover, political parties, which had previously ignored the German feminist movement altogether, now felt increasingly constrained to incorporate at least some of its demands into their programmes. This was the case above all with the left-wing liberals, but other parties too felt obliged to voice their concern for women's welfare, even if they explicitly rejected the majority of feminists' demands.[36] By the mid-1900s, too, most newspapers in the centre and on the Left of the political spectrum ran a regular column on the feminist movement and employed special women correspondents to write it. In 1901 the radical feminist leader Minna Cauer noted the changing attitude of the press with some satisfaction, if also with a certain amount of cynicism:

> A decade ago, every woman who supported the entry of women into the universities was 'emancipated' ... About five years ago, even women who called themselves friends and acquaintances of the women's movement prophesied its downfall as middle-class women called popular assemblies in which statements were made on current affairs. Today, at least in the capital city, people are immediately dissatisfied and accuse the leaders of the women's movement of forgetting their duty if they do not take a public stand on notable events.[37]

The growing public acceptance of women's role in national life was marked not only by reforms such as the Law of Association in 1908 – which encountered virtually no opposition in this respect[38] – but also by the increasing concern even on the part of those who opposed female emancipation that women should enter public life on the right terms. It was for this reason that the conservative party tolerated the formation of an Alliance of Conservative Women in 1911,[39] that right-wing groups including the nationalist associations (*nationale Verbände*) formed women's sections, some of them dating back to the early 1900s,[40] and finally that right-wing politicians joined in 1912 to form the German League for the Prevention of the Emancipation of Women in order to mobilize *women* against the feminist movement, to show that the female

sex in Germany did not want to be emancipated.[41] Similarly, the conservative women who mobilized themselves and entered public life after the
reform of the Law of Association in 1908 did so explicitly in order to
counter the influence of radical feminists. As Paula Müller remarked,
writing to the local branches of the German-evangelical Women's League
on the advantages of joining the BDF in 1908, if the League did enter the
BDF, 'we would together with the moderate party, far outweigh the
radical and progressive elements; indeed, we would have a great majority
over them'.[42]

III

Changes such as those which took place within the feminist movement can
in fact only be fully understood by looking at the changes which were
taking place in the social position of the women of the middle classes who
formed the movement's social constituency. For behind the numerical
growth and political development of the feminist movement in the
Wilhelmine period lay important changes in the social and economic
position of middle-class women, changes which themselves reflected the
transition of Germany to a mature industrial society in these years. The
spread of girls' education in the 1870s and 1880s, the growth of an
adequate system of secondary schools for girls from the 1890s, and finally
the opening of the universities to women as full-time matriculated students
from 1902 (Baden) to 1908 (Prussia) – all this provided the basis for a
rapidly expanding female petty-bourgeois intelligentsia, most of whom
found employment in the teaching profession. In Prussia, for instance, the
number of women teachers doubled between 1861 and 1896, rising from
7,366 to 14,600.[43] Women teachers' pay was much lower than that of their
male colleagues doing the same work, the conditions of employment were
highly restrictive (they had to remain single, for example, or resign on
marriage), their numbers were limited by law, especially in the scientific
subjects, their qualifications did not have to come up to the standard
required of male teachers, and the higher teaching posts were barred to
them not only *de facto* but also *de jure*. In the Prussian reform of girls'
education which came into effect in 1908, it was ruled that at least a third of
the science teaching in girls' secondary schools had to be done by men, and
no woman was to be appointed to the headship of a girls' school. Women
teachers in boys' schools were unheard of, and co-education was dismissed
in Prussia as immoral. In general, too, women schoolteachers came from a
higher social background than that of their male colleagues; for the
daughters of academics, lawyers, officers and professionals, teaching was a
means of maintaining social status without marrying; for the sons of
artisans, shopkeepers, primary school teachers and white-collar employ-

ees, it was a means of social advancement. This social gap gave an added sharpness to the conflict between male and female teachers. It was commonly agreed that a numerically significant body of support for the German League for the Prevention of the Emancipation of Women came from schoolteachers, above all *Oberlehrer*, fearful of female competition. It was not surprising, then, that women schoolteachers, intellectually aware, economically independent, but neither socially nor economically nor politically equal with their male colleagues, provided the largest, most vocal and most active body of support for feminism in Germany in the late 1890s and early 1900s.[44] Many leading feminists began as schoolteachers or spent some of their time teaching in a variety of institutions. Contemporaries noted that women teachers formed the mainstay of active support for the feminist movement in Wilhelmine Germany. 'The most important and reliable troops in the federal army', remarked one antifeminist tract in discussing the composition of the BDF, 'are the women teachers' associations'.[45]

This assessment can be supported by the evidence of a list of the eighty-two members of the German Union for Women's Suffrage, Hamburg branch, which was submitted in the second year of its existence (1904) to the police.[46] It shows that six of the members were men (one medical specialist, two factory owners, a pastor, a merchant and a stockbroker), twenty-eight of the women were housewives (most probably married to men active in left-liberal politics) and forty-eight of the women were single. Of these latter, two lived off private incomes, four lived at home with their parents, and ten lived in the suburb of Altona, which came under Prussian jurisdiction, and so were not investigated. No less than thirteen were schoolteachers; four were accounts clerks, two were shopkeepers, and there was also a nurse, a painter, a receptionist, a dressmaker, a commercial student and a factory inspector's assistant. The predominance of schoolteachers among unmarried members is clear. Apart from the housewives and the schoolteachers, the main occupational group was drawn from the ranks of women white-collar workers, whose numbers were also expanding with unprecedented rapidity at this time. Like the schoolmistresses, the female salaried employees had formed their own professional association in 1889, and leading radical feminists such as Minna Cauer and Lida Gustava Heymann were active in organizing it on both a local and a national scale. The problems of this group of women – unequal pay and prospects compared with those of male colleagues, poor working conditions, restricted opportunities – were similar to the schoolmistresses', and the feminist movement profited from this in a similar way.[47] These two petty bourgeois groups formed the basis for the new wave of radical feminism which revivified the German women's movement from the mid-1890s until the passage of the Imperial Law of Association in 1908.

The expansion of German feminism into a mass movement which followed on the passage of this legislative enactment was achieved primarily through the recruitment of married women. While there was a high proportion of unmarried women in radical feminist organizations such as the German Union for Women's Suffrage, as we have seen, the picture in 'moderate' and conservative women's organizations was very different. Here the great majority of members and local officials tended to be married women, though the full-time leaders and organizers were generally not; obviously, running a household and family usually prevented married women from involving themselves in political and organizational life full-time. Moreover, after 1908 the social base of the feminist movement was diversified by the mobilization of the wives of civil servants, naval officers, industrialists, academics and other local dignitaries. The women's movement ceased to be a movement of the unmarried female petty-bourgeois salaried employee and became a wider movement, embracing the consumer interests of housewives and the social and political aspirations and concerns of the middle and upper ranks of the industrial and professional bourgeoisie, even indeed on occasion the aristocracy, the armed forces and the bureaucracy.[48] Within the rather narrower confines of the female suffrage movement, the mobilization of women from the industrial, commercial and managerial bourgeoisie of Silesia and the Rhineland – Germany's two major areas of heavy industry, where new groups were formed in 1909–11 – introduced a disruptive element, for it was precisely in these areas that opposition to universal suffrage within the female suffrage movement originated, and that the foundation of the right-wing breakaway German Alliance for Women's Suffrage (*Deutsche Vereinigung für Frauenstimmrecht*) was begun.[49]

The disintegrative effects of this were more than evident both in the break-up of the suffrage movement after 1908 and in the deep divisions and fierce controversies that threatened to split the BDF itself at the general assembly of the same year. On numerous occasions after 1908, too, the German-evangelical Women's League, perhaps the most important of the new 'Establishment' groups that joined the BDF after the passage of the Imperial Law of Association, launched strong attacks on BDF policy, above all on its support for female suffrage; it came close to leaving the BDF altogether over this issue in 1912.[50] In these circumstances, unity could only be achieved – as it was in 1908 over the abortion issue, in 1912 over the suffrage question, and ultimately in 1911–16 within the female suffrage movement itself over the question of a property franchise – by a substantial shift to the Right, masked by an increasing vagueness and fuzziness of aims and ideas and accompanied by the *de facto* abandonment of many of the movement's more radical goals. Already by 1912 the BDF had in practice declared its allegiance to the idea that became its official guiding principle in the subsequent revised programme of 1919: that women's task was to heal social divisions and unite the German nation in a national racial community (*Volksgemeinschaft*) above party and class. Clearly this was an attempt to bridge the social differences that were threatening to split the BDF. Equally clearly, however, it also marked a significant shift away from commitment to parliamentary and party-political means of regulating social conflict.

On a more general level these developments also reflected the growing social antagonism between the bourgeoisie and the working class. From a middle-class point of view, the problem with the demands advanced by the radical feminists was that the only political party to back them all was the SPD. Some of them, too, such as universal suffrage, equal pay for equal work, co-education, and equal rights for women within marriage, were felt by more conservative middle-class women to be playing directly into the hands of the Social Democrats by spreading egalitarianism through society, removing property qualifications for the vote, and undermining the stability of the authoritarian family.[51] Moreover, the Social Democrats themselves had a large, active and (after 1908) rapidly growing women's movement of their own, which consistently refused to co-operate with the bourgeois feminists and showed itself unremittingly hostile to middle-class liberalism while supporting most of the radical feminists' own demands.[52] It was in fact often difficult for outsiders to distinguish between the Social Democratic and radical feminist line on a number of important aspects of the woman question, all the more so in the years (*c.* 1896–1907) when the radical feminists were actively – though unsuccessfully – trying to recruit working-class women, issuing a stream of demands and petitions aimed at improving the lot of the woman factory worker, and giving active financial and moral support to strikes such as those of the women textile workers in Crimmitschau (1906).[53] As the SPD itself grew in size, and hostility to it on the right increased, middle-class women felt it increasingly important to distinguish their brand of feminism from the Social Democrats'. One opponent of universal suffrage within the German Union for Women's Suffrage remarked in 1912: 'What use is flirting with Social Democracy, what use is the fearful avoidance of an apparent "withdrawal" from the working-class women's movement, if this movement always declares that a deep gulf divides it from all bourgeois women?'.[54] More generally, they argued, it was dangerous for the feminists to align themselves with the Social Democrats in opposing the Wilhelmine state. Instead, they should seek integration in it, to stabilize it against the growing threat of social revolution which they perceived in the rise of Social Democracy and the spread of labour unrest.[55] Such integration appeared all the more profitable in view of the reforms granted by the state to women in the expansion of girls' secondary and tertiary education, the opening of the medical profession and the passing of the Law of Association.

235

By 1914 the women's movement had become integrated into the social and political fabric of Wilhelmine Germany in many ways. It was taking a full part in public life. Its congresses and assemblies were patronized by local mayors, officials and dignitaries. It contained many individuals, groups and organizations closely associated with the political and social Establishment. Most important of all, perhaps, it was being consulted by the government on questions of education and social welfare. Many of its members were active in local government institutions dealing with these subjects, and by 1914 the BDF was coming to be regarded by imperial and local administration as the representative of these women. As Gertrud Bäumer remarked in 1913, 'the state has come nearer to women, has become more alive and comprehensible to them'.[56] This process culminated in the government's request to the BDF to organize welfare services for women on the outbreak of war in 1914.[57] Integration in this sense amounted to far more than a mere response to any deliberate or unconscious manipulative strategy on the part of the authorities. It formed part of a general process that had been at work in Wilhelmine politics since the early 1890s – the extension of the political nation from small élites of local notables (*Honoratioren*) to encompass the entire population; the entry of the masses on to the political scene.

One of the influences prompting this development – which in its widest sense was the consequence of Germany's transition to industrial maturity – was the increasing intervention of the state in the everyday life of the people. As far as women were concerned, this manifested itself in growing government and administrative regulation of labour opportunities and conditions, education, food, health and drug legislation, and many other government enactments through which the state, as it were, entered the home. This was a major influence in politicizing women and bringing them into the public arena through their participation in local health, economic, welfare and education boards, the formation of Housewives' Associations, and the increased interest of all kinds of women's groups in questions of this sort. It also encouraged women to enter public life as defenders of the 'women's sphere and representatives of specifically female interests, rather than as crusaders for individual freedoms and equal rights with men in every walk of life.[58] As the women's movement came to an increasing extent after 1908 to represent the interests of married women and housewives as well as those of unmarried women, teachers, white-collar workers and professionals, so it shifted away from demanding equal rights on the basis of the freedom of the individual woman and her equality with man, towards an acceptance of women's role in society and an attempt to defend the interests of women within the confines of this role. This development was hastened by the tendency of the professional associations of women white-collar workers and schoolteachers to take support away from radical feminist associations as they grew in size, became more effective in protecting their members' interests and adopted an increasingly 'unpolitical' and trade-union orientation which took them in the end right out of the feminist movement altogether. The General German Women Teachers' Association (*Allgemeiner Deutscher Lehrerin-nenverein*), which had enjoyed the closest ties with the feminist movement in the 1890s and early 1900s, sharing in effect the same leadership, had by 1914 narrowed its horizons to encompass only questions directly affecting the position of women teachers; and in 1907 the Commercial Union of Female Salaried Employees (*Kaufmännischer Verband weiblicher Ange-stellten*), founded and controlled for many years by leading radical feminists, such as Minna Cauer and Lida Gustava Heymann, voted to sever its ties with the women's movement and to adopt a purely trade-union orientation. This development was not unconnected with the growth of Social Democratic attempts to unionize women white-collar workers. It undermined the position of radical feminism within the women's movement, as the social groups which had been the mainstay of its support began to see in professional and trade-union organizations a more effective means of representing their interests than the feminist movement had been able to provide.[59]

What the feminist movement was doing in the years 1908–14 was in essence adjusting its strategy for the defence of bourgeois social institutions which it had criticized in its radical phase. Radical feminism meant, for example, the criticism of existing family institutions. In 1896 the BDF had launched a massive campaign against the family law clauses of the civil code then being debated in the Reichstag.[60] In 1902, by attacking the state regulation of prostitution, it had aligned itself with Social Democratic allegations – above all, with those made by the SPD leader August Bebel in his widely read book *Woman and Socialism* – that the bourgeois family was a hypocritical sham whose economic and contractual basis provided the major reason for the spread of prostitution in the late-nineteenth century.[61] In 1905–6 the ideas of the radical feminist Helene Stöcker gained increasing currency in the radical wing of the feminist movement; Stöcker supported equal rights for unmarried mothers and illegitimate children, argued against 'traditional clerical-ascetic moral teaching', and propounded a 'modern, individualist, scientific moral teaching' which she called the New Morality and which led her (among other things) to demand legal recognition of 'free marriages', the public distribution of contraceptives and the legalization of abortion.[62] In a more general way, the feminists' concentration on demanding more opportunities for women in public and professional life implied that their role in the family was second-best to an active personal career. Women's emancipation meant to a considerable degree their emancipation from the family. After 1908 the BDF repudiated this individualist attack on the bourgeois family and affirmed its commitment to existing family institutions. It condemned extra-marital sexuality, opposed the legalization of abortion and the public availability of contraceptives, and launched a fierce attack on the ideas of Stöcker and her associates. Similarly, as we have seen, after 1908 the suffrage movement withdrew from its alignment with the SPD in demanding universal suffrage and came round to the defence of existing property franchises.[63]

These changes did not signify a simple reversion to the acceptance of the status quo. On the contrary, the BDF continued to campaign for reforms. After 1908, the reforms it wanted no longer aimed at the legitimation of bourgeois social institutions through democratizing them (as, for example, in Stöcker's plea that her ideas sought to create a 'higher form of marriage' in which husband and wife would be equal in every way).[64] They aimed instead at legitimizing them by extending their existing functions, by enabling them to do more of the things they were doing already. Thus the bourgeois family was to produce more children, to receive more support from the state, to gain more moral authority (through the suppression of extra-marital sexuality), to have a wider appeal to women who at present stayed unmarried, and finally to have more 'racial value' through the barring of marriage to alcoholics, the mentally ill, the physically handicapped, the hereditarily diseased or the 'racially inferior'.[65] Similarly, the property franchise (which in many parts of Germany, above all in Prussia, was the main political institution preserving the parliamentary strength not only of conservatives but also of liberal and middle-class parties and keeping the Social Democrats from power) was to be strengthened by extending it, not vertically down the social scale, but laterally, across it, to the women of the propertied classes, thus further reducing the relative voting strength of the Social Democrats.[66] One implication of this, of course, was the reform of the civil code of 1900 to allow women to control their own property within marriage and so enable them to fulfil voting qualifications. The BDF, then, was still committed to the reform of the social and political institutions of Wilhelmine Germany. It did not accept the status quo. On the contrary, it was still dissatisfied with many aspects of Wilhelmine society – the declining birth rate, the official sanctioning of immorality in the state regulation of prostitution, the legal barriers to married women's possession of property, and so on – as with many other features of the Wilhelmine social and political system, above all of course the restriction of voting rights to men. It was not least in the hope of securing reforms such as these that the BDF committed itself to full support of Germany's effort in the First World War and to the organization of welfare services under official auspices. When the opportunity eventually presented itself in 1917–18, the BDF was not slow in presenting its own demands for the 'political–social transformation' of Germany in the postwar era.[67] To what extent these demands were actually met is of course another matter; certainly, without the Revolution of 1918, it is unlikely that many of the BDF's demands would have been fulfilled, and altogether implausible to suppose that the most controversial of the women's movement's proposals, the enfranchisement of women, would have met with any more approval than it did up to the end of October 1918.[68]

IV

The example of the feminist movement, then, underlines the inadequacy of conventional interpretations of liberalism in Wilhelmine Germany. To approach liberal or middle-class groups in Wilhelmine society merely under the aspect of their contribution to a negative continuity leading to the triumph of Hitler in 1933, or a positive one leading to the advent of the Social Democratic–liberal coalition government in 1969, necessarily does major violence to the complex dynamics of their historical development. Both theories of continuity bring with them a selective approach which distorts the reality of Wilhelmine society. Above all, perhaps, they involve a simplistic theory of the relationship between politics and society which reads back social developments from political ones in an unreflective way, and infers general characteristics of social classes from the characteristics of political organizations which are assumed to represent them. Because the feminist movement (it is argued, for example) was progressive, therefore it arose out of social developments – the involvement of women in economic and public life – that were also progressive. Alternatively, because many right-wing extremist political groups drew their members from the *Mittelstand*, it is assumed that the *Mittelstand* – or the petty bourgeoisie – possessed uniformly reactionary political views.[69] Yet, as we have seen, it was women's involvement in the petty-bourgeois occupations of primary school teaching and white-collar work that provided the social basis for the radicalization of the feminist movement around the turn of the century.

The models of continuity advanced by Wehler and Zmarzlik in fact break down at several points when applied to the feminist movement. It is certainly clear that the feminists' move to the right after 1908 constituted a significant step along a road which would lead them to a qualified acceptance of Nazi rule in 1933.[70] But it was only a step. Other events, such as the Revolution of 1918, the inflation of 1923 and the economic and political crises of 1929–33, had to occur before the potential susceptibility to the appeal of fascism created after 1908 could be actualized.[71] Although the allegation that Hitler was carried to power by the votes of women is a myth,[72] it is undeniable that the feminist movement did nothing to educate the Protestant middle-class women who formed its constituency to support democracy and develop a critical attitude towards fascist ideology.

239

By 1930 most of them were probably voting for the Nazis.[73] Yet to present this as the result of political seduction by manipulative pre-industrial élites is highly misleading.

Three distinct arguments are in fact involved here. The first of them concerns the idea of manipulation. Although it has been argued that the attention of the middle classes was diverted away from emancipation and reform by social imperialism or repressed through the technique of negative integration and other varieties of social control, this involves, as we have seen, an implied contradiction between emancipation and reform on the one hand, and social control, national enthusiasm and political integration on the other, which is simply not applicable in the case of the feminist movement. The major factor in precipitating the feminists' move to the Right was a *reform*, the Law of Association of 1908, which was genuinely emancipatory and integrative. It admitted into the feminist movement the kind of Establishment women who were opposed to female emancipation in every country, for the wives of military and naval officers, civil servants, and other notables, were no more likely to embrace the feminist cause in Britain or America than they were in Wilhelmine Germany.[74] It was after the admittance of these women that the feminist movement became nationalistic, not before, a development which in no way stopped it agitating for political and social reform, though it changed the nature of the reforms for which it agitated and the reasons it gave for wanting them. In addition to this, as we have seen, there were social changes taking place both in the situation of housewives and in the position of middle-class working women which provided an additional impulse for the feminists' retreat from the radical ideas of the liberal individualists. Even if it were correct to see the development of the feminist movement in the Wilhelmine period in terms of a continuity leading directly to 1933, therefore, the continuity involved would not be one of political manipulation.

Secondly, the manipulative model of continuity also implies that the middle classes were potentially capable of espousing emancipatory ideologies, indeed that in the normal course of events they were almost bound to do so, had they not been diverted towards authoritarian ones instead. The problem here is to demonstrate the existence of such a 'normal course of events'. The usual solution has been to point to other industrializing countries – notably the USA – and show that in these countries the middle classes did espouse emancipatory ideologies. This is far from easy to establish in the case of women's emancipation, however. In all countries, the feminists were a small minority even among the women of the educated middle classes; and the German women's movement, far from being insignificant by international standards, was by the outbreak of the First World War the third largest in the world, after Britain and the USA. Numerical contrasts appear only when we look at female suffrage movements. The German suffragists, 2,500 strong in 1908, rose to 14,000 in 1914, but by that time they were divided into three mutually hostile factions. By contrast, the National American Woman Suffrage Society, 17,000 strong in 1905, reached 75,000 by 1910 and 100,000 in 1915. However, it would be wrong to leap to the conclusion that these figures demonstrate that American women had in some way fulfilled their potential for emancipation while German women had not. The expansion of the American female suffrage movement only occurred because the movement abandoned liberal individualism, rather as German feminism was doing at the same time, and directed its appeal consciously towards white Anglo-Saxon Protestant women who wanted enfranchisement to counter the influence of the growing numbers of male immigrant and black voters – indeed, the American feminists began explicitly arguing for the disfranchisement of these two groups. The increasing appeal of feminism was thus linked with the increasing racism and anti-democratic tendencies of the movement. The parallel with the German case was striking.[75]

Finally, what lies at the root of the models of continuity employed by both Wehler and Zmarzlik is the concept of modernization: the difference between the two models can in fact be simply expressed by saying that while Wehler believes that Germany's modernization was retarded (above all through the manipulations of the 'pre-modern' élites), Zmarzlik argues that there were important instances of modernization taking place in Wilhelmine Germany which Wehler has overlooked (including the rise of feminism). More precisely, both would probably agree that modernization was taking place in the economy but not in the political system; the dispute arises in the crucial area in between, in the structure of society. It is for this reason (among many others) that these historians have turned to social history rather than political or economic history for solutions to the problem of the prehistory of Nazism. Yet once more, neither argument is really applicable in the case of feminism and female emancipation. Leaving aside for the moment the many problems associated with the concepts of 'modernization' and 'modernity',[76] it is clear that both models of continuity involve an equation of these concepts with the idea of emancipation. Of the two phases of the feminist movement discussed in the present essay, however, it is indisputable that the latter was the more 'modern'. The liberal individualist plea for equal rights for woman as a free and independent personality was a characteristic not of feminist movements in general but only of a phase in their development. In Germany as in America this phase ended with the transition of society to industrial maturity. Feminists such as Gertrud Bäumer explicitly argued, like her contemporaries in the USA, that individualist concepts of equal rights were outmoded; what was really modern was the situation in which women did not try to establish their independence from the family but rather built upon the role they played in family life, dignified it, secured the support of the state for it, and in turn used this role as a base from which to extend a 'motherly' influence over society.[77] These ideas were an initial theorization of an important part of what later came to be dubbed by its critics as the 'feminine mystique', which was to reach its apogee in the countries of the Western industrial world in the 1950s.[78] Both the women who dominated the German feminist movement in its more radical period before 1908 and the more conservative women who flocked into the movement in the last six years before the outbreak of the First World War had moved towards a more 'modern' position in endorsing this view. As in America, this turning away from individualism towards collectivism signified that society had entered the era of advanced capitalism, in which pre-industrial élites and 'pre-modern' modes of thought were declining in influence. In this more general sense, then, Zmarzlik's critique perhaps has more to offer than its liberal bias might at first sight suggest.

NOTES

1 H.-U. Wehler, *Das deutsche Kaiserreich 1871–1918* (Göttingen, 1973), esp. pp. 227–39.
2 T. Nipperdey, 'Wehlers "Kaiserreich": Eine kritische Auseinandersetzung', *Geschichte und Gesellschaft*, vol. 1, no. 4 (1975), pp. 539–60; Nipperdey's critique is far more subtle and wide-ranging than can be adequately conveyed in these few introductory remarks.
3 H.-G. Zmarzlik, 'Das Kaiserreich in neuer Sicht?', *Historische Zeitschrift*, vol. 222 (1976), pp. 105–26, Zmarzlik, 'Das Kaiserreich als Einbahnstrasse?', in K. Holl and G. List (eds), *Liberalismus und imperialistischer Staat: Der Imperialismus als Problem liberaler Parteien in Deutschland 1890–1914* (Göttingen, 1976), pp. 62–71. See also D. Düding, *Der Nationalsoziale Verein 1896–1903* (Munich and Vienna, 1972).
4 Zmarzlik, 'Kaiserreich in neuer Sicht?', pp. 118–19.
5 It is perhaps worth noting that women as a group make no appearance whatever in Wehler's book, not even in his discussion of the role of the family (pp. 123–4), which is concerned with the 'father–son relationship'. For Bebel's book, see H.-J. Steinberg, *Sozialismus und deutsche Sozialdemokratie* (2nd edn, Bonn, 1972), p. 158, n. 38. For women voters in the Weimar Republic, see G. Bremme, *Die politische Rolle der Frau in Deutschland* (Göttingen, 1956).
6 M. Twellmann, *Die deutsche Frauenbewegung im Spiegel repräsentativer Frauenzeitschriften, Ihre Anfänge und erste Entwicklung 1843–1889* (Meisenheim am Glan, 1972), Vol. I; H. W. Puckett, *Germany's Women Go Forward* (New York, 1930), pp. 139–40; *Jahrbuch der Frauenbewegung 1914* (Berlin and Leipzig, 1914), pp. 12–14.
7 G. Bäumer, 'Die Geschichte des Bundes Deutscher Frauenvereine', *Jahrbuch der Frauenbewegung 1921* (Leipzig and Berlin, 1921). The claim of half a million (which seems to be the source of the figure quoted in Zmarzlik, 'Kaiserreich in neuer Sicht?', p. 118), was in fact a wild exaggeration (see n. 30, below).
8 Biographies of Auguste Schmidt, Betty Naue, Auguste Förster, Anna Simson, Marie Stritt, Henriette Goldschmidt, Jeannette Schwerin, in Deutsches Zentralinstitut für Soziale Fragen, Berlin-Dahlem, Archiv des Bundes Deutscher Frauenvereine (hereinafter ABDF) 2/1/1–4. Stenographic report of 1902 Congress in ABDF 16/1/2.
9 *Centralblatt des Bundes deutscher Frauenvereine* vol. 9, no. 7 (1907), pp. 49–51; ABDF 5/VIII/1: Stritt and Pappritz to Gesamtvorstand, 14 Apr. 1907 (dealing with objections).
10 Stenographic report in ABDF 16/1/5, pp. 365–468.

11 Ibid., pp. 365–468. The assertion by U. Linse, in his otherwise excellent article 'Arbeiter-schaft und Geburtenentwicklung im Deutschen Kaiserreich von 1871', *Archiv für Sozialgeschichte*, vol. 12 (1972), pp. 233–6, that the BDF supported legalized abortion, is shown by the stenographic report of the debate in the ABDF (which Linse failed to consult) to be erroneous.

12 ABDF 2/1/1: Salomon to Bensheimer, 7 Apr. 1909 (for the description of Stritt as 'one-sidedly radical'; the rest of the file, marked 'not to be shown to outsiders', contains the minutes and correspondence relating to Stritt's enforced resignation).

13 G. Bäumer, 'Was bedeutet in der deutschen Frauenbewegung "jüngere" und "ältere" Richtung?', *Die Frau: Monatsschrift für das gesamte Frauenleben unserer Zeit*, vol. 12, no. 6 (1905), pp. 321–9 (one of the earliest statements of Bäumer's views). See also the lucid exposition of these theories by A. Salomon, in Countess of Aberdeen (ed.), *International Council of Women: Report of Transactions of 4th Quinquennial Meeting, held at Toronto, Canada, June 1909* (London, 1910), pp. 212–13.

14 See speeches of Marie Baum (for BDF Vorstand) and Marie Lischnewska, and final accepted resolution, in ABDF 16/1/5, pp. 365–468 (1908 general assembly); propaganda for 'racial hygiene' (including disfranchisement or even sterilization of mentally subnormal, cripples, alcoholics, and so on), in Staatsarchiv Hamburg (hereinafter St A. Hbg), Politische Polizei, S9001/I: Versammlungsbericht 22 Oct. 1912; *Die Frauen-bewegung*, vol. 17, no. 14 (1911), p. 110; *Frauenstimmrecht: Monatshefte des Deutschen Verbandes für Frauenstimmrecht*, vol. 2, no. 5 (1913), pp. 93–4; *Zeitschrift für Frauenstimmrecht* (Beiheft der 'Frauenbewegung'), vol. 6, no. 7 (1912); *Das kleine Journal*, 5 Aug. 1912 (cutting in Bundesarchiv Koblenz, Nachlass Adele Schreiber-Krieger, Pak. 25). These examples could easily be multiplied.

15 Thus cf. the discussion of arrangements for the 1914 BDF general assembly in ABDF 5/XVI/2: Baumer to Agnes Bluhm, 4 Apr. 1914.

16 Brief accounts in A. Kirchhoff, *Zur Entwicklung der Frauenstimmrechtsbewegung* (Bremen, 1916); M. Lischnewska, *Die deutsche Frauenstimmrechtsbewegung zwischen Krieg und Frieden* (Berlin, 1915).

17 Detailed (but wildly prejudiced) accounts in R. Deutsche and F. Sklarek (eds), *Zur Krise im Bund für Mutterschutz* (Berlin, 1910); H. Stocker, *Krisennache: Eine Abfertigung* (The Hague, 1910). Extensive documentation in Bundesarchiv Koblenz, Nachlass Adele Schreiber-Krieger, Pak. 1–3 (183 numbered Vorstandsprotokolle and 367 numbered letters). Eminent supporters who resigned included Werner Sombart, Anton Erkelenz, Friedrich Naumann, Lily Braun and August Forel.

18 This interpretation is perhaps most accessible in H.-U. Wehler, 'Industrial Growth and Early German Imperialism', in R. Owen and R. Sutcliffe (eds), *Studies in the Theory of Imperialism* (London, 1972), pp. 71–92; Wehler, 'Bismarck's Imperialism 1862–1890', *Past and Present*, vol. 48 (1970), pp. 119–155. A major aim of social imperialism, according to Wehler, *Das deutsche Kaiserreich*, p. 173, was to function as a 'conservative policy of diverting and taming attempts at reform which endangered the existing system, such as were incorporated in the emancipatory forces of liberalism or of the organized socialist labour movement, by diverting them abroad'. The discussion in the preceding paragraphs of this essay should have established the potential of the feminist movement as such an 'emancipatory force', and the social and political threat it posed to the existing system. I am following here one of the lines of criticism set out in G. Eley, 'Defining Social Imperialism: Use and Abuse of an Idea', *Social History*, vol. 1, no. 3 (1976), pp. 265–90; Eley, 'Social Imperialism in Germany: Reformist Synthesis or Reactionary Sleight of Hand?', in I. Geiss and J. Radkau (eds), *Imperialismus im 20. Jahrhundert: Gedenkschrift für G. W. F. Hallgarten* (Munich, 1976), pp. 71–86.

19 *Hamburgischer Correspondent*, 7 Oct. 1910 (cutting in Deutsches Zentralinstitut für Soziale Fragen, Berlin-Dahlem, Helene-Lange-Archiv (hereinafter HLA), Box 57); I. Remme, 'Die Internationalen Beziehungen der deutschen Frauenbewegung vom Ausgang des 19. Jahrhunderts bis 1933', PhD. thesis, Free University of West Berlin, 1955, pp. 37–40.

20 Ibid., pp. 50–63. See also L. G. Heymann and A. Augspurg, *Erlebtes-Erschautes: Deutsche Frauen kämpfen für Frieden, Recht und Freiheit 1850–1940* (ed. M. Twell-mann, Meisenheim am Glan, 1972). For Stritt's views, see Remme, 'Die Internationale Beziehungen der deutschen Frauenbewegung', p. 9.

21   ABDF 4/2: 'Erklärung des Bundes Deutscher Frauenvereine zur Organisation der Gegner'.
22   As the 'Erklärung' (see n. 21) demonstrated. For the 'Anti-League', as it was known, see St A. Hbg, Politische Polizei, S18848: cuttings of *Hamburger Nachrichten* 8 June 1912; *Hamburgischer Correspondent* 12 June 1912.
23   G. Bäumer, *Lebensweg durch eine Zeitenwende* (Tübingen, 1933).
24   The civil code (*Bürgerliches Gesetzbuch*), which came into force in 1900, was arguably more important, but far from constituting an improvement for women, it actually worsened their legal position in some respects. See A. von Zahn-Harnack, *Die Frauenbewegung – Geschichte, Probleme, Ziele* (Berlin, 1928), pp. 39–43; M. Weber, *Ehefrau und Mutter in der Rechtsentwicklung* (Tübingen, 1907), pp. 331–41. For the importance of the *Reichsvereinsgesetz* for the feminist movement see *Report of the Fourth Conference of the International Woman Suffrage Alliance* (Amsterdam, 1908), pp. 100–1.
25   Examples of its use against the SPD in *Sozialdemokratische Parteitagsprotokoll 1906*, pp. 404, 409; and against liberal feminists in St A. Hbg, Politische Polizei, SA 593/II: Heymann to police, 14 Mar. 1903, 19 Feb. 1908; *Der Abolitionist*, vol. 6, no. 2 (1907), p. 18.
26   *Statistik der Frauenorganisationen im Deutschen Reiche*, Reichsarbeitsblatte, Vol. 1 (Berlin, 1909), 'Deutscher Verband für Frauenstimmrecht'.
27   M. Wegner, *Merkbuch der Frauenbewegung* (Leipzig and Berlin, 1908), gives a total of 120,000 individuals belonging to the BDF, but this figure probably includes about 20,000 men. See n. 30, below.
28   Archiv des Deutsch-evangelischen Frauenbundes, Hanover, B1: A. von Bennigsen, 'Ausführungen Paula Müllers über die Stellung des DEFB zur Politik' (Vorstandssitzung, 5 Feb. 1913); Zahn-Harnack, *Frauenbewegung*, pp. 298–301; ABDF 5/IV/5: Bäumer to Vorstand, 5 Sept. 1912, 10 Sept. 1912, 20 Oct. 1912; ABDF 5/IV/5: 'Resolution des Ausschusses des Deutsch-evangelischen Frauenbundes', 13 Dec. 1912.
29   ABDF 16/II/2: Gesamtvorstandssitzung, 7–8 Mar. 1913.
30   The BDF's peculiar method of counting the same members in different categories as if they were different individuals resulted in a claimed membership roughly double the real number of women in the BDF. For the mathematics of this, see my book *The Feminist Movement in Germany 1894 – 1933* (London, 1976), pp. 193–4.
31   Figures in *Jahrbuch der Frauenbewegung 1912, 1913, 1914* (Leipzig and Berlin, 1912–14); St A. Hbg, Politische Polizei, S9001/I: cutting of *Hamburger Fremdenblatt*, 8 Oct. 1911; Universitätsbibliothek Rostock, Nachlass Käthe Schirmacher: Schirmacher to Schleker, 24 Mar. 1911 (I owe this last reference to the kindness of Amy Hackett, New York).
32   L. Elm, *Zwischen Fortschritt und Reaktion: Geschichte der Parteien der Liberalen Bourgeoisie in Deutschland 1893–1918* (East Berlin, 1968), p. 234.
33   For the Progressives and the BDF, see Zentrales Staatsarchiv (hereinafter ZSA) Potsdam, Fortschrittliche Volkspartei, Nr. 20: II. Parteitag 4–7 Oct. 1912; Nr. 36/I: Geschäftsführender Ausschuss, Protokoll, 4 Nov. 1912; Nr. 37, pp. 203–6: Zentralausschuss Protokoll, 21 Nov. 1910; Deutsches Zentralinstitut für Soziale Fragen, Berlin-Dahlem: Helene-Lange-Archiv 57: 'An die liberalen Frauen!', pamphlet, Sept. 1912. The south German liberals Conrad Haussmann and Friedrich Payer were especially hostile to female suffrage (see St A. Hbg, Politische Polizei, S9001/II: cutting of *Hamburger Fremdenblatt* 10 Oct. 1906; ZSA Potsdam, Nachlass Friedrich Naumann, Nr. 59, pp. 98, 100, 230). For the National Liberals, see St A. Hbg, Politische Polizei, S9001/I: cutting of *Vorwärts*, 11 Oct. 1911; Lischnewska, *Deutsche Frauenstimmrechtsbewegung*, pp. 15–16, 25; Zahn-Harnack *Frauenbewegung*, p. 287.
34   For these reforms, see Puckett, *Germany's Women Go Forward*, and Zahn-Harnack, *Frauenbewegung*.
35   E. Flexner, *Century of Struggle: The Women's Rights Movement in the United States* (Cambridge, Mass., 1966), pp. 113–30, 156–92, 215–21; I. Dahlsgård (ed.), *Kvindebevaegelsens hvem-hvad-hvor* (Copenhagen, 1975), entries for Denmark (pp. 190–227), Norway (pp. 316–28) and Sweden (pp. 329–42).
36   For the left-liberals, see Zahn-Harnack, *Frauenbewegung*, pp. 287–9; ZSA Potsdam, Nachlass Naumann, Nr. 59, pp. 247–51 (Protokoll der Vortstandssitzung des Wahlvereins der Liberalen, 8–9 Jan. 1907).

37 *Die Frauenbewegung*, vol. 7, no. 21 (1901), p. 161.

38 The admission of women to political life seems to have been accepted practically without discussion by all parties involved in the preparation of the *Reichsvereinsgesetz*; other aspects of the law, such as those dealing with the admission of minors or the use of foreign languages, proved highly contentious.

39 Zahn-Harnack, *Frauenbewegung*, pp. 298–301.

40 These consisted almost entirely of the wives of local notables (see lists in *Jahrbuch der Frauenbewegung* (Leipzig and Berlin, 1912–14).

41 L. Langemann and H. Hummel, *Frauenstimmrecht und Frauenemanzipation* (Berlin, 1916). NB the inclusion of a female in the authorship of this anti-feminist tract, issued by the Bund zur Bekämpfung der Frauenemanzipation.

42 Archiv des deutschs-evangelischen Frauenbundes, Hannover, B1: Müller to Ortsgruppen, 19 Aug. 1908.

43 See J. Zinnecker, *Sozialgeschichte der Mädchenbildung* (Weinheim and Basel, 1973), esp. pp. 46–8; H. Beilner, *Die Emanzipation der bayerischen Lehrerin, aufgezeigt an der Arbeit des bayerischen Lehrerinnenvereins (1898–1933): Ein Beitrag zur Geschichte der Emanzipation der Frau*, Miscellanea Bavarica Monacensia, vol. 40 (Munich, 1971).

44 For the vast social and economic gulf between primary and secondary school teachers in general, see F. K. Ringer, 'Higher Education in Nineteenth-century Germany', *Journal of Contemporary History* vol. 2, no. 3 (1967), p. 128.

45 Langemann and Hummel, *Frauenstimmrecht und Frauenemanzipation*, p. 9.

46 St A. Hbg, Politische Polizei, S9001: Bericht, betr. Feststellung des Vorstandes und der Mitglieder des deutschen Vereins für Frauenstimmrecht, 21 Nov. 1904.

47 Heymann and Augspurg, *Erlebtes-Erschautes*, chs. 1–3; E. Lüders, *Minna Cauer Leben und Werk. Dargestellt an Hand ihrer Tagenbücher und nachgelassenen Schriften* (Gotha, 1925), entries for 1907. Beilner, *Emanzipation der bayerischen Lehrerin*, gives information on women schoolteachers' unions, as does H. Lange, *Lebenserinnerungen* (Berlin, 1921). The archives of the Allgemeiner Deutscher Lehrerinnenverein are housed in the Deutsches Zentralinstitut für Soziale Fragen, Berlin-Dahlem. On white-collar workers, it is also worth noting that the major white-collar union, the Deutschnationaler Handlungsgehilfenverband, was rabidly anti-feminist, and sponsored publications such as the tract by W. Heinemann cited below, n. 51.

48 Thus compare e.g. the figures for the Union for Women's Suffrage given above with the membership of the moderate Verein zur Vertretung geistiger Interessen der Frau (later, Verein für Fraueninteressen), Munich, which had 516 members in 1902. Of these, only 207 were unmarried. Twenty members were the wives of army officers, fifty-two were members of the nobility. The association also included the wives of the Bavarian SPD leader Georg von Vollmar and of the racist ideologue Houston Stewart Chamberlain, and in the 1890s the poet Rilke also belonged for a time. (A. Hackett, 'The Politics of Feminism in Wilhelmine Germany 1890–1918', PhD thesis, Columbia University in the City of New York, 1976), pp. 298–300

49 Frauenstimmrechtsverband für Westdeutschland, *Grundlagen des Stimmrechts* (Solingen, 1911): an attack on universal suffrage by Rhenish-Westphalian branches of the German Union for Women's Suffrage at its 1909 congress led to Düsseldorf, Köln, Hamm, Duisburg, Hagen, Solingen and other branches forming the equal suffrage *Frauenstimmrechtsverband für Westdeutschland*, which joined right-wing Silesian dissidents in a new national organization in 1911. See *Frauenstimmrecht!*, vol. 1, no. 7 (1912), p. 158; ibid., vol. 1, no. 12 (1913), p. 277; HLA 50: *Jahresbericht des Frauenstimmrechtsverbandes für Westdeutschland 1912*; St A. Hbg, Politische Polizei, S9001/II: cutting of *Berliner Tageblatt*, 24 Oct. 1909.

50 See n. 38, above.

51 The best and most explicit statement of these arguments is to be found in M. Bahnson, *Ist es wünschenswert, dass der §3 aus den Satzungen des Deutschen Verbandes für Frauenstimmrecht gestrichen wird?* (Bremen, 1912). These arguments were also, of course, much favoured by anti-feminists. See esp. W. Heinemann, *Die radikale Frauenbewegung als nationale Gefahr!* (Hamburg, 1913).

52 W. Thönnessen, *The Emancipation of Women: The Rise and Decline of the Women's Movement in German Social Democracy 1863–1933* (London, 1973).

53 cf. comments of workers recorded in St A. Hbg. Politische Polizei, S9001/I: Wirtschaftsvigilanzberichte, 3 May 1903, 1 July 1903.

54 Bahnson, *Ist es wünschenswert . . .?*, p. 5.

55 This was in effect the message put across by Gertrud Bäumer, following Friedrich Naumann (Baumer, *Lebensweg*, shows Bäumer's strong admiration for Naumann and his ideas).

56 G. Bäumer, 'Frauenbewegung und Nationalbewusstsein', *Die Frau*, vol. 20, no. 7 (1913), pp. 387–94. See also *Jahrbuch der Frauenbewegung 1913* (Leipzig and Berlin, 1913).

57 U. von Gersdorff, *Frauen im Kriegsdienst* (Stuttgart, 1969), pp. 15–37.

58 These arguments were first advanced, in an American context, by A. S. Kraditor, *The Ideas of the Woman Suffrage Movement 1890–1920* (New York, 1965).

59 These developments were accompanied by a withdrawal of radical feminists from professional organizations to concentrate on the struggle for the vote. See in general Lüders, *Minna Cauer*; and n. 47, above.

60 St A. Hbg, Politische Polizei, S5466/I: cuttings of *Hamburgischer Correspondent*, 7 June 1895, *Berliner Tageblatt*, 30 June 1896

61 See my article, 'Prostitution, State and Society in Imperial Germany', *Past and Present*, vol. 70 (Feb. 1976), pp. 106–29.

62 Bundesarchiv Koblenz, Nachlass Adele Schreiber-Krieger, Pak. 1: Referat über den Vorrag von Helene Stöcker, 27 Nov. 1908; Pak. 3, P28a: Flugblattentwurf 'Zur Aufklärung!'; Pak. 3, P49: Vorstand der Ortsgruppe Berlin, 1 Nov. 1908; Internationaal Instituut voor Sociale Geschiednis, Amsterdam, Collection Henriette Fürth: Stöcker to Fürth, 20 Oct. 1905; *Die Frauenbewegung*, vol. 13, no. 3 (1907), pp. 20–1.

63 For BDF views on sexual morality in the Bäumer era, cf. ABDF 5/XVI/2: Bäumer to Max von Gruber, 13 July 1914; ABDF 5/XII/6: Scheven to Bäumer, 10 Feb. 1911.

64 St A. Hbg, Politische Polizei, S9000/I: cutting of *Hamburger Fremdenblatt*, 4 Oct. 1905.

65 See n. 14, above.

66 This function of female suffrage was of course familiar in other countries as well: cf. Kraditor, *Ideas of the Woman Suffrage Movement*.

67 BDF, *Die Stellung der Frau in der politisch-sozialen Neugestaltung Deutschlands* (Berlin, 1917).

68 As late as the afternoon of 8 Nov. 1918 the introduction of female suffrage was still being resisted by the majority of the Interfraktioneller Ausschuss. See E. Matthias and R. Morsey, *Die Regierung des Prinzen Max von Baden*, Quellen zur Geschichte des Parlamentarismus und der politischen Parteien, no. 1, Vol. 2 (Düsseldorf, 1961), pp. 571–3, 593, 598–9, 602, 606–9.

69 See the useful discussion in D. Blackbourn, 'The *Mittelstand* in German Society and Politics, 1871–1914', *Social History*, vol. 4 (Jan. 1977), pp. 409–33.

70 For BDF attitudes to the National Socialists in 1932–3, see esp. ABDF 16/II/5: Sitzung des engeren Vorstandes, 13 June 1932; ABDF 1/A/2: documentation on 'Auflösung des Bundes'.

71 See the discussion in Evans, *Feminist Movement in Germany*, pp. 235–75.

72 R. J. Evans, *Comrades and Sisters. Feminism, Socialism and Pacifism in Europe 1870–1945* (Brighton, 1987), pp. 157–95.

73 Before 1930 most of the BDF members supported the German Democratic Party (*Deutsche Demokratische Partei*, or DDP), German People's Party (*Deutsche Volkspartei*, or DVP), or DNVP and there is no reason to suppose that they were any more loyal to these parties than were the men who deserted them by the million for the Nazis in 1930–3. See *Jahrbuch des Bundes deutscher Frauenvereine 1932* (Leipzig and Berlin, 1932), for a discussion of political preferences of BDF member associations in the late 1920s.

74 There is a good discussion of conservative women in Britain in B. Harrison, 'For Church, Queen and Family: The Girls' Friendly Society 1874–1910', *Past and Present*, vol. 61 (Nov. 1973), pp. 107–38.

75 See above all Kraditor, *Ideas of the Woman Suffrage Movement*, pp. 7–8, 66–73, 125–38, 202–3, and *passim*.

76 See D. C. Tipps, 'Modernisation Theory and the Comparative Study of Societies: A

Critical Perspective', *Comparative Studies in Society and History*, vol. 15 (1972), pp. 199–226.

77 Bäumer, 'Was bedeutet in der deutschen Frauenbewegung "jüngere" und "ältere" Richtung?' (n. 13, above).

78 cf. B. Friedan, *The Feminine Mystique* (London, 1963).

8

'Red Wednesday' in Hamburg: Social Democrats, Police and Lumpenproletariat in the Suffrage Disturbances of 17 January 1906

Sometimes a historian's interest in a subject is sparked by an unexpected documentary find, and so it was when the political police file on Dr Anita Augspurg, a leading 'radical' feminist of the pre-1914 era, landed on my desk in the Hamburg State Archives early in 1971, as I was gathering material for my dissertation on the women's movement in Imperial Germany. Surprisingly the file contained relatively little on Augspurg's feminist activities; instead, it was full of detailed documentation on a charge of libel brought against her by the local police in 1906. It appeared that during mass Social Democratic demonstrations held on 17 January that year to protest against the city authorities' decision to revise the property and income qualifications for the local franchise upwards, thus reducing the power of the working-class vote, Augspurg had led a small group of feminists in a demonstration of their own for female suffrage. In the course of these events, she had had occasion to observe numerous acts of violence and brutality perpetrated by the police against the Social Democratic demonstrators. Augspurg was never one to hesitate when it came to the defence of civil liberties. The following day she published a long and detailed denunciation of the police's behaviour in the local Social Democratic daily, the *Hamburger Echo*. This brought on her a charge of libel, which she defended by calling over a hundred witnesses to attest the accuracy of her observations. So damaging were their revelations that the trial was stopped well before they had all been heard. The documents relating to the trial were collected in Augspurg's personal police file and three other substantial *Akten*, and they revealed a fascinating picture of social and political conflict. On completing my work on feminism, I took up this material once more, and started to read around in the area of 'social protest' and collective violence. It soon became clear that the disturbances of 17 January 1906 in Hamburg did not fit conveniently into the general interpretations which were beginning to be advanced in this field. Moreover, the disturbances proved to be one of those incidents which lead into much larger questions of social structure and political change. At the time, there was not only an almost total absence of scholarly work on collective violence in Imperial Germany, but also very little available on urban history, or, indeed, on the relationship of the organized labour movement to the mass of the working class. In this sense, the following chapter can be taken as a case-study illustrating some of the general points made in Chapters 5 and 6. It was first given in an abbreviated form to the Social History Society conference on 'Crime, Violence and Social Protest' held at Birmingham in January, 1977, and I am indebted to the audience for criticisms and suggestions. Thanks are also due to Geoff Eley, Dick Geary and Karin Hausen for their helpful comments on an earlier draft, and to Claus Stukenbrock for guiding me through the material in the Staatsarchiv Hamburg on which it is based. A summary of the paper and following discussion appeared in *Social History Society Newsletter*, no. 2 (spring 1977), pp. 7–8, a fuller version was printed in *Social History* vol. 4, no. 1 (1979), pp. 1–31, and an abridgement appeared in German in Jörg Berlin (ed.), *Das andere Hamburg* (Cologne, 1981) under the title 'Wahlrechtsraub, Massenstreik und Schopenstehlkrawall' (pp. 162–80). This chapter reproduces the *Social History* version, with some small alterations of detail, some minor cuts restored, and an additional note on the novel *Helmut Harringa* incorporated into the text. As Chapter 4 makes clear, recent work on 'social protest' has moved beyond the quantitative approach criticized here, but the essay stands among other things as an argument for the rewards that can be gained from an approach based on the individual case-study.

I

The 1970s have seen a dramatic revival of social history in Germany after decades of neglect.[1] Inevitably, however, German historians are taking up many of the central problems of social history with the methods and theories current at present, without having experienced many of the crucial debates and discussions which took place in other countries in the 1950s and 1960s. In most cases, too, they are acquiring their initial theoretical orientation from the USA rather than from Britain or France, despite the well-developed tradition of social history in these latter counties. A particularly striking example of this can be found in the field of crime and 'social protest'. The pioneering studies of Rudé, Hobsbawm and Thompson in this country[2] were virtually without parallel in West Germany; the challenge posed by their methods and arguments was not taken up. As West German historians are opening up this field of inquiry, they are doing so largely through the wholesale importation of social science methods currently in vogue in the USA. The leading influence here has been the quantitative approach pioneered by Charles Tilly (and, for

Germany, by his brother Richard).[3] In this essay, I want to argue that this approach has a number of serious drawbacks. Principal among these is the fact that by compiling aggregate series of data about incidents in which violence was used by more than twenty people, it detaches each act of 'collective violence' from its determinate historical context and in doing so obscures rather than illuminates the origin and meaning of violent action. This approach makes it difficult if not impossible for the historian to understand why some groups used violence as a form of protest while others did not (for non-violent protests do not enter the Tillys' picture at all). Nor does it take into account the changing implementation and effectiveness of state repression; at some times and in some circumstances the state may consider it more necessary than at others to repress collective protest by force, while on the other hand a decline in violent protest may simply reflect improved state repression and indicate an increase rather than a diminution of social tension. Moreover, as Karin Hausen has pointed out:

> In so far as one believes that protest is a form of articulating people's interests, one must at least admit that it is valid to ask how the protesters were affected by economic developments, how their concrete work and living situation improved or worsened. Aggregate data on the level of the nation state do not even provide a starting-point from which to answer this question. The study of smaller units of investigation would therefore, in this case, far from being a step back, constitute a methodological advance.[4]

This chapter seeks to illustrate these points through a detailed analysis of a single – though highly complex – instance of violent crowd action which took place in Hamburg on 17 January 1906. After discussing this specific case – chosen among other reasons because according to Richard Tilly no violent crowd actions took place at all in Hamburg between 1882 and 1913[5] – I shall return in a concluding section to the lessons which the method of approach I adopt has to offer the study of riot and social conflict in general.

II

In January 1906 Hamburg was a federated state in its own right within the German Empire, separate from Prussia, though in practice subordinate to it in most respects. It had already for some time been in the throes of rapid expansion and industrialization, a process evident in the growth of its population from 622,530 in 1890 to 763,349 in 1900 and to over a million in 1910; by this last date, too, there were more than half a million people living in suburbs and outlying districts which were not counted as part of Hamburg's population because they came under Prussian jurisdiction. The industrial expansion that lay at the root of this massive increase in population was based on shipbuilding, not only for the city's rapidly growing mechant marine but also for the new German navy being created under the leadership of Alfred Tirpitz from the turn of the century onwards. The boom in shipbuilding brought with it the growth of numerous ancillary industries, notably in metalworking and engineering. At the same time the continued expansion of Hamburg's role as the major entry port for imported goods into Germany gave rise to an increasing number of industrial concerns devoted to processing imported raw materials. Finally, the city's prosperity itself generated employment for building workers, labourers in demolition and construction, and other trades.[6]

The growth of the new working class formed the basis for the rise to prominence in Hamburg of the Social Democratic Party of Germany (*Sozialdemokratische Partei Deutschlands*, or SPD), whose members were drawn overwhelmingly from their ranks. Already since 1890 the party's support had been great enough to ensure it safe and uninterrupted control over the three Hamburg seats in the Reichstag, the Imperial German legislature.[7] But Reichstag elections were based on universal suffrage for all adult males. Local elections, to the Hamburg *Bürgerschaft*, or Citizens' Assembly, were based on a restricted franchise. In Hamburg, as elsewhere, the reason why most people were denied the vote was that they possessed little or no property. Thus in order to qualify for the right to vote in Hamburg in 1890, a man had to be a citizen, a right for which he had to pay a considerable sum of money in the form of a citizenship fee, and he had to pay taxes above a certain minimum rate. As a result, the Hamburg electorate in 1892 numbered a mere 23,645 out of a total population of over 600,000 living within the borders of the city-state.[8] The justification for such a restriction was again by no means peculiar to the city fathers of Hamburg. It lay in the widely held belief that only men of property could be trusted to act responsibly in determining the welfare of the state. Those without property had no stake in the affairs of the community; they could be bribed with money, or they could be led astray by irresponsible agitators who were only interested in their own advancement. Those who had nothing to lose, in other words, had no more interest in the well-being of Hamburg than they had in the well-being of Timbuctoo. The property-owners, on the other hand, could be trusted to have the interests of the propertyless at heart, because if the latter rebelled they would lose everything. In Hamburg, moreover, the property-owners, who were to a large extent from merchant families, could also argue that since the welfare of the whole community depended on the city's commerce and trade, those who were most actively involved in it were the only ones in a position to know what was in the general interest in this respect.

251

The problem with this argument was that property-owners naturally tended to have their own interests at heart much more than those of the rest of the community. Without the danger of their representatives in the Senate – the eighteen-man body whose members, elected for life by the citizens' assembly, formed the government of the city – being voted out of office by popular opinion, there was no real check on their economic and political egoism. Anyone who visited Hamburg in the 1890s and walked the few hundred metres from the plush 'villa district' of Rotherbaum and Harvestehude down into the grimy, tumbledown, often flooded, old quarter of the town near the harbour, where tens of thousands of poor workers' families lived in overcrowded, squalid and miserable conditions, would immediately be aware of the shocking contrasts of wealth and poverty which the existing political system of the city in practice did so much to maintain. If the propertyless had no voice in the affairs of the state, it was hardly surprising in reality that little was done to alleviate their lot. The most striking evidence for this was provided by the appalling cholera epidemic of 1892, in which well over 8,000, mostly poor people died within the space of a few weeks. The main cause of the epidemic was the failure of the city to provide a proper filtrated water supply, so that the population, with the exception of those wealthy property-owners fortunate enough to possess private drinking-wells, had to rely on water taken direct from the river Elbe, at a point not far away from the main sewage outlet. After the major financial effort of constructing the new docks in the 1880s, the Senate was slow to provide the city's inhabitants with a new water supply, and, though construction of one had begun at the end of the 1880s, its completion was still nowhere in sight by 1892. The result was that Hamburg gained the unhappy fame of being the only western European city to experience a major cholera epidemic in the last quarter of the nineteenth century; every other major town in western Europe had begun to take adequate precautions well before the discovery of the cause of cholera by Robert Koch in 1884.[9]

The result of the cholera epidemic, which placed Hamburg in the full glare of world public opinion, was to compel the senate and the citizens' assembly to reform the suffrage. In 1896, after much debate, the citizenship fee was dropped and the minimum qualification for the attainment of citizenship was set at an annual income of 1200 marks sustained over a period of five years or more. This was still far more than most workers could afford. For one thing, 1200 marks was considerably above the average annual wage of a manual labourer at that time. Even more important was the fact that few workers in those days were able to enjoy regular employment. Firms habitually dismissed their employees in times of recession; and many forms of employment were casual in nature, above all in the docks, which formed such an important source of employment for Hamburg workers: here, men were hired to deal with ships as they came

in, and if there were few ships, as in winter, then there were correspondingly few hirings. Finally, illness, which was naturally common among the
poorer classes, led to yet more fluctuations of earnings. Yet, despite all
this, the number of citizens began to increase once more, reaching a total of
almost 60,000 by 1904. Many of these were petty-bourgeois property-
owners. But a good number were also evidently members of the working
class: 12,000 out of the 13,500 new *Bürger* registered between 1901 and
1903 were indeed wage or salary earners rather than property owners.[10]

Despite the continued restriction of the local Hamburg franchise, the
growth of the working class, the increasing prosperity of the city and the
reform of the suffrage in 1896 combined in 1901 to ensure the election of
the first Social Democratic representative in the Citizens' Assembly, Otto
Stolten. In 1904 Stolten was followed by twelve more representatives of
his party.[11] Under the rules of 1896 it was already impossible for the SPD
ever to obtain a majority of the Assembly seats, for half the seats were in
fact reserved for notables (*Honoratioren*) and house-owners (*Grundeigen-
tümer*). However, as soon as the SPD could secure as many as 40 seats out
of the total of 160, which certainly seemed within the bounds of possibility
if the registration of workers as citizens continued at the same pace as in
1896–1904, then its representatives in the Citizens' Assembly would be
able to block any change in the Hamburg constitution, which required a
two-thirds majority in favour of any amendment.[12] Moreover, the presence of thirteen Social Democrats in the Assembly from 1904 on was
already a serious enough development in the eyes of the Senate. Hitherto
the Assembly had scarcely been the scene of party-political debates in the
modern sense. The political groups (*Fraktionen*) in this body, rather than
corresponding to national political parties, represented differing economic
interests within the property-owning élite. The purpose of the Assembly's
deliberations was generally held to be to strike a balance between the
interests of property-owners, merchants, shipbuilders and so on, so that a
relaxed, gentlemanly mode of discussion, compromise and a general
willingness to do a deal with the other party were the order of the day.[13]
Hamburg, in short, was ruled by what German historians know as
Honoratiorenpolitik, the politics of notables.[14] The coming of the SPD
ended this cosy atmosphere and introduced a new note of political polemic
and social criticism into the Assembly's debates, which the majority of
members found profoundly distasteful and disturbing. As an organized,
professionally run and aggressive political party, it was a new element in
Hamburg politics. With its attacks on free enterprise and its support for
labour unions, it thoroughly alarmed Hamburg's mercantile ruling class.[15]
Worse still, the SPD by virtue of its thirteen seats was beginning to be
entitled to representation on the various commissions and committees of
the Assembly. Such bodies often included representatives of the Senate
and sometimes dealt with matters of government which the senate

regarded as highly confidential.[16] Thirteen SPD deputies, in short, represented a disturbing factor in the political scene; forty or so, it appeared to the Senate, would mean that the old way of doing business would be ended once and for all. As the official historian of Hamburg, Ernst Baasch, put it, a further increase in the number of SPD deputies would constitute a serious threat to the 'undisturbed further development of the Hamburg state'.[17]

In the early months of 1905, therefore, the Senate and the conservative leaders in the Assembly held a number of secret meetings at which they worked out a way of preventing this from happening. The results of these deliberations were published on 14 May 1905: the Senate proposed to revise the franchise to prevent 'political power from falling more and more into the hands of the unpropertied classes'.[18] During the course of the year the original proposals were modified in a number of respects, and they received a number of additions which made the final Suffrage Bill a document of considerable complexity. The most important clauses of the final Bill, published on 24 December 1905 (a date calculated, of course, to avoid public notice and discussion, or at least to postpone it as long as possible), proposed that the electorate should be divided into two classes. Those with an income of over 2500 marks per annum were to elect forty-eight deputies. Those with an income of between 1200 and 2500 marks per annum were to elect twenty-four. Another eight were to be elected by the citizens of the outlying rural areas without respect to income class. With minor amendments in the franchise, the deputies elected by property-owners and notables were to remain, likewise the minimum qualification for citizenship (an income of 1200 marks per year sustained over five years). Moreover, in order to prevent the SPD from securing all twenty-four seats available to the second class, the Bill proposed the introduction of proportional representation. These proposals were justified with a series of allegations against the Social Democrats, who were charged with hostility to the state, opposition to the growth of commerce on which its prosperity rested, indifference to the aspirations of the individual citizen, ingratitude towards the efforts of the state to improve the lot of the worker, and so on.[19] In attempting to restrict as far as possible the small number of Social Democrats in the Citizens' Assembly, it was expressing its contempt for the majority of Hamburg's inhabitants, whose support for the SPD it evidently believed was the result of gullibility or ignorance and therefore was not be be taken seriously. The result would be a perpetuation of the grossly unequal society of the time and a continued emphasis on trade and profit to the detriment of social reform and freedom of choice for the majority of the people. The proposal constituted a public insult to the intelligence and independence of mind of the ordinary inhabitant of the town. Hamburg's masses therefore looked to the Social Democrats to do something to stop the proposal.

The party, naturally enough, was thoroughly conscious of its responsibility. It decided in the first place to take all possible practical steps to defeat the proposal. This meant, to be realistic, stopping it from securing the support of the Citizens' Assembly. Thus the SPD issued appeals to the bourgeois deputies in the Assembly to vote against the proposal (which, eventually, a number of them did). During the debate on the proposals, which began on 17 January, the SPD deputies did everything they could to delay the proceedings by tabling numerous amendments and making long speeches.[20] Important though these tactics were, however, they did not satisfy the aspirations of the mass of the party's supporters. Understandably enough, they wanted to do something to influence the situation themselves. The Social Democratic leadership in Hamburg was not particularly radical, and it shared in full the party's general disinclination to risk provoking the wrath of the authorities and bringing about a return to the days of the Anti-Socialist Law (1878–90), when the party had scarcely been able to operate openly at all. However, the pressure for extra-parliamentary action from its members was enormous. The SPD's protest against the 'suffrage robbery' was expressed in a steadily mounting crescendo of propaganda in the *Hamburger Echo*, its daily newspaper, in mass-circulation leaflets and posters, and at numerous popular assemblies held during 1905. The campaign, in which strong though vague calls to action were frequently reiterated, reached its first climax in a series of sixteen simultaneous mass meetings held on 5 January 1906. At a number of these meetings, it became clear that the party's membership interpreted the call to action as a call to a general strike; some also thought of a mass public protest outside the town hall, where the Senate and Assembly met. As later accounts made plain, the initiative for such actions came from the ordinary party members rather than from the local party leadership.[21] Nevertheless, when the Assembly finally settled on 17 January 1906 as the date on which the debate on the Suffrage Bill was to be held, the Social Democrats decided to follow these calls to action, and organized a series of eight mass meetings to coincide with the beginning of the debate.

These events were taking place in an atmosphere of considerable political excitement. The tension which the Social Democratic propaganda and the simultaneous campaign of the Bill's supporters helped create in Hamburg was heightened not only by similar events elsewhere in Germany but also by the steady stream of news from Russia about the liberalization of the political system in the course of the 1905 Revolution – news which increased the sense of frustration in the SPD and the sense of apprehension in the authorities.[22] Moreover, at the SPD's national congress at Jena in September 1905, the party had also resolved that the mass strike was an effective weapon against reactionary measures such as the restriction of the franchise.[23] This resolution gave the local SPD leadership official party backing for its decision to follow its members' calls to action and to use the occasion to stage Germany's first political general strike.[24] The protest meetings were to be held not as usual in the evening but at four in the afternoon, during normal working hours. The Hamburg SPD was led by orthodox Social Democrats, not by radicals. They made it quite plain that the intention was not to stay off work indefinitely, nor even all day on the 17th January, but rather simply to finish work early in order to attend the meetings. The strike was planned as a demonstration of the SPD's power and of the commitment and self-sacrifice of its supporters, not as a direct bid to press the Citizen's Assembly to withdraw its proposals by crippling the city's economy. The workers would attempt to resume their jobs the next day, though the SPD was aware that lockouts and dismissals were likely to be staged by the employers as reprisals. Nevertheless, despite its strictly limited nature, this was the first political general strike to be called by the SPD, and as such it aroused the apprehension of the authorities still further. As it turned out, it also aroused the expectations of the workers more than the SPD leadership intended. Because of the *political* rather than *social* focus of German historiography, the strike has formed the main object of interest for historians as well, perhaps understandably in view of the general political significance and controversiality of the mass-strike debate in these years. The demonstrations which followed the strike have in contrast received little attention.[25] It is one of the contentions of this essay that, of the two, it is the demonstrations which were the more interesting and ultimately also the more significant.

III

Early in the morning of 17 January 1906 the Hamburg SPD sent its men round the docks and distributed thousands of leaflets urging the workers to strike in protest against the 'suffrage robbery' and to attend the popular assemblies to be held later in the day. The result, claimed the party's leaders in the city, far exceeded expectations. As things turned out, this was no mere cliché of SPD propaganda. Hamburg's dockland in the late afternoon of 17 January was later said to have been 'quieter than on a Sunday'. No boats could be seen plying their usual trade on the Alster, the lake that separated the centre of the city from some of the plusher middle-class suburbs. Factories, shipyards and building sites were still.[26] The massive response to the party's call to strike was impressive and encouraging, but it also proved to be the beginning of the SPD's problems. At four in the afternoon, eight separate mass protest meetings were to begin. The liberal Hamburg newspaper, the *General-Anzeiger*, reported that in 'almost all the workshops' in the docks the workers had given notice that they would lay off at two in the afternoon. Elsewhere there was reported to be less solidarity and considerable fear of dismissal. But building workers, it was reckoned, were likely to attend in especially large numbers, since work on construction sites generally stopped at 4 p.m. anyway.[27] Already at four, in fact, the meetings were filled to overflowing. The police later reckoned that there were 3,000 people at the Hammonia Variety Hall in St Georg to hear Emil Fischer, an SPD deputy in the citizens' assembly; 2,500 people at Strathmann's Halls, and 2,200 at Buckowicki's in Mühlenkamp. These numbers were still small compared with the crowds attending the other assemblies: between 5,000 and 6,000 at Hallwachs' Hall in Eimsbüttel; 5,000 at Springborn; and similar numbers at the other three meeting-places (Sieberling's, Denecke's and Bock's Gesellschaftshaus in Rothenburgsort). Very few women were observed by the police at these gatherings. Outside all the meeting-places, huge crowds gathered, unable to secure admission because the meetings were already full. Altogether the police estimated that 24,000 people were present at the actual assemblies, but this was clearly an underestimate: even the police's own figures for the individual meetings yield a total attendance of over 30,000. According to the SPD daily newspaper in Berlin, *Vorwärts*, there were 30,000 at the assemblies and another 50,000 outside.[28]

The intention of the organizers was no more than to impress the citizens' assembly with the sheer size of the meetings. As Adolf Bartels, one of the SPD deputies in the Citizens' Assembly, told his audience at Sieberling's,

> We are a well-disciplined party and we want to demonstrate, to demonstrate effectively. We want to show that we are well-disciplined, and that we do not want a violent struggle, and will not let ourselves be provoked into one ... Now I would like to express the wish that this mass demonstration will give these people even at the eleventh hour the impression that the workers of Hamburg are prepared for once to risk a struggle for their right to vote.

'These people' – the bourgeoisie – were to be impressed, it is clear from the context, by the 'struggle' which the workers risked in staying away from their work, not by any violent scenes on the streets. From the very start of the assemblies, however, it was apparent that the vast crowds, having forfeited their pay and very possibly their jobs by leaving work early, were not going to be content merely with listening to speeches. They wanted action. Their resolve was fortified by the fact that the weather was unusually clear, fine and warm and also by the beer that was served at the assembly halls (according to the usual custom at political meetings in Germany) and drunk, it was reported later, in considerable quantities. In all the gatherings, cries of 'To the town hall!' were constantly audible from the floor. Every time a speaker mentioned the town hall, where the debate

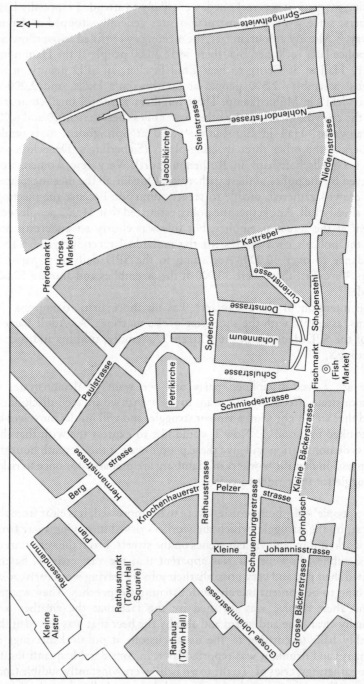

Figure 8.1 City Centre, Hamburg, 1906.
Source: Staatsarchiv Hamburg, Plankammer.

on the Suffrage Bill was taking place, he was answered by shouts of 'That's where we want to go!'. Alarmed at the militant mood of their audiences, the major speakers went out of their way to warn them to be cautious. 'We are really much too law-abiding to do anything rash', was the optimistic opinion of the chairman of the assembly at Sieberling's. 'We don't want any conflicts', the audience at Strathmann's was warned. 'Leave the meeting and show that we stand on the ground of lawfulness', advised the chairman of the Rothenburgsort assembly. Similarly, the meeting at Springborn's ended with an appeal to the crowd to proceed 'in a peaceful manner', and the speaker at Buckowicki's concluded by saying to his listeners, 'I want to ask you to be as quiet as possible, so as not to provoke violence'. Only in the case of the meeting in St Georg, addressed by Emil Fischer, was there no report of any attempt made to calm the crowd on the part of the leading officials. The local SPD leaders, however, did not follow the example of the top men, and clearly to some extent shared the mood of the crowds. In Eimsbüttel, once the main speakers had finished, the local party leader, Ziemer, could be heard inviting the audience to go for a 'promenade' to the town hall, though he also made it clear that in doing so he was going against the official line of the party leadership in Hamburg. Similar advice was probably given less ostentatiously at the other meetings, for subsequent events revealed that the local party members had appointed stewards to supervise the march to the town hall. In contrast, all the top SPD officials, with the exception of Emil Fischer, made every effort to calm the crowds, as even the police reports showed, though the total effect of their speeches, which were replete with references to the Russian Revolution, probably had the opposite effect. If it was obvious to them that they could not stop the crowds going to the town hall, at least they could try to ensure that they went in an orderly fashion. Nevertheless, it was already apparent even before the meetings ended that matters had now escaped their control.[29]

The meetings finished between 5.30 and 6 p.m., and the crowds began streaming from all of them towards the town hall. The police had considered from the start that demonstrations before the town hall were likely, and they had laid their plans well in advance. All police leave had been cancelled. Off-duty policemen had been ordered to report to their police station at 4.30 p.m. The plan was to post a strong force in front of the town hall itself, and to place smaller contingents in the nearby streets. The policemen gathering at the stations of Neuerwall, Hafenmarkt, Raboisen and Dammtorstrasse were to be held in readiness to reinforce the main body of law officers, who were to meet at the town hall at five. Already by 4.30 p.m. however some five hundred small boys aged '2 to 12' had gathered before the town hall in the Rathausmarkt (Town Hall Square). (See Figure 8.1.)

They were milling about in front of the town hall when the main

259

contingent of police arrived – 175 constables on foot, 25 mounted, 12 sergeants (*Wachtmeister*) and two staff sergeants (*Oberwachtmeister*), led by Lieutenant Niemann. Seeing the children, Niemann ordered his men to clear the square, in conformity with his orders that all gatherings of people in the area should be dispersed. Still following his orders, he then sealed off the entrances to the market. The trams had been ordered not to stop in their usual place on the east side of the market, but were still allowed to pass through the square at that end. So too was other normal traffic. In front of the town hall doors, Niemann posted a reserve of 25 mounted police and 20 police on foot.[30] Already by this time his superiors, alerted by reports of the unexpectedly high attendance at the SPD assemblies, realized that he would have to be reinforced. They called the majority of policemen on the beat elsewhere in the city to the Town Hall, leaving the greater part of Hamburg unpatrolled. By 5.30 p.m. practically the entire police force of the city was assembled in or near the Town Hall Square.[31]

Shortly after 6 p.m., the crowds began to arrive after walking into the city centre from the SPD assemblies, most of which had been held in outlying working-class areas. After attempting unsuccessfully to break through the police cordon, some of the crowd began throwing stones and empty bottles – evidently many of them had not only been drinking at the meetings but had also refreshed themselves on the way. At about 6.30 p.m., when the last of the crowds was arriving from the most distant of the meeting-halls, Niemann decided that the cordon at the junction of Bergstrasse and Hermannstrasse was in danger of breaking, and sent reinforcements, which were insulted, hooted and whistled at, and pelted with empty bottles.[32] Niemann ordered his men to draw their sabres or truncheons and to drive the crowd back. At the same time, he also sealed off the eastern side of the Town Hall Square, because some of the demonstrators were trying to evade the police cordon by jumping on to passing trams. The trams had by this time almost ceased to run, since after 6 p.m. it proved almost impossible for them to penetrate the thick crowds surrounding the Rathausmarkt, which was where most of the trams turned round. The crowds were now stretching from the Petrikirche to Jungfern-stieg. They seem to have had no aim save to impress the citizens' assembly deputies in the town hall with their numbers and commitment. Some of them sang songs or listened to improvised speeches. Eventually at 8 p.m., with trams logjammed all along the approaching streets, the tram company suspended all its services in central Hamburg until further notice.

At this point, Major Gestefeld, who was in overall command of police operations, decided that more reinforcements were necessary, and that it was time to attempt to relieve the pressure on the police lines around the Town Hall Square by a direct attack on the crowd. He called in the mounted police from the Raboisen station and they proceeded to clear the crowd back to the outer edges of the Town Hall Square. At about 8 p.m., having completed this task, they then went on to the offensive, and, drawing their sabres, they began to clear Rathausstrasse, where the crowds were a good deal thicker. By 8.30 p.m., slashing at everyone in sight with their sabres, they had cleared the Rathausstrasse and established new cordons at the far end,[33] as well as in the Schauenburgerstrasse.[34] By the Petrikirche, some of the demonstrators regrouped, and after singing the 'Workers' Marseillaise'[35] and listening to some brief impromptu speeches on the 'suffrage robbery', they began to march up Bergstrasse and along Jungfernstieg, singing workers' songs and occasionally stopping to listen to more speeches. Coming up against a police cordon, they marched via Grosse Bleichen to Klopstockstrasse, where they stopped outside the house of Dr Johann Burchard, Burgomaster of Hamburg and president of the senate. Burchard was generally considered to be an opponent of the suffrage reform, and indeed had voted against it in the Senate. The crowd, estimated variously at 1,000 or 3,000 strong, gave him three cheers, and Burchard came out to address them from the balcony of his house. After rousing them to give three hurrahs for 'our dear Hamburg, our father-city', he urged them to go home and bid them good night. Though they did not seem to have been unduly dismayed by Burchard's paternalistic attitude, the crowd nevertheless did not heed his advice, and after more cheering many of them returned not to their homes but to the demonstration still going on at the Petrikirche. While this more disciplined group had been marching to and fro, the situation around the town hall, where the main crowds were still milling about, had become steadily more violent and confused. Shortly after 8.30 p.m., after successfully clearing Rathausstrasse, the police launched a strong attack on the mass demonstrators thronging Schmiedestrasse. An eyewitness complaining of the police's behaviour in the SPD newspaper, the *Hamburger Echo*, some days later, gave a vivid impression of the scene:

Just before half-past eight I came through Schauenburgerstrasse with a colleague and met three friends at the junction with Schmiedestrasse. We talked for about ten minutes about the events of the evening, and among other things discussed the blameless and friendly attitude of the police. Suddenly, and quite unexpectedly for us, the policemen stationed at the opening of Schmiedestrasse launched an attack. The crossing was almost blocked by the trams, which were following each other so closely that it was impossible to escape quickly. I was pressed up against a moving tram and reached Schulstrasse under its protection. Here I met three of my colleagues again, at the side of the Johanneum. But scarcely three minutes had elapsed before a second attack followed the first. The crowd rushed in wild haste to the Fischmarkt. I stayed at the side of the Johanneum; a mounted policeman sprang on to the pavement opposite me, into the midst of the people standing there;

constables on foot joined him; the flashing sabres and the cries of the people had got everybody very worked up. Then, very loudly, one could hear the cry go out: 'Party members don't stay here – go home!'

And indeed now, at about 9 p.m., the SPD stewards made repeated attempts to persuade the crowds to disperse. Their appeals, according to eyewitnesses, were met with 'scorn and ridicule' (*höhnische Redensarten*).[36] But the diminished size of the crowd an hour or so later showed that they had had an effect.

The centre of gravity of the struggle now moved towards the Fischmarkt (Fish Market). The police attempting to clear Schmiedestrasse were pelted with empty bottles, thrown, so it was reported, from the upper-storey windows of a building under construction – most of the bottles hit the crowd rather than the police, thus increasing the general panic. Assailed by bottles from above and drawn police sabres from the side, the crowd, with much shouting and whistling, turned on the police, dragging them from their horses or throwing them to the ground. Nevertheless, by 9.30 p.m. the police were pushing the scrimmage down Schmiedestrasse into the Fish Market and the narrow streets of the surrounding area. Calling upon fresh reinforcements, Lieutenant Niemann, who had taken personal charge of the operation, managed to arrive at the Fish Market not long after 9.30 p.m., after an extended battle in which the crowd had torn guard-rails from the trams, overturned dustbins, and thrown these and anything else that came to hand. Witnesses heard repeated choruses of the 'Workers' Marseillaise' coming from the crowd while all this was going on. At about 10 p.m. the remnants of the column that had marched to see Burgomaster Burchard reappeared on the scene, after marching with Niemann's permission into Paulstrasse. The result was that they were driven into Domstrasse, a narrow street that led into the Fish Market at the other end. Here they demonstrated against the offices of the *Hamburger Nachrichten*, a conservative newspaper. In the meantime, Niemann had decided to clear the Fish Market. With eight mounted policemen he cleared the area, while another eight, led by a sergeant, cleared Schulstrasse. The result was that a part of the crowd – now much diminished in numbers – was driven from various directions into the three smaller streets leading off the Fish Market: Domstrasse, Curienstrasse and Schopenstehl. Niemann realized the folly of blocking off these streets from both ends, but the result was that the crowds milling about in them were constantly joined by others from neighbouring streets. The mounted policemen made repeated attempts to clear these streets from the Fish Market end, but they were foiled by improvised barricades and then driven back by a hail of stones, bottles, dustbins and their contents and lids. The crowd called the policemen 'bloodhounds' and 'cossacks', and one witness even reported hearing gunshots (a rather unlikely story). After several unsuccessful attempts to clear these streets, Niemann realized that he was leaving the town hall approaches unguarded, and withdrew his men to the Fish Market.[37]

As soon as the police departed, the crowds in Schopenstehl sent a hail of stones flying at the gas-lit street-lanterns, putting them all out. Immediately the street was plunged into darkness. People hurled stones at the shop windows and began to loot. The owner of a jewellery shop in Schopenstehl later testified that at 10.30 p.m., when the police withdrew and the lights went out, a stone came flying through his shop window, then two more, then

a proper bombardment was opened, so that the window-pane was totally smashed to pieces. The metal blinds were torn down, and the iron bars were broken off by several people pulling on them and forcing them out of the metal frame. As soon as the window was destroyed and the iron bars broken off, greedy fingers grabbed at the watches and gold in the display ...

These experiences were shared by many shopkeepers in the street, among whom there were several jewellers.[38] In a nearby street, Brandstwiete, the crowd lit a bonfire from the contents of rubbish bins. The fire brigade arrived at about 11 p.m. to put out the fire and was greeted with hoots, whistles and a hail of stones and bottles. Four of the firemen received slight injuries. No sooner had they retired, having extinguished the fire, than it was lit again. They returned 25 minutes later and put it out to the accompaniment of catcalls and whistles. On their way back to the fire station they extinguished two more street fires in the locality. Meanwhile, someone had destroyed the fire alarm in Niedernstrasse, and the fire officer sent to replace it was driven away by the crowd.[39] Ten plate-glass windows were smashed in the Exchange Bank building in Brandstwiete, and windows had already been broken in Schmiedestrasse in the course of the battle that had taken place there earlier in the evening.[40]

From the police's point of view these developments put an altogether more serious complexion on events. Property was being destroyed. At 11 p.m., on hearing of the looting and destruction, the forty mounted policemen at the Petrikirche rode to Schopenstehl, cleared away the barricade and drove out the crowd. All police stations were alerted by telegraph and a force of 150 police was quickly gathered outside the town hall – mostly, it may be surmised, men who had formed the cordon round the Town Hall Square earlier in the evening, before the centre of the disturbances had moved to the Fish Market area. They can thus have enjoyed barely an hour's rest during the whole evening; while Niemann and his mounted police had been in continuous active service for six hours without any refreshment or respite.[41] By now, in other words, the police were undoubtedly tired, angry and not a little panic-stricken, realizing that things had escaped their control and fearing the worst. The police force outside the town hall split into five groups and rushed through the streets around Schopenstehl, breaking up the remaining crowds by force. They met with little resistance. At a quarter to midnight they ran into a group of fifty people in Kattrepel, who attacked them with stones, allegedly urged on by a man who shouted, 'Up with the anarchy! Down with the dogs of the senate! Let's go, friends, down with the spiked helmet!' The police counter-attacked with drawn sabres and the crowd dispersed, singing the 'Workers' Marseillaise'. Another group of sixty in the Pferdemarkt (Horse Market) was similarly broken up.[42] By this time in fact all the crowds had dispersed; many had evidently heeded the advice of the SPD stewards to go home. Apart from the two groups in Kattrepel and the Horse Market, there were only isolated individuals or groups of two or three people left in the streets by 11.30 p.m. It was these people who now bore the brunt of the police's fury.

Of the many individual instances of police excesses reported later, some stand out as being particularly dramatic. At 11.30 p.m., as the police were clearing the Niedernstrasse, some people took refuge in the Lunau Bar, where the regulars were sitting enjoying a quiet drink. Twelve policemen burst in after them with drawn sabres, and fell upon the drinkers at the tables, hacking at them with cries of, 'Out with you, you bandits, you rabble!' The customers fled as quickly as they could, but not quickly enough to escape injury. One of them, a 76-year-old man, died later from sabre wounds and shock. The police claimed later that they had been pelted with empty beer mugs from the bar (or even, in one improbable story, with *full* beer mugs). This seems unlikely, since the bar had a plate-glass window that could not be opened and was not broken, and could only be entered through two sets of doors.[43] Other incidents included the case of Georg Wittmann, a 22-year-old joiner, south German in origin, and therefore particularly offensive to the local patriotism of the Hamburg police, who hacked him to the ground and kicked him, calling him a 'Bavarian dumpling' (*Knödelbayer*). Wittmann was taken from the Fish Market, where the incident occurred, to hospital, but died later from the effects of a sabre cut of such savagery that (according to a post-mortem examination) it had smashed the back of his skull in.[44] Similar incidents occurred around midnight in Domstrasse, Schulstrasse, Jungfernstieg and other now almost empty streets. Witnesses reported seeing groups of policemen fall on individual pedestrians or drive out people sheltering in doorways with sabre blows. An official messenger from the town hall was attacked by the police while he was going through the streets on official business.[45] A deaf man, unable to heed the warning cries that the police sometimes uttered, or to sense their presence if they approached him from behind, later recounted that he had been repeatedly attacked by policemen wielding sabres while he was on his way home.[46] A young middle-class man, son of a citizens' assembly deputy, reported later experiences that must have been typical of many less well placed than he to complain about them:

> I was at the assembly chamber on 17 January, in the public gallery. After the debate I wanted to go with some friends to drink a glass of beer in a restaurant near the Klostertor railway station. As I came to the Fish Market, I saw forty to fifty policemen, but almost nobody else there. Reichenstrasse, which borders on the Fish Market, was almost empty of people. As we went past it, a mounted policeman suddenly rode up to us with his sabre drawn and shouted at me, 'You rascal, you're another one of them!' and hacked mightily with his sabre at my head and at every part of my body ... At the same moment I was encircled by eight constables on foot, who also drew their sabres and struck at me with the naked blade. I eventually succeeded in fleeing into a bar. The policemen stormed in after me and drove me out of the pub again. Back in the street I was once more surrounded by about eight policemen and soundly beaten with their sabres. Finally I managed to escape. The mounted officer chased me and repeatedly struck me with his sabre from his horse ... I ran to the Klostertor railway staion and looked for a police station there to have my wounds bound ... After I had met up with my friends, we went up to a group of policemen to ask them where the nearest police station was. 'On the moon,' was the answer.[47]

While this was going on, men, women and children could be seen fleeing through the streets, in many cases streaming with blood from sabre wounds. On-duty pharmacists and physicians were kept busy into the small hours attending to people's injuries. One noted that he had bound the wounds of twenty-three people during the course of the early hours of 18 January, including those of a 10-year-old boy who had had the ends of several fingers chopped off by a police sabre.[48] By about 1.30 in the morning, however, all was still once more, and the remaining policemen returned to their stations and thence to their beds. The streets were finally quiet, and an uneasy peace descended over Hamburg.[49]

IV

As dawn broke on 18 January, the police, the press and the people of Hamburg began to take stock of the night's events. The right-wing press unanimously presented the occurrences of 17 January, which they dubbed 'Red Wednesday', including the looting and the violence, as a 'dress rehearsal for revolution', planned in advance by the Social Democrats, and only stopped from developing into something worse by the bravery of the police.[50] Pride of place was given to the policemen injured in the riot, for whom the conservative *Hamburger Nachrichten* opened a fund for public donations.[51] The first editions of the right-wing press to carry the story all asserted that one policeman had been killed. This story, which was pure fabrication, based on a wrongly coded wire, was quickly withdrawn in later editions. The liberal *Berliner Tageblatt* and *Frankfurter Zeitung* followed the right-wing line in their earliest post-demonstration editions and also printed the story of the dead policeman.[52] Only later did they go over to a more differentiated view, begin to distinguish between the demonstration and the looting, and include some criticism of the police.[53] The editorial of the conservative *Hamburger Nachrichten* on the affair saw an immediate parallel with the Russian Revolution. Its later editions of 18 January carried the following comments:

> Hamburg has thus been granted the melancholy fame of having constituted the arena for the first revolutionary scenes to be staged on the Russian model by the revolutionary party in Germany; for what has so far happened in Dresden, Chemnitz etc. cannot stand comparison with the events which took place here yesterday evening and during the night. As it appears from the descriptions in our second morning edition today, yesterday's events lacked none of the features which are characteristic of the Russian Revolution: the mob attacked the police, wounded policemen in large numbers, killing two[!], broke into shops, looted, built barricades, set things on fire and so on.

A repetition of these events, the paper declared, was more than likely. The Social Democratic masses were not interested in political rights; all they wanted was 'the key to the safe'; they preferred breaking and entering, robbing and looting, to argument and discussion. This was a foretaste of what could be expected if the Social Democrats took power, the paper concluded; the whole thing had been carefully planned from beginning to end.[54] These views were mild in comparison with those sent in to the conservative press by panic-stricken readers in the days following the riot. 'Citizens of Hamburg!' declared one reader of the *Hamburger Fremdenblatt* on 20 January. 'When you have rats in your houses, and they are about to cause the foundations to collapse, is it not your damned duty and obligation to put the useless animals out of their existence?'[55] Policemen, urged a writer in the correspondence column of the *Hamburger Nachrichten*, should be armed with carbines and bayonets; another letter advocated the employment of 'a large pack of strong, fierce police dogs' (*bissige Polizeihunde*), while a third put the case for the use of fire hoses.[56] Outside Hamburg, the press of the radical Right declared that the riots had been the work of 'Jewish agitators', whose sole concern had been to steal and rob.[57]

In a further editorial, the *Hamburger Nachrichten* warned of further 'attempts at a *putsch*' which might result in whole areas of Altona, Harvestehude and Rotherbaum (middle-class parts of the city) being 'laid waste'.[58]

These judgements were shared by the police. A report written almost immediately after the riot indicated the line that they would take. 'The apparent progress of the Russian Revolution', it began,

> gives the leading German comrades no peace. Perhaps, they think, the revolution, which according to Bebel is already near, might be brought about now by similar activities. Bebel spread this view at the party congress in Jena and at the international conference in Brussels. Hamburg was to provide the opportunity for such triumphs through the coming debate on the Suffrage Bill. It was probably to arrange this tactic that Bebel came to Hamburg in November last year, although he claimed he only wanted to discuss his views on the general strike with the Hamburg comrades. Already at the beginning of this month it became known that at the time Bebel held a secret meeting with the leading comrades in a bar here . . .

In this meeting, continued the report, both the strike and the subsequent demonstration had been planned. Although in public the Social Democrats had warned against street demonstrations, this was only to deceive the police. The events of 17 January proved that their purpose all along had been to take the town hall by storm and terrorize the citizens' assembly into rejecting the Suffrage Bill.[59]

The SPD in its turn did its utmost to dissociate itself from the affair. As early as 19 January an article in the Social Democratic *Hamburger Echo* suggested that the police were indirectly responsible for the looting and the violence because they had withdrawn patrols from the 'criminal quarter' around Schopenstehl to reinforce their cordon around the town hall and so allowed the 'mob' to run riot without check. Subsequent editions of the paper went further and claimed that the police had deliberately encouraged these criminal elements in order to provide themselves with an excuse for establishing a police state in Hamburg with the total repression of the labour movement. Many of those who had 'arranged' the disturbances were said by the SPD press to have been police informers. These articles earned the *Echo*'s editor, Wabersky, five months in gaol for libelling the police – his sixteenth conviction and his third prison sentence for this kind of offence since he had become editor ten years previously. Wabersky subsequently managed to get his sentence reduced to twenty days on appeal, by which time he had already sat in prison for forty-two days.[60] Just as readers' letters to the right-wing press expressed views even more extreme than those of the papers to which they wrote, so many of the SPD rank-and-file were a good deal more bold in their criticisms of the police than the *Echo* dared to be. Letters to the press voicing such sentiments were impossible because of the danger of prosecution (right-wing letter-writers of course ran no such risk).[61] But the police agents who toured the Social Democratic bars of Hamburg in disguise, and noted down the conversations of the customers, managed to sample some fairly strong comment in the days after the riot. 'Sensible people such as ourselves', remarked one worker of the local population in Uhlenhorst and Barmbek, 'stayed quiet'. Others, such as eight dockers overheard in another bar, asked, 'Since when has it been the fashion among us organized workers to indulge in robbery and looting?'. It was the 'mob', they concluded, who had been responsible, and the police were to blame for not putting a proper guard on the 'criminal quarter'. Some workmen were even heard to opine that the police themselves had smashed in the windows of the jewellers' shops with their sabres in order to discredit the SPD. If the police had been hoping to hear any glorification of violence or revolution in these bars, they were certainly disappointed.[62]

These conflicting interpretations of the events of 17 January reflected not only differing political attitudes but also differing theories of social relations and political action. The police and the right-wing press operated on the assumption that crime and revolution were intimately connected, indeed quite indistinguishable. Collective violence could only have one object: it was a political act, aimed at gaining political power, organized and planned in advance. The purpose of political power was to enable the propertyless to loot the possessions of the well-off. The warnings of the Jena party congress and the 1905 Revolution in Russia were only too clear. The revolutionary phraseology of the SPD was taken at its face value, and the party was regarded as little more than a criminal conspiracy to overthrow the existing system of property relations. The behaviour of the 'mob' indeed was an additional reason for disfranchising it. The police's own behaviour on the other hand was regarded in this view as almost invariably rational, their aggression designed solely to prevent criminal acts from being carried out; and indeed all criticism of the police's behaviour on the night of 17 January was met with libel suits from the police, who were uniformly successful in this tactic. Investigations were started against one police constable for assaulting a town-hall messenger, but they came to nothing.[63] The SPD operated on what was superficially at least a very different set of beliefs, the Marxist theory of the *Lumpenproletariat*. As Marx and Engels had observed in the *Communist Manifesto*, describing the possibility of non-proletarian social groups joining the revolutionary movement, the 'dangerous class', the social scum, that passively rotting mass thrown off by the lowest layers of the old society, may, here and there, be swept into the movement by a proletarian revolution; its conditions of life, however, prepare it far more for the part of a bribed tool of reactionary intrigue.[64] This was how the SPD viewed the riot, while the prosecutions of its own members that followed were attacked as evidence of 'class justice'.[65]

Yet in fact the Social Democrats' explanation of the origins of the riot was in many ways a mirror-image of that advanced by the police. The riot was seen by both sides as the product of a conspiracy arranged in advance and carried out for primarily political reasons. Like the police, the SPD was eventually obliged to abandon this view. As we shall see, the police failed to convict any SPD members for taking part even in the riot, let alone the looting, and they were eventually forced to fall back on the more general assertion that the party had been indirectly responsible for these events because they would not have taken place without the strike and the mass meetings which had followed. This was undeniable, but it did not really explain very much. It was also a very long way from the original assertion that the whole affair had been planned and carried out by the SPD from beginning to end;[66] similarly, in the trial of Wabersky, the editor of the *Hamburger Echo*, for libel, the defence failed to produce a single scrap of even the most circumstantial evidence that police informers had been at work in Schopenstehl. It had to fall back on the assertion that the *Echo* had never made such a claim. The SPD as a whole was forced to retreat to the less specific theory that the disposition of the police's manpower on the night in question had left Schopenstehl unpatrolled and so created the opportunity for the looting.[67] This too was undeniable, but it also failed to explain very much either, and it was a very different matter from the original claim that the police had arranged the whole affair with the *Lumpenproletariat* in advance. Both the police and the SPD, therefore, began with similar interpretations, but were forced to retreat from them by the requirement of the judicial system for hard evidence and the desire of the press for hard facts.[68]

A view lying somewhere between these two extremes, interestingly, was provided by a work of fiction published soon after. The immensely popular novel *Helmut Harringa*, by Hermann Popert, which was published in 1910 and had sold 293,000 copies by 1923, contains a chapter which is in all probability based on the events of 17 January 1906.[69] Popert, a judge in Hamburg, was a leading anti-alcohol campaigner. For a long time he was close to the left-liberals. The scene in his *Helmut Harringa*, set in Hamburg, begins in Niedernstrasse, which swarms with a crowd of young layabouts, 'dirty old men' (*schmutzige Greise*), prostitutes, and 'the miserable brood of the sunless alleyways and poison-laden rear houses' which characterize the area. A disturbance occurs, and a policeman (Henning by name) is cut off by the crowd, which lays siege to police station no. 7 (Depenau). The policemen draw their sabres and hack away at the crowd, which yells with rage and redoubles its efforts, while all the time being supplied by prostitutes with liberal quantities of beer. The empty glasses are thrown at the police who, battered and bleeding, are driven back, unable to rescue their comrade, officer Henning. The mob senses victory:

> Panting heavily, they surround the brave sons of the lower German land, picked men from the wooded villages around Hamburg, from the Vierlanden, Hanover and Holstein. Against them [i.e. the police], in a disorderly throng, all those from whom the big city has burnt out human feelings: the dross of the Germans, Poles as well, and riffraff from Italy and Asia Minor.

At this point, however, Ludwig Thormann, the leader of a Social Democratic gymnastic club meeting nearby, hears the noise of the battle and comes to the rescue: 'In a sharp tone of command ... he cries: "Whoever is an organized worker must now help the police!"' With cries of 'bravo', seventy socialist gymnasts, joined by the dozen or so genuine *workers* in the crowd, set to and rout the mob. They all feel that 'It must be so. Order must stand by order, organization by organization. Against disorder and chaos, which are death for all.' The scene is remarkable for the number of the obsessions of the German middle class which it manages to pack into a few pages: drunkenness, rampant sexuality, racial degeneration, dirt, crime, violence, the mob, the trusty German peasant, the evils of the big city, the Asiatic peril, the virtues of discipline, organization and order, the threat of the layabout, the courage of the police. It was precisely this characteristic indeed which made the book so popular. Most remarkable of all – and what distinguished the liberal Popert from the political Right – was the recognition that the SPD could function as a bulwark of order – a view which was to be amply vindicated in 1918–19. The immediate reason why the SPD gymnast Thormann comes to the rescue of the beleaguered policeman Henning introduces another classic theme: the army as a unifying social force. Thormann remembers that while he was a conscript in the army, Henning, then a regular sergeant in his platoon, rescued him from certain death. The immense popularity of the book is perhaps indicative of the spread of social anxiety among the German middle classes at this period.

V

On the morning of 18 January 1906, the Hamburg police, shaken by their experiences of the previous evening, and convinced that revolution was only just around the corner unless they acted quickly and decisively, imposed a total ban on open-air meetings and insisted that the SPD call off its planned participation in a nationwide series of demonstrations set for

21 January. All restaurants, pubs and bars in Schopenstehl, Niedern-strasse, Kattrepel, Mohlenhofstrasse, Springeltwiete, Altstädterstrasse, Fischertwiete and Depenau were ordered to close at 3 p.m. every day until further notice.[70] At the same time as taking these precautionary measures, the police set about re-establishing their authority by arresting those whom they regarded as responsible for the outrages of 17 January. On the assumption that anyone hit by a police sabre must have been committing a crime, detectives and constables sallied forth and arrested everyone seen wearing bandages. Lists of admissions to the casualty wards of local hospitals on 17–18 January were obtained, and those treated for sabre wounds were apprehended. The ambulance department of the fire brigade supplied a list of sixteen people whose wounds they had bandaged on the night in question. All of these save two had head wounds; the other two were wounded respectively in the leg and on the hand. All of them were arrested.[71] In a typical incident – one of many such – an officer reported that 'Schumacher was walking about with a bandaged head and stands in suspicion of having taken part in the riot'. The unfortunate Schumacher, naturally, was arrested.[72] Additional culprits for the riots were acquired through denunciations. One man, for example, was denounced, probably maliciously, by the mother of a 22-year-old girl he employed in his shop.[73] A married couple were denounced in graphic detail by their landlady, who said that they had thrown rubbish at the police, the woman had attacked them with her umbrella, and her husband had beaten a constable to the ground.[74] Again, the motives of the denunciator seem, to say the least, open to suspicion. One anonymous letter denounced four people at once.[75] Further candidates for arrest and interrogation were supplied by the police overhearing 'suspicious' conversations. Shortly after the riot, for example, a member of the metalworkers' union was walking home from his shipyard one day with a workmate and discussing the events of the 17th. As the word 'revolution' left his lips, a passing policeman jumped off his bicycle and arrested him. Back at the police station, the officers of the law gathered round him and shouted, 'You rascal! You want to beat up our colleagues, do you? You've thrown bricks at them, have you?' Thereupon they began hitting and kicking him. Brought to trial, the worker was accused of shouting, 'Up the Revolution!' and of pushing the policeman off his bicycle and assaulting the police officers at the station. He was found guilty only of the first offence, which earned him a week in gaol.[76] Taken as a whole, measures such as these yielded a large quantity of prisoners.

It was scarcely surprising, given the premisses on which the police based their policy of arrest, that many of those apprehended soon had to be released. The denunciations were in many cases revealed as malicious, and the minimum evidence necessary to make even a formal charge possible was also lacking in a number of instances.[77] Eventually some fifty people were brought to trial. They came before the courts about three months after the riot, having spent the whole of the intervening period in gaol.[78] The trials provided the opportunity for the renewal of the arguments that had followed immediately upon the riot itself. Commenting on the first of the two major trials, the right-wing newspaper *Die Post*, generally recognized to represent the views of heavy industry in Germany, alleged that those involved in the rioting and looting had not been common criminals but working men in their Sunday suits. 'Among the thirty accused, only one was a regular customer in the thieves' dens; all the rest were at the mass meetings, they were suffrage demonstrators. It is obvious that we are dealing with Social Democrats.'[79] The Social Democratic *Hamburger Echo* repudiated these 'lies'. Among the twenty accused in the second trial, it declared, only one was 'organized', and he was acquitted. In fact, the actual records of the trials reveal that both these statements were misleading. Among the thirty accused in the first trial, only four belonged to trade unions. Three of them were accused of riotous assembly and looting: one of these denied the charges outright, and the other two admitted looting but said that they had found the stolen goods on the street and had simply picked them up. Two of the three were members of the dockers' union; the other belonged to the construction workers' union. None of them had previous convictions; all of them received prison sentences of between five and ten months.[80]

The star of the trial was the fourth of the organized workers in the dock, Emil Stange, a journeyman plasterer, arraigned as a 'ringleader' who had led attacks upon the police. Stange, the only one of the fifty accused in the two trials who was a member of the SPD and had actually been to the protest meetings, had, like a number of the other accused, spent much of the evening of 17 January drinking. He was said to have led a troop of rioters, shouting repeatedly, 'Up with anarchy! Down with the dogs of the Senate!' The allegation is interesting evidence of the police's inability to distinguish Social Democrats from anarchists; the latter had in fact long since been expelled from the SPD and were a tiny, mostly bourgeois intellectual grouping in Germany. The accusation against Stange was highly implausible. Later on, it was alleged, Stange smashed in the window of a shop belonging to one Herr Langbehn, whose identification provided the basis for his arrest. Amid general applause from the right-wing press, Stange was sentenced to two years in prison. But this was not the end of the affair. Stange appealed; Langbehn had acted out of malice, he said, and the other witnesses (mostly police) who claimed to have seen him in the riot had been 'mistaken'. Stange's lawyers produced fresh evidence that he had entered a bar in a drunken state at 10 p.m. and had proceeded to drink eight half-litres and fifteen smaller mugs of beer; he had staggered out some time later, 'so drunk' (*derart seines Bewusstseins beraubt*) that he could no longer walk properly. His defence was that he had been too intoxicated either to lead a band of rioters or even to throw a stone at a window, let alone hit it.

With the collapse of the case against Stange, nothing was left of the police's attempt to enforce on events their original conception of a planned rehearsal for revolution.[81] Of the investigating magistrate's original category of eight among the sixty-five people initially charged as being 'obviously influenced by the Social Democrats, had taken part in meetings etc.', not one was left by the end of the affair.[82] Of course, one must qualify this conclusion by one further consideration. Although the police clearly failed in their attempt to pin charges on SPD and union members, this may not have been an entirely accurate reflection of the real state of affairs. Those arrested would most likely have realized under interrogation that they would be lost if they admitted belonging to the labour movement, and so would have denied being SPD or union members whatever the circumstances. Still, it remains unlikely that many of those eventually found guilty were, in fact, active in the Hamburg labour movement; membership could also be established by the police in other ways, and clearly further investigation yielded but meagre results.

Several of the others accused in the two trials were also acquitted: these included three dockers, a waiter, a railway worker, a bookbinder and a clerk who was a member of the extreme right-wing German-national Commercial Employees' Union. Those eventually found guilty provided strong backing for the SPD's allegation that the affair had been the work of the *Lumpenproletariat*. They included Heinrich Rudolph, a docker, and his wife Elise Rudolph, a prostitute with numerous convictions for contravening the vice regulations; both of them were said to have led troops of rioters shouting, 'Cut the policemen down'! and Elise Rudolph was alleged to have rolled a dustbin lid and thrown a stone at the police. Another docker found guilty was Karl Leeck, a well-known regular of a so-called 'thieves' den' in the Fish Market area. He had eight previous convictions for begging and two for theft. Friedrich Kadner, a boatman with three previous convictions for theft and one for begging, was convicted of looting; his defence was that he had been pressed up against the jeweller's window in Schopenstehl by the crowd! Others convicted included Karl Kloodt, a dock haulier, with one previous conviction for actual bodily harm, who claimed in defence that he had been incapably intoxicated on 17 January; Fritz Rehmers, an apprentice smith, with three previous convictions for theft, who admitted taking thirteen pairs of earrings, six bracelets, two gold watches and much more besides; Christoph Jauszius, a building worker with two previous theft convictions, arrested trying to sell a stolen watch – his defence was that he had seen everyone in the Schopenstehl grabbing what they could, so he had simply joined in (taking, among other things, two bracelets, five brooches, nine rings and twenty-two silver watches!); Franz Angelstory, unemployed,

Table 8.1 Social Composition of Workers Convicted of Riot and Looting in the 'Red Wednesday' Trials in Hamburg, 1906

Occupation	No. convicted	Occupation	No. convicted
Building worker	2	Locksmith (H)	1
Journeyman plasterer	1	Apprentice locksmith (H)	1
Mason's workman	1	Apprentice smith (H)	1
Digger	1	Granary worker (H)	4
Docker (H)	3	Manservant	3
Boatman (H)	1	Domestic servant ('boots')	1
Carter (H)	1	Part-time maid	1
Warehouse worker (H)	1	Telephone worker	1
Lighterman (day-labourer) (H)	1	Cigar maker	1
Stevedore (H)	1	Market worker	1
Ship-cleaner (H)	2	Card-cutter	1
Storehouse-worker (H)	1	Schoolboy	1
Boiler-cleaner (H)	1	Errand-boy	1
Casual labourer (H)	2	Work-boy	1
Labourer (H)	1		

Note: H – probably worked in harbour area.
Source: L1930–1/I: Rittner und Genossen; L1930–1/I: Dörrenhaus und Genossen.

who also pleaded guilty to looting; Johannes Drewes, a labourer with convictions for receiving stolen goods, burglary and resisting arrest; Wilhelm Linne, a docker arrested when seen with bandaged sabre wounds, convicted previously for begging, theft and receiving;[83] Max Nieber, an unemployed docker who 'lived in the thieves' dens' and admitted being on the streets from 9.30 p.m. on 17 January (after drinking solidly since 6 p.m.) until five in the morning of 18 January; Leo Hoppe, a domestic servant with a police record, said to have spent the whole evening in Schopenstehl, denounced after bringing a sackful of stolen goods into a 'thieves' den' in Niedernstrasse by one 'Berliner Jonny'; Karl Lembke, a casual labourer with convictions for theft and other offences, arrested because of his sabre wounds; Franz Stegmann, a card-cutter with eleven convictions for theft, receiving and other crimes, arrested because of his bandaged arm; Hans Grumme, a market worker with sixteen convictions for a wide variety of offences including burglary and wounding; and Robert Pesch, a locksmith, also a regular in the 'thieves' dens' with seventeen convictions including several for wounding, theft, fraud and *lèse-majesté*.[84]

Many of these people were inhabitants or habitués of the so-called 'thieves' dens' around Niedernstrasse. This area, where the looting and barricade-building had occurred, was in fact well known as a criminal quarter. 'In order to understand the riot in Niedernstrasse and Schopen-stehl,' a Berlin newspaper reminded its readers, 'one must remember that Niedernstrasse forms the centre of a quarter which can scarcely have a rival

in Germany for its structural condition and the nature of its inhabitants.'
The houses, it went on, were old gabled buildings whose upper storeys
shut off the light from the narrow streets. They were dark, decrepit and
insanitary, rents were very low and the area had attracted the 'work-shy'
and 'those who avoided the light of day'. Even the police did not feel safe
there at night, and always – exceptionally – went in groups when they
patrolled the area. Narrow alleyways and passages led from the streets into
a maze of courtyards where it was possible for criminals to evade the
clutches of the police for an eternity. It was well known for criminals from
as far afield as London to take refuge there when the English police were
on their tracks – an unusual sidelight indeed on Hamburg's much-vaunted
'special relationship' with England.[85] A reporter sent by another newspaper to inspect the area on the morning after the riot (18 January) painted
an even more lurid picture. 'Only now and then', he wrote,

> could one observe in one of the dark alleyways which led to the
> notorious inner courtyards one of those idle, puffy criminal faces
> peering out ... The light-shy rabble remained concealed in their lairs in
> the courtyards and rear houses. These passages – like dark caves – lead
> from the street to the narrow backyards.... Anyone who went alone
> and without due care into such a narrow alleyway could quickly be laid
> cold there in the dark. It was also these passages that offered the rioters
> the safest refuge in the revolt. If the mounted police sprang towards
> them, the demonstrators ran into these alleyways, and then from this
> safe base threw their knives and beer bottles at the horses and riders.

The reporter was clearly doing his best to make a dramatic story out of a
scene of total inactivity. Much of his story, including the knives thrown at
the police, was pure imagination. Characteristic too was his equation of
the demonstrators with the criminal underworld; the paper he was
reporting for was the extreme right-wing *Hamburger Nachrichten*.[86]

Nevertheless, there was a kernel of truth in these picturesque accounts
of the area in which the riot had reached its climax. The reporter's
description of the physical aspect of the district was accurate enough. The
area was well known to the police as the haunt of criminals. Not only did
the police force all the bars in the area to close at 3 p.m. in the period
following the riot, but also, when an international criminology conference
had met in Hamburg the previous year, the police had chosen this very
district to show the participants when asked to give a conducted tour of a
'criminal quarter'. The SPD *Hamburger Echo* commented sarcastically
that the police's time would have been better occupied in putting a more
adequate guard over the area.[87] Nor were the disturbances of 17 January
1906 the first such occurrences in the district. In May 1890 a strike by gas
workers had plunged much of the city into darkness, including Steinstrasse

and Speersort, where shop windows were smashed and passing trams pelted with stones. The riot spread to Niedernstrasse and the other streets in the area and went on after dark for the best part of a week. Thousands of spectators had come from the rest of the city to view the spectacle, and parties of young ladies and gentlemen were reported to have hired rooms in the Speersort, where they caroused in the safety of first-floor chambers and were heard through the open windows singing 'merry songs' (*lustige Tafellieder*) and cheering on with loud hurrahs the pitched battles taking place below them between the police and the 'howling mob'.[88] On 18 January 1906 so many spectators arrived to view the scene of the riot that the police felt obliged to chase them away with their sabres once more. Double rows of policemen closed off the entrances to the Fish Market after 6 p.m.[89]

On this date, indeed, not only the events of the night before but also the area in which they had taken place were the object of some curiosity for the people of Hamburg. Until 1896 much of the inner city had been covered with similar rookeries. These old-established and overcrowded areas had been inhabited by the working classes, who needed to be close to the harbour, which formed almost their only source of employment. Labour in the Hamburg harbour was organized on a casual basis, with men being hired *ad hoc* to deal with ships and cargoes as they came or went. The coming of industrial capitalism to Hamburg in the 1890s brought about important changes in the labour market and also in the social geography of the city. The rationalization of labour practices in the habour – one of the main results of a long, bitter and celebrated strike in 1896 – gave more steady employment to a minority, while greatly reducing work opportunities for the rest. New industries sprang up which gave employment on a fixed basis in developing industrial areas on the city boundaries. The new industrial proletariat so created enjoyed a steadily rising level of real wages after 1896, and lived in newly created working-class suburbs on the outskirts of the city – the areas in which the SPD meetings of 17 January were held. A rapidly growing network of tram routes and local railways provided them with cheap and regular transport to their work. In 1896–7 the Senate began a large-scale slum clearance scheme which concentrated initially on the area known as the *Neustadt* (new city), frequently liable to flooding. It had also been the scene of violent clashes during the great port strike of 1896. By 1906, therefore, the old rookery around the Fish Market and Niedernstrasse was a socially and geographically isolated area, almost the last such quarter untouched by the improving hand of the Hamburg Senate, and inhabited largely not by the 'work-shy', if such people existed, but by those workers who still needed to be close to the harbour in order to find employment – the residue of the casually employed harbour workforce. By 1906, ten years after the rationalization of port labour, these had become economically increasingly marginal – a process that may be read in the fact that many of the port workers convicted for their part in the events of 17 January – and they formed roughly half of all those convicted – possessed previous convictions not only for theft but also for begging.[90]

It is at this point that the distinction between the different phases of the disturbances of 17 January 1906 becomes crucial, both for the evaluation of the list of convicted persons and for the assessment of the significance of the evening's events in a wider and more general sense. It is clear that a fundamental qualitative difference existed between the violence and looting in the area around the Fish Market between 10 p.m. and 11 p.m., and the much larger-scale but less violent and destructive disturbances that took place around the town hall during the preceding four hours. For different reasons, neither the police nor the Social Democrats were prepared to admit the validity of this distinction – the police because they wanted to pin the responsibility for the looting of the later phase on to the participants in the earlier demonstrations, the Social Democrats because they wanted to pin the responsibility for the violence that had occurred in the earlier phase on to those who had carried out the looting later on. A clear distinction between the two phases emerges, however, both from the SPD accounts of the evening and from the police papers and trial documents. The arrests and trials in particular provide strong evidence for the validity of this distinction. For the major *political* trials to arise out of the disturbances were, in fact, not those of the actual participants but rather related to another series of incidents altogether, in which leading Social Democrats in Hamburg were accused of *incitement*. This second set of trials is of less interest for our purposes because it merely repeated the arguments that had been put forward in the Social Democratic and in the conservative press in the period immediately following the riot. But, as far as the authorities were concerned, it provided the main 'evidence' of SPD responsibility for the events of 17 January.[91] In the trials of the *participants*, the concern of the police was to convict those *directly* responsible for the offences against *property*. Violence and public disorder were secondary; so huge had been the crowds, so hectic the evening, that any serious move against the *rioters* was clearly out of the question.

It was the police's concentration on the looters to the relative exclusion of other offenders that led to the failure of their attempt to find Social Democrats to convict in these trials. The principles on which the police based their policy of arrest for riotous assembly – injuries, bandages, denunciations etc. – were so ludicrously inadequate that they were bound to yield meagre results in terms of eventual convictions. Arrests for looting on the other hand were easier to effect, because the police could use known contacts in the criminal underworld, plus raids, incidents of people trying to sell stolen watches etc., to apprehend at least a good proportion of the culprits, though of course by no means all. The looting and receiving

indictments were altogether more solid than those for riotous assembly
(*Aufruhr*). Twenty-four of those eventually convicted (a majority) were
convicted for looting or receiving, and all except four of those pleaded
guilty. Most of those accused of riotous assembly denied the charges and
claimed they had merely been carried along by the crowd. Of those
acquitted at the trials, seven had been accused of riotous assembly but only
one of a property offence. Nearly all of those against whom the charges
were eventually dropped had initially been arrested for their alleged part in
the riot.[92] Of course, by their very nature, riotous assembly charges are
easier to deny than theft or receiving charges. Moreover, the routine
procedures operated by the police in their search for arrests were likely to
be more successful where those with previous convictions were concerned
than with those who had none; and they were certainly more rational and
effective in the case of property offences than in the case of riotous
assembly, as we have seen. Still, even when these considerations have been
taken into account, it remains overwhelmingly likely that the
economically marginal substratum of the 'criminal quarter' was heavily
over-represented in the looting and destruction that accompanied the final
stages of the events of 17 January, for by 10.30 p.m. the rioters had
dwindled to a small group, probably only several hundred strong: many
more could not all have crowded into the narrow area where the events
took place; those concerned in the Schopenstehl, according to eyewitnesses, probably numbered no more than fifty; and the actual scale of the
looting itself was not very large. Without doubt a number of the culprits
got away; but it seems equally likely that few of them belonged to the
respectable working classes, and that a majority of those responsible were
in fact brought to book.[93]

VI

It is obviously impossible to reach even this degree of certainty about the
participants in the major part of the evening's events. It seems probable
that shipyard, port and building workers responded most strongly to the
strike; but, though these almost certainly formed the majority of the
audiences at the protest meetings held at 4 p.m., and constituted the bulk
of participants in the subsequent demonstrations, it is no longer possible
to gauge with any accuracy how many of them were party members, how
many were actually in employment, or how many took part in the
bottle-throwing and other violent incidents that occurred during the
confrontation with the police. Nor is it possible to reach any precise
conclusions about the kinds of workers involved. What can be said with
some certainty, however, is that the great mass of the demonstrators were
to a greater or lesser degree supporters of the SPD, and above all,

committed to equal suffrage, the issue around which the strike and demonstration centred. Several influences were involved in producing the massive support which these people gave to the SPD's call for a protest against the 'suffrage robbery'. Economic depression certainly played a part. January, for example, when the Hamburg riots of 1906 took place, was a month of high seasonal unemployment both in the building trade and in port work (the latter due to the annual freezing-over of the river Elbe, Hamburg's main outlet to supplies and markets in the German hinterland). The main participants in the demonstration of 17 January and the strike that preceded it, building, shipyard and harbour workers, provided the mainstay of the Hamburg SPD itself, which in 1911–12, for example, contained over 6,000 building workers, 4,000 woodworkers, 7,500 metalworkers, 6,000 transport workers (mostly employed in the harbour) and 8,000 unclassified labourers, many of whom probably found employment on building sites, in shipyards, or on the waterfront. Apart from the 8,000 women members of the party, these groups made up the overwhelming bulk of SPD membership in Hamburg at this date.[94] In the celebrated Berlin disturbances of 1892, in comparison, the main participants in the early stages were building workers thrown out of work by seasonal unemployment (the riots took place in February).[95]

Apart from this general economic background, there was another social influence at work. These various disturbances, and the gap they revealed between worker militancy and SPD legalism, may also have been an expression of a generational conflict. Many, if not most, participants in the looting certainly seem to have been what participants described as 'adolescents' (Halbstarke or Halbwüchsige). It is of course an obvious point that the old and the middle-aged seldom take part in riots of this kind. Nevertheless, those convicted for the Schopenstehl disturbance do seem to have been relatively young. The concept of 'adolescent', given the fact that physical maturity was attained later then than now, can be taken perhaps to refer to those in their late teens and very early twenties. The average age of those convicted in the two major trials following the Hamburg riot, for example, was 22 years and 6 months, and the majority were younger (the statistics being distorted by a very few participants of considerably greater age). The median age was in fact only 20. The press, including the Social Democratic press, was dismissive of these youths, who were regarded as 'delinquents' out for some violent fun, or easily led by more experienced elements from the Lumpenproletariat. It is impossible to generalize about the age of those involved in the earlier demonstrations, and this might indeed have been somewhat higher. Younger workers' commitment to the suffrage may have been relatively weak, given the fact that the minimum age for voting in the Citizens' Assembly elections was 25. In any event, the age gap did reveal a genuine problem: the SPD never succeeded in establishing a youth movement of its own on a secure basis; those groups it did manage to set up, both before and during the First World War, showed a constant tendency to align themselves with the radical opposition within the SPD and were always being disciplined by the party leadership, a policy which usually resulted in splits, secessions and membership losses. It is at least possible, therefore, that the indiscipline of the crowd during and after the meetings which inaugurated the evening's events had part of its origin in a generation gap, giving a foretaste of the more marked generational conflict that was to emerge between the youthful supporters (and leaders) of the German Communist Party and the increasingly middle-aged Social Democrats during the Weimar Republic.[96]

By themselves, however, these influences were of course insufficient to provoke mass demonstrations on the streets. Before this could occur, a *political crisis* was necessary. Thus in 1905 tensions between the working class and the government had been heightened by the Russian Revolution and the Suffrage Bill, while the Berlin *Moabiter Unruhen* ('Moabit disturbances') of 1910 can only be understood when seen against the background of several months of mass demonstrations, street marches, leafleting and speech-making by the SPD on the democratization of the Prussian suffrage law. The final political contingency in the series was of course that of 1918, when the loss of the war and the reform of the constitution provided the political impetus to set in motion a far larger mass movement, fuelled by economic distress and social tension far graver than in 1901 or 1906. The Revolution of November 1918 has often been seen as little more than the expression of war-weariness, the violence that accompanied its eventual suppression as the consequence of the brutalization of the masses through their experiences in the trenches. Yet the events of 1918 did in fact bear a strong resemblance to the lesser disturbances of previous years, suggesting the existence of longer-term social and political continuities underlying the pattern of periodic mass insurrection. On 6 November 1918 a general strike broke out in Hamburg, the railway stations were occupied, imperial emblems were torn down and red flags hoisted all over the city, and the army officers were arrested by the troops. A workers' and soldiers' council was formed, and it demanded the release of political prisoners, freedom of speech and other reforms. Elections for a properly constituted workers' and soldiers' council were held in the factories, docks and shipyards on 8 November; the council met on 9 November and elected a presidium which by 12 November had taken over full power in the city from the old government, which was officially disbanded. These revolutionary acts were carried out under the leadership of the Independent Social Democrats, a new political party which had seceded from the official SPD the previous year because it opposed the party's support of the war. The leader of the Independents in Hamburg, Heinrich Laufenberg, had adopted a consistent policy of trying to mobilize the unorganized and non-unionized labour force, above all among the port workers and metalworkers, against the established Social Democrats, and in this effort he seems ultimately to have been successful.[97]

A crucial difference between the events of 1906 and those of 1918 thus lay in the presence in 1918 of a revolutionary leadership prepared to take advantage of the militancy and desire for action of the working masses, as the SPD was not. All accounts of the revolution give particular prominence to the role of the leadership of the Independent Social Democratic Party in Hamburg in the removal of the agents of the existing order and the assumption of governmental power. In 1906, by contrast, the crowds milling about before the town hall had no real idea of what to do; few of the police's allegations were less plausible than that of a concerted plan to storm the town hall. The main concern even of the unofficial SPD stewards was to control and discipline the crowds and eventually to send them home. Nevertheless, even in 1906 the relationship between leaders and masses was not merely one of restraint versus militancy; after all, it was the SPD leadership in the city which had arranged the demonstration in the first place, and there can be little doubt that the party's propaganda had helped convince the workers of Hamburg of the injustice of the 'suffrage robbery'. Of course, the demonstrations had their recreational dimension; and the role played by drink is also evident from the documents, though so little stigma was apparently attached to this in Imperial Germany that neither the right-wing press nor the SPD itself seems to have felt any need to pay particular attention to it.[98] The basic motive for the demonstration among the Hamburg working classes was clearly provided, however, by a deep urge for equality and a genuine sense of outrage at the prospect of disfranchisement; it was this, and not any simple desire for excitement, that prompted them to jeopardize their jobs by participating in the general strike, and to take part in the lengthy protest meetings that preceded the demonstration.

When the workers marched into the town, it was not with any intention of committing acts of violence. The press, of course, singled out violent incidents, and indeed, as we have seen, seized upon the false report of the killing of a policeman with a zeal and promptitude that could scarcely be exceeded in the mass media of the present day. So pervasive and persistent is this concentration on the violent elements in the demonstration by the newspapers whose reports form a large part of the sources on which any account of the disturbances must rest, that it was impossible to break completely free from it in the account given in Section III of this chapter. Certainly violent incidents occurred; even the SPD made no explicit attempt to deny this or to dismiss the reports of bottle-throwing, attacks on police horses etc. as fabrications, though it did its best to ignore them. But if one reads between the lines, and takes into account the huge size of the crowds, what becomes apparent is the relatively restrained nature of the crowd's behaviour until the police attacks reached their height. A similar restraint in the use of violence would be observed in the revolutionary crowds of 1918. The crowds were committed and enthusiastic, and they showed their political convictions by singing repeated choruses of the *Arbeitermarseillaise* and listening to frequent speeches on the 'suffrage robbery'. But their convictions did not lead them to indulge in unprovoked violence and aggression.

Long before 1906, however, the SPD party leadership had come to distrust the depth and power of these convictions which it had helped to foster. It constantly insisted that it was a law-abiding party which rejected violence and sought instead to achieve the social revolution through the ballot-box.[99] If violence occurred, it was the work of *provocateurs* or *Lumpenproletariat*. As early as 1892, for example, several days of rioting, looting and destruction in Berlin were attributed by the SPD newspaper *Vorwärts* to the *Lumpenproletariat* acting in collusion with the secret police.[100] Two decades later, little had changed. Several days of violent riots in Berlin in 1910, the celebrated Moabit disturbances, were again condemned by the SPD, which once more described them as the work of the *Lumpenproletariat*, and did its best to bring them to an early end. While criminal elements may well have been involved, however, the Moabit disturbances seem actually to have involved a genuinely working-class community;[101] and on 'Red Wednesday' in Hamburg too, the action that took place before about 10 p.m. was in all probability the work of the SPD's own supporters. In adopting this hostile attitude to popular disturbances, the SPD was losing touch with the potential for militancy of the classes which it claimed to represent, militancy which found expression in frequent outbursts of spontaneous collective protest, both political and industrial, at moments of high social and political tension.[102] A characteristic indicator of the SPD's own attitude during the Hamburg demonstration in 1906 was the formation of the well-disciplined column which marched off to visit the bourgeois politician Burgomaster Burchard and congratulate him on his popular opposition to the 'suffrage robbery'; these men may well have represented the most active and loyal of the party's own members, and at any rate they were certainly organized on the march by local party officials, whose main concern seems to have been to reassure the city's bourgeoisie, through its representative Dr Burchard, of the peaceful intentions of the party and the commitment of its members to 'our father-city Hamburg'. These men were, however, only a minority of those present at the demonstration; most of their comrades preferred a more active and less deferential mode of expression for their grievances.[103]

The failure of the police and the authorities to come to a realistic assessment of the attitude of the SPD party machine was thus one of the strangest features of the events of 17 January 1906, not least in view of the lengthy history of Social Democratic legalism. To a large degree the attitude of the police was formed by the polarized form of the political dialogue, made more extreme by the events of the previous year, above all the Russian Revolution and the Jena general-strike resolution. But the police were clearly unable to cope with the situation in practical terms as well. In the riot of 1906, the police were evidently inadequately prepared to deal with the phenomenon of a mass demonstration involving several thousand people and lasting for a number of hours. They failed to negotiate with the SPD stewards, who would have been more than prepared to come to an arrangement,[104] or to provide sufficient manpower to enable policemen on duty to be replaced from time to time. Much of the blame for the police excesses after the demonstration can be attributed to the fact that the officers involved had been on duty for several hours without a break even for refreshments. The role of the police in the disturbances was in fact one of amplification rather than control. Had they decided simply to maintain their cordons round the town hall, the crowd would probably have dispersed, either of its own volition or under the influence of the SPD leaders. By deciding to clear the streets, the police precipitated the deterioration of the situation. Later on, by driving the crowd into the 'criminal quarter', the police provided the stimulus and the excuse for the looting that took place. Their indiscriminate attacks on the crowds and (after 11 p.m.) on individuals further alienated the working class and reinforced its sense of solidarity. The end result of the police's action was to heighten social tensions rather than to calm them. In this sense, the disturbances should be seen as *transactions* in which the two sides interacted and responded to each other's actions, rather than a simple series of crowd *actions* and police *reactions*, as the right-wing press tried to portray them.

In the short term, 'Red Wednesday' caused the Hamburg Senate to feel itself altogether justified in pushing forward with its proposals to restrict the Assembly's franchise. After numerous attempts by SPD representatives in the Assembly to delay the proceedings, the conservative deputies eventually succeeded in pushing through the measure by the end of January, with a majority merely three votes above the required two-thirds; the final ratification took place on 28 February.[105] In the long term, however, the results were to be very different. Indeed, the weakness, unpreparedness and brutality of the police can perhaps be seen as evidence of their consciousness of the fragility of the social order which it was their job to defend. Hamburg's population had expanded so rapidly, and its social structure changed so profoundly, in little over a decade, that the police had been altogether unable either to increase their manpower or to adapt their tactics to keep pace; 1906, it can be argued, illustrated their awareness of this weakness. By 1918 demoralization had become comlete, and the police simply abandoned control of the streets to the revolutionary crowd.[106]

VII

Incidents such as that of 17 January 1906, though seemingly isolated and, in terms of achieving their aims, apparently futile, illuminated in a uniquely dramatic way many of the strains and tensions that underlay the placid surface of Wilhelmine society. When analysed in detail against their contemporary economic, social and political background they suggest continuities which, but for outbursts such as these, might have remained concealed. It is for this reason, among others, that an 'index of social tension' cannot be convincingly constructed from a computation of the frequency of 'social protest' or violent collective action.[107] The only way to achieve an understanding of the nature and depth of social conflict in any society is to examine the participants in the conflict and the conditions in which the conflict took place. The correlation of quantifiable economic trends with instances of political violence may seem a possible short-cut. But this method of procedure omits the vital area in between the trends it discusses – that of *social* change and *social* structure. A series of events such as those recounted earlier in this chapter is not readily explicable in terms of an index of 'social protest' vaguely related to global changes in the standard of living, the statistical rate of increase in the total urban population or the growth of industrial production. Even if significant correlations could be established in these areas, their explanatory power would be minimal. What is required is the employment of appropriate concepts.[108] In this essay, I have tried to do this by using the familiar concepts of class conflict and relations of production to analyse the social and economic determinants of the events under examination. In attempting to use the historical context to explain why violent crowd actions of various types occurred, I also hope I have contributed to an understanding of the historical context itself. This surely is the proper justification for the case-study approach.

This understanding of the meaning and purpose of the case-study which I have tried to argue by example is very different from the function of the case-study in the methodology of pure quantification, where it serves as no more than an element in the construction of aggregate series and indices. A major weakness of this latter approach, it has been pointed out, is that it only *counts* individual incidents of 'collective violence'; it does not *weigh* them, so that a hundred incidents involving thirty people appear a hundred times more important than one incident involving thirty thousand people.[109] This fault could perhaps be corrected, and the correction built into the computation of statistical correlations. But this was not the case in the Tilly's work (*The Rebellious Century*), a fact which seems symptomatic of a more profound theoretical inadequacy. The Tillys argue that aggregate studies are necessary because it is impossible to generalize from a few individual case-studies, though they do concede that an accumulation of a large number of individual case-studies would be very helpful to them in their task of making their generalizations firmer.[110] Only quantification, they claim, permits generalization. It would be a sorry fate for the present essay to be regarded as yet another case-study in this manner, as no more than an additional pinch of grist for the Tillys' generalizing mill. It could only be regarded as such on the basis of a crudely positivistic view of history: a single instance of collective violence is a single 'fact' and therefore cannot be generalized from; a thousand instances are a thousand facts and therefore can be generalized from.

A single instance, in this view, is largely the outcome of chance: only the broadest trends are capable of rational explanation in terms of historical determination. What I have tried to show in this essay is that there is an intermediate area between detailed empirical research and large-scale generalization on the basis of quantitative study. This gap, so conspicuous in the positivistic account of the Tillys, can only be bridged by the use of theories and concepts specifically designed to operate at this intermediate level of causality.[111] Using the notions of class conflict, changes in the relations of production and so on, it is possible to render even so specific a series of events as those of 17 January 1906 intelligible in terms of historical determination. As Perry Anderson has written:

> There is no plumb-line between necessity and contingency in historical explanation, dividing separate types of enquiry – 'long-run' versus 'short-run', or 'abstract' versus 'concrete' – from each other. There is merely that which is known – established by historical research – and that which is not known: the latter may be either the mechanisms of single events or the laws of motion of whole structures. Both are equally amenable, in principle, to adequate knowledge of their causality.[112]

NOTES

The documents used in the preparation of the detailed analysis in this essay are all housed in the Staatsarchiv Hamburg. The four main sets of files used are classified as: Politische Polizei S3496; Politische Polizei S14139; Landgericht, 1930–1/I; and Senat Cl. VII, Lit. Me, No. 12, Vol. 20a. To avoid unnecessary repetition these files will be referred to in these notes as S3496, S14139, L1930–1/I and Senat . . . 20a respectively. Newspaper titles will be abbreviated as follows: *AZ* for *Arbeitgeber Zeitung*, *BT* for *Beliner Tageblatt*, *DP* for *Die Post*, *DZ* for *Deutsche Zeitung*, *FZ* for *Frankfurter Zeitung*, *GAH* for *General-Anzeiger* (*Hamburg*), *HC* for *Hamburger Correspondent*, *HE* for *Hamburger Echo*, *HF* for *Ham-*

burger Fremdenblatt, HN for *Hamburger Nachrichten*, VW for *Vorwärts* and VZ for *Vossische Zeitung*.

1 For further elaboration of these points on the development of West German historiography, see Introduction and Chapter 1, above; also the introduction to R.J. Evans (ed.), *Society and Politics in Wilhelmine Germany* (London, 1978), pp. 11–39; G. Eley, 'Memories of Underdevelopment: Social History in Germany', *Social History*, vol. 6 (1977), pp. 785–91.

2 The classic works of the 1950s and 1960s include G. Rudé, *The Crowd in History* (New York, 1964), E. P. Thompson, *The Making of the English Working Class* (London, 1963); G. Rudé and E.J. Hobsbawm, *Captain Swing* (London, 1969); the last-named work, though based on detailed local research, also contains suggestive examples of ways in which statistical methods might be used.

3 C., R, and L. Tilly, *The Rebellious Century* (London, 1975), with references to numerous articles relating to this general synthesis. The influence of this approach can be seen in the special issue of the journal *Geschichte und Gesellschaft*, vol. 3, no. 2 (1977) devoted to the theme of 'social protest', edited by Richard Tilly and carrying an article by Charles Tilly and assessments of the Tillys' work by others. See also R. Wirtz, 'Sozialer Protest und "Collective Violence" in Deutschland im 19. Jhdt', *Sozialwissenschaftliche Informationen für Unterricht und Studium*, vol. 4 (1975), pp. 6–12.

4 K. Hausen, 'Schwierigkeiten mit dem "sozialen Protest": Kritische Anmerkungen zu einem historischen Forschungsansatz', *Geschichte und Gesellschaft*, vol. 3, no. 2 (1977), p. 263.

5 Tilly, *The Rebellious Century*, p. 211; but the figures in the table do not add up. Perhaps there is an arithmetical error or a lapse in proof-reading.

6 cf. E. Baasch, *Geschichte Hamburgs 1814–1918* (Gotha and Stuttgart, 1924–5), Vol. 2; J. Schult, *Geschichte der Hamburger Arbeiter 1890–1918* (Hanover, 1967); R. A. Comfort, *Revolutionary Hamburg: Labor Politics in the early Weimar Republic* (Stanford, Calif., 1966).

7 Schult, *Geschichte der Hamburger Arbeiter*, p. 69.

8 A. Bebel, *Die Sozialdemokratie und das allgemeine Stimmrecht* (Berlin, 1895), p. 39.

9 See my *Death in Hamburg: Society and Politics in the Cholera Years 1830–1910* (Oxford, 1987).

10 U. Seemann, 'Die Kämpfe der Hamburger Arbeiter gegen die Verschlechterung ihres Wahlrechts in den Jahren 1905/6', *Wissenschaftliche Zeitschrift der Universität Rostock*, vol. 10, no. 1 (1961), p. 65.

11 Schult, *Geschichte der Hamburger Arbeiter*, pp. 69–78.

12 Seemann, 'Kämpfe der Hamburger Arbeiter', p. 65.

13 Comfort, *Revolutionary Hamburg*, ch. 1.

14 See G. Eley, *Reshaping the German Right: Radical Nationalism and Political Change after Bismarck* (London, 1980), ch. 2.

15 Comfort, *Revolutionary Hamburg*, ch. 1.

16 Seemann, 'Kämpfe der Hamburger Arbeiter', p. 65.

17 Baasch, *Geschichte Hamburgs*, Vol. 2, p. 111.

18 Ibid., p. 288.

19 Seemann, 'Kämpfe der Hamburger Arbeiter', pp. 80–5.

20 Ibid., pp. 98–9.

21 *Jahresbericht der vereinigten Vorstände der drei sozialdemokratischen Vereine und Einzelberichte, Geschäftsjahr 1905* (Hamburg, 1906).

22 L. Stern (ed.), *Die Auswirkungen der ersten russischen Revolution von 1905–1907 auf Deutschland*, Archivalische Forschungen zur Geschichte der deutschen Arbeiterbewegung, Vol. 1, Nos. 1–2 (Berlin, 1954–6).

23 C. E. Schorske, *German Social Democracy 1905–1917: The Development of the Great Schism* (Cambridge, Mass., 1955), pp. 42–5.

24 Ibid., pp. 45–7.

25 Ibid., p. 47; also Schult, *Geschichte der Hamburger Arbeiter*, pp. 69–79 (very inaccurate).

26 *Jahresbericht der vereinigten Vorstände.*

27 S3496: *GAH*, 18 Jan. 1906.

28 Ibid., *VW*, 19 Jan. 1906.
29 L1930-1/I: Versammlungsberichte, pp. 13–42; S3496: *HF*, 19 Jan. 1906, no. 15; *HC*, 18 Jan. 1906, no. 31.
30 Senat ... 20a: Police chief to Senate, 16 Feb. 1906; Speech of state prosecutor at trial; S3496: *HC*, 25 Apr. 1906, no. 208; L1930-1/I: Polizei, Abt. VII – Bericht über die Vorgänge am 17. Jan. 1906; S3496: *GAH*, 18 Jan. 1906.
31 Senat ... 20a: Polizeidirektor – Ergänzung des Berichts über die Vorgänge am 17. Januar 1906 bezüglich der Krawalle im Schopenstehl, 6 Feb. 1906.
32 Senat ... 20a, 16/1: Anlage. Drucksache f.d. Senatssitzung, 55, 13 Feb. 1906. Every hit, it was alleged, was greeted by wild cheering (S3496: *HF*, 18 Jan. 1906, no. 15).
33 S3496: *HC*, 18 Jan. 1906, no. 31; *DZ*, 19 Jan. 1906; Senat ... 20a: *HC*, 25 Apr. 1906 (Speech of State Attorney).
34 Some reports described these events as having taken place an hour or so earlier, but it is clear from other evidence that they were mistaken.
35 The 'Workers Marseillaise' (*Arbeitermarseillaise*), by Jakob Audorf, was the most important Social Democratic song. From 1875 onwards it was customarily sung at the close of every party congress. Its first verse began: 'Onward you, who respect right and freedom, all of you gather round our flag, even though lies surround us with darkness our bright dawn will soon be arriving' (G. A. Ritter, 'Workers' Culture in Imperial Germany: Problems and Points of Departure for Research', *Journal of Contemporary History*, vol. 13, no. 2 (1978), pp. 186–7.)
36 S3496: *HF*, 19 Jan. 1906, no. 15; *HE*, 21 Jan. 1906; *HE*, 23 Jan. 1906, no. 18; *HC*, 28 Apr. 1906, no. 213; *GAH*, 19 Jan. 1906, no. 15; *DZ*, 19 Jan. 1906 (quoting *HN*); *HF*, 19 Jan. 1906, no. 15. The long quotation is in S14139: *HE*, 22 Nov. 1906, no. 812.
37 S3496: *GAH*, 20 Jan. 1906: *HC*, 18 Jan. 1906, no. 31; *HC*, 28 Apr.; Senat ... 20a: Polizeihauptmann – Ergänzung des Berichts über die Vorgänge am 17. Januar, 6 Feb. 1906; Drucksache 53 (nr. 12); Drucksache 23.
38 Senat ... 20a: *HN*, 22 Jan. 1906.
39 L1930-1/I: Feuerwehr 48/06, 17 Jan. 1906.
40 L1930-1/I: *HC*, 28 Apr. 1906, no. 214.
41 Relief was effectively impossible because of lack of numbers. For further consideration of this point, see the concluding paragraph of Section VI.
42 Senat ... 20a: Anlage zu 14, Untersuchungsrichter V bei dem Landgericht, betr. d. Tumult von 17 Jan. 1906, 7 Feb. 1906; *HC*, 25 Apr. 1906 (Speech of state attorney). For a full account by Major Gestefeld and others directly concerned, see L1930-1/I: Polizei Abt. VII, Bericht über die Vorgänge am 17. Januar 1906.
43 Lunau'sche Gastwirtschaft incident reported in Stenographische Berichte über die Sitzung der Bürgerschaft zu Hamburg im Jahre 1907, 9. Sitzung der Bürgerschaft, am 18. Feb. 1907 (Herr Blume); also S3496: *VW*, 6 Feb. 1907.
44 S14139: *HF*, 21 Nov. 1906.
45 S14139: *HN*, 21 Nov. 1906.
46 Ibid.
47 S14139: *HN*, 22 Nov. 1906.
48 S14139: *HN*, 21 Jan. 1906.
49 For the timing of the end of the evening's events, see S3496: *HC*, 19 Jan. 1906.
50 S3496: *AZ*, 21 Jan. 1906, no. 3.
51 S3496: *HN*, 28 Jan. 1906, no. 69. By 4 Feb. 1906, the sum of 13,359 marks, 10 pfennigs had been collected – a testimony to the wealth of Hamburg's bourgeoisie as well as to its gratitude to the police.
52 S3496: *DP*, 19 Jan. 1906, *BT*, 18 and 19 Jan. 1906, nos. 32–4. See also S3496:*VZ*, 18 Jan. 1906, no. 29; *FZ*, 19 Jan. 1906, no. 18.
53 This was above all the case after the events of the following November, when details of police brutality emerged during a trial in which one of the police's critics was being arraigned for libelling the force: cf. S14139, *passim*. Early editions of the liberal *Neue Hamburger Zeitung* carried not only the 'shot policeman' story but also a story that another policeman had been thrown off a bridge into one of Hamburg's canals by the mob (S3496: *Neue Hamburger Zeitung*, 18 Jan., no. 29).
54 S3496: *HN*, 18 Jan. 1906, no. 44; *GAH*, 20 Jan. 1906 (quoting *HN*).
55 S3496: *HF*: 20 Jan. 1906, no. 16.

Rethinking German History

56 S3496: *HN*, 21 and 25 Jan. 1906.
57 S3496: *HE*, 30 Jan. 1906 (quoting *DP*).
58 S3496: *HN*, 21 Jan. 1906. (Burgomaster Burchard's house was in this area.)
59 L1930–1/I: 1017/06 IV, 18 Jan. 1906.
60 S3496: *HE*, 19 Jan. 27 Apr. and 13 Mar. 1906.
61 For discussion of the operation of press censorship against Social Democratic newspapers, see A. Hall, 'The War of Words: Anti-socialist Offensives and Counter-propaganda in Wilhelmine Germany 1890–1914', *Journal of Contemporary History*, vol. 11 (1976), pp. 11–42; Hall, *Scandal, Sensation and Social Democracy* (Cambridge, 1977).
62 S3496: Wirtschaftsvigilanzberichte 4(a), 4(b), 4(h), 4(k), 4(l), 4(m).
63 Polizeibehörde I, DU 55/1906: Disziplinaruntersuchung.
64 K. Marx and F. Engels, *Collected Works*, Vol. 6 (London, 1976), p. 494.
65 For a discussion of 'class justice', see K. Saul, *Staat, Industrie, Arbeiterbewegung im Kaiserreich* (Düsseldorf, 1974), pp. 189–282.
66 For an analysis of those prosecuted and convicted, see Section V, below.
67 See n. 60, above, for references.
68 For a discussion of the social and political function of judicial procedures designed to ensure 'fairness' at this level, see D. Hay, 'Property, Authority and the Criminal Law', in Hay *et al.*, *Albion's Fatal Tree: Crime and Society in Eighteenth-Century England* (London, 1975), pp. 17–63.
69 H. Popert, *Helmut Harringa* (47th edn, Dresden, 1923), pp. 61–80.
70 S3496: *HN*, 21 Jan. 1906, no. 52. The demonstrations took place in many parts of Germany; Hamburg was an exception. See Schorske, *German Social Democracy*, pp. 46–9.
71 L1930–1/I: Feuerwehr 481/06.
72 L1930–1/I: Retent 1460/IV.
73 Fall Seefeld: L1930–1/I: Retent 1526/06 IV.
74 Fall Schön: L1930–1/I: Retent 1791–06/IV. Other denunciations are filed in L1930–1/I, and include Fall Nellstein, Retent 2010/06/IV; Fall Natzel, Retent 2159/06/IV; Fall Fuhls, Retent 1976/06/IV.
75 L1930–1/I: Retent 1371/06/IV.
76 S3496: *HE*, 1 Mar. 1906.
77 cf. the analysis of denunciations in R. C. Cobb, *The Police and the People. French Popular Protest 1789–1820* (Oxford, 1970), pp. 3–17.
78 Those arrested but not tried also spent a considerable time on remand for questioning (i.e. in *Untersuchungschaft*), and the effects of this should be borne in mind when reaching a final assessment of the effects of the affair on the populace.
79 S3496: *DP*, 4 May 1906.
80 S3496: *HE*, 8 May 1906.
81 S3496: *HC*, 28 Apr. 1906; Landgericht B, 1930–1/III: Antrag auf Wiederaufnahme des Verfahrens in Strafsachen des Emil Stange.
82 Senat ... 20a: Anlage zu 14 – Untersuchungsrichter 7 Feb. 1906, Abschr.
83 L1930–1/I: Rittner und Genossen.
84 L1930–1/I: Dörrenhaus und Genossen.
85 S3496: *BT*, 21 Jan. 1906, no. 47.
86 S3496: *HN*, 19 Jan. 1906, no. 46.
87 S3496: *HE*, 19 Jan. 1906.
88 Senat ... 20a: *HN*, 4 Feb. 1906.
89 Senat ... 20a: HF 19 Jan.
90 For these aspects of the general background to the affair, see Schult, *Geschichte der Hamburger Arbeiter*; Baasch *Geschichte Hamburgs*; H. Speckter, 'Die grossen Sanierungsmassnahmen Hamburgs seit d. 2. Hälfte des 19. Jahrhunderts', *Zeitschrift für Raumforschung und Raumordnung*, vol. 6 (1967), pp. 257–68; F. Tönnies, 'Hafenarbeiter und Seeleute in Hamburg vor dem Streik 1896–97', *Archiv für Gesetzgebung und Politik* (1897), pp. 673 ff.; E. Francke, 'Die Arbeitsverhältnisse im Hafen zu Hamburg', *Jahrbuch für Gesetzgebung, Verwaltung und Volkswirtschaft im Deutschen Reich* (1898), pp. 943–50. See also J. Reincke, *Die Cholera in Hamburg* (Hamburg, 1893), offprint from *Deutsche Medizinische Wochenschrift*, vols. 3–4 (1893), esp. p. 14.

288

91 For an example of such a political trial, see S5883, trial of Louise Zietz (one of the most active SPD speakers in Hamburg) for incitement (*Aufreizung*).

92 Sources in nn. 73, 74 above.

93 It is perhaps worth noting that there was no question of large-scale crime being involved in the affair; organized crime in Hamburg had its headquarters in St Pauli; the Schopenstehl area was better known for petty crime.

94 Schult, *Geschichte der Hamburger Arbeiter*, pp. 285–6.

95 A. Lange, *Berlin zur Zeit Bebels und Bismarcks* (2nd edn, Berlin, 1982), pp. 728–9.

96 Median age compiled from sources in nn. 73, 74. See also Schult, *Geschichte der Hamburger Arbeiter*, pp. 315–23; and R. N. Hunt, *German Social Democracy 1918–1933* (New Haven, Conn., 1964), pp. 89, 241–59.

97 Schult, *Geschichte der Hamburger Arbeiter*, pp. 315–57; H. Laufenberg, *Die Hamburger Revolution* (Hamburg, 1919); F. L. Carsten, *Revolution in Central Europe 1918–1919* (London, 1972), pp. 33–4, 323–35; and esp. V. Ullrich, *Die Hamburger Arbeiterbewegung vom Vorabend des 1. Weltkrieges bis zur Revolution 1918/19*, 2 vols (Hamburg, 1976).

98 The role of drink in such events, and in German working-class culture in general, urgently needs closer investigation. Political meetings such as the demonstrations of 17 January 1906 were usually held in large beer-halls, with alcoholic refreshments being served; empty beer bottles seem to have been a favourite weapon of the crowd in the ensuing disturbances, and several of the accused pleaded in mitigation or as a defence that they had been incapably drunk by the middle of the evening. More generally, it was still customary at this time for dock workers and other labourers to drink quite heavily during working hours. Interesting evidence of the contrast with the British labour movement in this respect is provided by the reports of members of a British workers' delegation to Germany in 1910–11. One delegate remarked on the 'very great number of barrels of beer' at an SPD May Day gathering near Frankfurt; another commented that workers in a German factory he visited 'had pots of beer at their side' as they worked; 'it was a very strange sight, and one which we do not see in our own country'. (*Reports on Labour and Social Conditions in Germany: Working Men's Tours*, vol. 3, no. 3 (1910–11), p. 12.) See also E. Lucas, *Arbeiterradikalismus: Zwei Formen von Radikalismus in der deutschen Arbeiterbewegung* (Frankfurt, 1976), pp. 92–8.

99 See e.g. the discussion in G. A. Ritter, *Die Arbeiterbewegung im Wilhelminischen Reich* (Berlin, 1959), p. 221.

100 Lange, *Berlin zur Zeit Bebels*, pp. 728–9.

101 H. Bleiber, 'Die Moabiter Unruhen 1910', *Zeitschrift für Geschichtswissenschaft*, vol. 3 (1955).

102 For a more general discussion of worker militancy, see D. Geary, 'The German Labour Movement 1848–1919', *European Studies Review*, vol. 6 (1976), pp. 297–330.

103 This incident is briefly recounted above, p. 261.

104 On one occasion, stewards actually did reach a limited accommodation with the police: the leaders of the march to Dr Burchard's house, on returning with their column of followers to the town centre, and finding their way blocked by a police cordon, managed to persuade the police to let them through without hindrance, on the understanding that they would behave peacefully (see S3496: *HF*, 19 Jan. 1906; *HE*, 21 Jan. 1906). This, and the efforts the stewards made to disperse the crowds after 9 p.m., suggests a willingness to negotiate which the police evidently failed to take advantage of.

105 Seemann, 'Die Kämpfe der Hamburger Arbeiter', pp. 98–100.

106 It should be added, however, that the crowd in 1918 numbered among it many ex-soldiers, and that the relative strength of the police had been depleted by the war; from 1914 to 1918 the main burden of maintaining law and order within the borders of Germany had fallen on the army. Moreover, the 1918 crowd possessed easy access to arms and ammunition, altogether unavailable in 1906. cf. Ullrich, *Die Hamburger Arbeiterbewegung*.

107 See R. Tilly and G. Hohorst, 'Sozialer Protest in Deutschland im 19. Jahrhundert: Skizze eines Forschungsansatzes', in K. Jarausch (ed.), *Quantifizierung in der Geschichtswissenschaft* (Düsseldorf, 1975). Later historiography – notably that influenced by mainstream Social Democracy – has consistently played down the incidence of

collective violence in Wilhelmine Germany. For a good example of this, see the account of the Hamburg suffrage demonstration in Schult, *Geschichte der Hamburger Arbeiter*. In so far as they depict the Wilhelmine period as one of decline in social tension and collective violence, R. Tilly *et al.* are continuing this line of interpretation. East German historians have devoted some attention to riots, but no systematic studies have been made. In this respect, H. Bleiber, 'Die Moabiter Unruhen 1910', *Zeitschrift für Geschichtswissenschaft*, vol. 3 (1955), pp. 173–81, virtually the only serious attempt at an analysis of a violent crowd action in Imperial Germany, is a disappointment.

108 That is to say, statistical correlations are meaningless without a theory of causality. In this respect, Tilly and Hohorst's reply to their critics, rejecting the argument that their approach suffers from a lack of theory, has nothing new to offer (G. Hohorst and R. Tilly, 'Sozialer Protest, Gewalt, Rebellion und die Kritik: Bemerkungen zu H.-G. Haupt und K. Hausen', *Geschichte und Gesellschaft*, vol. 3, no. 3 (1977), pp. 418–21).

109 Hausen, 'Schwierigkeiten', p. 263.

110 Hohorst and Tilly, 'Sozialer Protest, Gewalt, Rebellion', suggest that the operational costs of the purely quantitative approach are lower than those involved in studying a large number of individual cases. When measured in terms of significant results, however, it is more plausible to argue, with Hausen, that in this case at least, 'the price paid in order to work with quantitative methods in research on the history of protest is very high, perhaps too high' (Hausen, 'Schwierigkeiten', p. 263).

111 See in this respect the discussion of the riot of 8 February 1886 in London in G. Stedman Jones, *Outcast London. A Study in the Relationship between Classes in Victorian Society* (Oxford, 1971), pp. 291–5, an event with many parallels to the disturbances discussed in this chapter (origin in a socialist political meeting, predominance of dockers and building workers, time of year, attack on symbols of property and reaction, ensuing bourgeois panic, and so on), the major differences being the absence of a strong police force and the indiscriminate nature of looting; in the Hamburg riot, looting was specifically directed at a limited number of jewellers' shops. More generally, cf. Robert J. Holton, 'The Crowd in History: Some Problems of Theory and Method', *Social History* vol. 3, no. 2 (1978), pp. 219–33. The absence of any reference to Germany in Holton's article, which takes several countries into consideration, is a telling comment on the state of research.

112 P. Anderson, *Lineages of the Absolutist State* (1974), p. 8.

Index

Abraham, D. 57
  neo-Marxist analysis of Weimar
    Republic 77–9
Adenauer, K. 32, 34
Agrarian League 48
agrarian life-style
  and religious rituals 139, 144
Alliance of Conservative Women 231
Anderson, M. 57
  political biography of Ludwig
    Windthorst 63–5
Anglo-German relations 69–72
anti-Semitism
  Hitler's policy 29
  in pre-war Prague 86–7
  of Bavarian peasantry 48, 82
  of Nazi Regime 82
Augspurg, Anita
  police libel case 248
authority
  and German national character 157, 158,
    159, 184
  enforcement and evolution of police
    powers 163–5
  resistance to by subordinate classes 178
Ayçoberry, P. 57, 65
  study of Nazism 66–7

Bartels, A. 257
Bäumer, G. 221, 226, 228
  feminine mystique theory 241–2
Bavaria
  Catholic church influences 135–6, 140,
    147
  study of resistence to Nazism 79–83
Bebel, A. 198, 199, 224, 237
Berlin 49, 146
  police force 173
Bismarck 31, 37–8, 39, 40, 57, 63, 64, 65,
    97, 106
  attempt to limit independence of
    Catholic Church 147
Blackbourn, David 7, 23
  critique of structural continuity thesis
    99–103
    analysis of theoretical problems 103–8
Blasius, D.
  studies of law and order in Prussia
    167–8, 170, 175
Bochum
  case study of social structures 83–6
bourgeois
  definition problems 117

  legal ideology 117
  rules and values 111–12, 203
bourgeois revolution
  concepts of 100
  effects of failure 101–2
  in England and France 104–5
  in Germany 105–7, 110, 113
  Marxist definition 104
bourgeoisie 118
  antagonism with working classes
    235
  feudalization of 42, 72–3, 96
  power and penal practice 170
Bracher, K. D. 67
Broszat, M. 57, 67
  study of Nazi rule 68–9, 80
Bülow, B. Von 58
  Bulow Block 1906–9, 48, 63, 148
  influence on Wilhelm II 62–3

capital punishment 169
capitalism 114, 118
  and changing social structures 119
Catholic Centre Party 147–8
  and the Peasant Leagues 48
  Bulow Block 1906–9 48, 148
  changing political alignments 49
  role in Reichstag 63–4
  significance in Wilhelmine Germany
    48–9
  see also Windthorst, L.
Catholic Church 130–1, 135–6, 140
  and the peasantry 146
  influence in trade union movement 149
  persecution in early German Empire 147
  social and political institutions 147–8
  study of popular decline and revival
    140–2
Cauer, M. 231, 233, 237
Cecil, L. 61
chancellors 39
  see also Bulow, B. von
cholera epidemic
  in Hamburg 252
Churchill, Winston 95
citizenship fee
  for right to vote 251, 252
"class justice" 211, 269
Cobb, Richard 4
Cohen, G. 57
  study of Germans in Prague 86–7
Cole, T.
  study of von Bülow 63

Commercial Union of Female Salaried
  Employees 237
Communist Party 118
  see also West German Communist Party
"continuity thesis" 26, 55, 56–7, 97–8, 158
  and concept of manipulation 240–1
  and concepts of modernization 241
  as distorted historical perspective 48
  criticisms of 99–103, 108–9, 223
Crew, D. 57
  study of Bochum 83–6
crime and punishment
  effects of repressive law and order
    strategies 168
  in England and France 168–70
  of lower classes 176–7
  see also penal reform
criminality
  and social tension 176
  "social" 177–8
  see also theft
cultural activities
  and bourgeois values 112, 206
  of working class 202–4, 209–10
cultural associations
  of the labour movement 207
cultural institutions
  as socializing agents 204

Darwinism
  influence on European politics 29
  influence on feminist movement 226–7,
    228–9
decision-making
  chaos in Third Reich 67–8
Deist, W. 76
  study of Wilhelm II's military entourage
    61–2
democracy
  and liberalism 115–16
  see also suffrage
Democratic Alliance 230
dictatorship 57, 63, 66
duelling 110–11

East Germany
  historiography influences on West
    Germany 35
  opposition to the Third Reich 80
economic depression
  as factor influencing social protest 279
economic growth
  social consequences of 72
education
  control by the church 132–3
  for women 231, 232
  political influences on policy 24–5
electoral systems
  income as minimum voting qualification
    205

  see also citizenship fee
Eley, Geoff 7, 23, 57
  critique of structural continuity thesis
    99–103
  analysis of theoretical problems
    103–8
  study of the German Right 73–7
elites
  "feudal" ethos 96
  manipulation of political system 72–3,
    94–5
  ruling class and the foundations of Third
    Reich 37, 38–43, 222–3
Eulenburg, P. 58
  influence on Wilhelm II 59–60
Evangelical-Social Congress 228
Eyck, E. 58

fascism 99, 119, 239
  historical research 3
  revival 3, 24
Fatherland Party 74
Federal Republic of Germany
  modernization process 44
federalism
  and political issues 114
Federation of German Women's
    Associations 225–6
  internal divisions 234–5
  opposition to female suffrage 230
  political influence 236
  reform policies 238–9
  support for "national identity" policy
    228
  traditionalist doctrine 226–7, 237–8
feminism
  and political developments 222
  anti-feminism movements 231–2
  feminist mystique theory 241–2
  in Hamburg 9
feminist movement
  as a focus for historical research 5,
    221–2, 239–41
  commitment to nationalism 228, 229
  influence of education reforms and
    women teachers 232–3
  political significance of 225, 231
  radical 228, 233, 235, 237, 239
  radical wing decline 227
  recruitment of married women 234
  rise of 6, 223–5
  sexual liberation movement collapse
    227
feudal ethos
  and German elites 96, 110
  of German industrial magnates 112–13
  values 109
Filbinger, Hans 24
Fischer, Emil 257

Fischer, Fritz 3
  study of German First World War aims
    32–3
foreign policy
  influence of public opinion 71–2
France
  history studies 4
  political structures and bourgeoise
    revolution 105
  law, order and penal practice 169–70
Franco-German reconciliation policy 32

General German Women's Association 225
General German Women Teachers'
  Association 237
general strikes
  Hamburg "suffrage robbery" protest 256
  Hamburg 1918 280–1
generational conflict
  as factor influencing social protest
    279–80
German Alliance for Women's Suffrage 234
German Empire 39, 45
  governmental difficulties 194
  religious belief 130–1
  under-representation of Catholic
    Community 149
  see also Weimar Republic; Wilhelmine
    Germany
German Historical Institute 67
German League for the Prevention of the
  Emancipation of Women 228, 231
German mentality 1
  see also spirit of submission
German National People's Party 74, 230
German Union for Women's Suffrage
  membership 233, 234
German Women's League 230
Great Britain
  historiographical traditions 45–6
  law, order and penal practice 168–70
  Marxist historians 4
  study of labour movement history 193
  work on German history 3–4, 6–8,
    15–16, 23–4

Hamborn
  violence and crime 172
Hamburg 250–1, 258
  Augspurg police libel case 248
  bourgeois liberalism 9
  cholera epidemic 252
  citizenship fee 251, 252
  criminal quarter 274–6
  feminism 9
  general strike 1918 280
  independence in Wilhelmine period 47
  industrialization, employment and social
    change 276–7

local electoral system 10, 205, 251
  restrictive senate proposals 254, 283
Social Democratic Party protest at
  "suffrage robbery" 255–9, 281
police force 171–2
  criticisms of 267–8, 283
  post-riot measures and policy of arrest
    270–1, 277
  riot strategy 259–65, 268, 283
  weakness and loss of control 283–4
religion 146
Social Democratic Party membership
  279
Social Democratic representatives in
  citizens assembly 253–4
suffrage reform 252
suffrage riots 10, 259–65
  analysis of different phases and
    behaviours 277–82
  arrests and trials 271–4, 277–8
  as revolutionary action 268–9
  right-wing press reactions 265–67,
    274–5, 281
Heinemann, President 24
Heuss, T. 110–11
Heymann, L. G. 233, 237
Hickey, Stephen 23
Hildebrand, K. 67
Hirschfeld, G. 57
historical scholarship 1, 3, 4–5, 6–8
  biographical approach 55–6, 57, 58–65,
    89–90
  and political atmosphere 44–5, 97–8
  British 45–6
  diversity of approaches 87–8, 89
  German 8, 10–15, 25, 31–2, 33–6, 43–8,
    46–7, 56, 79, 97, 98, 103–4, 107, 192,
    193–4
  influence of history of feminism 221–2
  international dimensions 88–9
  on the German mentality 156–61
  politicization of 25
  structuralist approach 57, 68, 77–9, 90
  see also social history
"history from below"
  and British historiography 46
  and local initiative 11
  concept of 7
History Workshop movement 5
  German 12–13, 14
Hitler, Adolf 28, 42, 57, 89
  anti-Semitism 29
  as totalitarian dictator 65–6, 68
  background 29
  importance of personal appeal 30
  interpretations of role in atrocities 67
homosexuality
  and the Wilhelm entourage 59
Housewives' Association 236

Hull, I.
    study of Wilhelm II 59–61
Huttenberger, P.
    analysis of cases of Nazi resistance 82

Imperial Law of Association
    significance for the women's movement
        229, 230, 240
Imperial League Against Social Democracy
    230
Independent Social Democrats 280–1
indoctrination 41
industrialization
    and state intervention 236
    influence on decline of collective
        violence 180
    influence on religious belief 143, 146–7,
        150
Institute of Contemporary History,
    Munich 79
International Association for the History
    of Crime and Justice 10
International Council of Women 228

Jerome, J. K.
    observations on German mentality 160–1
Jewish people
    persecution and mass murder 82

Kaiserreich see Wilhelmine Germany
Kehr, E. 36, 104, 197
Kennedy, P. 57
    study of Anglo-German relations 69–72
    study of foreign policy of Wilhelm II 61
Kershaw, I.
    study of Jewish persecution 82
Kettenacker, L. 57
Kohut, T. 58
    psychohistorical study of Wilhelm II 59
Kulturkampf 63, 147

labour movement
    culture 206–7
    influence of Marxism 195
    links with Social Democratic Party 193,
        195, 196, 198
    rejection of liberalism 194–5
    role in stabilizing the social system 204–5
    sociological bases to historical studies
        192–4, 201, 202, 206
Laufenberg, Heinrich 280–1
law and order
    attitudes towards 159–60, 182, 211
    enforcement problems 170–1
    Prussian strategies 167
    resistance to 212–13
    see also legal positivism
law reform
    and bourgeois principles 116–17

see also Imperial Law of Association
League Against Social Democracy 41
legal positivism 162
leisure activities
    of Social Democratic subculture 202–3
    of working class 208–9
Lerman, K.
    study of von Bülow 58, 62–3
liberal values
    changes and rise of Nazism 5
liberalism 5, 97, 107, 194, 239
    abandonment by feminist movement
        226–7, 229, 230
    and democracy 115–16
Liebenberg Circle 59–60
Liebknecht 198, 199
local issues
    as focus for social historians 13–14
    and the "alternative constituency" 11
Luther
    and German national character 157

Marxism 37
    as focus for labour movement history
        193
    in historical scholarship 4, 7, 34, 35,
        77–8, 90, 93, 98, 104–5, 107
    challenge to structural continuity
        thesis 100–3
    in modern German history 119
    view of bourgeoisie 106, 108
Mason, T.
    study of the Third Reich 67
"mentality"
    as focus for social history 127, 156–61
middle-classes
    and liberalism 145, 227
    manipulation theories 240
    social reforms and position of women
        232
    view of Hitler 30
    see also bourgeoisie
modernization
    and collectivism 242
    in Federal Republic 44
    in German Empire 44
    without Revolution 96–7
"modernization theory" 94, 95, 241
Moltke
    influence on Wilhelm II 60
Mommsen, W. J. 57, 67, 103
    study of German decision-making
        69
"moral economy" 177
Müller, P. 230, 232
Munich
    decline as cultural centre 49
    intellectual freedom in Wilhelmine
        period 47

nationalism
 influence on women's movement 228,
  229
 radical nationalists 37, 76, 77, 87
 social history case study 86–7
national-socialism
 historical foundations 26, 27, 36, 42
 rise of 29–30, 31, 74, 102
 see also Hitler, Adolf; Nazi Regime
nationalist pressure-groups 74, 75, 76, 78
 see also Navy League
Naumann, F. 229
Navy League 75, 76
Nazi Regime 28
 centrality of the dictator 66
 collaboration with 82
 historical interpretations of 65–6, 66–7,
  98
 internal chaos 68–9
 legacy of beliefs as influence on social
  historians 129
 resistance to 79–82, 83
 rise of 37
Northcliffe, Lord 95

Peasant Leagues 48
peasantry
 decline of moral and religious standards
  135–6
 role of religion in everyday life 131–2
 social control through the church 132–4
 superstition and popular belief 136–9
 wood thefts 177–9
penal reform 169–70
People's Association for Catholic Germany
  147, 148
personality
 in historical research 55–6, 57
 of Hitler 30
 of Wilhelm II 61
police
 brutality and Augspurg libel case 248
 brutality in Hamburg riot 264–5
 bureaucracy 173
 controls over prostitution 10, 211–12
 effectiveness of powers 166–7, 182–3
 effects of intrusive police presence 160–1
 inefficiency 171
 lack of training 173
 militarization 173–4
 origins of powers 163–5, 194
 strategy in Hamburg riot 259–64
  failure 282–3
  post-riot measures and policy of arrest
   270–1
political development
 dominance of ruling elites 94–5, 97, 103
 influence of historical experiences 24,
  25–6

influences of socio-economic structures
  10, 90–1, 118–20
 "primacy of internal policy" concept 34
 see also continuity thesis
political ideology
 as ersatz religion 152–3
political influences
 on historical research 44–5
 on social protest 280–1
political mobilization 5, 28, 73, 74, 75
 of petty-bourgeoisie 47–8
 of the Right 42, 74
 of women 236
 through diversionary tactics 41
political parties
 effects of failure of bourgeoise revolution
  102
 influence of feminist movement 231, 235
 manipulation by ruling elite 40–1, 94–5
 stance of female suffrage movement 227,
  230
 see also Catholic Centre Party; Social
  Democratic Party
political structures 115
 and the German mentality 184
Popert, Hermann
 novel based on events of Hamburg
  suffrage demonstrations 269–70
power
 of bourgeoisie 105–6
 of police 163–5
 of ruling elites 94–5, 222
prisons 168
proletariat
 culture 209–10
 "of rags" 213, 273
 values 10
 see also working class
prostitution
 state control 10, 211–12
 uncontrolled 183
Protestant Church 142
 effects of industrialization 143, 146–7
 in Prussia 130
 secularization 145–6
Prussia
 authoritarian controls 158–9
 control of German Empire 39, 47
 Junkers 109–10
 persecution of Catholics 147
 religion 130

racism 38
 see also anti-Semitism
religious belief 1, 152
 and gender 151–2
 and opposition to feminist movements
  228
 and social class 143–6

religious belief *cont.*
  as ideology of legitimation 37
  as instrument of social control 131–6
  as socially divisive force 113–14
  decline 28, 143, 150
  peasant 137–9, 146
  "popular" 139, 140–2, 153
  role in everyday life 131–2
  social history of 125, 128–30
  see also Catholic Church; Protestant
    Church; secularization
repression 40
  as factor in social protest and violence
    250
Revolution 1848 105–6, 107
  failure 96–7
Revolution 1918 280
Richter, Eugen 24
riots 205, 282
  case study of Hamburg suffrage
    demonstrations 259–65
  explanations of origins of Hamburg
    demonstrations 268–9
  socio-economic factors 279–80
Ritter, Gerhard 25, 32, 66
  study of rise of national-socialism 26–31,
    45
    criticisms of 36–8
Röhl, J. 57, 58
Roth, G.
  sociological study of Social Democrats
    195–201

secularization 142–4, 145, 150–1, 153
  among Catholics 149
  between working-class men and women
    151–2
  sociological study of 128
shipbuilding
  Hamburg industrialization and
    prosperity 251
social anthropology
  as base for social history studies 13–14,
    126–7
social class
  and German mentality 184
  and political ideology 100
  and religious belief 143–6
  conflict 284
  of workers convicted in Hamburg riot
    trials 273–4
social consciousness
  functionalist interpretation of 202
  relevance of historical experiences 25
social control
  by the church 132–3, 136
  resistance to 134–5
Social Democratic Party of Germany 2,
  118, 162, 184

anti-violence policies 282
attitudes to social and political issues
  199, 238–9
attitudes to working class culture
  214–16
effects of bureaucratization 205–6
effects of policies of ruling elites 43
explanation for Hamburg riots 267–9,
  281
functionalist sociological view of 201–2
involvement of women's movement 191,
  235
-liberal coalition 34, 97, 200
organizational bureaucracy 199
own women's movement 235
political evolution and legitimation 200
prominence in Hamburg 251, 253–4,
  279
rejection of liberalism 195
research institute 25
social divisions 197–8
"subculture" 10, 191, 193, 196, 198,
  202–3
social groups
  as a focus for historians 4–5
social history 1, 13, 126–7, 129
  case-study methodology 284–5
  high politics perspective 45
  locally based 11, 57, 79, 83–6, 90
  of criminality 167–8, 170, 175
  of everyday life of working class 207–8
  of nationalism 86–7
  of religion 125, 128–30, 139
  of social protest 249–50
  of Wilhelmine Germany 50
  working seminars on 8–9
social imperialism 48, 49
  as a diversionary technique 41, 227–8,
    240
social mores
  embourgeoisement of 111–12
social movements 11
social protest 2, 179
  Hamburg suffrage demonstrations 248,
    256–9
  as basis for novel 269–70
  in West Germany 34
  see also riots
social structures
  in capitalist society 118
  in continuity model 241
  in industrialized community 83–6
social tension 181
  and criminality 176
  and violence 180
  concepts of 181–2
socialist ideology 37
  as a criminal offence 162
  as ersatz religion 152

sociology
  as base for social history studies 13, 35,
    56, 126–7, 191
  functionalist interpretation of labour
    history 192–4, 201
  limitations of functionalist viewpoint
    201–2, 206
Sombart, N. 57, 58
"spirit of submission" 1, 156, 158, 184
  and state coercion 166
Stange, Emil 272–3
state absolutism 162
  effects of 163
  evolution of police power 163–5
Stöcker, Helene 237
Stolten, Otto 253
Strauss, Franz-Josef 24
Stritt, Marie 225, 226, 228
suffrage
  reform in Hamburg 252
  "robbery" by Hamburg senate 254–6,
    283
  universal 116
  see also women's suffrage movement
superstition and witchcraft 138–9, 140

Tenfelde, K.
  study of Bavarian mining village 81–2
theft
  as modern crime 174
  relation to criminal violence 174–5
  wood 177–9
Third Reich 79–80
  decision-making 67–8, 69
  Imperial Germany as foundation for
    38–43, 223
  studies of atrocities 67
Tilly, Charles 249, 285
Tilly, Richard 250, 285
Tirpitz, Alfred 251
  role in Navy League 76
totalitarianism theory 66
trade unions 206
  attitude to pilfering 214, 215
  Christian 149
  collective bargaining agreements 113
  links with women's movement 237
  relationship with Social Democrats 43
Treaty of Versailles
  effects on internal German politics 29
  war guilt clause 32

United States of America
  academic influence of 35
  migration and development of German
    sociologists 193
University of East Anglia
  Working Seminars on social history of
    Germany 8–9, 15

vagabondism 170–1, 183–4
values
  crisis in Weimar Republic 94
  feudal 109
  working-class 10, 204, 214, 215
  see also religious belief
Veblen, T. 94
Vietnam War 3
violence
  as a political act 268
  collective 179, 180, 182
  decline in relation to theft 174–6
  related to social tension 176, 180, 282
  related to urban growth 172

Weber, Max 35
Wehler, Hans-Ulrich 8, 36
  interpretation of the origins of Nazism
    36–8, 45, 158, 222–3
Weimar Republic 97, 222–3
  crisis of values 94
  failure of 27, 29, 99, 118, 201–2
  neo-Marxist structural analysis of 77–9
West German Communist Party
  ineffectiveness of 98
  labour movement history 193
West Germany
  historical influences on political
    strategies 24–5
  influence of American sociology on
    intellectual legitimacy 193–4, 200
  political crisis and social unrest 34
  Social Democracy and liberalism 97
  view of past historical events 98
Wilhelm II 31, 32, 37, 57, 58
  anti-feminism 225
  attitude to England 59
  homosexual entourage 59
  influence of Bernard von Bülow 62–3
  influence of Philipp Eulenberg 59–60
  influence of Moltke 60
  military entourage 60, 61–2
  personality 61
  role in foreign policy 61
Wilhelmine Germany 6, 47
  compensation and indoctrination
    strategies 41
  feudalization of the bourgeoisie 42
  foreign policy 61
  historical research 6–7, 50
    biographical approach 57
    structuralist approach 57
  influence on modern German political
    development 223
  political manipulation 40–2
  political structure 115, 222
  repression 40
  rise of national socialism 42–3, 74
  support of Catholic Centre Party 48–9

Windthorst, Ludwig 24, 148
  biographical study 63–5
Wittmann, Georg
  death in Hamburg riot 264
Women's League 228, 229–30, 234
women's movement 2, 224, 240
  political integration 236
  retreat from emancipatory feminism
    226–7
  significance of Imperial Law of
    Association 229, 230, 240
  Social Democratic 10, 191, 235
  see also feminist movement
women's organizations 225–6
women's suffrage movement 229
  break-up 234
  growth 230
work relations
  and function of leisure activities
    208–9
working class
  attitudes to the law 211, 213–14

contravention of bourgeois norms
    214–15
  culture 206–7, 209–10
  deviance 210–11, 214–15
  diversity of experience and attitudes 50
  in Social Democratic subculture 203–4
  interaction with labour movement 208–9
  resistance to legal restrictions 212–13
  social history studies of everyday life
    207–8
  values 10, 204, 214, 215
World War I
  Franco-German agreement on origins 32
  Germany as instigators 33, 69, 72
  social effects of 27–8
World War II
  post-war intellectual debate 2–3

Zehr, H.
  study of violence and theft 174–5
Zeldin, Theodore 4
Zofka, Z. 82